INVENTING THE CHURCH

RELIGION, CULTURE, AND PUBLIC LIFE

RELIGION, CULTURE, AND PUBLIC LIFE

SERIES EDITOR: SETH KIMMEL

The Religion, Culture, and Public Life series is devoted to the study of religion in relation to social, cultural, and political dynamics, both contemporary and historical. It features work by scholars from a variety of disciplinary and methodological perspectives, including religious studies, anthropology, history, philosophy, political science, and sociology. The series is committed to deepening our critical understandings of the empirical and conceptual dimensions of religious thought and practice, as well as such related topics as secularism, pluralism, and political theology. The Religion, Culture, and Public Life series is sponsored by Columbia University's Institute for Religion, Culture, and Public Life.

Gods in the World: Placemaking and Healing in the Himalayas, Aftab Jassal

Prophetic Maharaja: Loss, Sovereignty, and the Sikh Tradition in Colonial South Asia, Rajbir Singh Judge

An Impossible Friendship: Group Portrait, Jerusalem Before and After 1948, Sonja Mejcher-Atassi

Moral Atmospheres: Islam and Media in a Pakistani Marketplace, Timothy P. A. Cooper

Samson Occom: Radical Hospitality in the Native Northeast, Ryan Carr

Karma and Grace: Religious Difference in Millennial Sri Lanka, Neena Mahadev

Perilous Intimacies: Debating Hindu-Muslim Friendship After Empire, SherAli Tareen

Baptizing Burma: Religious Change in the Last Buddhist Kingdom, Alexandra Kaloyanides

The Sexual Politics of Black Churches, edited by Josef Sorett

At Home and Abroad: The Politics of American Religion, edited by Elizabeth Shakman Hurd and Winnifred Fallers Sullivan

For a complete list of books in the series, please see the Columbia University Press website.

INVENTING THE CHURCH

THE PULL OF THE PAST IN ECCLESIAL POLITICS

BÉNÉDICTE SÈRE

Translated by
CAROLINE WAZER

Foreword by
CAROLINE WALKER BYNUM

Columbia University Press   *New York*

Publication of this book was made possible in part by funding from the Institute for Religion, Culture, and Public Life at Columbia University.

Columbia University Press
Publishers Since 1893
New York   Chichester, West Sussex

L'invention de l'Église © Presses Universitaires de France/Humensis, 2019
Translation copyright © 2025 Columbia University Press
All rights reserved

Library of Congress Cataloging-in-Publication Data
Names: Sère, Bénédicte author | Wazer, Caroline translator
Title: Inventing the church : the pull of the past in ecclesial politics / Bénédicte Sère ; translated by Caroline Wazer ; foreword by Caroline Walker Bynum.
Other titles: Invention de l'Église. English
Description: New York : Columbia University Press, 2025. | Series: Religion, culture, and public life | Includes bibliographical references and index.
Identifiers: LCCN 2025012988 (print) | LCCN 2025012989 (ebook) | ISBN 9780231218382 hardback | ISBN 9780231218399 trade paperback | ISBN 9780231562225 ebook
Subjects: LCSH: Church history—Historiography | Church history—Middle Ages, 600–1500 | Church history—Modern period, 1500–
Classification: LCC BR138 .S4713 2025 (print) | LCC BR138 (ebook) | DDC 282.09/02—dc23/eng/20250610

Cover design: Milenda Nan Ok Lee
Cover images: PVDE/Bridgeman Images and WikiCommons
GPSR Authorized Representative: Easy Access System Europe, Mustamäe tee 50, 10621 Tallinn, Estonia, gpsr.requests@easproject.com

CONTENTS

Foreword to the English Translation,
by Caroline Walker Bynum   *vii*
Preface to the English Translation   *xi*

Introduction   1

1 Conciliarism: From Historical Reality to
Historiographical Crystallization   15

2 Constitutionalism: A Stake of
Political Modernity?   57

3 Collegialism   83

4 Rethinking Reform: The History of Reform
and Antireformism   105

5 Anti-Romanism and Its Hitherto Unrecognized
Medieval Roots   133

6 Modernism's Challenge to the Middle Ages: Between Medieval
Studies and Medievalism   155

vi 🕉 CONTENTS

7 Infallibilism: Anatomy of a Misinterpretation   175

Conclusion   195

Acknowledgments   201
Notes   203
Bibliography   261
Index of Names   307

FOREWORD TO THE
ENGLISH TRANSLATION

CAROLINE WALKER BYNUM

This is a remarkable book. It is extremely clearly written and argued, without jargon or trendy gestures yet powerful in its intersection with current debates over the nature of religion, of the Catholic Church, of how one should reason from historical sources, and how one should (indeed must) use the past in contemporary argument. It is based on a wide range of scholarship in French, English, and German. In two chapters, British or American medievalists (e.g., Charles McIlwain, Brian Tierney) are the major figures, and in several others the major works with which the book is in dialogue (e.g., those of Étienne Gilson, Marie-Dominique Chenu, and Gerd Tellenbach) are well-known in translation to English-speaking historians. Sère's book should be of relevance to current debates in and about the Catholic Church, but also far more broadly to our current American predicament in trying to decide how to interpret foundational documents (such as the American Constitution) and in deciding how far historians and scholars should marshal the past to address current issues, as, for example, in the lively debate of the moment over historical "presentism."[1]

Sère spells out her argument clearly in her introduction, explaining that hers is not a work about the reception of sources from the European Middle Ages or about medieval history per se, nor is it a viii ⁊ FOREWORD TO THE ENGLISH TRANSLATION

treatment of the contemporary Roman Catholic Church. Rather it arises from her puzzlement—a puzzlement that should strike scholars generally—that contemporary academic studies of religion, of the Middle Ages, and of the Catholic Church, especially as it has emerged from Vatican II, agree so little in either detail or in broad claims and theses with the actual documentation from the Middle Ages. In her conclusion, she makes a few suggestive remarks about how the modern, often distorted use of medieval sources (especially those from the fifteenth century) might be replaced not just by much closer attention to the actual archival and printed material of the medieval period itself but, more importantly, by a much broader history of knowledge (with attention to how the past is constructed in each subsequent age) or by a history of the pastorate or of the Church as it actually operates and lives in the larger world of politics, values, and society.

In each chapter, Sère presents the historiography of an idea, important in nineteenth-, twentieth-, and even early twenty-first-century debate over the nature of the Church ("Church" broadly understood), a critical reading of the actual sources (at least from the thirteenth century forward) on which the modern (sometimes contradictory) positions have been based, and an assessment of how and often why contemporary usages are distorted. The seven topics she treats are conciliarism, constitutionalism, collegialism, reformism, anti-Romanism (resistance to the primacy of the pope in Rome over the whole Catholic Church), modernism, and infallibilism. The conclusions in the analyses of the seven topics are not parallel, and indeed this is one of the strengths of the book, although in no chapter does Sère find that modern use of medieval sources simply remains true to the medieval meaning and context. For example, in the chapters on conciliarism (the longest treatment in the book) and collegialism, she shows that arguments at Vatican II about the role of bishops vis-à-vis the pope had little if anything to do with the conciliar movement of the Middle Ages or with its understanding of bishops or of the church as a "college" or a corporate body. In the chapter on infallibility she shows that medieval uses of the idea were almost the opposite of the idea of papal infallibility that was promulgated at Vatican I, yet Vatican I did not "invent" the idea (as is often said). The intent of the medieval idea was, however, to prevent a pope from invalidating the positions of a previous pope. The chapter on modernism is a savvy analysis of nineteenth- and twentieth-century "Thomism" and anti-Thomism that can be usefully read by anyone interested in the history of modern philosophy, demonstrating as it does how ideas, far from being pure ratiocination done in the classroom or a faculty study, are always reflections of fundamental values and the movement of ideas in the world.

In sum, at a time when English-speaking readers are grappling with fundamental problems concerning how one should interpret, reconstruct, and argue from all sorts of documentary materials from the past, here is a book that does exactly the work and provides exactly the model we need. The entire book is a refutation of some current ideas about simply imagining or "making up" the past, simply using it for present noble (or ignoble) purposes, or simply ignoring it. Far from a book about Catholic history (although it is certainly that), Sère's approach proves a model of historical argument at its best.

PREFACE TO THE ENGLISH TRANSLATION

When I conceived, developed, and wrote this book in Paris between 2016 and 2018, following the completion of my habilitation thesis in 2015 and its publication in 2016, my goal was to understand a fundamental tension: Why were Church history textbooks—designed for undergraduate students and written in a synthetic style—so at odds and so discordant with the archival materials I was analyzing as a historian? I began to question the significant gap between the official narrative (as presented in textbooks and magisterial accounts) and the reality captured in the sources themselves.

Reading textbooks from other historiographical traditions—particularly from American, British, Italian, and German perspectives—I encountered similar explanatory frameworks for the historical phenomena I was studying: the Great Western Schism, ecclesiology, reforming councils, the papacy, and opposition to the pontiff. Yet these frameworks were embedded within distinct national narratives, each shaping its own official version of events.

To challenge the grand French narratives and highlight the dissonance between textbooks and sources, I examined how other historiographies addressed the same phenomena. It became evident that these national narratives, too, relied on their own official versions,

xii ❧ PREFACE TO THE ENGLISH TRANSLATION

often equally distant from the historical sources. My aim was to enrich French scholarship by introducing diverse perspectives, particularly from the United States, into French academic discourse. I sought to make these discussions resonate with French intellectual traditions and the textbooks we provide to students. Scholars like Charles McIlwain, Brian Tierney, and Francis Oakley are central to this project because the American school developed a distinctive and fertile approach to medieval ecclesiology.

Today, this book is being translated by Columbia University Press for an Anglo-American audience. This shift highlights a new role I now assume: that of a reverse intermediary, introducing debates from French historiography into an American context, sharing its syntheses, methodologies, and even its blind spots. In addition to rethinking the Franco-centric lens through which historical narratives have been presented, I aspire to initiate (virtual) conversations between figures such as Marie-Dominique Chenu and Brian Tierney, Yves Congar and Francis Oakley, Cary Nederman and Gustave Thils, Thomas Prügl and Alain de Libera, Étienne Fouilloux and John Van Engen, Gerd Tellenbach and Charles McIlwain, and Sylvio De Franceschi and Giuseppe Alberigo.

This process underscores how the meaning of a book evolves with its audience. Readers shape the work. They make a book. While I cannot yet predict how American readers will interpret this book, I have gathered insights from the courses I've taught as a visiting professor at Columbia University's Department of History and at the Jewish Theological Seminary since 2022, as well as from conversations with colleagues—medievalists, historians, biblical scholars, and religious studies experts—in New York and beyond. One recurring theme has emerged: History is often misused, both by the Church and in secular contexts. The use of history is always rife with misrepresentations.

A similar book could be written, in the same vein, about the U.S. Supreme Court. Its recent rulings on presidential immunity bear a

PREFACE TO THE ENGLISH TRANSLATION ☙ xiii

striking resemblance to the doctrine of papal infallibility, particularly when presidents are embroiled in lawsuits or criminal investigations. Legal reasoning in such cases often hinges on interpretations of the U.S. Constitution, particularly around executive privilege and the balance of powers, allowing history to justify these rulings. Precedents such as *Nixon v. Fitzgerald* (1982), which affirmed a sitting president's immunity from civil damages for official acts, have set a legal framework that is continually referenced in modern cases. Yet, much like in Church history, this selective reuse of historical precedents can distort the past and produce misleading narratives.

The story of the seven "isms" illustrates how concepts become entrenched and disconnected from their historical roots. We see how primary sources are often manipulated to serve contemporary needs. Just as the Catholic Church draws on its foundational texts to legitimize its authority, the U.S. Constitution serves as the cornerstone of political legitimacy in America. It becomes essential to ask how each generation interprets these texts, and how they distort them to fit the needs of the present.

This raises an important question for the historian: Should we engage in political activism and impose contemporary sensibilities on the past, or should we resist presentism and allow historical sources to speak for themselves? The answer is crucial for understanding the role of history in today's world.

To conclude this preface, I would like to take this opportunity to express my deep gratitude to Caroline W. Bynum, without whom this English edition would not exist, and to Barbara H. Rosenwein, whose thoughtful insights and enduring friendship have been invaluable to this work.

INVENTING THE CHURCH

INTRODUCTION

The historian must constantly learn to detach himself from the prevailing discourse of the institution he studies, especially when that institution wants to convey—and even manages to convince itself—that the tradition to which it refers is history itself.

—Claude Langlois, *Le continent théologique. Explorations historiques* (Presses Universitaires de Rennes, 2016), 40

This study arose from a question. Why are academic textbooks so discordant with the primary source documentation of the Middle Ages? More precisely, how might the gap between the fifteenth-century archival documentary sources and the official narratives of the same period—the narratological frameworks of which have circulated (perhaps unintentionally) through textbooks used to teach religious history and Church history—be understood? This contrast in narrativities demands pause.

The starting point of this book is engagement with archival sources and knowledge of texts from the late Middle Ages. However, the book is not directly aimed at deploying the contents of these texts in service of an interpretive goal. Instead, it seeks to take a certain distance from the "Church" as object, as well as from the traditions of

2 &? INTRODUCTION

"religious history" and "Church history." The book holds up the "Church" as an object of study not by delving into the content of its *history*, but rather by following the traces of its *narrative* or, more precisely, the *creation of its narrative*.

I thus envisage the Church as an object of study not in the sense of religious history, much less ecclesiastical history, but instead at the confluence of political history, the history of doctrinal categories, the history of political modernity, the history of constructions of classical concepts in the history of political ideas, and the history of conceptual appropriations and paradigms that have shaped our understanding of the present through the prism of a past, whether recent or distant. The political is constructed through the ecclesial. By means of a critical historiography, this book investigates the gestation of the political. Indeed, by retracing how the Church continually manipulated accounts of its own past in order to construct its memory and to create a narrative, I shall show how the Church invented itself through a constant back-and-forth between the Middle Ages and modernity—or, rather, between the Middle Ages and contemporaneity.

The grand narrative of the Church was constructed after the events concerned took place. "Church history" as it can be read in textbooks is, therefore, no more than an optical illusion resulting from the need of the Church to narrate its past differently, according to the sensibilities of the present. While examining how the Church itself was telling its own story, I use the term "Church" to mean something different from the ecclesial. By means of critical distance and painstaking reconstructions of layers of narrative, we see the ecclesial genesis of political modernity. The subject here is thus less ecclesial and religious than it is a revision of our perception of the ecclesial genesis of political modernity; it offers a Middle Ages without the Church. Such is the intellectual framework of my approach.

The reader will thus move constantly back and forth between the Middle Ages and modernity as archival sources from the medieval

INTRODUCTION ❧ 3

period—particularly its final centuries—are consistently confronted with more recent narratives. To reiterate: In this approach it is the discursive gap that creates meaning, the Church's self-narration being something distinct from the history of the Church.

The time-honored construction of grand teleological narratives—for example, those from the Enlightenment era or the Whigs—is well-known. Historians have for some time now denounced these grand narratives, these vast historiological constructs in which the teleology of progress serves as the key to understanding history. Linear interpretations, ideological interpretations, idealizing interpretations—all have already been deconstructed by historians of the debates around secularization, theories of modernization, or, recently, the political stakes of periodization.[1] However, to understand the gap between archival research and the narrative given by textbooks of religious history, it is important to trace the genealogy and construction of certain grand narratives after engaging with the archives of the fifteenth century.[2] Our perspective is not one of a counter-ideological (and hence polemical) offensive, but instead one of the hermeneutical utility of reconstituting genealogies and describing the resulting historiographical configurations quasi-phenomenologically and even through stylization. We might thus better situate the continuities and discontinuities, the antecedents and parallelisms, the filiations and their usages in service of an improved historiographical reflexivity. To be sure, the question of the medieval legacy imposes itself, along with the inevitable question of modernity. How did the modern world emerge out of the medieval world? How did the passage, the transition, the crossing of the threshold play out? But rather than a new interrogation into the theory of secularization, which has by now been fully addressed,[3] we ask: How has our contemporary world made use of the Middle Ages? By giving voice to the Middle Ages so that it might speak about our contemporary world, with its debates and its passions, this book constantly alternates between the fifteenth century and the nineteenth and twentieth centuries. Through this constant interplay, it traces the establishment of historiographical constructs over the long term in order to trace the constitution of narratives and counternarratives, legitimizations and reuses, linearities and ruptures, reappropriations and suppressions, and manipulations and misinterpretations.

This book, therefore, is not a survey, a textbook, or a didactic work on the history of the Church. It is also not a monograph based on unpublished primary sources. Rather, it presents itself as a series of essays that rely on an ensemble of very recent studies and enter into dialogue with more classical or older works in order to give rise to bold and perhaps risky theses, to stimulate questions, but also to challenge received knowledge and to provoke reflection based on seven "isms," like so many acts of temporalization or dynamic highlightings of realities.[4] In its seven chapters the book attempts a critical reconstruction of conciliarism, constitutionalism, collegialism, reformism, anti-Romanism, modernism, and infallibilism. Each chapter questions the origin of the concept (the ism), its inheritance from the past (whether continuous or interrupted), and its repetition and reuse in contemporary times. This questioning takes place within a constant interplay between archival documentary sources and academic grand narratives, which are the concretization of earlier traditions.

Each chapter poses the question of legacy, since each is situated between the Middle Ages and contemporaneity. Thus, the historiographical debate could be styled a mirror-image gesture showing the continuity or rupture or both in the history of each concept. Was the ism continuous or discontinuous? For each the continuist historians emphasize what they see as a long process, whereas the discontinuists, often agents of a counternarrative, focus on ruptures and the reversibility of the objects or actors in question.

INTRODUCTION ❧ 5

Hence our questions: Is contemporary conciliarism the legacy of the conciliary theories of the fifteenth century? Is it a movement exogenous to the Church and, thus, in rupture with the long tradition of the Church, or is it a movement with roots tapping into canon law since the twelfth century, roots eminently endogenous to the ecclesial tradition because they come from its very heart? Is modern constitutionalism the continuation of medieval ecclesiological conciliarism? Does collegialism, so central to theological discussions at the time of Vatican II, have medieval roots, and if so, what are they? Was reformism, a concept central to the history of the medieval and modern Church and laden with historical significance, embraced by the contemporary ecclesiology of the Conciliar Fathers, or was it avoided, dismissed, or even circumvented? Was anti-Romanism, a historiographical category in modern and contemporary history, not also a reality of the medieval period, an unexplored aspect of its historiography? The long-term religious crisis of modernity—would this not, as Marie-Dominique Chenu has suggested, have had parallels in the crisis of 1270–1277, when the Church faced intellectual modernity in the form of Aristotelianism, especially the radical kind?[5] And should the Middle Ages therefore be considered not the foil to the modernist crisis and the antimodernist paradigm, but rather the setting for a dress rehearsal of the vicissitudes of the Church's relationship with intellectual modernity? As for infallibilism, the exigencies of narratological linearity led to the drawing of legitimacy for the tradition from the Middle Ages, even if it has now been shown that the contemporary understanding of infallibilism is a historical misinterpretation: The infallibilism of the Middle Ages was fundamentally anti-pontifical.

The mirror images of continuism and discontinuism in the historiographical debate are compounded by the fact that it is possible to speak of a double continuism and a double discontinuism. Indeed, in

6 � INTRODUCTION

the grand narratives this is not only a question of continuity between the medieval period and the modern/contemporary period, with the issues of periodization to be understood as issues of power or the illusions of ruptures as theorems of secularization. It is also a question of continuity—or discontinuity—between the disciplinary fields of the religious and the political: Is political constitutionalism an extension of ecclesiological conciliarism? What does the state owe to the Church in terms of state dynamism and political innovation? Is it secularization, or a blank slate? Is modernity itself a radical new beginning, or is it a cryptic extension of Christianization? What place does an ecclesial-Christian Middle Ages occupy in Western modernity? These questions imply two historiographical crises. The first is the crisis of periodization, in the sense that Kathleen Davis has shown to be no more than a gesture of power on the part of modernity. The second is the crisis of disciplinary boundaries, the lines of which the young field of history of knowledge seeks to interrogate in order to better account for a new coherence of areas of knowledge.[6] The sole ambition of pointing out this dual crisis is to better understand the medieval legacy in its contemporary usage. The constant back-and-forth between the late Middle Ages and the nineteenth and twentieth centuries is meant to give us a better understanding of our relationship with contemporaneity, and in particular the relationship between our contemporaneity and religious matters.

This is why the validity of often questionable historiographical interpretations of the Middle Ages is less interesting for the purposes of the present book than the heuristic value of identifying and analyzing contemporary interpretive projections on the "screen" of the Middle Ages. What is of interest to the present reflection is making intelligible readings that are, historiographically, dubious. In their intersections and collisions, these readings shed new light on modernity.

SEVEN ESSAYS ABOUT ISMS

The seven chapters are all linked together in a tightly woven fabric of interpenetration and narratological construction. The same may be said of conciliarism in its own right, for in a sense conciliarism formed the basis of the other isms. Indeed, it is a model for tracing the construction of grand narratives. If defined as an instance of control, conciliarism limited monarchic power—in this case, pontifical power. However, this definition should be qualified. It is true that, hardened by the era of the Council of Basel, a time when conciliar theories radicalized during a moment of conflict between the pope and the Conciliar Fathers, historiography rapidly established the fifteenth century as a century of reformist councils and the golden age of conciliarism. But that golden age perished quickly, according to the official Roman version of the narrative, with death spasms caused by the Second Council of Pisa, and it ultimately came to a definitive end with the Fifth Lateran Council. According to the official magisterial interpretation, therefore, conciliarism was merely a revolutionary episode and an accident of history. For the proponents of an official counternarrative, on the other hand, it was a golden age that persisted underground and proved to be a long-term movement. Far from being dead in the fifteenth century, conciliarism in fact fed the English parliamentarism of the sixteenth and seventeenth centuries, and even the different types of democratic constitutionalism that existed up to the nineteenth and twentieth centuries, before finding new life in the 1960s with the "new conciliarism" at the start of Vatican II.

Along with collegialism and reform, conciliarism presents itself as a type of counterpower to and limitation of absolutism. It feeds anti-Roman sensibility as a pole of resistance to Roman pontifical and monarchical primacy, in the same way that modernism is the other

8 ❧ INTRODUCTION

pole of resistance, in an intellectual sense, against Roman supremacy. Moreover, conciliarism and pontifical infallibilism are two principles in tension, just as the *Haec sancta* (1415) and *Pastor aeternus* (1870) may be understood to be in tension, since the council considered itself to be the infallible authority.

When reading the archives, however, the common version of an official narrative—that of the "politics of forgetting" in the face of conciliarism and its counternarrative—enters into dissonance with the reality of the sources. This was a reality much more complex, more sinuous, and less linear than that reflected in modern narratives. Two examples—Pierre d'Ailly and Jean Gerson—show this clearly. Consecrated as "conciliarists" by posterity, neither of the two men was entirely so in his respective evolution. For both figures, a scrupulous reading of the sources reveals the extent to which the myth of conciliarism was constructed wholesale by a partisan narratology: through a skillfully orchestrated archival arrangement for the former, and through the selective memory of posterity for the latter.

Was constitutionalism shaped—or not—by medieval conciliarism, this ecclesiological version of the proto-constitutionalism of the Church? This was the debate at the heart of a historiographical configuration that maintained a double continuism: one continuism from the medieval period to the modern period, and the other from the ecclesiological field to the political field. As a result, the question arises of whether political modernity is, or is not, based on an ecclesiological substrate. "From Gerson to Grotius," Figgis wrote; Brian Tierney specified, "from Gratian to Grotius."[7] The slow emergence of constitutional processes over the long period stretching from the twelfth to the eighteenth centuries went hand in hand with the slow emergence of the state and, for some historians, gave weight to ecclesiological models in the conceptualization of the modern state. Others, by contrast, have seen no continuity between one and the other: no filiation, no genesis of modern constitutionalism

INTRODUCTION ❧ 9

in the modern period. After all, there was no state in the medieval period.

Thus, the debate has pitted adherents of continuism and discontinuism in deadlocked opposition. The question of political theology explodes around, or behind, the constitutional theme. In this sense, the political theology of Carl Schmitt, the Nazi political theorist, is what one might call resolutely antimodern. Like both reformism and anti-Romanism (and, undeniably, like conciliarism), constitutionalism has participated in constructing a *limitatio* to the absolute power of the pontiff, or, in other words, constructing the idea of a counterpower.

Collegialism is understood in the contemporary perspective, which is to say that of the Fathers of Vatican II, as meaning an episcopal collegialism. The contemporary theologians have drawn the roots necessary for the linearity of their narrative from the medieval past, thus affirming their narrative's legitimacy. However, they established the tradition at the cost of a historical "forcing." The history of collegialism as it was written at the time of Vatican II remains a history of theologians, which is to say a history of doctrines. It also remains a history conditioned by the magisterium, in the lineage of the "ecclesiastic policy of forgetting" that ignores the dark hours of Church memory, such as the episcopalist current at the Second Council of Pisa, for example. This is a history that requires harmonizing the constitutionalist tendencies contained in the notion of collegialism, as defended by the progressive faction of the council, with a hierarchy and respect for primacy, revised after the composition of the dogmatic constitution *Lumen gentium* by the adherents of pontifical monarchism. The collegialism of the 1960s was, above all, cut off from the history of medieval practices, which are clear from the medieval sources and documentation, with its capitulary, canonical, municipal, and even synodal and conciliar assemblies. This was not an episcopal collegialism. Such a thing clearly never existed in the Middle

Ages, contrary to what contemporaneity has managed to claim. As with infallibilism, something entirely different was meant, despite the use of the same term and the efforts to construct a linear narrative.

The notion of *reformatio*, or what we would know by the modern term "reformism," also presents a violent contrast between its medieval usage and its modern and contemporary evolution. This was a multivalent term throughout the medieval period, culminating in a powerful stream in the fifteenth century, particularly at the time of the reformist councils. That contrasted with the times when the term was used on its own to signal an authentic political program within the Church, a piece on the chessboard of the ecclesiological propositions of the time. Beyond the rupture of the Reformation, in the sixteenth century, what was at stake at the time of Vatican II was the discrediting and semantic circumvention of the term. *Aggiornamento* was preferred instead, signaling the repression of *reformatio*. According to Yves-Marie Congar, regardless of whether reform was true or false, its connotations were too subversive and dangerous. Because reform, like conciliarism, constitutionalism, collegialism, and anti-Romanism, is a concept involving the limitation of power, specifically of pontifical power, the term arouses suspicion. Because reformism, like modernism, aims not to break with the Church but rather to question it and to make it evolve, to transform it, the term has been lightly dismissed. Reformism always provokes an antireformism in the ecclesial world, reinforced by the establishment of the dogma of infallibility, for which reform has neither pertinence nor necessity. The twentieth century has shown that between reform and the Church there exists a passionate relationship woven with semantic charges and discharges, reappropriations and avoidances, attractions and repressions.

Anti-Romanism combines all the trends of ecclesial constitutionalism in resistance to Roman primacy. Because it adopts this posture of counterpower through rebalancing, contestation, and critical distance in the face of monarchic omnipotence, anti-Romanism, like

INTRODUCTION ❦ II

conciliarism, constitutionalism, and collegialism, aims to protect against and prevent the abuse of absolute centrality. Like the other isms, anti-Romanism induces a binary in an ideologically constructed reflectiveness: Romanism/anti-Romanism; modernism/antimodernism; infallibilism/anti-infallibilism. The discrepancy between a reading of the sources of the fifteenth century, especially those of the Great Western Schism, and the historiographical configurations of the twentieth century also remains strong here. In this case, however, the route from one period to another has an inverse evolution. While historical research has rendered anti-Romanism a modern and contemporary category, with no expression in prior periods, the archives of the fifteenth century speak of it as if it were a tangible reality: hatred of the pope, hatred of the pontifical office, personal hatred of Benedict XIII (1396–1422), etc. Although it is not a category that has been accounted for in the Middle Ages historiographically, its presence in the period is nevertheless validated by the sources. Late medieval anti-Romanism makes sense, although it is neglected in contemporary historiography and official accounts that, nevertheless, tend to show that the charge against centralized and absolute power began much earlier than the sixteenth and seventeenth centuries and was much broader than merely the ecclesial sphere. Anti-Romanism is a form of anti-absolutism that has also weakened ties between the king and his subjects.

Because it can be read as the intellectual version of political counterpower and the *limitatio* of Roman pontifical power, modernism is itself close to the political principles of conciliarism, constitutionalism, and collegialism. As a sensibility of resistance and critical thinking, it is fundamentally similar to anti-Romanism in its relation to the Roman center, to the point that it is possible to see convergence in modernism's postures of resistance to the regimes of institutional centrality and intellectual veridiction. Like anti-infallibilism, to which it may be compared and of which it is a contemporary, modernism puts into question and into crisis the regimes of veridiction avowed by the central body, whether theological or historical. Anti-infallibilism and modernism make way for critical thought and reject Roman intransigence. In the complex history of modernism, the Middle Ages are unique in that they were reinterpreted in the sense of medievalism, an antimodernist paradigm necessary for the fuller elaboration of modernism. Through this twisting of narratives into an era that never was, the Middle Ages therefore become the revealer of contemporary passions—their precipitate. This is why performing closer readings of controversies (those of the thirteenth century, in this case) leads to the discovery of parallels between the crisis of 1270–1277 and the modernist crisis of 1907. The mechanisms of resistance and censure attest to a long-term religious crisis in the relationship between the Church and intellectual modernity, even when the two historiographical traditions do not intersect.

As it was developed in the nineteenth century, infallibilism is in a sense "a new idea," to use Claude Langlois's phrase.[8] But this new idea needed historical roots. The thurifers of pontifical infallibilism, unsurprisingly, tapped the Middle Ages to fill this need for roots. There, they read the genesis of an idea, with the result that the contemporary narrative presents all the characteristics of linearity and continuity. The concept and its partisans thus equipped themselves with a strong advantage in the lively controversy that took over the period from the final third of the nineteenth century until Vatican II. Upon a closer reading of the authors of the fourteenth and fifteenth centuries, however, it becomes clear that infallibilism was not the same thing in the Middle Ages as in the nineteenth and twentieth centuries. The contemporary understanding of medieval infallibilism is the history of a misinterpretation. In fact, in the fourteenth century, in the context of debates over evangelical poverty, the concept of infallibility was at the heart of a conception of the limitation of pontifical power: It was about protecting the traditions of the

Church by preventing popes from invalidating, at their discretion, the decisions taken by past pontiffs. Infallibility was a constitutional safeguard against the arbitrariness of pontiffs. In the fifteenth century, infallibility was exclusively a question of the infallibility of the council. Suffice it to say that William of Ockham and Simon de Cramaud would only have been infallibilist in the sense of an anti-pontifical infallibilism. The relationship of contemporaneity to its own memory thus has led to distortions of history and manipulations of its medieval past. As closely as possible to the fifteenth-century understandings of the sources, this book points out the contrasts in narrativities: One is a linear narrativity of the infallibilist reinvention, and the other issues from the texts themselves, in rupture with this linearity.

1

CONCILIARISM

From Historical Reality to
Historiographical Crystallization

Narratological constructs concerning the council and conciliar theories served as the starting point for the grand constructions of the official historiography of the fifteenth century. Through the constitutionalism of their political propositions and their historical implementation during the first half of the fifteenth century, in fact, the council and conciliar theories became real, attractive, and convincing alternatives to ecclesial government at a time when the papacy had scarcely recovered from the upheavals of the century. The issue was thus a major one: It was necessary to tarnish the memory of an episode that had humiliated the monarchic omnipotence of the pontiff and his image. The historiographical operation needed to rewrite the events.

FIFTEENTH-CENTURY CONCILIAR THEORIES

The Familiar Framework of Conciliar Facts

"The fifteenth century was the century of the council, just as the thirteenth century had been that of the exaltation of the papacy and the fourteenth that of Avignonian centralization," Jean-Louis

16 &) CONCILIARISM

Gazzaniga wrote in a 1984 article about appeals to the council.[1] The time of the Great Western Schism and the so-called reforming councils was a time of trouble and of ecclesiological questioning. The density of conciliar events was the occasion for diverse experiments: at Pisa (1409), Perpignan (1408–1409), Cividale (1409), Rome (1413), Constance (1414–1418), and Basel (1431–1449). The chronology of the emergence of the conciliar idea is well-known, as is its theorization, thanks particularly to the work of Hermann Josef Sieben, who identified a vast ensemble of treatises as so many theories regarding the council's authority.[2]

In broad strokes, the scenario has been established in textbooks and other works of religious history: The first appeals dated to the years 1379–1380, with the treatises of Henry of Langenstein and Conrad of Gelnhausen, on the one hand, and considerations in the form of scholastic questions posed by Peter Flandrin, Pedro Tenorio, Pierre Ameilh, and Petrus Boeri, on the other. After this first wave and a period of silence imposed by the French monarchy there came the time of the University of Paris and its theological faculty, starting in 1394. The so-called path of the council (*via concilii*) faded, making way for the resolution of the schism through the resignation of at least one of the two popes (or the "path of resignation," *via cessionis*). In the years 1404–1407, the partisans of the *via cessionis*, recognizing the path's failure as a solution to the schism, turned toward the conciliar idea.

At this time, appealing to the council was a sign of belonging to the "*via cessionis* party." Such was the case for Simon de Cramaud and Jean Courtecuisse. Around 1408–1409, with the convocation of the Council of Pisa, following the double cession of the respective cardinal colleges, many personalities joined the movement, tired of the stubbornness and inertia of Benedict XIII, and of obedience to Avignon. Among the disappointed were Pierre d'Ailly and Jean Gerson. After the enthusiasm of Pisa came the bitterness of its outcome as a third pope was elected without the removal of the other two. The council was not supported by a strong secular authority. At the same time, obedient councils occurred (Perpignan, Cividale, Rome).

In 1414, Sigismund, king of the Romans, in the manner of the Christian Roman emperors, convoked the Council of Constance, which opened on November 1 of that same year. The council brought together all of Christianity: prelates, academics, and doctors as well as prominent laymen. The European monarchs sent their delegates. The council was structured by nation. It asserted itself under Sigismund's authority, especially following Pope John XXIII's flight to Schaffhausen on March 20, 1415, after which the council decided that it would continue even without a pope. Some days later, on April 6, 1415, the culmination of conciliar affirmation was articulated in the decree *Haec sancta*: According to it, the ecumenical council is inspired by the Holy Spirit; its power comes directly from Christ and it represents the entire Church; the pope is bound to conform to it. The council therefore becomes the authority with control over the pope. Another decree, called *Frequens*, followed on October 9, 1417, and imposed regularity in conciliar meetings. The council became the regular governing body in the Church (even if its rule was not subsequently applied). On November 11, 1417, Martin V was elected pope. This was the end of the Great Western Schism. Many councils were convoked and assembled to apply the decree *Frequens*: Siena-Pavia in 1423, Basel in 1431. The Council of Basel again devolved into drama and set Pope Eugene IV in violent opposition against the Conciliar Fathers. The episode continued in a tormented and radicalized atmosphere until 1449.

The outline of events is well-known, then, as are the treatises and the theorists. The implications of conciliar theories had bearing on the limitation of monarchic pontifical power, which Jean Gerson insisted must be tempered. The council was conceived of as an organ of control. In this sense, it might become an organ of reform.

The decree *Haec sancta* stated as much: The council has authority over the pope in that it might control him. At Basel, the most radical of the Conciliar Fathers went the furthest in interpreting the decree in the sense of a superiority of the council over the pope. Born in this context was the term "conciliarism," which was probably used for the first time by Lorenzo d'Arezzo, author of *Liber de ecclesiastica potestate*.[3]

Which Realities of Conciliarism? The Examples of Pierre d'Ailly and Jean Gerson

The historiographical posterity of the political theories of the time created a golden age out of the fifteenth century. Conciliar actions, authors, and treatises were quickly erected as a paradigm of conciliarism whose model must have dated from this moment. Pierre d'Ailly and Jean Gerson became the incontestable theorists of conciliarism, ahead of John of Segovia or Nicholas of Cusa. But, returning to the texts more closely, a gap between the official version of conciliarism as it appears in the historiography and the complexity of the words and trajectories of the authors must be acknowledged.

Turning to the case of Pierre d'Ailly, we might rightly ask whether he was a conciliarist.[4] When we examine his texts from 1380 to 1420, we may see the nonlinear development of his political thinking about the council. His evolution was marked by reversals, ruptures, and rallies. Pierre d'Ailly was more politician than ecclesiologist: His conciliar stance was driven solely by the pressing needs of the moment and the practical realities at play. His was a conciliarism of circumstance more than of conviction. But the image of the "conciliarist Pierre d'Ailly" came precisely from archivistic manipulations that he himself orchestrated. He produced an optical illusion

CONCILIARISM ❧ 19

rather than an exact reflection of his real doctrinal production. In fact, in 1411, when Boniface Ferrer, prior general of the Carthusians, publicly insulted and made allegations against him in a treatise against the Council of Pisa, Pierre d'Ailly, then a cardinal, had to defend himself. He did this with the *Apologia concilii Pisani* in 1412. To better justify himself, he began by defending the council under attack, the Council of Pisa, and by casting himself as the champion of conciliarism. But, thanks to the council's records, it is known that Pierre d'Ailly was absent at the times of major decisions, under the pretexts of diplomatic missions or illness. Hélène Millet has convincingly shown that "he adhered to the party of the union legitimately assembled in the council, but not in the way in which the council had believed could put an end to the Schism."[5] His conciliarism was therefore neither certain nor complete.

In this treatise, the cardinal above all attempted to defend himself against accusations of fleeing or fighting against the council. He needed to restore his image as a coherent thinker free of self-contradiction. Revisiting his writings, he highlighted everything that could be read as leaning toward conciliarism, pointing out allusions and remarks in order to rewrite his doctrinal itinerary and reshuffle the chronology of his membership in the council. According to this narrative, which can be refuted by a careful reading of his texts of the 1380s and 1390s, he had endorsed the path of the council since the beginning of the schism. It was his writings that justified him, he proclaimed. Hence the significant archival reshuffling that he carried out. In the *Apologia concilii Pisani*, he quoted himself almost exhaustively in order to make his trajectory appear coherent and to erase his own reluctance to take the plunge into conciliar doctrine. He rewrote his own texts, such as the *De materia concilii generalis*, first written in 1402 and reworked in 1416. In his office, he had his collected writings copied into compilations. He corrected and annotated them in the margins. In short, the state of the archives reflects Pierre d'Ailly's own desire to provide his contemporaries and posterity with an image of himself as the conciliarist he had never been in reality.

The position of Jean Gerson, better known than that of his master, presents similarities. Posterity has consecrated Gerson as *the* conciliarist of the fifteenth century, without concession or regret.[6] The conciliar—which is to say conciliarist—ecclesiology of the Parisian chancellor was invoked from the fifteenth century to the middle of the twentieth, and again, in the early twenty-first century, in Philippe Denis's 2014 book.[7] The interpretations of the chancellor's work may be traced across centuries, movements, authors, and their doctrines. The question is what the successive appropriations of Gerson through these texts might tell us, and what meanings might be drawn from rereadings of his work.

Like Pierre d'Ailly, Gerson considered the conciliar solution only in terms of the grand ecclesiological movements of the moment, within the very specific context of events of the time. In fact, within the ecclesiology constructed by Gerson on the subject of conciliar realities from 1391 to 1418, three conciliar theories can be distinguished: The first is conciliarism by way of papalism (with the council remaining the instrument of pontifical supremacy, 1391–1402); the second is conciliarism by way of anti-subtractionism (1402–1409); finally, the third, that seen at Constance, is conciliarism by way of conviction (1409–1418). Historians, the modern commentators, have retained only one stage of this progressive evolution of and plasticity in Gerson's conciliarism: its maturity— that is, the Gerson of the years 1409–1418, the complete Gerson, the convinced conciliarist. This is the Gerson of the *De potestate ecclesiastica*, the treatise that gathers his major conclusions and states his ecclesiological constitutionalism: The council must limit and regulate the pope's use of *plenitude potestatis*.[8] How should this selection be understood?

CONCILIARISM ❦ 21

Regarding his ecclesiological work, Gerson himself was able to provide instructions to his readers. In ecclesiological matters, at the end of the treatise *De auferibilitate sponsi* he advised reading three works together: the *De auferibilitate sponsi* itself (1415), the *Tractatus de unitate* (1409), and the famous sermon delivered before the pope at Tarascon, *Apparuit gratia* (1404):

> Ecce ergo viginti considerationes quodam ordine geometrico se sequentes, quae junctis aliis sedecim quarum cujuslibet initium est Unitas ecclesiastica, additis quoque aliis quatuor dudum Tarascone praedicatis, redduntur quadraginta considerationes.
>
> (Behold, then, the twenty points following each other in a certain geometrical order, which, when joined to the other sixteen, the beginning of each of which is about ecclesiastical unity, and the addition of the other four already preached in Tarascon, make forty points.)[9]

The twenty points of the *De auferibilitate*, to which Gerson added the sixteen points of the *Tractatus de unitate* and the four points of the sermon at Tarascon, thus made a total of forty points. With this assertion Gerson presented himself as an antipapalist at least, if not a full conciliarist. Gerson only selected texts that expressed resistance to the pontiff, with the sermon at Tarascon marking the start of his path. This image of a non-papalist (which he had not always been) is therefore skewed. It is, however, the image that he himself wanted to leave to posterity.

A close look at the manuscript tradition reveals that Gerson's recommendation was not followed in reality. Of the forty-three manuscripts containing at least one of the three works, not a single one includes all three together. In other words, Gerson's recommendation was neither heard nor implemented. Posterity adopted other criteria for assembling collections. The archival state of the manuscript copies, in fact, seems to follow the principles of compilation based on *auctoritas*, or the reputation of the famous author, more so than on thematic principles, which here would be ecclesiological. To put it another way, the manuscripts did not copy the texts based on their functions in the disciplinary field of ecclesiology, as Palémon Glorieux sought to do when classifying Gerson's works into thematic volumes. In contrast to Glorieux, and especially in contrast to Gerson's wish, there was no regrouping of texts based on themes of ecclesiology or conciliarism. As Daniel Hobbins has convincingly shown, the assembling of collections and copies was instead based on the author's name. It was Gerson's *auctoritas* that counted in compiled volumes.[10] It was the receiving audiences who decided the criteria of compilation, and not the recommendations of Gerson himself. They respected Gerson as a theological authority and spiritual guide.[11] In contrast to Pierre d'Ailly, the complete works of Gerson are therefore the basis of all systematic study concerning him, and have been so since shortly after his death.[12]

In the context of Bellarmine's challenges to Gerson's orthodoxy,[13] and in the wake of the outbreak of anti-Romanism in Venice led by Paolo Sarpi (1606), Edmond Richer (1559–1631), a syndic of the Faculty of Theology of Paris, undertook the defense of the chancellor and claimed to present the purest doctrine of the Paris school according to a "typically French theological-political sensibility."[14] He collected under the name "Paris school" the major adherents to conciliar theories from the fifteenth century until the beginning of the sixteenth—namely, Pierre d'Ailly, Jean Gerson, Jacques Almain, and John Major, sometimes stretching back to the fourteenth century to include John of Paris. In the anonymously published edition of 1606 he collected the complete works of Gerson and the principal treatises of the other cited theorists.[15] In 1611, he published in Latin the treatise *De ecclesiastica et politica potestate*, which was translated into French in 1612 as *De la puissance ecclésiastique et politique* (On ecclesiastical and political power).[16] The text was intended to be an abridgement of the doctrine of the theological faculty of Paris, or the "Paris school," on the question of the relationships between civil power and ecclesiastical power in the anti-Roman context of the Bellarminian theory of the *potestas indirecta* of the pope *in rebus temporalibus*—namely, the right of the pontiff to intervene insofar as spiritual interests demand.[17] Gerson is explicitly cited in it only twice,[18] although the introduction claims to build on the work of "l'Eschole de Paris."[19] Richer's thesis therefore claimed to rely on Gerson to defend a constitutionalism of the conciliar type, with an aristocratic conception of the power of the Church. In it, the government is mixed: the monarch is the legislator, the aristocracy the executor branch. The sovereignty of the community of the faithful must be defended against pontifical absolutism. Monarchy is therefore constitutional, which is to say limited and controlled. From this first foundational thesis of his politico-ecclesiological theory, Richer advanced to a second foundation: the defense of the rights of priests, the successors to the seventy disciples from the Book of Luke. This was a form of presbyterianism.

Starting in 1612, Richer was challenged, condemned, blacklisted, and dismissed. The leading expert on his works and his most formidable adversary was André Duval (1564–1638), a representative of Catholic zealotry and a pro-Roman doctor who was closely connected with the nuncio Ubaldini.[20] In his attack, Duval forged the polemical category of "Richerism": He claimed that Richer had distorted the teachings of the Paris school. He accused Richer of having misrepresented Gerson. His undertaking was to defend Gerson against Richer and to reclaim Gerson in the service of justifying a monarchical Church. His ecclesiology was ultramontane. From here, issues of appropriation shaped the controversy. Richer claimed to continue Gerson's work, and Duval intended to rehabilitate the true Gerson. This was how, hardened by controversies, the conciliarist Gerson presented by Richer and Richerism appealed to the Jansenist, Gallican, and parliamentary movements. In 1682, while writing the *Quatre*

24 ∾ CONCILIARISM

articles de la Déclaration du clergé gallican, which venerated pontifical primacy, Bossuet denied pontifical absolutism and the infallibility of the pontiff.[21] He reaffirmed the prestige of the great conciliarists, the validity of the *Haec sancta*, and the teachings of the Paris school, even if he placed more emphasis on episcopal dignity than on conciliarism.

In 1706, Louis Ellies du Pin relied on Richer's edition when preparing a new edition of the complete works of Gerson. A year later, the same du Pin wrote a commentary on Bossuet's *Déclaration* of 1682, titled *Traité de la puissance ecclésiastique*, referring to the Paris school, for which the general council was superior to the authority of the pontiff: The commentary's references to d'Ailly and Gerson are numerous.[22] Du Pin combined conciliarist, Gallican, and Jansenist sensibilities. In the eighteenth century, Jansenists and parliamentarians saw Richer as one of their own. They conceived of a conciliarist constitutionalism based on his words, to the point that his work inspired the writing of the Civil Constitution of the Clergy in 1790.[23] A type of Jansenism that emerged in the 1750s, which Catherine Maire calls "judiciary Jansenism" in her works, is well represented by the figures of Mey and Maultrot, lawyers at the Parlement of Paris starting in 1733, canonists, and Jansenists who were interested in Richer and Richerism.[24] The two authors professed a radical conciliarism based on Ockham, Gerson, and Almain. This made room for canon law, a central component of their argument. Maultrot defended Richerism in the context of the imminent expulsion of the Jesuits from the French kingdom in the same year, 1763.

Finally, the nineteenth century saw a long eclipse of the Gersonian authority in the ecclesiological Catholic world. But at the same time, some Protestants appropriated the chancellor, whom they framed as a reformist precursor in a facile teleology. All Protestant theological seminaries discussed the "pre-reformer" Gerson. A clear illustration of this is the title of a work by Émile de Bonnechose,

Réformateurs avant la Réforme, XVe siècle: Gerson, Jean Hus et le concile de Constance, avec des considérations nouvelles sur l'Église gallicane depuis le grand schisme jusqu'à nos jours (Reformers before the reform, fifteenth century: Gerson, Jean Hus, and the Council of Constance, with new considerations about the Gallican Church from the Great Schism to our time).[25] The *Dictionnaire de théologie catholique* expressed concern over this Protestant appropriation of the French chancellor, despite the lack of attention paid to him by Catholic historiography over the course of the nineteenth century. The entry for "Gerson (Jean le Charlier de)," composed contemporaneously to the entry for "Gallicanism," was written by Louis-Joseph Salembier (1849–1913). The author, a Catholic priest, expressed annoyance at this Protestant appropriation and denounced the reclamation:

> Extenuating circumstances can be pleaded in Gerson's favor. He had been instructed by men who were none too stable, and had made a close study of William of Ockham, the most evil genius of the fourteenth century. As we have seen, Gerson was generally more sensible and moderate in practice than in theory. D'Ailly and Gerson are accused of having been the fathers of Gallicanism and, from a certain point of view, this is not incorrect. Let us note, however, to be fair, that when it came to the first subtraction of obedience, in 1398, these so-called leaders of anti-pontifical opinions played no part.[26]

Salembier not only justified Gerson and sought to rehabilitate him but was also, perhaps, unique in intuiting the complex evolution of Gersonian ecclesiology instead of expressing certainty that Gerson's conciliarism was either linear or uniform. Above all, according to Salembier, even if Gerson seemed sulfurous, he was not overly so, and Catholicism could lay claim to the man without shame. Salembier warned against the editions of Gerson's works produced by Richer and Louis Ellies du Pin, which he wrote were "prepared under the influence of Gallican ideas and with a view to religious polemics."[27] In short, the Gallican and Protestant appropriations of Gerson by Von der Hardt, Richer, and du Pin damaged the chancellor's memory—which Roman Catholicism nevertheless needed, just as it needed that of Bossuet. As an *auctoritas* canonized in an academic sense, if not by Rome, Gerson's name had become an intellectual guarantee—more so than an ecclesiological one—that was endowed with a powerful legitimizing role. One might almost say that Gerson's name functioned as an empty *auctoritas*, one that produced ideological effects. Or, rather, it was an empty reference, the contents of which had been neutralized but that still functioned connotatively with real efficacy.

The conciliar myth is therefore far from reality: Conciliarism is a historiographical construct that must be deconstructed.

THE POLITICAL HIJACKING OF CONCILIARISM IN THE MODERN ERA

In the sixteenth century, the dynamism of conciliar theories came, above all, from the reuse of a model borrowed from the preceding century's "golden age of conciliarism," rather than from theological content or ecclesiological development.

Starting with the Second Council of Pisa (1511–1512) and its counteroffensive, the Fifth Lateran Council, the conciliar organ was very quickly instrumentalized as a tool of political pressure, a "weapon of deterrence," in Jean-Louis Gazzaniga's words, or an "essential safety valve," in those of Olivier de La Brosse. More than a religious body, the council was, above all, a political weapon: "In the arsenal of the time, the threat of the council had the value of a large piece of artillery."[28] The memory of the reformist Councils of Constance and, especially, of Basel, painful for the papacy, permitted French kings to brandish threats of a council each time the balance of power between them and the pope grew tense, as happened during the reigns of Charles VII, Louis XI, and Charles VIII. Louis XII, in his conflict with Pope Julius II over French ambitions in Italy, moved from the traditional threat to actual implementation: With the support of five French cardinals, he assembled a council at Pisa in 1511. The matter at hand was a denunciation of Julius II's noncompliance with the *Frequens* decree, and thereby a condemnation of the pope.

The failure of the Second Council of Pisa is well-known: Poorly attended (seven cardinals, two archbishops, and twenty-four bishops) and hardly representative (the prelates were all French; none were Italian), the council was forced to retreat to Milan, to Asti, and then to Lyon. It was accused of resembling a conciliabule, its near homonym, or even of being a "rump parliament" (F. Rapp) in which only bishops devoted to Louis XII were seated.[29] The council closed ingloriously in 1512, and that same year Julius II, in response, convoked the Fifth Lateran Council. Its location was significant. Julius II intended to serve as the effective chair of the council and to set its agenda, in the manner of the pontifical councils of the twelfth and thirteenth centuries. The texts produced there were not decrees but pontifical bulls set forth by the pope himself after conciliar approval. With the episode of the Second Council of Pisa and the Fifth Lateran Council, historiography declared "the agony of conciliarism" and "the definitive victory of the papacy."

Today, however, the episode can be better explained: The so-called victory of the papacy was not so much a unilateral achievement as an error in political tactics. In the conflict between Julius II and Louis XII, the imbalance of power resulted from a bad choice of arena. Although he could have remained master of the military arena, Louis XII committed the double error of veering into ecclesiological and spiritual spheres, that of the council. Above all, he put into action

28 ∞ CONCILIARISM

what should have remained merely a threat, something that had been a consistent policy of the Valois kings since Charles VII, when "the strength of Julius II in the Fifth Lateran Council was that he was on his terrain, on his own terrain."[30] The instrument of the council as a political tool ought to have remained in the form of a threat; once executed, it turned into a diplomatic failure, especially because Louis XII, ultimately proving faithful to his predecessors' policy, secretly came to an accord with the pope. Jean-Louis Gazzaniga has explained that the French king rapidly lost interest in the council as soon as it met, despite having fought to convene it, because neither the king nor the pope wanted a schism.[31] The king of France had every reason to come to an agreement with the pope.

We also know that conciliar sensibilities persisted almost everywhere: within the Sacred College, in the universities and religious orders, and in the bureaucratic services of the state, but also from the Curia to the Rota and the consistory. Conciliarism remained perennial among the cardinals, who committed themselves to making the council work in cases where the pontiff did not do so. The movement was certainly not a unified doctrine, nor were its objectives and functions even theorized. Still, one strong idea out of the entire legacy took hold: the idea that pontifical jurisdiction should by no means remain the sole governing body in the Church.

For the French historian Alain Tallon, it was in 1518 that things reached a tipping point. He rightly distinguished between conciliar theology as ecclesiology and conciliarism as an ideological and political movement.[32] What came to a halt in 1518 was conciliar theology—namely, its ongoing study or living ecclesiological elaboration. Tallon spoke of a "theological poverty" and the "vagueness of conciliarist theses defended at the time" as well as the "intellectual decadence of conciliarist ecclesiology in France after 1518."[33] He saw several indications of this, among them the lack of a new edition of Gerson's ecclesiological work despite the constant reissuing of his pastoral works throughout the period.[34] The arguments after 1518 were limited to determining who was "above" or "below" the pope or the council. The great scriptural and patristic texts used in the age of the reformist councils were no longer mentioned.

Far from being attributable to the Reformation, the decline of conciliar theories was due more to the contemporaneous perception of the French monarchy. The monarchy was wary of the conciliar legacy, which it saw as double-edged; royal absolutism had more in common with pontifical absolutism than with academic conciliarism, episcopal conciliarism, or parliamentary conciliarism of the Gallican type. It is evident that conciliarism's potential was too subversive for Valois absolutism, underpinning a collusion of interests between the two forms of absolutism: "the kings contented themselves with a virtual council, a means of pressure and negotiating tactic" against the papacy.[35] This was because in the sixteenth century the Valois monarchy sought to distance itself from the pope as well as from its own theologians and academics. It aimed to subdue the Church within its kingdom. This explains the policy of concordats.

The pontifical monarchy was not monolithically anti-conciliarist. A tripolarity existed, with the pontiff representing one pole, the Curia the second, and the conciliarists the third. The alliances among and between these poles changed over time. The curialists could, in certain years, opt to protect the council against the pope, and the Sacred College could devote itself to the mission of replacing a defective or corrupt pope by means of the council, as happened in the time of Alexander VI Borgia. In the middle of the Fifth Lateran Council, Felinus Sandaeus, auditor of the Rota, and Jacobazzi, dean of the Rota, concluded that by virtue of the right of devolution, the council could be convened without the pope.[36] At other times, it was the pope who wielded the council as a tool against the views of a conservative, anti-conciliarist Curia.[37] Sometimes a council was evoked but, because neither party actually wanted one, collusion between the pope and the Curia hindered its realization. Whether in the French court or in Rome, the Manichaean struggle between Papimanes and Papifigues evoked by Rabelais in book 4 of *Pantagruel* never took place in actuality.[38] Conciliarism remained, above all, an ideological movement that instrumentalized the council as a virtual counterpower. As a weapon it was effective, and the complicity between absolutisms remained well underground and efficient.

For this reason, Francis Oakley and James H. Burns refused to speak of a decline of the conciliarist movement.[39] They attested to its vigor in the 1510s and after 1518, asserting that conciliarism's dynamism came from its historical reuse, not from its theological elaboration, and that the legacy of the councils had never been revived to this extent in the High Middle Ages. The Gallican tradition exhumed the Visigothic, Merovingian, and Carolingian councils, which had been convoked and presided over by kings such as Clovis and Charlemagne. Nostalgia for a time of deliberative and parliamentary assemblies lay at the heart of the establishment of monarchical absolutism and, in its own way, participated in that development.

Conciliar theory and the ideology of conciliarism after the fifteenth century have been analyzed in the context of modern states and nascent absolutisms. They can only be understood outside this political reading with difficulty. In one sense, following Paolo Prodi, the council might almost be conceived of as a hindrance to the establishment of modern states.[40] From this perspective, the council was not a political structure adapted to its times; it was more like a fossil from another age, a fossil that would introduce constitutionalism into the ecclesiology and political theory of the time.

THE 1960S TO THE 2010S: A NEW "GRAND NARRATIVE"

The "New Conciliarism" of the 1960s

When, on January 25, 1959, John XXIII announced the convocation of a council for the year 1962, he created an unprecedented stir. This is well-known. From 1959 until the end of Vatican II, studies on the council and conciliarism exploded. This was what Francis Oakley dubbed the "new conciliarism." For Yves Congar and his circle, a 1960 volume titled *Le concile et les conciles*, resulting from a colloquium at Chevetogne, marked its start.[41] In Italy, Germany, the United States, and Spain, studies multiplied. What might be observed, however, is an insular, nation-based historiography, without real international dialogue. Over the course of decades, specialists retreated into their respective national territories.

In the 1970s, German *Konzilienforschung* was extremely prestigious and dynamic. The names of Regimius Bäumer, Walter Brandmüller, Hermann Josef Sieben, and Hans Schneider suffice to show that, in a certain sense, the Germanic world was at the forefront of scholarship concerning conciliarism.

Grand editorial and scientific undertakings took place. The periodical *Annuarium historiae conciliorum* was founded by Remigius Bäumer and Walter Brandmüller; Johannes Grohe has taken over as editor. In the late 1970s, the book series *Konziliengeschichte* was also founded by Walter Brandmüller; it is currently edited by Peter Burns (Bamberg) and Thomas Prügl (Vienna). To date, it has put together more than sixteen very erudite volumes, among them the seven prestigious works of Hermann Josef Sieben (the most recent published in 2017). A parallel undertaking was the publication of a *Lexikon der Konzilien* edited by Peter Burns, Ansgar Frenken (Ulm), Johannes Grohe (Rome), and Nelson H. Minnich (Washington, DC). In Italy, studies in the wake of the Bologna school flourished starting in the 1980s, with Giuseppe Alberigo's magisterial *Chiesa conciliaire: Identità e significato del conciliarismo* published in Brescia in 1981. In the United States was Brian Tierney, and in the same vein in the United Kingdom, the British scholar Francis Oakley set the tone for studies on conciliarism. His works from 1969 to 2003 (even 2016) established the *doxa* for the historiography of the council. Through these forty years of publications, Oakley crystallized and popularized the binary approach to conciliarism.

The Binary Vision and Narrative Crystallization in the "Oakley Moment"

Already in 1976, Hans Schneider demonstrated in a classic book that the decree *Haec sancta* offers the best vantage point from which to study the polarizations of conciliarism.[42] Indeed, for the purposes of locating the ongoing ideological construct or the "invention of conciliarism," the Council of Constance, and especially the decree *Haec sancta*, which issued from its fifth session, on April 6, 1415, serves as a fine example of the deployment of this "conciliar drama." Ecclesiological and historiographical polemics have focused on this text and this moment in order to elaborate their respective arguments, as well as their signals of belonging and ecclesial identity, even into our own day.

Starting with the studies and controversies that surround the *Haec sancta*, it is possible to trace the polemical framework of the historiographical narrative. The schema is a binary one: For the partisans of pontifical monarchy, conciliarism was no more than an accident, a revolutionary episode in the life of the Church. Following the Council of Basel, the movement was extinguished and disappeared. This was the famous "agony of conciliarism." For the partisans of the council, on the other hand, conciliarism was a movement that, after its fifteenth-century golden age, went underground but continued to be fed by authors and intellectual currents until well into the mid-twentieth century. The writing of these two histories was, in both cases, an issue of a theology rooted in tradition—hence the ideological manipulation of what this tradition entails. History has been used in service of an ideological position, something true for both camps. Diving into the details will permit us to takt account of this construct at work.

The Ecclesiastical Version of a "Politics of Forgetting," or the "Pontifical Camp"[43]

One historiographical strain—the official, ecclesiastic one—has tended to deny the persistence of conciliarism and to limit its existence to the fifteenth century. This negationist reading has its roots in that century, starting with Juan de Torquemada (d. 1468), who, well before the *Summa de ecclesia* (ca. 1453), attributed the origins of conciliarism to the heretical teachings of William of Ockham and Marsilius of Padua, adding that Pope Martin V did not recognize the *Haec sancta*. From here, this papalist—or "philopapal," to use a phrase of Thomas Izbicki[44]—historiography progressed in stages. In 1439 in Florence, Pope Eugene IV, *sacro approbante concilio*, definitively condemned the Council of Basel's interpretation of the doctrine of Constance and the decree *Haec sancta* regarding the superiority of the council over the pope. Promulgated on April 20, 1441, Eugene IV's bull *Etsi non dubitemus* relied heavily on Torquemada. It affirmed, following the theologian, that the founders of this diabolical impiety were Marsilius of Padua, John of Jandun, and William of Ockham.[45] In 1460, Pius II thundered forth with the bull *Exsecrabilis*, which forbade appeals to the council against the pope and defined conciliarism as a *pestiferum virus*.[46]

In 1511, the Second Council of Pisa, founded on the principle of regularly convened councils with episcopal scope, met and suspended the pontifical authority of Pope Julius II. In response, Julius II convoked the Fifth Lateran Council, which opened on May 3, 1512. For the Roman historiography, this crisis consecrated the "victory of the papacy" and the triumph of pontificalism. The Second Council of Pisa was annulled by the Fifth Lateran Council, and the 1516 bull *Pastor aeternus* signaled the end of the conciliar era, the bull declaring that the pope had the right to convoke, transfer, and dissolve the council.[47] The council was no longer either a threat or a reality. It became an "ecclesiological fossil," in Oakley's words, "lodged deep in the lower carboniferous of the dogmatic geology."[48] The theologian Cajetan, relying on the teachings of Thomas Aquinas and Torquemada, ideologically consecrated the triumph of the papacy through his defense of centralized monarchy, particularly in chapters 20 through 22 of his *De comparatione auctoritatis papae et concilii*.

At the end of the nineteenth century, with the revival of Old Catholic theology and the triumphs of pontifical primacy and the dogma of infallibility, theologians redeployed the narratological framework of conciliarism. Still associated with the image of the enemy, conciliarism was, in this interpretation, no more than a revolutionary episode in Church history, heterodox and exogenous, an unfortunate aberration that ended in the 1440s with the triumph of the papacy over the council. As evidence, no entry on conciliarism appeared in *The Catholic Encyclopedia* of 1908, only an entry titled "Councils (General)." In this entry, the Council of Pisa is omitted, the Council of Constance is declared legitimate only after the pope of Roman obedience, Gregory XII, formally convoked it, and Basel is considered ecumenical only up to its thirty-fifth session, which is to say after the fall of Pope Eugene IV was proclaimed by the Conciliar Fathers.[49] In the *Dictionnaire de théologie catholique*, Pisa, Constance, and Basel are excluded from the list of ecumenical councils, which jumps from

Vienna (1311–1312) straight to Florence (1439–1445).[50] In 1947, Angelo Mercati, prefect of the Vatican Library, established the official list of the succession of pontiffs in the *Annuario pontificio*, basing it not on historical criteria but on theological criteria, those of Vatican I. He excluded the Pisan lineage, which had previously been recognized in the lists annually published between 1913 and 1946, without any historical basis and without any recognition of the scholarly community of historians, who unanimously affirmed the impossibility of dealing with it. Hence it was possible, in 1958, for Angelo Roncalli to adopt the name John XXIII even though it had already been used by Balthasar Cossa, who was elected pope in the Pisan line in 1410.

The Conciliarist Counter-Memory of the 1960s

Certain milestones running contrary to this magisterial, ecclesiastic, and negationist historiography were established starting in the nineteenth century. In 1818, Henry Hallam stated that the Council of Constance and the decree *Haec sancta* were respected by the majority of the faithful and ecclesiastics north of the Alps.[51] In 1867, Bernhard Hübler framed Constance as a major departure, and in 1869, Ignaz von Döllinger described it as "the most extraordinary event in the whole dogmatic history of the Christian Church."[52] More decisively, John Neville Figgis, in the distinguished 1907 contribution to the history of political thought that resulted from his Birkbeck Lectures, defined the decree *Haec sancta* as the "most revolutionary official document in the history of the world."[53] Although Figgis offered an important reassessment of conciliarism, of which the decree *Haec sancta* remains the paroxysmal expression, he nevertheless did not call into question the revolutionary origin of the movement.

The year 1955 was the other major milestone in this establishment of a counter-memory. It was in this year that Brian Tierney published

36 ∾ CONCILIARISM

his *Foundations of the Conciliar Theory*. Contrary to what had long been believed, Tierney showed that conciliar ecclesiology was neither revolutionary in its origins nor rapid in its decline. Fundamentally, he showed that conciliarism had very deep medieval roots that reached to the twelfth century. It was not a product of the fifteenth century, as Figgis had claimed and as the ultramontane monarchists had taught. Instead, the true roots of conciliarism were to be found in canon law and its twelfth-century commentators. An initial school surrounding Huguccio believed that a heretic pope was ipso facto removed from office. A second school, which sprang up around Alanus Anglicus and Johannes Teutonicus, held that a heretic pope was not discharged ipso facto, but must instead be referred for a verdict and then a deposition by a council, a body of higher jurisdiction in matters of faith. Furthermore, because conciliar theory drew its ecclesiology of *communio* from the synodal practices of the Church in its earliest centuries, its practices were reiterated in Gratian's *Decretum* and enriched by corporatist theories put to the test in the twelfth and thirteenth centuries. Finally, regarding the thought of John of Paris in his 1301–1302 *Tractatus de potestate regia et papali*, Tierney wrote of "the most consistent and complete formulation of conciliar doctrine before the outbreak of the Great Schism."[54] Thus, Tierney refuted the political-theory origins of conciliarism: In his work, William of Ockham and Marsilius of Padua are not positioned as the medieval origins of conciliarism. The former could not have had influence because he was not truly conciliarist. The latter did not have influence because his radicalism was too extreme.

By thus relocating the sources of conciliarism, Tierney, without initially having meant to, considerably rattled the claims of the Roman historiography. As long as its traditional sources were identified as Marsilius of Padua and William of Ockham, both of whom had been declared "heretics" by the Church, conciliarism was marked by its

CONCILIARISM ❧ 37

heretical origin and became—logically, but also tactically—condemnable. It remained an accident, exogenous to the essence of the Church. When Tierney shifted the origins of conciliarism from heretical philosophies to the most orthodox of certified canonists, he contributed to restoring conciliarism's orthodoxy and its endogeneity to both Church history and the very essence of the Church. He rendered conciliarism "a logical culmination of ideas that were embedded in the Law and doctrine of the Church itself."[55] For many, the book was conclusive.[56] It paved the way for the decade that followed, the 1960s.

The 1960s saw the emergence of a revival of conciliar ecclesiology, a context that the Anglo-American school of research on councils (Walter Ullmann, Brian Tierney, Francis Oakley) dubbed the "new conciliarism." Three elements supported the emergence of this current: the four-hundredth anniversary of the Council of Trent, the revival of studies in the history of medieval canon law, and especially the convocation—to general surprise—of the Second Vatican Council by Pope John XXIII on January 25, 1959, with an opening date of October 11, 1962. The pope's announcement stimulated a wave of publications on the history of ecumenical councils and their role in the Church. Many focused on the Council of Constance, and especially the decree *Haec sancta*, a veritable polemic if there ever was one. Indeed, two authors contributed to laying the groundwork for an authentic questioning of the official position on the *Haec sancta* and, consequently, the official positions on the Council of Constance and conciliarism.

In 1959, upon the request of a confrere, the Benedictine Paul De Vooght undertook the task of verifying whether the *Haec sancta* had been approved by Popes Martin V and Eugene IV. The question of the approbation of the decree by the popes of the era was critical because it allowed for an understanding of whether the theologians of the time had validated the conditions for acceptance of the decree as dogma, and whether the popes had perceived it as such. From this starting point, De Vooght published a series of articles on the validity of the decree and the Council of Constance, as well as on the powers of the council and on conciliarism. The articles were gathered into a single volume, published in 1965 as *Les Pouvoirs du concile et l'autorité du pape au concile de Constance*.[57] Referring to the works of Walter Ullmann and Brian Tierney, De Vooght sought to remain a historian in his analyses and refused to offer theological conclusions in his work. He affirmed that the decree *Haec sancta* met all the necessary conditions to constitute a dogmatic decree, which Martin V and Eugene IV approved. He provided numerous pieces of evidence: Martin V severely corrected King Alfonso V of Aragon, who, by continuing to support Pedro de Luna, violated "salutary decisions made by the Council of Constance for the reunification of the Church."[58] In the 1970s, subsequent works confirmed the findings of his early articles.[59]

In 1962, Hans Küng, a Swiss theologian and professor at Tübingen, advanced the same conclusion in his *Strukturen der Kirche*, translated into English in 1964 as *Structures of the Church*: What the *Haec sancta* defends is not a radical conciliarism that reduces the pope to nothing more than an executive tool subordinate to a conciliar parliamentarism, but instead a different form of superiority with respect to the pope. In this interpretation, the council was an authority of control in cases where a pope might fall into heresy, schism, or some other offense.[60] The *Haec sancta* was therefore well received by the popes of the era, proof that the decree was perceived as valid and dogmatic. Küng evoked the historiographical and ideological misunderstandings linked to an overinterpretation of the term "conciliarism":

> With all its justified emphasis on the superiority of the *pope* the militant anti-conciliarist, anti-reformationist, and anti-Gallican position

of the Church and of theology has at the same time frequently made it unnecessarily difficult rightly to recognize and to take seriously the proper and traditional meaning of the superiority of a *council.* Admittedly, in view of the present linguistic protocol of the Church, it is very misleading to speak in an unqualified way of a Council's superiority over a pope. A superiority of this kind, in general, would be understood in the sense of an heretical extreme conciliarism and is rightly rejected. Although it is not disputed by anyone, today we are often too little aware of the fact that this can also be understood in a thoroughly orthodox way, namely along the lines of statements made by canonists concerning the pope's loss of office and the confirmation of this fact by a council.[61]

Küng highlighted two propositions on the ecclesiological level, to the detriment of the Roman historiography: (1) The conciliar theory of the Council of Constance was not an invention of Marsilius of Padua and William of Ockham, since Tierney had shown that the principles of conciliarism were based on medieval canon law; and (2) the conciliar theory of Constance was not buried by the Council of Basel, but persisted within the Church after it, despite all objections. These were the same theses Francis Oakley developed consistently from 1974 to 2016.[62]

The two authors had marginal positions in the field until the 1970s.[63] For example, Congar's position on the subject was that the approval of the popes was reserved. For Eugene IV, Constance was formally valid but must be understood in the papalist sense, identified with Tradition.[64] He added, "Speaking historically, one cannot say that the doctrine of the decree *Haec sancta* received the approbation of the popes. Incidentally, according to its own doctrine, the Council of Constance never needed approbation of this type, and never sought it."[65] The question therefore arose of what tradition and history were. As the editor of Paul De Vooght's collection *Unam sanctam*, Congar included a warning in his introductory note at the beginning of the work: "Dom P. De Vooght's study presents itself both as a conclusion for history and as a problem for theology."[66] Congar, however, aligned himself with the Roman historiography, refusing the theological problem despite the strength of the historical conclusion.[67]

A response came without delay, as soon as 1965. The pontifical supremacy camp reaffirmed the standard traditional historiography. In this line of thought, the Council of Constance violated the principles of the First Vatican Council. The decrees *Haec sancta*, on the superiority of the council, and *Pastor aeternus*, on pontifical infallibility, entered into conflict. How could one simultaneously conceive of the affirmation of a body of control over the pope, on the one hand, and, on the other, the reaffirmed supremacy of pontifical infallibility? Debates focused on the question thus formulated: Was the decree *Haec sancta* an emergency measure taken in the context of a crisis? The issue consisted of identifying the dogmatic value, and therefore the enduring validity, of the decree.

Joseph Gill, as a young man, made himself an advocate for the classic thesis.[68] Rector of the Pontifical Oriental Institute in Rome, known for his studies of the Council of Florence, Gill reiterated the long tradition of rejecting the legitimacy of the Council of Constance after the promulgation of the *Haec sancta* and warned against the revival of the conciliarism of past centuries in his own day. He explicitly named Paul De Vooght among the "conciliarists of today." Later textbooks would repeat a phrase of Joseph Gill's regarding the *Haec sancta*: "It was conciliarism in its most extreme form."[69] Likewise, Isfried Pichler and even Heinz Hürten represented the conservative traditional interpretation linked with Joseph Gill.[70] They strongly criticized the works of Paul De Vooght and Hans Küng. As evidence, these authors wrote of the end of the schism through the resignation of Gregory XII, the only legitimate pope according to them. Only

CONCILIARISM ❧ 41

this resignation could render possible the end of the schism without the need for any other conciliar action against the true pope. The affirmation of a Roman lineage on the part of the magisterium, however, remains a theological theory whose historical truth is impossible to demonstrate. All a historian can say is that nobody knew who the true pope was in 1415.

After Joseph Gill's riposte, the two sides split into "emergencists" and "nonemergencists": the former believed the decree *Haec Santa* was an emergency measure, and therefore a decree with a scope limited by circumstance, and the latter believed the decree had permanent validity and scope within the Church. For Hubert Jedin, in 1963, the decree was "an emergency measure intended to prevent the dissolution of the council after the flight of John XXIII."[71] Because he followed the Roman decisions as to the succession of the popes of the Great Western Schism, Hubert Jedin did not see John XXIII (the fifteenth-century one) as an incontestable pope. Thus, he believed, the decree should be taken not as universal but as an emergency measure. For the German historian and theologian of the councils, it was the Council of Basel in 1439 that had granted the *Haec sancta* an absolute dogmatic value and declared the superiority of the council over the pope as a truth of faith. On this subject, Francis Oakley warned that it should be seen not as a work of history but instead as a contribution to an ecclesiological discourse. Also around 1965, August Franzen, a theologian and priest at Cologne, picked up the same thesis: The *Haec sancta* only became dogmatic in 1439 in Basel due to its reinterpretation in the sense of a radical conciliarism. Until that point, it had been no more than an emergency measure.[72] Regimius Bäumer agreed with this assessment.[73] Both disciples of Hubert Jedin, before whom they defended their doctoral dissertations in the 1950s, the two German Catholic theologians, Franzen and Bäumer, had skewed readings of Brian Tierney: On the one hand, they insisted upon the radical conciliarism seen in the work of Marsilius of Padua and William of Ockham, which had been adopted at Basel. On the other hand, they saw in Constance a moderate conciliarism better qualified as "conciliar theory." They validated Tierney's decretist reading of the case of a heretic pope expressed in the *Haec sancta*, but they were silent regarding the contribution of the decretalists to conciliar theory.

In the same Roman and pontificalist line, Walter Brandmüller, a German priest and historian who became a cardinal of the Catholic Church in 2010 after having been president of the Pontifical Committee for Historical Sciences from 1998 to 2009, wrote of the Council of Constance as the site of a virtuosic pragmatism and of the *Haec sancta* as a "hasty and unnecessary" decree,[74] a decree that was not dogmatic, in any case, but merely canonical. For these authors, in the tradition of the school of Heinrich Finke, conciliarism was a disastrous liability.[75] Brandmüller described his ecclesiology as an "authentically Catholic, hierarchical, sacramental conception of the Church."[76] In a review of Brandmüller's work, however, Jürgen Miethke wrote of a narrow and papalist ecclesiology.[77] He characterized Brandmüller as a "partisan of the papalist system with a strong tendency to legitimize the Roman perspective."[78] Ultimately, the logic ran, if the *Haec sancta* were linked to a historical emergency context, then the measure, even if valid, would be non-irreformable, meaning it was without permanent validity for the Church—the papal supremacy reaffirmed in Vatican I would therefore be preserved. For the Roman Catholic historiography, it was theologically necessary to render the *Haec sancta* an emergency measure without lasting scope, notwithstanding the historical facts. According to this historiographical reworking, the decree does not belong to Catholic doctrinal tradition; it should not count.

The third part of the controversy took place in the 1970s. Paul De Vooght and the school around Brian Tierney clarified their terms in the context of the response in and around 1965, itself a response to the historical milestones erected by De Vooght and Küng at the beginning of the 1960s. Paul de Vooght repeated Küng's arguments with a clearer aim of refutation. For him, the decree *Haec sancta* was neither an expedient (*eine Notstandsmassnahme*, literally "an emergency measure") nor a simple disciplinary measure. Instead, it conveyed a veritable doctrinal position. It was not intended to be applied only in extraordinary circumstances.[79]

In terms of his career, Francis Oakley could be described as a champion of the counter-memory of conciliarism. The "Oakley moment" crystallized the binary narrative of the historiography. In Brian Tierney's sphere of influence, Francis Oakley historically reaffirmed that conciliarism had continued to exist within the Church since the fifteenth century. It was perhaps underground but nevertheless remained lively in the regions north of the Alps until his own day. For Oakley, the *Haec sancta* therefore indeed had a dogmatic validity that was inscribed in the theological roots of its time: The decree said no more than what moderates (Franciscus Zabarella, Pierre d'Ailly, Jean Gerson) had been saying for a long time already.[80] In other words, the decree was the most perfect and greatest accomplishment of conciliar theory.[81]

Another member of the American school of research on councils, Thomas Morrissey, a student of Brian Tierney and a professor of canon law at New York University, reexamined the conditions under which the document was produced, concluding that, for its contemporaries, there was no doubt that the decree was valid. That the Council of Basel had reaffirmed the dogmatic validity of the *Haec sancta* was at that time already considered a truth of faith.

To dispute the dogmatic validity of the *Haec sancta* was, therefore, to dispute the canonicity of the Council of Constance and the force of conciliar theory. The two historiographies are set face-to-face. The historiography of a politics of forgetting, which denies the persistence of conciliarism after the fifteenth century out of fear of a threat to

44 ❧ CONCILIARISM

pontifical supremacy, is the so-called Catholic, Roman, curialist, ultramontane, or papalist historiography. On the other hand is the historiography—also Catholic, but more anti-Roman—of a conciliar counter-memory affirming the persistence since the fifteenth century of conciliar ideas with origins in the twelfth century, which traversed the sixteenth, seventeenth, and eighteenth centuries before arriving, intact and enriched, at Vatican I in the late nineteenth century, with Henri Maret as their ultimate representative, and even stretching into the heart of the twentieth century.[82] This is the historiography of the Anglo-American school, of which Francis Oakley was the best advocate and the most zealous popularizer starting in 1969 and continuing through the 1980s, 1990s, and 2000s.[83]

Several remarks on this crystallization of the narrative must be made. In his popularization of a conciliarist counter-memory, Francis Oakley defended a diluted form of Catholic anti-Romanism typically found in Anglo-American milieus, the same milieus that have dominated the historiography of anti-Romanism and especially canonical anti-Romanism. This said, it is necessary to note that, since the 1950s, American Catholicism has remained relatively well integrated with Roman and curial milieus. The major international conferences in canon law are now dominated by Americans—though they were previously influenced by German canonists and by Stefan Kuttner—and their proceedings published by the Vatican. Certain anti-curial critiques of the historiography have been pronounced in highly integrated institutional frameworks. Thus, Avery Dulles (1918–2008), an American Catholic priest and a Jesuit, closely associated with the experts of the Second Vatican Council and the "new theology," embodied the Atlanticist turn of the Holy See by becoming the first North American theologian to receive the honor of being named a cardinal. He participated in the American dimension of debates on Catholic anti-Romanism even within a Roman-approved framework. Is it better, therefore, to speak of anti-Romanism or, instead, of parties within Romanism?

A second remark is necessary. In France, the Anglo-American historiography did not have a foothold. The Oakleyan narrative is curiously absent from French textbooks of religious history: Oakley is at best occasionally quoted, but more often he is not included. Certainly, religious history textbooks, from elementary to advanced, are skewed as a genre, constructed through uncritical repetition. However, French surveys have established the Roman narrative through reuse, filiation, repetition, borrowing, and concretion by copying. The Roman historiography has been exported into French historiography through chunks of arguments and quantities of stereotype. An entire generation of French historians missed Oakley. One example among others is the *Dictionnaire historique de la papauté*, edited by Philippe Levillain and published in 1994, followed in 2002 by an English translation, *The Papacy: An Encyclopedia*. With Olivier Guyotjeannin, Philippe Levillain wrote the entry on "Conciles oecuméniques."[84] The passage on Constance is a negation of the works of Paul De Vooght and a profession of faith in the ultramontane vulgate that began with Torquemada:

> The Council of Constance (1414–8) was considered an ecumenical council in its final sessions (42nd to 45th), after the election of Martin V (1418). He wished to end the Great Schism by proclaiming the impossibility of its dissolution before the reform of the Church "in its head and its members," giving birth to the so-called "conciliarist" theory. Its decrees, adopted during the 3rd, 4th, and 5th sessions, were never, however, approved by the popes or recognized by the Church.[85]

All elements of the vulgate are present in this passage: the nonvalidity of the sessions prior to the election of Martin V and Pope Martin

46 &) CONCILIARISM

V's non-approbation of the decrees of the third, fourth, and fifth sessions. On the other hand, just a few pages later, the entry "Conciliarism," written by Aldo Landi, integrates all the historical studies of the 1960s (De Vooght, Tierney, Fink, Sieben, Black, and Alberigo). Against the papalist vulgate, Landi states in that entry that the *Haec sancta* was not a measure borne of crisis or urgency; rather, the decree's function of control over the pope was intended to be permanent.[86]

Another equally representative editorial undertaking is the *Histoire générale du christianisme*, published in 2010 under the direction of Jean-Robert Armogathe.[87] Walter Brandmüller was commissioned to write the entry devoted to the Council of Constance. When he titled his entry "Les soubresauts de l'institution ecclésiastique" (The upheavals of the ecclesiastical institution), Brandmüller was referring to the conciliar episode of the end of the Middle Ages. It should be kept in mind that this double volume on the general history of Christianity was an undertaking begun twenty years previously at the Presses Universitaires de France. It aimed to be international, with half of its contributors (thirty-two out of a total of seventy-three) from outside France. The goal was to cross-fertilize different intellectual and historiographical perspectives and to shift away from dependence on exclusively French references. It should be recalled, however, that the undertaking was coordinated by three French historians. The volumes did not hesitate to tackle and discuss controversial subjects. Under the aegis of Armogathe, there was a clear basis for the perspective that repeatedly emerges in the work like a leitmotif: Christianity permeates all social constructs; it is the explanatory model of societies, cultures, and the Western system of thought in its conceptual structures. Certainly, starting in the introduction, the authors deny any confessionality in their project. Are they, however, exempt from belonging, in some sense, to a certain strain of Roman Catholicism accented with the defense of orthodox Christianity? Although this question could be asked of many chapters and entries, it can no longer be asked of those written by Walter Brandmüller, who at the time had recently been named cardinal by Benedict XVI.

Brandmüller's words here pick up the narratological framework of the historiography of the years around 1965, based on the *doxa* of Vatican I regarding pontifical infallibility. To a degree, this falls within the lineage of Joseph Gill, the symbol of this representation: Brandmüller shares the same vision of the conciliar episode "from Vienna to Lateran V"[88] and the preeminence of the figures of Marsilius of Padua and William of Ockham at the origins of a "revolutionary project in the constitution of the Church."[89] Brandmüller restores to the two condemned authors their accountability for the heretical origins of the conciliar movement. Next, the idea that the decree *Haec sancta* was approved without a pope, *sede vacante*, is aimed at weakening the decree's scope and validity. "It was not at Constance but at Basel that one dared to present the superiority of the council over the pope as a truth of faith, to depose Eugene IV, and to name an antipope, Felix V, in the person of Amadeus VIII, Duke of Savoy,"[90] contrary to what many decades of discussions have attested: that the decree has been a truth of faith since Constance. Juan de Torquemada is quoted abundantly.[91] Stereotyped items follow: the triumphant recovery of the pontifical monarchy, the Fifth Lateran Council, and the "canonical and political overcoming of the conciliarism that had reared its head in the anti-pontifical *conciliabulum* of Pisa in 1510–1511."[92]

The 2010s: The Return to a Politically Grounded Conciliarism

With Cary Nederman, politics have returned to the field of conciliar historiography. The American historian, an expert in the history of ideas and political theory, has sought to challenge Brian Tierney's long-standing thesis. By attributing canonical origins to conciliar theories, Tierney contributed to rendering those theories endogenous in the Church, against the ultramontane manipulation that consistently attributed to conciliarism's origins the political theories of Marsilius of Padua and William of Ockham. However, in a swing of the pendulum, Cary Nederman has taken up John N. Figgis's original idea, according to which the conciliar movement is not only an ecclesiological choice but, above all, a political theory due to its constitutionalism. The conception of the conciliar movement in terms of political theory is attributable to Figgis and his disciples, of whom the most famous was Charles McIlwain[93] and the most successful popularizer George H. Sabine.[94] Ultimately, what Nederman has attacked is the "Tierney moment," the moment of the Church's endogenous reappropriation of a form of constitutionalism, conciliar theory. Nederman has questioned the impact of medieval ecclesiology on the formation of modern constitutionalism. He has insisted upon recognizing that Gerson, who was neither canonist nor jurist, was anchored in the most characteristic political traditions of the Latin Middle Ages: "Only by neglecting the intellectual foundations of Gerson's conciliarism is it possible to attribute distinctively modern constitutional ideas to his writings."[95] Perhaps, even, historians were mistaken in considering Gerson central to the conciliarist movement.[96]

Influenced by Cary Nederman and following the lead of Jürgen Miethke, who in 1996 restored the importance of Ockham among the conciliarists,[97] Karl Ubl took another step forward in the refutation of continuism. He denounced the thesis of continuism in conciliary theories from the fifteenth century to the present, which is to say the entire historiography of the counter-memory advanced by Brian Tierney and Francis Oakley. Through the case study of John of Paris, who had only a meager canonical education, Karl Ubl argued that the canonists of the thirteenth and fourteenth centuries contributed nothing to conciliarism. According to Ubl, for John of Paris

CONCILIARISM ☙ 49

the elaboration of conciliar thought had been no more than a pure reaction to pontifical centralism and absolutism—a reaction, not a continuity. In other words, conciliarism was more of a rupture than a filiation. Against Tierney, Ubl affirmed that there was no canonical source for the conciliarism of the fifteenth century. Fundamentally, what Karl Ubl sought above all to critique was the Catholic appropriation of the American concept of constitutionalism. In other words, he refuted the connection made by Tierney between constitutionalism and conciliarism: For Tierney, "One might indeed argue that the resemblances between the conciliar theories and the constitutional experiments of secular States were due partly to canonistic influence in the secular sphere."[98] He also refuted the counter-teleology described by Oakley regarding the continuity of conciliar theories, following Tierney. In support of his demonstration and following Cary Nederman, Karl Ubl made a clear distinction between medieval constitutionalism and modern constitutionalism. He has distinguished between conciliarism and constitutionalism in order to return to the sources of political theories, for example Gerson's.[99] Against Tierney, Ubl has discussed the "modernity of medieval ecclesiastical law." He has preferred to locate the roots of conciliar theories in medieval political philosophy, in the same sense that Charles McIlwain, an admirer of John Figgis, spoke of medieval constitutionalism. For Ubl, Catholic historiography, even the anti-Roman kind, took the concept of constitutionalism and applied it to conciliarism—this is, according to him, what Francis Oakley and Kenneth Pennington did. Constitutionalism, however, is difficult to export beyond the history of American political philosophy, from which it originated. In sum, Ubl's thesis has aimed to show that Christianity had neither origin in nor influence over political theories of the limitation of powers.

The whole debate remains useful for comprehending the different individual interpretations of the meaning of ecclesiology, but the most interesting aspect of the debate remains how the fields are constituted in politics and ecclesiology: To what extent might ecclesiology be legitimately dissociated from the field of politics? The history of this pairing and its discursive construction should be interrogated.

The Gamble of Erudition, and a Path Out of the Binary Schema

Recent scholarship has gambled on returning to the original texts and sources as a path out of secular and binary historiographical controversies. Four authors may serve as examples: Michiel Decaluwé, Thomas Prügl, Sebastian Provvidente, and Émilie Rosenblieh.

After noting the lack of a reliable edition of the text of the *Haec sancta*, Michiel Decaluwé established a new edition in 2006.[100] From the 1960s until the 1980s, a raft of publications on the Council of Constance and conciliarism, as well as on the decree *Haec sancta*, showed that scholars had always been at odds over the interpretation of the decree but had never questioned the reliability of the philological establishment of the text. Alberigo studied the *Haec sancta* more than anyone, reconstructing three stages in the composition of the decree, with modifications made between March 29, 1415 (fourth session), and April 6, 1415 (fifth session). He presented the decree as a product of circumstance, written for a specific occasion, but never posed the question of identifying the authors of the decree. When Walter Brandmüller and Thomas Morrissey disputed the meaning of the clause "etiamsi papalis existat," the former read "etiam si papalis existat" in the text of the *Conciliorum oecumenicorum decreta*, while the latter read "etiam si papalis."[101] Each was convinced he was reading the authentic and correct text. Brandmüller insulted Morrissey by accusing him of distorting the text. Each of the two protagonists based his reading on a different textual tradition and a different edition of the text. Michiel Decaluwé has revived the textual traditions of the decree beginning with the manuscripts and incunables, and then moving on to the first movable-type printings: Von der Hardt, Mansi, and Jedin in the *Conciliorum oecumenicorum decreta* (hereafter *COD*). He proved that the *COD* used the edition of Von der Hardt, not that of Mansi. Von der Hardt published the text of the Wolfenbüttel manuscript, which contained the acts in the form in which they were reissued at Basel. But he also published the texts of two manuscripts from Vienna, which according to Crowder are unreliable. At any rate, there exist three different manuscripts of the decree. It appears that Von der Hardt relied on the two Vienna manuscripts to establish a second version of the *Haec sancta*, which was the one used for the *COD*. In other words, the version of the text in the *COD* is less reliable than the first version of the *Haec sancta*, which was based on the Wolfenbüttel manuscript. Philologically, the text is therefore already questionable. In order to establish a reliable critical edition, Michiel Decaluwé, for his part, relied on several manuscripts from the Vatican Library, all dating from the fifteenth century. Among them, four contain the journal of Guillaume Fillastre and three the journal of Cerretanus, including the text of the *Haec sancta*. Decaluwé proposed a critical edition, something no previous scholar had attempted, despite the intensity of the controversy. This appeared in 2006.

Thomas Prügl has also approached the controversy through a critical return to the sources. In a substantial article published in 2011, he relied on four of them to move the matter forward: Juan Palomar, Jean Mauroux, Jean de Vincelles, and Pierre de Versailles.[102] A partisan of the pope, Palomar gave a shocking interpretation of the decree *Haec sancta*: The decree was situated within the tradition of the development of canon law regarding the limits of pontifical power and, as such, needed to be incorporated and received, not suppressed. Thomas Prügl's idea was to show, contrary to Brandmüller's interpretation,

52 ᔆᕠ CONCILIARISM

that many of the pope's supporters welcomed the *Haec sancta* in the fifteenth century, and that Brandmüller's reading of the *Haec sancta* as an emergency or necessary measure was the result of a historical misinterpretation. For Palomar, as for many papalists, the *Haec sancta* remained a good standard in the event of the pope acting irresponsibly or in error. Prügl insisted upon showing that the *Haec sancta* was in line with tradition. For Palomar, it was even in line with a conservative ecclesiology! This was a reversal of Brandmüller's position.

Jean Mauroux, Latin patriarch of Antioch and president of the French nation at the Council of Constance, wrote a treatise titled *De superioritate inter concilium et papam* in 1434. Mauroux was a long-standing partisan of the pope. He did, however, recognize the authority of the *Haec sancta* as the foundation and most important document of ecclesiology. At no point did he call into question the authenticity or the Catholicity of the Synod of Constance and its decrees.[103] For him, the conciliarist reading of the decree was an *opinio communis*. In his genealogical reconstruction of the interpretation of the *Haec sancta* by its contemporaries, Prügl showed that the interpretative rupture took place after Jean Maroux, with the work of Nicolas Albergati, the spokesperson for the legates of the pope. Albergati criticized the conciliarist interpretation of the decree. This was the first time the decree was called into question on account of its interpretation. To Albergati, it was necessary to "follow the decree according to the readings of saints and scholars." He asked for an "authentic" interpretation and demanded a "traditional" reading. Prügl specified, however, that this reading was not the same traditional meaning meant by Palomar. Hence the problem Prügl identified regarding the question of "tradition": To what degree does the theological claim of adherence to tradition overlap with historical facts? In other words, what link exists between tradition and history in the ideological stakes of polemicists and theorists?

Thomas Prügl's methodology therefore went further than that of Francis Oakley and the North American school because Prügl retraced the contemporary debates in order to grasp the points of rupture and the front lines. He meticulously returned to the sources of the time and unearthed new ones. Jean de Vincelles, abbot of Saint-Claude in the Jura, was a successor to Cardinal Albergati. He was present at Constance as procurator of Cluny Abbey. His writings concerned the question of the struggle for the presidency of the council. He affirmed that the *Haec sancta* ran contrary to the "traditional" prerogative of the Apostolic See. Playing on the ambiguity of the decree, he proposed to direct and reduce it for a restricted interpretation by making it "antiquis juribus et dictis sanctorum conformare" (conform to the ancient laws of the saints). By this, he intended to reaffirm the jurisdictional primacy of the pope, which had been called in to question at Basel. Fundamentally, his perspective was anticonciliarist, and it fed the great stream that arose in pontificalist historiography. Along the same lines, Pierre de Versailles, bishop of Digne, had worked as a young theologian to combat Jean Petit's theses at Constance, in close collaboration with Jean Gerson. He was Charles VII's legate at Basel and one of the few to defend the rights of the Apostolic See at the request of Nicolas Albergati and Jean de Vincelles: He, too, demanded that the *Haec sancta* be reinterpreted in the light of tradition. Like Jean de Vincelles, Pierre de Versailles sought to render the decree an emergency measure tied to the context of Constance, and therefore to remove the decree from Church tradition. Prügl returned to the sources of the controversy and the moment of interpretive ruptures. For apologists, both ancient and modern, tradition is not univocal.

Sebastian Provvidente, on the other hand, took a gamble on recontextualizing the decree *Haec sancta* by taking into account judiciary practices, trials, and depositions that had previously been overlooked.[104] Concerning *Notstandstheorie* (the "emergency measure" theory), which is to say in reaction to Walter Brandmüller in particular, Sebastian Provvidente noted the historiographical desire to harmonize the canon *Prima sedes a nemine judicatur* with the reality of historical facts. Provvidente saw this harmonization as a hermeneutic forcing that tended to distort and reduce historical data to canonical principles.[105] However, he added, the partisans of *Notstandstheorie* never recognized that there existed within the Church a line of thought that affirmed the necessity of a public process of deposition in the event of a heretical pope: "According to the *Notstandstheorie*, there was no room for a deposition process of a pope as this would go against the principle of *Prima sedes a nemine judicatur*."[106] This tradition, however, has its origins in the *Summa de jure canonico* of Alanus Anglicus (early twelfth century), for which the *Apparatus jus naturale* became a classic reference on the subject. For Provvidente, it was this procedural line that the Conciliar Fathers chose to follow in order to depose John XXIII, the legitimate pope who had convoked the council and was only later deemed a heretic.[107] In his *De auferabilitate papae*, Gerson insisted that a heretic pope was not discharged ipso facto, as in Huguccio's thesis, but that a human deposition was necessary.[108] This position was conservative in the sense that it allowed the conciliar body to compensate in cases of institutional weakness. Because the principle of a deposition process was evoked by Ockham in his fourteenth-century battle against the pope, it was rejected by Catholic historiography, of which Brandmüller has been a notable representative.[109] Provvidente's proposal to study judicial practices along with ecclesiological debates could allow for a better understanding of how the Conciliar Fathers envisaged the text of the *Haec sancta* itself and the conciliar theories of their time. This approach would require expertise in the trial of Jean Hus and the ability to draw connections between judicial mores and the ecclesiological perceptions of the time among the Conciliar Fathers.

CONCILIARISM ❧ 55

Émilie Rosenblieh, an expert on the Council of Basel and the judicial proceedings of this conciliar era, also returned to the sources. In particular, she unearthed a little-known manuscript, Paris, BnF, lat. 1511.[110] This manuscript preserves the records of the hearing and the evidence produced against the pope between July 26, 1437, and October 17, 1438, making it possible to understand how the Council of Basel instructed the second trial of Pope Eugene IV, which began in July 1437. Anxious to affirm its jurisdictional primacy over the papacy, the council elaborated a new conception of pontifical heresy based on the violation of canons and conciliar decrees. On the testimony of twenty-nine witnesses and various pieces of evidence, the pope was accused of violating the ancient canons, especially those of the Council of Chalcedon, the sacrality of which had long been recognized, and above all those of Constance, with the *Haec sancta* in first place. He was declared "an assiduous violator and contemptor of the sacred synodal canons."[111] This historical episode makes it clearer than ever that the decree *Haec sancta* was an ecclesiological issue: The institution of the Council of Basel brought conciliar authority up to date just as the decree intended. Embodying the sacred authority of the assembly, the Council of Basel justified the primacy it claimed at the top of the ecclesiastical hierarchy.[112] It put the *Haec sancta* into action by deposing a pope who had resisted it. How, in these conditions, might the reception of the Council of Basel by the triumphant papacy of later centuries, which willingly forgot the episode, be understood?

Regarding conciliarism, Paul De Vooght made a disconcerting remark in 1960: "It could very well be that this immense quarrel over conciliarism has not served much purpose." He added, "Reaching the end of its course, the conciliarist adventure left Catholic doctrine in the same place it had found it at its birth." After these extensive investigations, it might therefore be tempting to ask: All that fuss for this? In any case, the scope of the historical object "conciliarism" seems to conceal its own heuristic fruitfulness elsewhere.

For our purposes, conciliarism has been a privileged viewpoint from which to unravel the construction of the grand narrative that was the official historiographical account of the fifteenth century. Because the Roman historiography was constructed out of a painful and, frankly, shameful episode in the papacy, it is possible to trace how the theme became an object of banishment and a "politics of forgetting" in order to better understand how grand narratives can thus be determined not only by issues of power, but also of honor. The shame of the episode was the foundation of the official narratology, and also the foundation of the counternarrative that resulted from it. Although the history of conciliarism cannot yet be considered a peaceful history—will it ever be?—the subject of conciliarism allows the historian to grasp the abysmal problem of the relationship the Church has established with its own memory and its own history.

2

CONSTITUTIONALISM

A Stake of Political Modernity?

Eugenius IV is the forerunner of Louis XIV.
—John Neville Figgis, *Political Thought from Gerson to Grotius,*
1414–1625: Seven Studies (Harper, 1960), 41

In the history of the political thought of the Church, conciliarism was the anvil against which constitutionalism was forged. The question of how political models circulated from one sphere to another, from the ecclesial to the secular and vice versa, has been asked widely and continues to be asked today. At the heart of the link between ecclesiology and politics, the theme of constitutionalism serves as a viewpoint, perhaps an unexpected one, from which to examine the issue's stakes, circulations, academic periodizations, and disciplinary interfaces. These can be seen, for example, at the intersection of public law and political theory, or that of canon law and theology.

It remains difficult to establish a univocal definition of constitutionalism. One common denominator, in fact, is the *limitation of the actions of rulers*. Putting this into simpler terms, Charles McIlwain wrote that constitutionalism is the institution of a limited government.[1] However, understanding the semantic, political, geo-cultural, and legal evolution of the concept requires retracing its history, as there have undeniably existed multiple constitutionalisms depending on period, political culture, even language.

Behind the definition of constitutionalism and its conceptual scope, another unique debate seems to be hidden: that of political modernity. The theme of constitutionalism poses the question of the medieval legacy and its transition to modernity, leading to the following working question: Was political modernity itself based on an ecclesiological foundation or not? Three questions, variations on the same theme, articulate the problem differently: (1) Regarding the question of the origins of constitutionalism, and especially the medieval origins of constitutionalism, did the constitutional state emerge from the Middle Ages, or did it begin only with the modern era? John Figgis raised the question in 1907, and Brian Tierney later picked it back up. (2) Was there continuity from medieval constitutionalism to modern constitutionalism—or, rather, from conciliarism, the ecclesiological constitutionalism of the fifteenth century, to parliamentarism, the type of political constitutionalism found in seventeenth-century England? Brian Tierney devoted his entire career to arguing a double continuism, in both a chronological and a politico-ecclesiological sense. (3) Finally, could the question of modernity be articulated according to the terms of a theory of secularization, the extreme form of which is perhaps best expressed in Schmitt's term "political theology"—in other words, that "All significant concepts of the modern theory of the State are secularized theological concepts"?[2]

WHICH DEFINITIONS?

The term *constitutio* was originally a medical one, describing a state of being, the idea of order, the organization of a whole. A constitution, in its original sense, regulated the life and movement of the physical body.[3] Historically, the word was also connected to the domain of law, in which it designated a group of texts—pontifical or monastic—forming an authentic instrument. The *Carta caritatis* of Cîteaux Abbey, dating from around 1100, functioned as a veritable constitution.[4] The constitutions of the Dominican order were qualified as "cathedrals of constitutional law."[5] The word "constitutionalism" has its own, no less polysemous, history. Stéphane Rials examined its canonical origins and identified five spaces conducive to the emergence of a proto-constitutionalism in the chronology: the canonical space, the space of the anciens régimes, the space of private law, and finally the two major geographical spaces, England and North America (first colonial, then independent).[6] Starting in the thirteenth century, Italian cities and Western cities, each in their own way, more broadly offered models of a municipal proto-constitutionalism with all the qualifying mechanisms: election, unanimity, majority, secret ballot, mandate, restriction on the concurrent holding of multiple offices, the maxim *Quod omnes tangit*, deliberative dynamics, consensus, and representivity.

In the medieval and modern sources, the path to constitutionalism often operated through resemblances and synonyms. First and foremost, the texts spoke of *limitatio*: Government was limited, monarchy was limited, the papacy was limited. Another synonymy was that of "basic law." For Bossuet, there was a direct equivalence between "basic law" and constitutionalism. Likewise, the arena of mixed government and the theoretical field of constitutionalism are related, as James Blythe has shown: From Aristotle, Polybius, and Cicero down to the Middle Ages, the theme of mixed government has been a common site for types of political thought that resemble constitutional thought.[7] Claude de Seyssel wrote of checks or counterpowers. The famous pamphlet *Vindiciae contra tyrannos*, published in 1579 and translated into French in 1580, addressed the question of the nature

60 ✌ CONSTITUTIONALISM

of power and its checks, which is to say constitutional limits: It argued that *maiestas* should be limited and subject to law.[8] The Anglo-American authors evoked *checks and balances* or "the balance of powers," to use a phrase of Henry St. John, 1st Viscount Bolingbroke (1678–1751).

Seemingly uniquely, the German language justly accounted for the double sememe contained in the concept of constitution: *Konstitution*, referring to the legal sememe of "standard," and *Verfassung*, referring to the political sememe of the "organization of the state." Constitutionalism thus raises a legal-political double polarity: It is a limitation of power that gives the state its rights and its limits, its basic liberties and its checks. At the same time, it establishes the constitution as the supreme and basic standard. It is the apex of the hierarchy of laws, and for this reason it is perpetual, inviolable, irrevocable, and insusceptible to change. However, the balance of powers fluctuated from one period to another, as did the relationships between them. Olivier Beaud has traced their reversals, moments of rupture, fusions, and disjunctures.[9] According to him, the shift took place in the eighteenth century, and especially in 1748 with Montesquieu's *L'Esprit des lois*. The great caesura between premodern history and modern history took place at this moment, as signified by the passage from ancient to modern constitutionalism. Montesquieu's accomplishment, essentially, consisted of assimilating the concept of the constitution to Aristotle's Greek *politeia* and, consequently, politicizing the concept of the "constitution." By redefining the constitution politically, Montesquieu connected to it the ideas of liberty and the division of power (or "separation of powers"). For his part, Thomas Paine (1737–1809), in the United States, understood the constitution as the superior legal standard, the supreme law of the state, its basic law. He imbued the concept with juridical significance by defining it as "not the act of a government, but of a people constituting a government".[10]

A constitution is the act of the people in their original character of sovereignty. A government is a creature of the constitution; it is produced and brought into existence by it. A constitution defines and limits the powers of the government it creates. It therefore follows, as a natural and also a logical result, that the governmental exercise of any power not authorized by the constitution is an assumed power, and therefore illegal.[11]

This famous definition influenced the Abbé Sieyès, who was responsible for fusing the two meanings, political and legal: The constitution was both a certain arrangement of powers *and* a basic law.[12] Sieyès articulated the sovereignty of the nation and the constitution in order to establish boundaries and limits to absolute government, which he perceived as despotic. A constituted political body was thus a limited political body. The moment of the American Revolution and the French Revolution was characterized by a balance between the two semantic polarities. In the nineteenth century, however, this fragile balance exploded. With Hegel, there came the return of politics: There was no longer a *Konstitution*, or "supreme standard," but only a *Verfassung*, an "organization of the state"—that is, *politeia*.

A double trend resulted from this Hegelian legacy: On the left was that of the Marxists, for whom politics prevailed over legality; there, the constitutional standard was subordinated to economic and social relationships. On the right was the lineage of Carl Schmitt, for whom the constitution was the result of a "political decision" of the authoritarian type: Reasons of state prevailed over legal standards; the pure decisionism of an all-powerful ruler was deployed without limit. In Schmitt's 1928 treatise titled *Verfassungslehre*, it was no longer a question of *Konstitution* but only of *Verfassung*.[13] In the 1990s, Olivier Beaud closed his semantic analysis by posing a topical question. By that point, according to Beaud, the legal sense of "constitution" had prevailed over the political sense: Was this a crisis of constitutionalism?[14] As if the excess of constitutional positivism had become a form of anti-constitutionalism.

The geographical sensibilities and cultural meanings of the concept should now be considered. England has always been held up by historiography as a model of customary constitutionalism, a constitutionalism without a text, in which the limitation of power and monarchical government coexisted within a constitutional monarchy. According to the English model, what constitutionalism limits is the absolutism of power, not sovereignty. Regarding this teleological vision of British constitutionalism, the French historian Denis Baranger recently made the point (1999) that England is, in reality, not a model but, at most, an example.[15] Baranger sidestepped grand constitutional teleologies, those simplifications of Whig historiography, in order to revisit the constitutional history of Great Britain via the concept of "accountability," the vector of constitutional dynamics. The development of an executive responsible for maintaining the constitution marked a shift from monarchical power toward the ministerial community with effective and administrative responsibility, which, though not institutionalized, tended to efface the monarchy itself. The constitutional modality could thus be found in political life itself. As Baranger maintained, "For the English, their constitutional code is their history."

Among the major classifications of constitutional history, the United States offers the best example of constitutionalism with a written text. The charters of "incorporated" colonies prefigured the written constitution. Connecticut's *Fundamental Orders* established a decisive milestone in 1639. The Constitution of 1787 came to validate the 1776 Declaration of Independence: Here, the Constitution was an act of will that constituted a new political order. Or, rather, the establishment of the Constitution was the performative act that founded the people.[16] As Derrida put it, it was a "coup de droit."[17] From this point, there existed both a constitution in the American sense, meaning a founding act, and a constitution in the British sense, meaning a state of affairs or an order to which politics are subjected.

French constitutional thought, for its part, has largely been shaped by prevailing cultural conditions. From the start of the modern era, constitutionalism in France was thought of within the frame of absolute monarchic sovereignty. Hence, it immediately established itself as an opposition force: French constitutionalism became a constitutionalism of protest and combat. In France, the question has arisen of determining whether the country belongs to the written or customary type of constitution. Starting with the French Revolution, France has adopted fifteen written constitutions throughout its history, with the result that Carolina Cerda-Guzman wrote of a "constitutional frenzy that ultimately tends to underline the sometimes vain nature of the political significance of a written Constitution."[18] However, in the nineteenth century an emergent counterrevolutionary theme asserted that the Old Regime had a customary constitution based on immemorial standards, willed by God, insusceptible to modification, and higher than royal will. According to this view, the writing down of this constitution was nothing more than the reactualization of an idealized past reality, and God was the true constituent. The antiquity of these customary laws was seen as infinite, their origin quasi-mythical. The legitimist and counterrevolutionary constitutionalists thus articulated an unexpected but authentic constitutionalism that ran counter to the practice of a written or formalized constitutionalism that had resulted from the Revolution. Far from the counterrevolutionary reconstructions, the legal historian Albert Rigaudière, who chose the medieval genesis of constitutionalism as one of his fields of investigation, preferred to describe a "process of constitutionalization of rules" that took off at the end of the fourteenth century.[19] He identified a vast corpus of around forty texts dating from between 1378 and 1409 that were a "sort of constitution" for France; these texts stabilized standards, established procedures, and even normalized political practices.[20] Among these texts of constitutional value, the so-called ordinance of August 1374, which established the age of royal majority at thirteen, was qualified by Raymond Cazelles as "the first constitutional law of the French monarchy."[21]

Returning to the main thread, there have existed multiple constitutionalisms with definitions that have fluctuated according to the rhythm of geopolitical and cultural contexts. Among them are political and legal constitutionalisms; written and customary constitutionalisms; and British, American, German, and French constitutionalisms. These constitutionalisms all pose the question of the medieval and ecclesial legacies to modernity.

DOUBLE CONTINUITY OR DOUBLE RUPTURE?

The essence of the debate can be broken down into several formulations. Was there a constitutionalism in the Middle Ages, since the existence of a state is a necessary condition for the discussion of constitutionalism? If there did indeed exist a medieval state, as has been shown by thirty years of work around the genesis of the modern state at the end of the Middle Ages, in particular, was there a continuity between medieval constitutionalism and modern constitutionalism? And, finally, was there a continuity between ecclesiological constitutionalism of the conciliarist type and political constitutionalism of the parliamentarist type? Can the two continuities be made to intersect in an inevitable transition, as Figgis saw, from the conciliarism of the fifteenth century to the parliamentarism of the seventeenth century, from "Gerson to Grotius"[22] or, as Brian Tierney put it, from "Gratian to Grotius?"[23] Was there really a linear route from Constance to 1688, as Harold Laski suggested?[24]

The best viewpoint of all from which to measure the extent of the debate and to take in the respective positions seems to be the work of Brian Tierney, who, from 1955 to 2014, defended a single thesis, that of a radical double continuism: from medieval constitutionalism to modern constitutionalism and from ecclesiological constitutionalism to political constitutionalism. Tierney took as his starting point John Figgis's then provocative and lapidary assertion that the *Haec sancta* was the "culmination of medieval constitutionalism."[25] The intuition that there had been a continuity from Gerson to Grotius was posed by Figgis, a disciple of Maitland and Mandell Creighton, and was also noted by Gierke.[26] For Figgis, there was a continuity between fifteenth-century conciliarism and seventeenth-century English parliamentarism: He was the first to examine the relationship of ecclesiology to politics and the problems of continuity and discontinuity in the transition from medieval thought to modern thought. The only hole in Figgis's argument, according to Tierney, was that he did not consider conciliarism prior to the fifteenth century, which Tierney himself then undertook to do, moving from Gerson back to Gratian, from the conciliar theory of the fifteenth century back to its canonical foundations in the twelfth century.[27] Relying on Figgis's foundational and classic text, Tierney summarized his agenda as follows: "My task will be largely to supply some connective tissue linking the world of the twelfth-century lawyers with that of the fifteenth-century constitutional theorists whom Figgis discussed."[28] He thus insisted on thinking in the long term, from the twelfth to the seventeenth century, the period of the slow, uninterrupted emergence of constitutional process.

A generation after Figgis and half a generation before Tierney, Charles McIlwain's work, starting in the 1930s, provided fuel for Tierney's project.[29] McIlwain's contribution to the question was to reintroduce Roman law into the constitutional thought he studied.

66 ❧ CONSTITUTIONALISM

Far from according credit to the presupposed Teutonic origins of constitutionalism, providentially preserved in England's Common Law, McIlwain highlighted Roman law and civil jurisprudence at the origins of liberalism and constitutionalism in his debate with Esmain and Carlyle.[30] In his classic 1940 work, he followed Bracton, Fortescue, and Balde in distinguishing between the *rex* and the *lex*, whether *gubernaculum* or *jurisdictio*, and even unlimited and limited government as well as absolute monarchy and limited monarchy.[31] After 1933 and in 1940, for McIlwain this meant thinking of the state as safeguard against tyranny, which in his time meant totalitarianism, particularly Nazi totalitarianism. Because McIlwain maintained and defended the existence of a state in the Middle Ages, he sustained the reality of a constitutionalism that he called "ancient."[32] According to him, there was only one weakness in medieval constitutionalism: it was unsanctioned. It therefore existed but proved fragile. The law was not protected. What differentiated medieval constitutionalism from modern constitutionalism was, according to McIlwain, precisely the establishment of sanctions, or in other words the decisive passage from legal limitations on the power of the ruler to the political accountability of the government to the governed. In modern constitutionalism, the government became accountable to the law.[33]

In his reading of McIlwain, Brian Tierney pointed out what he thought was missing from this analysis—namely, a consideration of the Church, the ecclesial, and the ecclesiastic. Tierney proposed to address this omission by reattributing to constitutionalism its canonical—that is, ecclesiological—origins.[34] In a word, he conferred an ecclesiological endogeneity on constitutionalism. The double continuity on which Tierney worked was thus his main thesis, a thesis that appeared consistently in his rarely amended,[35] and broadly accepted,[36] body of work over the roughly sixty years that followed the first edition of *Foundations of the Conciliar Theory*, from 1955 to 2014.

Following Tierney, his students and close colleagues, especially those at Cornell University, furthered and expanded his thesis. In the 1970s, Antony Black worked on the concepts of consent and representation. For him, the councils were a sort of transition between medieval constitutionalism and modern constitutionalism, but also democracy.[37] James Blythe, a doctoral student of Tierney's at Cornell, strove to examine the theme of mixed government, on which he published a book in 1992.[38] In a very "Tierneyan" way, he intended to refute those who denied the influence of medieval ideas on the mixed constitutions of the seventeenth and eighteenth centuries: For him, the mixed constitution well and truly existed in the Middle Ages.[39] He concluded, "Early modern mixed constitutionalism is not primarily the result of a new revival of classical ideas, but rather a development of medieval thought."[40] Finally, Francis Oakley reused Tierney's double continuism in service of a systematization and history of the conciliarist counter-memory, which is to say of a constitutionalist continuism within the Church.[41] He belonged to the same historiographical and ideological lineage, with the anti-Roman sensibility inherent in American Catholicism, including in the study of canon law. As for Constantin Fasolt, he drew a parallel between the history of conciliar theory and the history of medieval parliaments, with particular focus on the maxim *Quod omnes tangit*.[42] In the movement led by Brian Tierney, it is therefore possible to identify an American historical school of constitutionalism in which continuity made sense. This sense of continuity was specific to English and, especially, American culture, referring to history in such a way that, for these American scholars, having a constitution meant having a history.[43]

France, which has been shaped more by a culture of rupture, nevertheless also produced historians with the same continuist intuitions. Gabriel Le Bras (1891–1970), for example, wrote on the canonical origins of administrative law starting in 1956.[44] Paul Ourliac (1911–1998) was the first to express such intuitions: For him, the canonical

68 &) CONSTITUTIONALISM

theories regarding pontifical monarchy that were articulated at the time of the Great Western Schism served as models for the theories of the French monarchy.[45] Patrick Arabeyre furthered this relationship between ecclesiology and constitutionalism, which is to say between royal absolutism and conciliarist theories, by distinguishing the geo-cultural sensibilities of medieval theorists. In the northern, more Gallican parts of France, conciliarist currents dominated. In the South, where more ultramontane sensibilities predominated—as, for example, in the universities of Toulouse, Montpellier, and Cahors, the land of "Southern Papalism"—absolutist currents prevailed.

In the same manner in which Patrick Arabeyre had studied Guillaume Benoît (1455–1516), Tyler Lange studied the jurist and parliamentarian Cosme Guymier (d. 1503), who, in his commentary on the pragmatic sanction, exposed his Gallican conception of Roman primacy and his conciliarist ideal of monarchy.[46] The chiasmus was there. Cosme Guymier intended not to contest monarchical power but to fight against absolutism; he intended to conform the French monarchy to the conciliarist theory of power in a sort of conciliar constitutionalism. Guymier's work in political science was useful for conceiving of the construction of an ecclesiology of the sort that allowed him to draw a parallel between the council and the Parlement of Paris, two similar forms of parliament-senate.[47] This was a sort of "Church Parliament," or *Kirchenparlament*, to use Hubert Jedin's term.[48] Tyler Lange insisted upon highlighting the continuism of Cosme Guymier, for whom "the kingdom was thought of in ecclesial terms."[49] For Guymier, monarchy was quasi-papalist, or "pontificalized," as Julien Théry would say.[50] The conciliarism that came from academic theorists and Parisian parliamentarians permitted the transfer of attributes and the power of the Church regarding the French monarchy. Constitutional law drew on canon law.

Still in France, in the disciplinary field of public law, the school around Stéphane Rials could also be counted as part of this return to

CONSTITUTIONALISM Ꮿ 69

the theological roots of modernity, parallel to Brian Tierney's work and Francis Oakley's systematization. In a programmatic article with a title referring to Tierney, Stéphane Rials studied the canonical origins of modern constitutional techniques, which he called the "canonical laboratory in the development of modern constitutionalism."[51] Like Tierney, Rials rethought the origins of modern legal thought in terms of a transfer from ecclesiology to politics, evoking "modernity as the secularization of a theology and an ecclesiology."[52] For him, the weight of ecclesiological models in the development of the modern state was substantial. This weight can be found in Laurent Fonbaustier's *La Déposition du pape hérétique. Une origine du constitutionnalisme?* (The deposition of the heretic pope. An origin of constitutionalism?).[53]

Further proof can be found in the original title of the legal thesis defended by Laurent Fonbaustier in 1998, under the supervision of Stéphane Rials: *Modèles ecclésiologiques et droit constitutionnel: L'institution de la responsabilité des gouvernants* (Ecclesiological models and constitutional law: The institution of the responsibility of rulers). In the manner of Brian Tierney and Francis Oakley, the author took as his starting point the same comparison that John N. Figgis, at the beginning of the twentieth century, had made between the Church crisis concerning the Council of Constance in the fifteenth century and the crisis of English kings during the political and constitutional revolutions of the seventeenth century. This heuristic comparison between the conciliar theories of the fifteenth century and the English parliamentarism of the seventeenth century invalidated the long "Whiggish" historiographical tradition, which in the nineteenth century distorted the interpretation of constitutionalism through its proclaimed teleological linearity.[54] Laurent Fonbaustier took care to specify that this was a constitution—a framework for the actions of rulers; checks on their power. Hence his working definition of constitutionalism: an effective framework for power, or even "the framework for the activity of those in power, in keeping with certain limits." Each in its own way, conciliarism and parliamentarism contributed to this legal development of the limitation of the arbitrariness of rulers. To address its purpose, the establishment (or origin) of constitutionalism, the author concentrated on one significant moment, the conciliar era of the fifteenth century at the time of the Great Western Schism, a time of major "constitutional crisis" within the Church. He devoted his study to the question of pontifical power, or, more precisely, to the question of the deposition of a defective, which is to say heretical, pope. The author focused on the ability of a community to use institutional mechanisms to react to behavior it perceived as abusive or wrongful on the part of its leaders. The stakes were high, because canon law stated from the outset (distinction XL, canon 6 of Gratian's *Decretum*) that "the pope is to be judge of all, but he himself is to be judged by none, unless he be found departing from the faith." This reflection on the heretical pope established a discussion about the limits of the pontifical power in the face of arbitrariness, the unshared domination of Gregorian inspiration, and pontifical absolutism. An approach to the management of power that was as much a matter of political science as it was of constitutional law slowly came to maturity.

To write about the advent of constitutionalism, Laurent Fonbaustier reaffirmed the contribution to the founding concepts of limited power of mystical images (*corpus mysticum*, mystical marriage); the *status generalis ecclesiae*, a sort of unwritten Church constitution; and limited power's central concepts (participation, consent, deliberation, election, representation, embodiment, delegation, sovereignty, sovereign assembly). He emphasized the constitutional dynamics that were stimulated by ecclesiological models and attempted to approach the question of the transfer, circulation, and transmission to secular authorities of ecclesiological models (the conditions of this transmission, the mobility of ecclesiastical personnel, the community of thought), as well as to evaluate this influence on secular structures.

Laurent Fonbaustier spent significant time on the responsibility of the pope in order to examine the concept's heterogeneous foundations (canonical, theological, secular, Aristotelian) and its institutionalization. He then studied the ecclesiological model of accountability as applied to secular structures in both French constitutional thought (the Gallican concept, neo-conciliarism, the Catholic Monarchomachs, the Protestant Monarchomachs) and Anglo-Scottish constitutional thought (English neo-conciliarism, Scottish constitutionalism, the parliamentarism of the English revolutions). This demonstration resulted in a sort of constitutionalist genealogy organized into three theses: (1) The medieval proto-constitutionalism transformed, more or less, into a modern constitutionalism (for example, in the forms of French Gallicanism or English and Scottish parliamentarism); (2) ecclesiological constitutionalism evolved into secular constitutionalism through the influence of the ecclesial sphere over the secular political sphere, or the "nagging question of the contribution of the Church to the emergence of individual rights"; and (3) conciliarism was a type of constitutionalism; it instituted the accountability of the pope before the conciliar assembly and progressively institutionalized the vicariate of the pope. The author thus defended the idea of the long-term existence of constitutional thought—Tierney's historical approach—for which he wanted to identify, in the crisis of the Great Western Schism, the moment of major theorization and impulse for the theme over the following centuries. Like Figgis, Laurent Fonbaustier regularly spoke of an "ecclesiological laboratory" and the "influence of the doctrines and practices of the Church on secular constitutionalism," of the place of the Church in the dynamics of Western constitutionalism.

Predominant due to the reception and diffusion of Tierney's work, this double continuity has, however, been contested, especially by those who have warned against the risks of anachronism. Harold Berman, in 1983, and Peter Moore, in 1986, pointed out that the councils of the fifteenth century were sometimes defined in an exaggerated and anachronistic manner as European proto-parliaments.[55] The controversy took shape with the work of Cary Nederman. A major partisan of the anti-continuist assault, Nederman has advocated a double discontinuism against those he dubbed the "neo-Figgists" (Brian Tierney, Francis Oakley, Antony Black), for whom constitutionalism's genesis was to be found in the ecclesiological thought of the Latin Middle Ages.[56] For the American philosopher, an expert in political science, there were no grounds to say that conciliarism had engendered modern constitutionalism. As evidence, he pointed to the ecclesiology of Jean Gerson, who, according to Nederman, remained anchored in the political traditions of the Middle Ages: Gerson's conciliarism would have come from medieval corporatism, in which the community was the source of political authority.[57] There was, therefore, neither a continuity nor a persistence of ideas. Nederman inverted the chronology: For him, conciliarism was no more than a version of medieval constitutionalism that had appeared earlier. In other words, the argument was inverted: The conciliar theories of the Church came from medieval theories of government.

Above all, Nederman saw a major rupture between medieval and modern constitutionalism, which included institutionalized checks on power: The conception of power was based on the office and not the individual; the limitation of leaders in the modern era was carried out through public control of state offices; the guarantee of personal rights and the free and individual consent of the governed to the government became the marks of modern constitutionalism. In the medieval period, checks on power were no more than moral ones: It was virtue that limited power and prevented it from turning into tyranny. The conception of government was a moral conception, and obedience to the law was a law of conscience for the leader. Gerson

CONSTITUTIONALISM ❧ 73

considered the limitation of pontifical power by focusing on the moral person of the pontiff and not the office. In the event of abuse due to a defect of personal qualities, Gerson proposed deposing the person of the pope. He did not, per Nederman, think of limiting the office. Medieval constitutionalism, then, remained an essentially religious and ethical system of limitations, which functioned as a constitution to limit the power of the king. In this sense, it was not comparable to modern constitutionalism, and it was not its origin. What Nederman attacked was, ultimately, the Tierney moment, which is to say the endogenous reappropriation through Catholic historiography of a form of conciliar constitutionalism. He called into question the impact of medieval ecclesiology on the formation of a modern political constitutionalism. For example, he argued that modern constitutionalism owed nothing to Gerson beyond an obfuscation of the origins of Gersonian conciliarism, which he saw as having developed out of the politics of the time more broadly, rather than out of ecclesiology.

Karl Ubl, the German medievalist, furthered Nederman's double discontinuism against Brian Tierney and his followers. Studying John of Paris, Ubl found the theory of consent present in Aristotle.[58] For the German historian, the canonists of the thirteenth and fourteenth centuries, such as Henry of Segusio or Innocent IV, contributed nothing to conciliarism, which emerged only within a corporatist tradition with strictly philosophical foundations. John of Paris, Ubl showed, also had no more than a very weak canonical education. Against Tierney, Ubl affirmed that there was no canonical source to the conciliarism of the fifteenth century. Conciliarism would have been no more than a pure reaction to the excessive centralism of the papacy: a reaction, not a filiation. Ubl then attacked the Catholic appropriation of constitutionalism, a concept of American origin. He refuted the connection Tierney had drawn, since 1955, between conciliarism and constitutionalism. At the same time, he refuted the counter-teleology of Oakley's narrative. Against these scholars, he cast doubt on the "modernity of ecclesiastical laws of the Middle Ages" and preferred instead to read a rooting of conciliar theories and medieval constitutionalism in the more strictly political philosophy of the Middle Ages. In sum, he saw it difficult to export constitutionalism outside the boundaries of the history of American political philosophy, the soil from which it had sprung. It was not to be found beyond political modernity. In a word, it could be said that, for Ubl, ecclesiology had neither great influence nor real impact on the modern political theories of the limitation of power and constitutionalism.

In parallel to the academic fields of philosophy and political history, represented here by Cary Nederman and Karl Ubl, respectively, the Tierneyan double continuism was also called into question by certain legal philosophers. The question was not so much about continuism per se as it was about the presence of a state in the medieval era. For many philosophers of law, the emergence of the state could only be a postmedieval phenomenon, as there was certainly no state in the medieval period, and, consequently, no constitutionalism. These legal philosophers were only able to conceive of modern constitutionalism from the moment at which the state came into existence, which is to say the sixteenth century. Against Charles McIlwain, who affirmed the existence of the medieval state and, thus, a medieval constitutionalism, Olivier Beaud, among others, granted a broad definition to "medieval constitutionalism" because, for him, there was no medieval state: "Ancient or medieval constitutionalism has become obsolete since the birth of the modern State."[59] He only understood constitutionalism in the strict sense for the modern era. The debate replayed the abovementioned scenario of Brian Tierney's refutation, via Gaines Post, of the theses of Meinecke, Kern, Gilbert, and Friedrich, all falling within the Hegelian-type legacy. According to these theories, the emergence of the state was only attested at the start of the modern era. As a foundation for

CONSTITUTIONALISM ❧ 75

his thesis, Tierney depended on the works of Ernst Kantorowicz and Gaines Post.[60]

THE QUESTION OF POLITICAL MODERNITY

Again, the issue at stake in the debate over double continuism and double discontinuism (ecclesiological–political and medieval–modern) indeed seems to be that of political modernity and the theory of secularization. Was political modernity based on an ecclesiological, and thus medieval Christian, foundation, or not? The theme of constitutionalism has continued to provide an excellent perspective from which to identify the theses of continuism and discontinuism.

Before Brian Tierney first articulated the continuist thesis in 1955, two German authors writing between the 1920s and the 1950s advanced the concept of "political theology." They did this, each in his own way, in order to think about continuity. Indeed, what was the measure of continuism for Carl Schmitt in his *Political Theology* (1922) and his *Theory of the Constitution* (1927)? How should one understand the now- famous adage "All significant concepts of the modern theory of the state are secularized theological concepts"? Schmitt's (1888–1985) constitutional thought was original, born in the context of early twentieth-century Germany, a very different context from the Anglo-American terroir discussed above.[61] In 1927, Schmitt wrote *Verfassungslehre* (Theory of the constitution). Constitutionalism was at the time a fashionable subject of study both politically (in context of the Weimar era) and epistemically (in the context of the rise of *Geisteswissenschaftlichen* anti-positivist sciences of the mind).

This strand of German constitutional history may be traced. Hugo Preuss, minister of the interior during the Weimar Republic, wrote the new constitution of the parliamentary regime and sought to counteract the authoritarian principles of the Second Reich as recorded in the so-called constitution of Bismarck. From this point, for Preuss, it was necessary to insist upon parliamentarism, liberalism, and even contractualism, and to reestablish federalism by fighting Prussian hegemony and the Germanism of a strong state. The Weimar Constitution was a reaction against the authoritarianism of Wilhelm II and Bismarck. Schmitt had a reactionary and even counterrevolutionary sensibility, however, and in 1927 he criticized the Weimar regime, liberal democracy, and parliamentarism. He opposed his own constitutional theory, in the anti-legislative tradition of Carl-Friedrich von Savigny (1779–1861), the founder of the historical school of German law, and above all in the legacy of Hegel and his constitutional realism. Hegel, in fact, defined the constitution as a "political law," which is to say as the sociopolitical regime of a country. His anti-Kantian realism consisted of placing political realities above legal standards. For him, the constitution should be read less in legal terms (the supreme law) than in political terms (the sociopolitical forms of a regime).

Through the mediation of Lorenz von Stein, Carl Schmitt endorsed Hegelian realism. Committed to this sensibility, he took on the political meaning of the constitution by defining it as the political being of the state (its *Sein*). For him, the constitution was more than a text—it captured society as a whole, hence its substantial connection to the people, or perhaps the spirit of the people, who gave themselves the constitution that best suited them. The constitution was the reflection of what the people wanted, the reflection of its real sentiments. Within the Hegelian legacy, however, Schmitt remained a statist, someone for whom the state transcended society. The German jurist then became an advocate for a strong German state. He demanded an effective sovereignty of the state, setting the real effectiveness of strong power in opposition to the ideal validity of legal normativity. In sum, for him, constitutional practice prevailed over the constitutional text. The constitution was a political reality more so than a normative idea.

Beyond the immediate German context of the 1920s, the constitutional theory of Carl Schmitt was more fundamentally rooted in an Augustinian vision of history, authorized by his radical and committed Catholicism. Far from any rationalism of the Aristotelian-Thomist type, Schmitt adhered to Augustine's voluntarism as applied to *jus divinum*, a voluntarism from which, among other sources, he forged a strong "decisionism." Because the state was the consequence of original sin, according to Augustine's teachings, Schmitt reiterated the necessity of the state as the guarantor of natural law and as a safeguard against the malignity of *post lapsum* man. Schmitt's "decisionism," like his political conceptions of the state and the constitution, were fundamentally marked by Augustinian theology and a providential vision of history. Olivier Beaud went so far as to write of a "metaphysics of the decision" that authorizes the leader to distinguish between good and evil. This decisionism was all the more necessary because it was providential, insofar as it was willed by God himself. In one sense, the state was the institutional and providential mediation desired by God—through divine decision—on the model of the mediator Church instituted by Christ in order to connect God and humans. For Schmitt, the Church remained the conceptual model for the state. His political thought was rooted in a theological interpretation with this decisive nuance: It was not a question of transposition from the theological realm to the legal-political one, but rather of a re-theologizing of politics and law, in the sense that Schmitt did not "secularize" politics.[62] He did not relieve it of its theological and providential dimension. The Schmittian constitution was thus thought of within the providential framework of a divine decision.

This re-theologized—rather than transferred—constitutionalism was, perhaps, constructed precisely as a reaction to the secularizing liberalism of the Weimar regime. As Schmittian exegetes have already said, Schmitt's thought was dialectical, constructed in reaction to and through conflict. Beaud wrote, "According to Schmitt, history obeys a dialectic of the struggle between friend and enemy."[63] Constitutionalism is itself eminently dialectic: It was, in a certain manner, constructed and reinforced in the twentieth century in reaction to absolutism and the dictatorship of positive law. If there was a "Schmittian continuism" through the re-theologizing of constitutionalism, it was a dialectical continuism, which is to say a continuism through conflict, because it arose from an Augustinian anthropology. Paradoxical in its essence, Schmittian constitutionalism in the Augustinian style was therefore anti-parliamentarian, antiliberal, and anti-contractualist, which is to say that it was a constitutionalism of paradox, in which it was the state itself that took guardianship over the laws, a strong state according to providentialist design or divine decision. One might almost say that it was an antimodern constitutionalism, in the sense that "political theology" is antimodern.

Another German interlocutor, more or less a contemporary of Schmitt, was Ernst Kantorowicz (1895–1963), who gave his *The King's Two Bodies* the subtitle *A Study in Medieval Political Theology.*[64] It seems likely that Kantorowicz intentionally cited the Carl Schmitt of 1922 between 1952 and 1957, the publication year of *The King's Two Bodies.*[65] The two men shared the same reactionary sensibility and the same appetite for a strong state. While working on his article "Mysteries of State,"[66] or on the fiction of the two bodies of the king, Kantorowicz did not argue that the political and secular sphere simply took up the Church's absolutist ecclesiology.[67] To be sure, the adage *Dignitas non moritur* came from canon law and applied to the pope: The Apostolic See never dies. But more profoundly, it seems that Kantorowicz's political theology drew its conditions of possibility from the Christian dogma of the incarnation.[68] It was the dual nature of Christ, both God and man, that permitted the fiction of a double body of the king: a

CONSTITUTIONALISM Ꮭ 79

mortal body and an immortal body. The state forged a secular mysticism not through transfer or transposition but through the substantial rooting of politics in religious substance. Far from being a "disenchantment" (a term used by Max Weber and Marcel Gauchet), Kantorowicz's political fiction was a "re-enchantment" through anthropology and the Christian symbols that, for him, irrigated politics. The modern state was built not so much through "secularization" (Weber) as through a decisive principle of analogy. The "continuism" between theological ecclesiology and politics articulated in the *Study in Medieval Political Theology* was thus based on the analogy between Christ and the emperor, and to a lesser degree between the pope and the emperor. The analogy came from the dogma of the incarnation, the foundation of it all. If, for Marcel Gauchet, Christianity was "the religion of the exit from religion"[69] because of the incarnation, it was for Kantorowicz the necessary condition for a "re-enchantment" on account of this same incarnation.[70]

What are the legacies of this German double continuism, Schmittian and Kantorowiczian? "All significant concepts of the modern theory of the state are secularized theological concepts." Modernists, thinkers of the modern age, historians and philosophers, have tended to focus their comments on the first clause of the quotation. In 1985, Jean-François Courtine studied the theologico-political configuration of the absolute state of the seventeenth century. In a substantial article, he described a "crypto-theological" character rather than a theologico-political character.[71] He emphasized the constant appeals theorists made to theological concepts in their definitions of the state. The *summa potestas* of the modern state was designed on the model of the *plenitudo potestas* of Roman sovereignty. "Eugenius IV is the forerunner of Louis XIV," John N. Figgis wrote, which Courtine quoted in translation as "Sans Eugène IV, pas de Louis XIV!"[72] "The Roman Church was the perfect prototype of an absolute and rational monarchy with a mystic foundation."[73] The absolute state was a quasi-Church.

Following Kantorowicz, Courtine taught that the rationalism and the mysticism of the state had intermingled, the absolute state being a mystical monarchy on a rational base and the pontifical state being a rational monarchy on a mystical base.[74] For the French philosopher, the political question was without a doubt a question of the ecclesiological legacy.

The second part of the Schmittian quotation—"from secularized theological concepts"—drew the attention of other scholars. The American ceremonialist school was the direct heir of Kantorowicz's teachings, particularly in the person of Ralph Giesey, but also in Sarah Hanley. Hanley reused the methodology of the great German historian, applying it to the liturgical practices of monarchs both medieval and modern. In these descriptions of political ritual, no place was accorded to Christian legacies. This was pure discontinuism, the subject of the debate launched by Alain Boureau against the American ceremonialists in 1991.[75] Boureau's critique aimed to restore these rituals to their place as Christian liturgical rituals transferred into the secular sphere by denying that the "constitutional ideology" recorded in royal ceremonies was an a priori fact without genesis or precedent. Ex nihilo, a "constitutional ideology that engenders itself."[76] He concluded, "It is impossible to think of celebration in the West, at least until recent date, outside the religious model."[77]

Finally, the "secularized concepts" related to constitutionalism have interested medieval historians in recent years. When he organized a scholarly conference in 2014, François Foronda gave it the title "Des chartes aux constitutions: Autour de l'idée constitutionnelle en Europe (XII–XVII siècle)" (From charters to constitutions: Concerning the constitutional idea in Europe [twelfth to seventeenth centuries]). This title signaled chronological continuism, but the content revealed no ecclesiological-political continuity; none of the twenty-five or so papers delivered at the conference dealt with ecclesiology, ecclesial institutions, or the theological universe. Here, there was no ecclesiology in thinking about the state. The origin of constitutionalism was envisaged in terms of contractualism. Having worked extensively on contracts a decade previously, Foronda conceived of filiation solely in terms of a chain of political causality.[78]

Jean-Philippe Genet, in 2008, concluded with a genealogy stretching "from contractualism to constitutionalism," "from implicit contract to explicit constitution."[79] A historian of England, Genet belonged to the current of the new constitutional historians, which included the school around Christine Carpenter (Edward Powell, John Watts, Helen Castor, etc.). According to these historians the constitution was not a text but a complex of political, social, and moral relationships.[80] It was the synonym of "political culture" more so than a textual foundation. Within this deliberately loose redefinition, Genet described a genealogy of the progressive revision of the "great charters" into privileges and fundamental laws. He pointed toward a universe of legal standards that, little by little, took on the status of the constitution. "Constitutionalism can start with a constitution, but also with a constitutional functioning never based on texts. Political action legitimates the constitution, not the other way around."[81] The discontinuism is striking here for the failure to take into account the ecclesiological roots of constitutionalism. Is this an assumed discontinuism, or discontinuism by repression? Such is the question that should, legitimately, be asked.

3

COLLEGIALISM

Was the "religion" of the seventeenth or nineteenth centuries of the same type that was in question in the Middle Ages?
—Michel de Certeau, "L'histoire religieuse au XVIIe siècle. Problèmes de méthodes," *Recherches de sciences religieuses* 57 (1969): 250

The connection between conciliarity and collegialism, or between synods and collegial forms, is part of the long history of relationships between Roman primacy and its counterpowers.[1] "Collegialism" was another name ("the new name for the classic theme," in the words of Sesboüe) for ecclesial polarity in the face of pontifical and monarchical polarity. It was an avatar of conciliarity, even of conciliarism, within the conflicting history of the tension between the Roman primacy and the Church as represented by its episcopate, its College of Cardinals, and the Conciliar Fathers, as well as within the history of the limits and the counterpowers that responded to Roman supremacy.[2] Collegialism formed part of the complex and multivocal history of constitutionalism. Taken together, conciliarity, constitutionalism, and collegialism once again raise the question of counterpowers, or in other words the legally defined limits to the power of the pope.

THE DISCURSIVE INVENTION OF "COLLEGIALISM" AT VATICAN II

"The debate over collegialism—a term otherwise ignored by Vatican II—was the liveliest debate of this council."[3] First of all, the definition given to collegialism by the experts and theologians of Vatican II should be remarked upon. What did the theological world of the time understand this word to mean? In paragraphs 19–27 of *Lumen gentium*, the term *collegium* (college) refers to everything relating to the collective body of bishops (*collegium seu corpus episcoporum* or even *ordo episcoporum*), including the bishop of Rome, by fact of their shared ordination ("in virtue of their common sacred ordination and mission," according to the text) and their hierarchical communion with the pope and among themselves:[4] "The order of bishops, which succeeds to the college of apostles and gives this apostolic body continued existence, is also the subject of supreme and full power over the universal Church, provided we understand this body together with its head, the Roman pontiff."[5]

The terms *collegium*, *corpus*, and *ordo* were used indiscriminately. The definition of collegialism as it is used in *Lumen gentium* was, therefore, as follows: The bishops of the universal Church formed a college, headed by s the pope, that was the successor to the college of the apostles, of which Peter had been the head.

According to Hervé Legrand's analysis, this definition implied three major changes in the relationship between the pontiff and his bishops.[6] The first change appeared in the very source of bishops' power. Up to that point, episcopal jurisdiction had derived from pontifical jurisdiction, with the pope communicating to the bishops their powers of order and jurisdiction. The revolution of Vatican II consisted of restoring a divine jurisdictional origin to the bishops: Henceforth, their power would come directly from Christ through their ordination. Christ entrusted bishops with the charges of sanctifying, teaching, and governing.[7] The bishops were consequently the "vicars and ambassadors of Christ";[8] they were "not to be thought of as vicars of the Roman Pontiffs."[9] As a result, the distinction between power of order and power of jurisdiction became obsolete. The second mutation in this definition to develop was that because the pope no longer conferred jurisdiction to the bishops, he thenceforth reserved certain privileges by virtue of his primacy. Finally, in order to bring this collegialism up to date, institutional liaisons were established. These included episcopal conferences, which "render a manifold and fruitful assistance, so that this collegiate feeling may be put into practical application."[10] These episcopal conferences referred explicitly to "Churches, established in various places by the apostles and their successors, [that] have in the course of time coalesced into several groups, organically united. . . . Some of these Churches, notably the ancient patriarchal Churches, as parent-stocks of the Faith, so to speak, have begotten others as daughter Churches."[11] The episcopal conferences were thus presented as the contemporary forms of the ecclesial meetings of the earliest days of Christianity.[12]

Unsurprisingly, *Lumen gentium*'s definition of collegialism has been the subject of abundant comment. As the original (since 1951) pioneer of a theology of the "college of bishops" and the coiner of the French term *collégialité*, which he based on *sobornost*, a concept in Russian Orthodox theology and spirituality, Yves Congar spilled the most ink on the subject.[13] Drawing on the decree's definition, he expanded its meaning. In one sense, collegialism permitted the local church to be thought of as a "realization of the Church," "a contribution to a unique reality": "The episcopate that each has received is possessed in its entirety by its respective bishop: just as each local church is simply a realization of the Church, not a simple circumscription of a whole, so too the episcopate, which each pastor exercises locally, is a participation in a unique reality that must be called *ordo*, *corpus*, or *collegium*."[14]

86 ∞ COLLEGIALISM

The divine origin of episcopal jurisdiction and, thus, the divine origin of collegialism have similarly been commented upon. That bishops received their jurisdiction from God and not from the pope was a claim from the era of the Second Council of Pisa (1511–1512), and it paradoxically resulted in the First Vatican Council.[15] Thereafter, any attempt to defend the contrary—namely, that jurisdiction was received from the pope—seemed to contradict all historical testimony. In his *Journal d'un théologien*, Congar spoke of "the historically untenable thesis that bishops received their jurisdiction through the pope."[16] Through this redefinition of origins, the arguments of history were invoked: Appeals were made to historical works, and the paucity of existing works on the subject was deplored. Congar invited an expansion of the field of study. It became necessary thereafter to write this history of collegialism: "For a thousand years, everything in this field has been seen and built from the papal angle, not that of the episcopate and its collegialism. Now *this* history, *this* theology, *this* canon law must be made. That is all."[17]

However, difficulties dominated in the interpretation of conciliar decrees. At the heart of the interpretive issue, it was necessary to introduce collegialism without attacking primacy—in short, without attacking the results of the First Vatican Council. Such was the tenor of the debates within the expert commissions, depending on trends and sensibilities. In his *Mon journal du concile*, Yves Congar revived their spirit, and even their words. He commented upon the strength of the curialist and ultramontane faction, as well as its presence and its weight: "There really is a gap in the Church between the curialists and everyone else! The whole weight of Vatican I still burdens us!!!"[18] He continued, "The curialists (Ottaviani, Browne, Staffa, Carli . . .) are doing *EVERYTHING* they can to prevent the episcopate from regaining rights that have been stolen from it."[19] To those names, it was necessary to add those of the Cardinals Siri, Parente, Jacono, Coutinho, Fares, Tromp, and Cocognani. For Siri, "bishops had authority only with and under the Roman pontiff. . . . Nothing can be gained from collegialism that diminishes the primacy."[20] For Jacono, it was necessary to "take care not to achieve primacy."[21] For Coutinho, "there was no episcopal college without the pope."[22] For Carli, "Everything must be handed over to the arbitrary will of the pope."[23] "Ottaviani begins to deny that the apostles constituted a college."[24] "Father Tromp wrote, mimeographed, and distributed a fairly long exposition against collegialism—vigorous and obtuse, legalistic and Bellarminian to the core—all conceived in the sense of the pontifical monarchy."[25] For Cicognani, "collegialism was the negation of primacy."[26] The insistence of the curialists began to influence the pope himself:

> Lately, the speeches Paul VI has been giving during public audiences have constantly returned to the absolute divine mission of the papacy. All this makes me think and fear that the pope, worried by the development of the idea of collegialism and expecting his pilgrimage to the Holy Land to provide some enlightenment on these questions, has brought back a reinforced awareness of being THE base of the Church, THE vicar of Christ. I see that the men of the Curia are working hard to make ultramontane theses prevail.[27]

The other trend was represented by Karl Rahner, Edouard Schillebeeckx, and Yves Congar. For them, "the supreme power over the universal Church is always collegial, but it can be exercised either collegially or personally by the head of the college. When exercised collegially, it is the council."[28]

In addition to the major tension at the center of the debates between primacy and collegialism, three ambiguities stood out from the decree. These ambiguities gave rise to questions, and even to impasses. First of all, there arose the question of the practical implementation and concrete realization of collegialism. Bernard Sesboüé summarized the

88 ❧ COLLEGIALISM

issue well: "It is difficult to see how collegialism could have a concrete reality outside the convocation of the Council. But the real problem posed by Vatican II is its exercise when the Council is not convoked."[29] Jean-Marie Tillard famously spoke of a "dormant collegialism": "Vatican II did not show us how in practice to combine the freedom of the Pope with the requirements of collegialism. . . . What we see at present is the papacy in action and collegialism lying dormant."[30]

A second ambiguity resulted from the free-floating association between collegialism and communion.[31] Congar brought the two concepts together in order to establish a strong link between them:

> Collegialism . . . concerns the very being of the episcopate of the Church, it translates its nature where there is a mystery of communion. On the subject of collegialism, we increasingly invoke the model of the Three Divine Persons who are one. . . . We cannot isolate one (collegialism) from the other (communion). There is a general principle of collegialism, through which legal collegialism is ontologically based in the profound nature of the Church as communion.[32]

For Congar, "it is within this ontology of communion that a theology of episcopal collegialism will be able to take root."[33] For Grootaers, commenting on Congar's work, "collegialism" had a legal sense, whereas "communion" had a moral sense.[34] The drift of this confusion, even if Paul VI denied it,[35] risked dissolving collegialism into a sort of affective fraternity without structural foundation. Paul VI wrote, "Collegialism is a clearly visible love that bishops must have for each other."[36] Suffice it to say that, in this respect, collegialism no longer held authority over pontifical primacy. Thereafter, all agreed to recognize "the central and fundamental concept in the conciliar documents" in the ecclesiology of communion.[37]

The third and final ambiguity, a corollary of the preceding one, was the syntagma of "hierarchical communion." It was Paul VI who

COLLEGIALISM ❧ 89

introduced the qualifier "hierarchical" into the acts of the council. "Communion is at the base of collegialism, which has hierarchy as a major characteristic."[38] At the core of the syntagma was the tension between the ecclesiology of Vatican I and the ecclesiology of Vatican II, and more precisely the tension between the Council of Constance and Vatican I. Congar sketched out a definition in an attempt to further harmonize "communion" and "hierarchical communion": "The one was *sub Petro* and the other *cum Petro*."[39] Hence the oxymoron of the syntagma: A hierarchically oriented communion was no longer communion in the original sense of the term.[40] It was an effort to balance, to summarize, and above all to restrain. Then followed the *Nota explicativa praevia*, or preliminary note, which Monseigneur Felici wrote, on the request of Paul VI, to clarify the interpretation given to the decree *Lumen gentium*'s third chapter, on collegialism. "The entire constitution must be read in the light of this note."[41] For Sesboüé, "the *Nota explicativa praevia* was destined to prevent any conciliarist-inspired deviation in the interpretation of the conciliar text."[42] It established the "Roman theology" of a conservative minority against the majority of the bishops and the proponents of biblical, ecumenical, and theological renewal. The text clearly states as much: "The College always and necessarily is understood together with its head because (the pope) retains intact in the college his office as vicar of Christ and pastor of the universal Church." And, later in the text, "It performs strictly collegial acts only at intervals and only with the consent of its head. The text says: 'with the *consent* of its *head*,' lest this dependence be thought of as though it were on someone *outside* the college: the term 'consent' evokes on the contrary *communion* between the head and members, and implies the necessity of an act which is proper to the head."[43]

Disappointments and dissatisfactions would fuel the rest of the history of post-Vatican ecclesiologies. Felici concluded the *Nota* with this flourish, which was intended to be historical: "This hierarchical communion of all the bishops with the Sovereign Pontiff is certainly a solemn teaching of Tradition."[44] Any hesitation lay in the "certainly." What was the actual historical content of the concept?

THE SEARCH FOR A HISTORICAL LINEARITY

The Texts

Although Congar and all subsequent interlocutors deplored the stark paucity of historical studies on the subject, the fundamental milestones of a theological history of collegialism might nevertheless be outlined, starting with Cyprian and then, for the medieval period, moving on to several passages in the works of Bernard de Clairvaux, Guillaume Durand, Gerson and d'Ailly, and Zabarella. For the modern period, there were few milestones aside from the work of Bolgeni (1733–1811). Broadly speaking, this was how the history was seen by the theologians of Vatican II. What might be said about this scenario, which was typical of the theologians' linear approach?

The history as recounted above is fundamentally incomplete. Conforming to the ideals of theological history, the concept of episcopal collegialism was projected onto the Patristic era of the fourth and fifth centuries. According to this narrative, Cyprian was the perfect theorist. In 1963, Jean Colson's study *L'épiscopat catholique. Collégialité et primauté dans les trois premiers siècles de l'Église* (The Catholic episcopate: Collegialism and primacy in the first three centuries of the Church) was published in the *Unam sanctam* series founded by Yves Congar. Three chapters in the book were devoted to Cyprian. The author emphasized the complementarity of the two doctrines, pontifical and collegial, in order to preserve the desired harmonization. The idea was to avoid undermining the conclusions of Vatican I, even if doing so required rhetorical contortion: "The unity and infallibility of the Catholic Church rest upon the complementarity of the apostolic college, which infallibly taught and directed the Church in unity, and Peter, the center and the infallible guarantor of the unity and infallibility of the faith of this college."[45]

Although he was a recognized expert in primitive Christian institutions, the author wrote a history of the ecclesiastical type.

Collegialism would thus have been present in the minds of the patristic authors (Basil, Chrysostom, Cyril, Ambrose, Augustine, Leo, Gregory). It would then have disappeared due to the breakup of ecclesial structures caused by feudalism. This feudal dispersion would have prevented any thought of collegial regrouping.[46] Then came Bernard de Clairvaux, who belonged to what might be called "the second feudal age." Within the trend of Dominican history, his protean *De consideratione* would have become one of the first cornerstone texts in favor of collegialism: "Recall St. Bernard writing his famous *De consideratione* to Pope Eugene III and speaking out against the growing abuse of Roman interference in the normal purview of the authority of the bishops. The idea of solidarity among bishops, of forming a single *college* or body for the evangelization of the world, would impose itself and constantly return to the Council (Vatican II)."[47]

For Congar, "the Middle Ages scarcely thought of the episcopate as anything but dispersed."[48]

More fundamentally than feudalization, episcopal collegialism as Vatican II defined and understood it was penalized by another type of collegialism: the collegialism of cardinals. This ecclesiology of the Sacred College, which was present in embryonic form in the work of Guillaume Durand but found its finest theorists in men like Pierre d'Ailly and Francesco Zabarella, cast doubt on thought surrounding episcopal collegialism. Congar described the risk quite clearly: "One of the reasons, and not the least, why the Middle Ages (at least starting in a certain period) hardly developed a theology of episcopal

92 ಔ COLLEGIALISM

collegialism was a sort of confiscation of the idea by the ideology of the college of cardinals."[49]

Beginning in the years of the Council of Vienna, 1311–1312, Guillaume Durand the Younger, in his *De modo generalis concilii celebrandi*, found a form of the limitation of the monarchical exercise of pontifical power in the College of Cardinals. He also built on an idea that had circulated since the time of Gregory VII, according to which cardinals, *pars corporis papae*, together with the pope formed the *ecclesia Romana*, the head of all other churches. In his work, Congar pinpointed a furtive allusion to the collegial power of bishops: "Durand was not a Gallican, but he desired a papal power that respected the authority of bishops, working *sub ratione*, taking their advice into account; he rejected *universalis episcopus* and *summus sacerdos* as titles for the pope and preferred instead to say *episcopus primae sedis*."[50]

Guillaume Durand's contribution was considerably enriched in the fifteenth century by the work of Pierre d'Ailly and Francesco Zabarella. For them, collegialism meant exclusively that of cardinals, *collegio cardinalium*,[51] and, occasionally, an application of collegialism to the conciliar representation of *universitas fidelium*. Between the two, there was no place for an episcopal collegialism. The idea of a shared power over the Universal Church could only be one of cardinals or councils. The two men wrote between 1408 and 1418. Named a cardinal in 1411, Pierre d'Ailly wrote his *De potestate ecclesiastica* in 1416. In the treatise, he—for good reason—advocated for a collegial regime based on the pope and his cardinals. The terminology is well-known: The cardinals co-assisted (*coassistunt*)[52] the pope, just as the apostles were co-assistants to Peter.[53] They were the coadjutors (*coadjutores*) of the pope,[54] a part of the pontifical body (*pars corporis papae*). The conception of power was just as oligarchic as it was collegial. The oligarchic element suggests a mixed government, in which the pope would be the monarchical element and the cardinals the "aristocratic" element in the sense of an oligarchy according to the

COLLEGIALISM ❧ 93

Aristotelian vulgate, in which mixed governments were better than simple governments. Also better was collegialism among cardinals, as opposed to episcopal collegialism, in the sense that the cardinals aimed for the good of the Universal Church whereas bishops aimed for the good of their particular church. According to the Aristotelian adage, the common good is more perfect than the individual good.[55]

Regarding Zabarella, Congar commented on the concept of collegialism's corporatist deviation. This deviation had its origins in the definitions of Hostiensis,[56] who had applied the corporatist theories of his time to the concept of colleges in the sense given to the definition by Roman law—that is, an association of men possessing the same charge and the same power (*coetus equalium*), an assembly of equals:[57] "The College of Cardinals had in fact become a real corporation, with the right to intervene in the admission of new members and the exclusion of colleagues, with the freedom to assemble, with a common fund, etc."[58] Hostiensis next applied the corporate theses to the relationships that existed between a bishop and his chapter, and also between the College of Cardinals and the pope.[59] The cardinals would, then, hold *plenitudo potestatis* along with the pope and, upon his death or in the event he was defective, they would have universal jurisdiction.[60] The connection with conciliarity, even conciliarism, was clear at this time, during the Great Western Schism. By quoting Hostiensis, Zabarella opened the door to the convocation of a council by the cardinals.[61]

Thought of as a meeting of the *universitas fidelium*, collegialism thus joined conciliarity. Gerson wrote, "The Christian Church in its totality is a single body, a college, and an authentic congregation because of the human status of Christ, even if the pontifical seat is vacant and even if it is impeded."[62] The Church as a *congregatio fidelium* was the definition of a true council according to the theologians of Constance. The perspectives of a *collegium* and a *congregatio* merged for the thinkers of the Great Western Schism: "The concept of a college no longer appeared 'stuck' on collegialism alone, but, without negating that definition, would now extend to all believers."[63]

Jean Gerson, the great fifteenth-century theologian of the Council of Constance, was perhaps the figure who came closest to thinking of episcopal collegialism in the theological manner of Vatican II. In contrast to his teacher and friend Pierre d'Ailly, Gerson was never named a cardinal or a bishop. He remained the chancellor of the University of Paris and a parish priest. Véronique Beaulande-Barraud has demonstrated Gerson's concern for limiting pontifical power in order to elevate local churches and to exalt bishops before papal omnipotence, particularly by defending parish priests against competition from the mendicant orders, which were known to aspire to be the pope's delegated militia.[64] Gerson aimed to redistribute the pastoral and sacramental forces of the ecclesial structure by anchoring his ecclesial vision in the *Ecclesia primitiva*, which linked episcopal government with synodal activity. One might almost speak of a Gersonian episcopalism similar to what existed in the Patristic era. Gerson insisted upon the hierarchical autonomy of bishops and their immediate jurisdiction over their flocks, without the intrusion of the pope: "The pope's plenitude of power is not, however, to be understood as meaning power in an immediate sense over all Christians, with the result that he could, at will, exercise immediate jurisdiction over them himself or though extraordinary means. Indeed, exercising such acts of authority would harm ordinaries who have more immediate, even the most immediate, rights over the flocks entrusted to them."[65]

The pope, therefore, held power that was mediated compared with the immediate authority of ordinaries. He could not contravene an episcopal judgment without ruining the sense of hierarchy by violating the jurisdiction of ordinaries.[66]

COLLEGIALISM ❧ 95

When they examined the texts, the theologians of Vatican II found material to reconstruct their own episcopal collegialism in the rights of ordinaries that Gerson defended. Indeed, although Gerson built on Pierre d'Ailly's perspective on the collegialism of cardinals,[67] he focused his attention more distinctly on the episcopal body. In the *De auctoritate concilii* (written between November 1408 and November 1409), Gerson evoked the authority of bishops: "In the event of the default of the pope and the cardinals by death or otherwise, or in the event of reprehensible negligence, the authority to unite the Christian religion is vested in the Catholic bishops."[68] Better, the community of bishops (*universitas episcoporum*)—or, perhaps, the college of bishops—was an infallible entity. Using the strong and rare term *inobliquabilis*, he wrote, "Universitas episcoporum est inobliquabilis secundum affectum et intellectum, nec est compossible Christi lege eos omnes collective desinere per mortem aut haereticare" (The community of bishops is unflinching according to affect and intellect, and it is not possible, according to the law of Christ, for all of them to collectively die or to fall into heresy).[69] Charles Moeller pointed out that Gerson was speaking of a community of bishops and a modality of their infallibility when this community was gathered.

Finally, Gerson used the term *collegium* in the context of a question of the infallibility of a universal episcopal college: "The college of all Christian bishops cannot err in faith nor be tainted by schism; this is what you must believe with certainty."[70] This infallibility arose from the Christly origin of the powers of the bishop: "The status of priests, like that of bishops, is part of the original and ordinary institution of Christ. It is shown that because the disciples themselves, who were succeeded by priests according to the glosses and canons, were ordained through the hierarchy and sent forth immediately by Christ, they received the power to hierarchize not from Peter but from Christ."[71]

96 ∞ COLLEGIALISM

After examining these texts, Charles Moeller noted the content of Gerson's words: "The text spoke of infallibility and the entire episcopate gathered in a general council, and it used the term *collegium episcoporum* to examine this doctrine."[72]

Gerson wrote all these texts in the context of councils, from Pisa to Constance. Chronologically, they were inscribed within the development of the authority of the council. The connection between conciliarity and collegialism was subtle. In the *De auctoritate concilii*, Gerson spoke of a *consilium Ecclesiae et episcoporum*.[73] Is it to be understood that there was only one council, the council of the Church and the bishops? Or were there two councils—the council of the Church (the council) and the council of the bishops (the episcopal college)? In the first case, the council should be understood as a representation of the Universal Church and also of the episcopal college. Later on, Gerson specified that the pope is subordinate to the Universal Church or to the college representing it.[74] Should it be understood that this college representing the Church was the council, with "college" here being a synonym for *concilium*? Or, rather, that the college was an entity independent from the council and that, consequently, the pope was subject to the council—the Universal Church—and to the college representing the Church? It remains difficult to attribute the capacity to represent the Universal Church to the episcopal college. Instead, *collegium* should here be understood as designating the council.

In sum, the connection between collegialism and representativity was strong: Whether conciliar, cardinal, or episcopal, the college was a representative body of the Universal Church.[75] For Gerson, in sum, collegialism—which was always thought of within the discursive context of conciliarity, even a conciliarity without a pontifical head—was one of the modalities of the *limitatio* of primatial power. A counterpower. Hence the consonance between collegialism and *reformatio* in a Gersonian sense: For Gerson, it was a question of returning power

COLLEGIALISM ∞ 97

to bishops so that they could lead the fight against heresy in the spirit of the *Ad abolendum*, which he quoted: "It is necessary to avoid as heretics those whose bishops have declared must be avoided."[76]

The Zones of Silence

The historical approach of the Vatican II theologians, however, sinned by omission. The history of collegialism was part of the "ecclesiastical politics of forgetting," which produced an ecclesiastical history conditioned by rejections of and reticence regarding its memories. The zones of silence are, therefore, numerous. In this history of episcopal collegialism, the Second Council of Pisa has remained perhaps the most overlooked council.[77] It was, however, the focus of the episcopalist movement's claims. How should this be understood?

The Second Council of Pisa (1511–1512) occurred within the context of the conflict between Louis XII and Pope Julius II. From the start, the convocation of nine cardinals, all of them French, followed Louis XII's anti-pontifical offensive. On the basis of the conciliar decrees *Haec Sancta* and *Frequens*, the council aimed to reaffirm the doctrines that had been imposed at Constance and Basel. On April 21, 1512, the Conciliar Fathers declared the suspension of Pope Julius II's pontifical authority. In response, Julius II convoked the Second Lateran Council, which was inaugurated on May 3, 1512. There, Poggio and Cajetan defended the pope against conciliar claims and against Gerson. Facing them, Giovanni Gozzadini (1477–1517) advocated a healthy conciliarism. In his *De concilio* of 1538, Domenico Giobazzi (1443–1527), in turn, refuted the conciliarist options. Almain and John Mair refuted Cajetan based on Gerson and the so-called School of Paris, which was then at its greatest extent. The Fifth Lateran Council (1512–1517) marked the triumph of pontificalism and the definitive victory of the papacy. The official Roman historiography definitively buried conciliarism at this point. What this historiography does not sufficiently relate, however, is the actions and demands that bishops expressed at the council. The bishops had sought to impose a limit to pontifical privileges by proposing a different counterpower than the council: the episcopal body. This was a question of establishing an episcopal sodality or confraternity (*episcopalis societas, confraternitas, sodalicium*) and of requesting from the pope that this confraternity have a common chancellor, a treasury, and the ability to hold regular meetings to discuss matters in the interests of bishops. The cold reactions of the pope and the cardinals, along with how they ended these demands by imposing the idea of perpetual silence, are well-known. This was the failure of the movement. With the bull *Pastor aeternus* in 1516, the Fifth Lateran Council reaffirmed, in stark contrast, that the pontiff had authority over all types of councils.

The demands resurfaced at Trent. Here, it was a matter of first defining the divine and non-pontifical origin of the power of bishops, and then of defining the relationship of the pope to the bishops. Though formulated in the sixteenth century, these demands went unfulfilled until the First Vatican Council, in a clear paradox, solemnly affirmed that bishops were successors to the apostles, thereby putting an end to episcopal demands through the recognition of the episcopate as a divine institution. The bad press of the Second Council of Pisa, and its place in the rubbish bin of ecclesiastical history, might therefore be better understood.

In addition to the omissions of ecclesiastical rearrangements, the major fundamental pitfall of this theologian-style history remains that it is a history of doctrines that fails to take into account the history of practices. The proponents of this type of history have focused on constructing the linearity of a historical narrative rather than examining the twists and turns of a history that is necessarily winding because it was pragmatic and lived.

THE GAP BETWEEN PRACTICES OF COLLEGIALISM AND THE OFFICIAL NARRATIVE OF VATICAN II

When he set out in search of medieval collegialism, Congar examined the texts of the canonists in addition to those of the major theologians. Jean d'André established a clear synonymy: "Universitas, communitas, collegium, corpus sunt quasi idem significantia" (University, community, college, and body have almost the same meaning).[78] He noted other equivalents in Azo's definition: "Collegium est personarum plurium in corpus unum quasi conjunctio vel collectio: quod generali sermone universitas appellatur, corpus quoque vulgariter apud nos consortium vel schola" (A college is a sort of conjunction or collection of many people in a single body, what in general language is called a *universitas*; among us, this body can also be commonly called a consortium or a school).[79] Congar found the legal definitions of the term "college" too broad and technical,[80] and he was never able to locate episcopal collegialism in them.[81] His strictly textual and doctrinal approach was unable to grasp the archival reality of institutions and communities in order to make sense of the practices of collegialism. The history of practices offers another way to locate a certain type of collegialism that was present in the Middle Ages—one that was not exclusively episcopal, to be sure, but close enough in its operating principles.

In the Middle Ages, the term *collegium* designated any society of individuals gathered for a common purpose. The current academic definition became attached to the word only very slowly, supplanting the periphrasis designating a house (*domus*) for poor students. Starting in the thirteenth century, the adjective "collegiate" designated a church served by a college or chapter of secular canons.[82] Originally, the chapters had been established in cathedral churches in the service of a bishop; later, they could be installed in other churches with foundations that served as a source of prebends for the clergy canons. It was these canons who became known as "collegiate." In 2009, Anne Massoni published her study *La collégiale Saint-Germain l'Auxerrois (1380–1510)*. In it, she specified the institutional, legal, and communitarian structures of the different collegiate bodies. The collegiate church was, according to Massoni, a community of clergy within which the chapter of canons was only one component, though not an insignificant one: "Founding assemblies were the moment at which the canons lived together as a body, not as individuals. It was in chapter that the group experienced its cohesion. This was the only place the canons met up together, since in the choir they found themselves intermingled with other clergy."[83]

Fundamentally, the canons in their assemblies practiced this ecclesial corporate life, this collegialism, to the point that the term *collegium* was sometimes used as an equivalent to *capitulum*.[84] Anne Massoni clarified the distinction:

> The two terms referred to different characteristics of the same reality. *Capitulum* meant the head, and the chapter indeed filled this function of being the head of the church, as seen in the decisions taken by the chapter. *Collegium* emphasized their collective character. The canons were "colleagues" in the sense that they never acted individually in chapter. . . . A college was not a chapter because the latter went beyond being a simple assembly; it was a body that had a collective existence with associated rights. A chapter was its own entity and not an aggregate of individuals. A chapter was more than a college: it was a body, and not only a group.[85]

Following this definition, Massoni has thoroughly examined how the canons practiced meeting in chapter. During assemblies, the speaking order respected the principle of seniority, with the most senior canon giving his opinion after the dean and so forth. Otherwise, deliberations were carried out under a system of the complete equality of voices.[86] Collegiate leadership, or the ability to decide together, was one of the characteristics of the status of canon.[87] The figure of the dean maintained complex relationships of hierarchical authority and collegial belonging with the rest of the chapter, being both their superior and their equal. Massoni wrote of the dean, "Like the pope among the cardinals, he was a *primus inter pares*, and his election, an issue for the canons, was significantly described as a 'conclave' in 1451. . . . The more complex nature of the reception of the dean shows that he was one canon among others, but also the most eminent."[88]

The situation differed based on geography. In the northern part of the kingdom of France, the bishop and the chapter remained two distinct institutions, but in the southern examples of cathedral chapters, the bishops remained a stakeholder in the chapter. A southern bishop was a full member of the chapter, a real *primus inter pares*. The history, indeed, differed depending on location.

Hélène Millet, for her part, has called attention to the existence of a monastic capitular collegialism. In the midst of the Great Western Schism, monks—especially Benedictines—were invited to many assemblies of the clergy: "For them, these repeated gatherings were a signal of a collective awakening that manifested itself in the decision, made at the assembly of 1406, to revive the tradition of general chapters organized by ecclesiastical province."[89]

Thus, during the time of the Great Western Schism the monastic orders took advantage of assemblies to support the French Church and to reconnect with their own deliberative traditions.

Alain Rigaudière compared the quest for collegialism with the practices of urban representative assemblies.[90] He went on to define representative assemblies as "Groups composed of representatives of a body, convened in periodic meetings and organized with a view to deliberating and making decisions on subjects of common interest."[91]

In these assemblies, there developed the techniques of expression and deliberation, decision-making and government. Rigaudière specified the multiplicity of the forms of these feudal assemblies known by various names: *curia, consilium, colloquium, congregatio generalis, parlamentum*. For Rigaudière, "the general assemblies of residents within the framework of the city played a fundamental role in the genesis of all other medieval assemblies in the progressive definition of their skills and the organization of their working methods."[92] Collegiate techniques were central to assemblies: the method of convocation, the preparation of lists of electors, mandates, proxies, delegation, the organization and management of debates, voting systems, the struggle against absenteeism and brigades, and sensitivity to public affairs and the common interest. Hence the intrinsic link between systems of assembly and collegialism, between synodality (in the etymological sense) and collegialism.

Is it possible at this point to come closer to locating a medieval collegialism of the episcopal type? In a 2015 survey titled *Les Évêques dans le royaume de France au XIVe siècle* (Bishops in the kingdom of France in the fourteenth century), Vincent Tabbagh observed the indisputable absence of collegialism from the corporate consciousness of the French episcopate in the late Middle Ages.[93] At the heart of the book is a question Tabbagh formulated in its introduction: "How to account for this historical strangeness—namely, that the French episcopate had none of the corporate consciousness necessary to implement collective action on a kingdom-wide scale? Why did the bishops not play the card of collegialism in order to set themselves up as a counterpower or decision-making entity with respect to the king or the pope?"[94]

There was no corporate consciousness among the French episcopate beyond collegiate membership. Why? A partial answer is that the episcopate chose to serve the royal state, an alliance with the monarchy that built up the state at the cost of the orders. By placing itself in the service of the monarchy, the episcopate renounced its own identity. Tabbagh has shown that the Gregorian moment ended because the monarchical state meant the sacrifice of the corporate consciousness of the bishops. He noted that the collegiate model functioned better in the chapters than in the episcopal context. The bishops seem to have experienced neither collegialism nor fraternity.

Hélène Millet made the same observation regarding the era of the Great Western Schism and, especially, the experiment of subtraction of obedience: "By agreeing to follow the royalty on the path of subtraction of obedience, the prelates were often accused of having sacrificed the independence of the Church to safeguard their own interests."[95] It must be said that, having become autonomous, the French Church gave itself over to the leadership of the king. The true esprit de corps therefore could be found more in a sense of belonging to a French clergy than in a sense of belonging to an ecclesial body of the episcopate. The assemblies of the clergy of France were where belonging was recognized and experienced: "The end point of the clerical assemblies, the decision to withdraw obedience, cannot be conceived without the existence of a minimum level of consensus and the sense of belonging to a coherent group for which it was possible to legislate. . . . It was only after becoming aware they represented the Church of the kingdom that the prelates believed they had the authority to proclaim themselves a conciliar assembly."[96] A type of collegialism certainly existed, but it was not an episcopal one; it remained synodal, even national, in nature.

It is difficult to find collegialism outside the realm of practices, and even within practices it is difficult to find a purely episcopal collegialism. Furthermore, it has even been shown that the cohesion of the episcopal body was the target of attacks from the pope's canonists, the same figures who developed the *plenitudo potestatis*.[97]

In sum, by looking for a more collegiate style of government in the medieval era, particularly in the decrees of Constance and the conciliarist movements of the fourteenth and fifteenth centuries, the theologians of Vatican II augmented the linearity of a narrative of conciliar counter-memory that served to reinforce their own position. Thus, medieval collegialism as it was conceived, studied, and interpreted through medieval constitutionalism remained a theological optical illusion that distorted the real history. It was necessary to seek the historical roots of the concept of "collegialism" in order to ground it in tradition. Likewise, it was necessary to avoid novelty to an extent that, to them, justified forcing the history to fit a chosen narrative, and also to sustain a position of continuism.

If medieval collegialism can be spoken of at all, it must be seen as anchored not within an ecclesial tradition but instead within practices of the sharing and balancing of power as well as the spirit of corporatism. As for a properly episcopal collegialism, it clearly never existed in the medieval period, contrary to what modern interpretations have wanted to make the Middle Ages say.

4

RETHINKING REFORM

The History of Reform and Antireformism

The term "reform," so coextensive with the life of the Church . . .

—Yves-Marie Congar, in *Cardinal Yves Congar. Écrits réformateurs*, ed.
Jean-Pierre Jossua (Cerf, 1995), 199

Few issues are more fashionable than this one.

—Pierre Toubert, *Les structures du Latium médiéval. Le Latium méridional et la
Sabine du IXe siècle à la fin du XIIe siècle* (École Française de Rome, 1973), 932n1

In 1964, during Vatican II, Étienne Delaruelle was commissioned
to write volume 14 of Fliche and Martin's *Histoire de l'Église*. The
volume concerned the fourteenth and fifteenth centuries and was
titled *L'Église au temps du Grand Schisme et de la crise conciliaire (1378–
1449)*. One entire section of it, the sixth, was devoted to "reform." In
a still-famous passage, he wrote, "In the history of the Church, the
word 'reform' was probably never used so often as it was between 1378
and 1449, when the word appeared in the most diverse texts from the
most diverse genres. The word—or rather, myth—was a term loaded
with emotional potential and whose dazzling prestige defied any
analysis or definition."[1]

Delaruelle continued this reflection by emphasizing the consub-
stantial link between crisis and reform: "Even if this word [reform]

in itself suffices and constitutes a program of government of the Church, the fact remains that the circumstances of the time meant it was constantly associated with the idea of schism."[2] Similarly, reform was associated with the reformist councils of the late Middle Ages, from Pisa to Basel: "The Conciliar Fathers presented themselves as reformers; the partisans of the Council of Basel recruited from reformist circles." Delaruelle concluded,

> In the late fourteenth century, there thus formed a "complex" of words, aspirations, projects, critiques, the common fund of all religious and even secular literature of this time: the same common places, the same judgments of the Church's past, whether recent or distant, and the same conceptions of its structure and institutions. Should historians today take these assertions at face value? To the contrary, we think that our role here is to criticize, which will serve as the subject of the first chapter.[3]

It would be an understatement to say that many textbooks in religious history were thereafter marked by this historical framework. It was not until the late 1980s (with the work of Gerd Tellenbach) and the 2010s (with that of Florian Mazel) that the first fissures in the traditional teachings on reform appeared. This was particularly true for one of the most famous of them, the so-called Gregorian reform.[4]

Four years later, in 1968, within the context of the discussion of reform at Vatican II, Yves Congar pointed out the astonishing fact that the term "reform" had been used just once in the decree on ecumenism. At most, the "current reformist self-criticism" was mentioned.[5] In general, the preferred term was *aggiornamento*, following Pius XII and John XXIII. Congar commented, "We are sometimes frightened by the word 'reform' because history has tragically associated it with real revolution. It seems that some sort of curse weighs upon it."[6] The historiography of this discrediting remains to be written. What Congar avoided saying explicitly was that, since the fifteenth century, reformism had also been associated with conciliarism against pontificalism. Hubert Jedin phrased it tersely: "Wer Reform will, sat Konzil" (Whoever wants reform calls for a council).[7] Similarly, Isnard Wilhelm Frank wrote of one fifteenth-century reformer, "Wer Reformer sein wollte, musste auch Konziliarist sein" (Anyone who wanted to be a reformer also had to be a conciliarist).[8]

GREGORIAN REFORM AS INVENTED BY THE NINETEENTH CENTURY

The works of Charles de Miramon have shown how the nineteenth century—initially Romantic, then liberal, and finally positivist—invented what is now referred to as the "Gregorian" reform. According to his article "L'invention de la Réforme grégorienne,"[9] the decisive end of the negative image of Gregory VII that had resulted from eighteenth-century Gallican and Jansenist historiography came with the 1815 publication of the first biography of the pope, written by the German Protestant historian Johannes Voigt (1786–1863).[10] According to Voigt, Gregory VII was a "hero of spiritual power," a reformer who had the brilliant intuition to separate the Church from the state and spiritual power from temporal power.

From that point on, the door was open for the Romantic movement to reuse the fashionable concept of "spiritual power" in the interest of developing a civilizational dynamic that guided people toward greater morality and happiness. Auguste Comte glorified Gregory VII as the founder of a Church that he considered ideal; Schleiermacher made him the representative of the liberty and autonomy of the Church; finally, Hegel completed this transition from histories of Gregory VII, the individual, to histories of the "Gregorian" age. With François Guizot's famous course of 1828, reform became a central concept—central, that is, for him and not for the medieval sources, since only four occurrences of the term can be found in sources from Gregory VII's time.[11] Reform was the religious version of what revolution has been for historians of liberalism, in the sense that it is always seen as a nodal point. Gregory VII was the great man, the charismatic leader who perceived expectations of reform in the society of his time. Better yet, reform itself became the hero of the narrative, supplanting the great man himself. Starting in this period, historians began to treat any type of reform positively.

THE CONTEMPORARY HISTORY OF *REFORMATIO*: A TRIPLE WARNING

Over the course of the twentieth century, three major historians contributed to forging a subfield of ecclesial historiography, that of reform. For the Anglo-American world, the Austrian scholar Gerhart Ladner constructed the study of *reformatio* based on historical foundations. Yves Congar conceived of the theological and ecclesiological foundations of reform. Hubert Jedin contributed to establishing reform as a legitimate subject for Catholic historians.

Gerhart Ladner and the "Ladner School"

Gerhart Ladner (1905–1993) was Austrian.[12] He studied in Vienna, Berlin, and Rome. A convert from Judaism, he left Europe for North America in the 1930s. He lived in Toronto in 1938, then taught at the University of Notre Dame (Indiana), Fordham University (New York) and, starting in 1963, the University of California, Los Angeles. Ladner was influenced by the great thinkers of the 1930s: Kantorowicz,

Peterson, and Curtius, to name a few. Many friendships guided his intellectual evolution. His interpretation of the twelfth century was influenced by his friendship with Giles Constable, who around that time was drawing connections between personal reform and institutional reform. Similarly, his interpretation of the late Middle Ages was marked by the influence and views of Étienne Gilson and Heiko Oberman. Ladner published his masterwork, *The Idea of Reform*, in 1959. From that point on, the history of *reformatio* became a new historical subdiscipline with its own foundations, methods, and starting point. The scholarship in the subdiscipline was mainly patristic. Because of Ladner's dual training in history and art history, his understanding of reform was informed by both fields.

What was the thesis of the work? Ladner started from the presupposition that change is inherent in nature and the human condition. The idea of *reformatio* as presented by the Fathers was rooted in the Pauline theology of personal renewal, which was itself based on Genesis 1:26: Man is created in the image and likeness of God. In Ladnerian continuism, this patristic conception of reform had a strong influence on later ideologies of reform over the centuries that followed. For Ladner, the origins of the Christian idea of reform could be found in the creation of man in God's image, an image lost with the fall of Adam and Eve. Ladner qualified this founding principle depending on whether it concerned Greek or Latin patristics. In the East, among the Greek Fathers, *reformatio* was a *restauratio* of the original image of God in man. This was a return to the paradisical state of Adam before the Fall. In the West, among the Latin Fathers, *reformatio* was a *reformatio in melius*, according to Augustine's expression: It was the return to a state better than what Adam had enjoyed in Paradise. The practical consequences of this distinction were immense. In the East, reform was connected to a process of purification and assimilation to Christ, a *christomimesis* with a dimension that was, above all, mystical. In the West, reform was more connected to individual conversion, to penitence in the non-sacramental sense of the term. The approach was individual, spiritual, and penitential.

Ladner's methodology was based on three guidelines. First, he emphasized the practical aspect of reform and its concrete measures. He understood reform as a correction, a link with tradition, even a conversion. Second, Ladner paid extreme attention to the terminology and images of reform: His philological analyses of reform, put into context, served as the axis and the force behind his methodology. Finally, Ladner distinguished reform from other types of renewal. As a genus, renewal—itself included in the category of change and transformation—contains two distinct species: rebirth and reform. Rebirth implies the sense of spontaneous changes ("vitalistic renewal"), whereas reform implies a conscious intentionality and not a spontaneous response or a need. Ladner listed four concepts of renewal: (1) a cosmological concept (the golden age and the various historical ages of empires); (2) a "vitalistic" concept: the growth and biological reproduction of the plant, animal, and human kingdoms; (3) a millenarianist concept linked to messianism, to utopias, to the idea of a total perfection; and (4) a symbolic concept of conversion and penitence—distinct from reform, but possible to combine with it.

Hence the Ladnerian definition of reform as "free, intentional and ever perfectible, multiple, prolonged and ever repeated efforts by man to reassert and augment values pre-existent in the spiritual-material compound of the world."[13]

The scope and impact of Ladner's 1959 work are still underestimated. Because it only dealt with the patristic period and late antiquity, the admiration it aroused among scholars of late antiquity and the High Middle Ages can be seen in the reviews of the work published between 1960 and 1962, including those of Henri-Irénée Marrou,[14] Herbert Antony Musirillo,[15] Robert Grant,[16] Christine

Mohrmann,[17] Heinrich Fichtenau,[18] Friedrich Kempf,[19] and Klaus Thraede.[20] Its audience among Austrian medievalists—Heinrich Fichtenau,[21] Herwig Wolfram,[22] Walter Pohl[23]—is easily understood considering Ladner's own origins and his links to the University of Vienna. Both Austrians, Wolfram and Pohl were also the editors of Ladner's memoirs, titled *Erinnerungen*.[24] The historians of various "renaissances," especially that of the twelfth century, also inspired Ladner's ideas, as did scholars of sixteenth-century reform.[25] Steven Ozment read Ladner through his student Louis Pascoe; in the same spirit, Heiko Oberman, a contemporary of Ladner, established an Institut fur Spätmittelalter und Reformation (Institute for the Late Middle Ages and the Reformation) at Tübingen.[26] The influence of Ladner and his book is also attested in the historiographical revival of studies on monastic reforms and observances in the fifteenth century, within the broader movement, now known as "the Catholic Reformation," that predated the schism of 1517. John Van Engen, an eminent disciple of Ladner, contributed to developing the linkage between individual reform and institutional reform, especially through his study of the *Devotio moderna*.[27] Finally, Ladner left his mark on political science by emphasizing the fact that reform was neither a renewal, nor a rebirth, nor millenarianism. Neither was it a "new start," or a return to the past or to the beginnings. Instead, reform was a change toward something truly new, something that had never existed before. This possibility of change could be experienced without violent rupture, which was to say that reform is not revolution. For Ladner, in contrast with Gerd Tellenbach or Karl F. Morrison, reforms did not lead to revolutions but instead belonged to an "imagery of renewal."[28]

Despite his plans, Gerhart Ladner never wrote his intended volumes on reform, which should have followed those on the Patristic era. He certainly wrote much about the Gregorian Middle Ages in various articles, as gathered in his *Selected Studies*, but there was no synthesis in book form for the later periods. His students, particularly those at UCLA, focused their work that might be described as Ladnerian (in both a philological and a methodological sense) on the remainder of the Middle Ages, especially the late Middle Ages. The most famous of these students were Phillip Stump, Louis Pascoe, and John Van Engen. Among them, Louis Pascoe was the great mediator between Ladner's generation and that of the Ladnerian medievalists. In 2012, Louis Pascoe, an American Jesuit, wrote, "After the Bible and *The Spiritual Exercises of St. Ignatius of Loyola*, the book that has probably most influenced me is Gerhart B. Ladner's *The Idea of Reform*."[29] The two met in 1956–1957, when Ladner became the supervisor of Pascoe's doctoral thesis, which took up the Ladnerian treatment of reform and the lexical and semantic study thereof. The thesis, titled *Jean Gerson: Principles of Church Reform*, was published in 1973.[30] For Pascoe, a student of Gerson, the end goal of theology was personal conversion. But the inverse remained true: Personal reform resulted from ecclesiastical reform.

In 2005, Pascoe devoted another volume to Pierre d'Ailly: *Church and Reform: Bishops, Theologians and Canon Lawyers in the Thought of Pierre d'Ailly (1351–1420)*.[31] Pascoe revisited the idea of hierarchy in Gerson's ecclesiological and, especially, conciliar thought by ruling out any specter of democratic or secularizing theory in it. For Pascoe, the conciliar theories of Gerson were a "hierarchical reform," in the sense of an institutional reform.[32] The council took a major role only in the implementation of the reform. Likewise, for d'Ailly, Pascoe strove to connect concrete reforms and the ideology of reform, unlike the biography by H. Millet and M. Maillard-Luypaert, which instead focused on the difference between Pierre d'Ailly, bishop of Cambrai, and Pierre d'Ailly, the reformist cardinal prelate at the Council of Constance, by taking stock of his actions: "It is one thing to conceive major reform projects, and another to put them into practice within the diocesan framework."[33] The same coauthors continued, "The results of the episcopate thus appear mixed. Pierre d'Ailly's reformist desire, which was displayed with great constancy throughout his life, came up against inevitable obstacles on the ground."[34] Aside from these works, Louis Pascoe's great merit lay in training a generation of medievalists in the Ladnerian school: Christopher Bellitto, Thomas Izbicki, David Flanagin, and Louis Hamilton, among others, all of them scholars of the Great Western Schism and reform in the late Middle Ages.

Yves Congar and the Critique of the Idea of *Aggiornamento* at Vatican II

In 1968, Yves Congar published a second edition of his major work *Vraie et fausse réforme dans l'Église* (translated into English in 2011 as *True and False Reform in the Church*), the first edition of which had appeared in 1950.[35] This publication revealed an attentive reading of Ladner. Ladner's teachings reached their fullest expression when Congar wrote, "The term 'reform' was first treated by the Fathers and by liturgy as a theme of Christian anthropology. It was essentially a question of the reconfiguration of man in the likeness of God, which sin caused him to lose. *Intus reformari*."[36] Following Ladner, Congar emphasized the reformation of the image of God within the Christian as an individual. However, Congar warned against an elementary reading of Ladner. For him, it was a question of not reducing ecclesiological reform to the spiritual reform of the individual, of oneself: "That is not enough," he wrote.[37] Openly influenced by the nineteenth-century German theologian Johann Adam Möhler, from whom he drew the definition of the Church as structure and life, he reminded his readers that structural reform should not be neglected.[38] Congar specified, "It is not a question of reforming abuses: there are hardly any. It is about reforming structures."[39] Such was Congar's great warning on the subject of Ladner.[40]

Faced with the general reluctance to use the term "reform" to describe the critical self-examination of the Church, Yves Congar sought to rehabilitate the term, presenting four characteristics and four conditions. According to Congar, the characteristics of reform are as follows: (1) The criticism must be sincere and true and lead to change without rancor, as the act of criticism is not infidelity but the greatest fidelity, and can be found at the true roots of the Church; (2) a reform must focus on what is essential, and not on secondary features; (3) the reform and its effects must penetrate parishes, which is to say it must reach the laity; and (4) the reform must be anchored in the tradition of the Church (*reditus ad fontes*). The four conditions of a non-subversive reform are (1) that it must be carried out in charity and pastoral service; (2) it must take place through dialogue and not diatribe—that is, in a spirit of unity; (3) patience is necessary for reform; (4) true renewal is a return to traditions (false renewal is novelty).

For Congar, *aggiornamento* was not enough. It was no more than a surface-level change, a superficial adaptation: "Our era of rapid mutation, of cultural change . . . calls for a revision of 'traditional' forms that goes beyond the level of adaptation or *aggiornamento* and is, instead, a new creation."[41] He added, "It is not enough to maintain what has been through adaptation; it is necessary to reconstruct."[42] Congar thus criticized the substitution of the idea of reform with that of *aggiornamento*. The term "reform" was used nine times at Vatican II, compared with sixty-three occurrences of the term "renewal," whereas in the proceedings of the Council of Trent the term "reform" can be read thirty times, compared with seven occurrences of "renewal." Vatican II therefore had a clear preference for registering renewal (*renovatio/renovare*) over reform (*reformatio/ reformare*). Related terms (*emendare, corrigere*) were also work-arounds for avoiding *reformare*. This seems to have been because, in John XXIII's eyes, the term "reform" was too steeped in history to be supported as such in the context of a project of renewal of the Church. Giuseppe Alberigo described "reform" as a "hot and controversial" term.[43] But it also demonstrated how reform suggested decadence, whereas *aggiornamento* refers to the forward march of a Church in the sense of the people of God shepherded by a pastor and inspired by the Holy Spirit. As Philippe Levillain explained, "The term *aggiornamento*, which has passed into the common political vocabulary, made it possible to discard the term 'reform,' so heavy with meaning in the singular and, in historical context, unpromising in the plural."[44]

Congar's *Vraie et fausse réforme dans l'Église* was almost condemned in 1952 because it used the word too frequently.[45] As Étienne Fouilloux explained,

> What, for John XXIII, could be the meaning of the term *aggiornamento* if not the euphemistic substitution for a proscribed word of a neologism he did not invent, but to which he will confer the value and vigor of an emblem? According to him, the Church he leads has a lesser need to confront the surrounding world through affirmation or condemnation than it does to update itself in order to better respond to new challenges thrown at it. . . . How can we not see this as a "new-look" reformism?[46]

He meant this to show that reforms also risked engendering revolutions, and the specter was menacing. Congar, however, knew the historical roots of the meaning of *reformatio*, which he invoked whether or not it was opportune, regardless of the context.

Hubert Jedin (1900–1980): Reform as Permanent Criterion in Church History?

In a now famous article written as an homage to Hubert Jedin, who had recently died, Giuseppe Alberigo took account of the German priest's contributions.[47] An expert at Vatican II and a prolific scholar of the history of reform, Jedin restored the field's broad historical scope. For three centuries, since Luther's schism—as with Cardinal Bellarmine (1642–1721) or Adolf Harnack (1851–1930)—many Catholics believed reform had been co-opted by the Protestant camp. Starting in 1951, however, Jedin reaffirmed the scope of the concept beyond its polemical and confessional use: Reform had been an act of the Church from its very beginning, and not only since Luther's act, or even in reaction to Luther's act.[48] Alberigo summed this all up with a single title: "Reform as a criterion of Church history."[49]

Reform, both as *reformatio* and in the Protestant sense of the term, held a central place in Jedin's work as a whole. Alberigo recontextualized this as follows.

> It is known that Jedin found himself confronted with reform from his early days as a Church historian. This was inevitable given his condition as a German Catholic, forced by birth to confront a condition of "divided faith," of parallel Churches, of close and daily confessional confrontation. In relation to these facts, the young Silesian priest very quickly adopted a critical attitude, striving to understand through historical analysis.[50]

Jedin approached the topic of reform by starting with analyses of events, employing a positive and inductive historical practice by verifying, confronting, accepting, or refuting any conceptual generalization.

Jedin belonged to the cultural context of the 1930s, 1940s, and 1950s, within which Catholic culture for the most part accepted the

Protestant co-optation of the idea of Church reform, to the point that Church reform and the Protestant Reformation were commonly considered synonymous, or at least connected (a situation aggravated by the existence of a single noun in Romance languages).[51] The official Roman Catholicism refused any request for renewal expressed by any type of movement (liturgical, ecumenical, biblical, for promotion of the laity, etc.). The defensive immobility of the Roman Catholic stance became all the more rigid when it was forced to face the triple front of the Bolshevik Revolution, the rise of fascism, and virulent anticlerical secularism. Alberigo continued, "In this context, the thematization of Church reform automatically had a Protestant or modernist tint in the eyes of Catholics, which is to say it was not something that could be proposed."[52] He added,

> It was within this context that Jedin undertook historical research, intending to subsequently push it further in order to completely overcome the prejudicial controversies that had conditioned the German (and not only the German) historiography of the origins of the Protestant Reformation. Throughout this evolution, Jedin concentrated his research around two theses: the Catholic Reformation as sister movement, rather than subordinate, to the Protestant Reformation, and the Council of Trent as an ambivalent event that was born as an assembly of the single Western Christian Church and that concluded with a new foundation of Roman Catholicism. Knowledge of these two historical phenomena will encourage us to gradually rediscover the full understanding of the concept of "reform" as a problem of the entire Church and all its confessions, as well as of the major moments of its history.[53]

In his masterwork on the history of the Council of Trent, Jedin returned to the Council of Constance and the life of the Church between Constance and Trent in order to shed light on what he called the "era of reforms," erasing the academic gap between the Middle

118 ❧ RETHINKING REFORM

Ages and modernity. "The awareness of the non-correspondence between the historical realization of the Church and what it 'should' have been is a sentiment as old as the Church," he wrote on the first page of *Storia del Concilio di Trento*.[54] This formulation went beyond the historical period in question, applying to the entire history of the Church. Jedin highlighted the historical context of reform initiatives in the lead-up to the Council of Trent. Alongside the official failure of the reform projects *in capite et in membris*, the self-reform of individual members was asserted. Jedin pointed to a real dynamic within the apparently official and monolithic label of "reform," which was in reality protean and plural. Jedin's remarks and summaries therefore went far beyond the period of the sixteenth century, his broad scope applicable to the entire history of the Church. In that history, he found scripted patterns in the dialectic between decadence (*deformatio*) and reform (*re-formatio*).

In the 1960s, under the impetus of John XXIII's proposal for an "update" (*aggiornamento*), and in the preconciliar and conciliar contexts of Vatican II, Jedin thoroughly discussed the theme of reform.[55] He recalled the definition of the Church as people in incessant movement through time: "A Church is not like a perfectly finished ship sailing on the ocean of time. It grows like a mustard seed, and therefore the concept of development not only can be but must be applied to the history of the Church."[56] What Jedin did not share was "a theory of decadence, which is to say of a progressive detachment of the Church from the ideal condition of the primitive Church, especially since the Church produced saints in periods of decadence, just as there were shadows during periods of flourishing."[57] Jedin specified, " 'Tradition' and 'progress' cannot be separated in the history of the Church. They form a pair of homogenous terms; tradition without progress would mean fossilization, while progress without tradition would be revolution."[58]

Reform of the Church thus proved to be the permanent criterion of Church history: "It is neither a temporary nor a cyclical phenomenon but a constant that historical criticism can take for granted as one of the major criteria of its own method."[59] Church reform was viewed as mirror-image pairs: decadence (*de-formatio*) and reform; reform and revolution; plan and realization, dynamics and reversibility. It was necessary to distinguish the start, the culmination, and the decline of any reform; the agents of reform (religious communities, councils, popes, or territorial Churches); the typical settings of reform (the head of the Church, the ecclesiastical apparatus, isolated groups of the faithful); and the causes (internal or external). "It is therefore not an inert instrument but a functional criterion for an increasingly adequate understanding of the life of the Church over time."[60] Hence the synergy, in the same years, of Jedin's works with those of Yves Congar and Gerhart Ladner.

Beyond the golden legend of Jedin as spun by his former student Alberigo, however, it is necessary to remember how divisive he was.

DEFINITIONS OF REFORM IN THE TIME OF THE FIFTEENTH-CENTURY COUNCILS

What link exists between *reformatio* at the time of the reformist councils and the way authors in the 1950s thought of reform? Can the fifteenth-century understanding of *reformatio* be perceived in twentieth-century ecclesiology? To the contrary, a gap can be observed between the two, which is to say between the archival sources of the late Middle Ages and the ecclesiological theories of the 1950s. What, in fact, was *reformatio* in the late Middle Ages?[61]

Reformatio, a Concept Based on a Theology of the Image

In the fourteenth century, *reformatio* was still understood on the basis of a theology of the image.[62] Theology of the image is a history of form: formation, deformation, and reformation presented as the successive stages in the history of salvation. Form and deformity—or deformation—are like two faces of the same coin: Man is created in the image of God (Genesis 1:26). He carries God's form within himself. He is informed by God. Sin deforms this image inside him. Because of original sin, man became deformed; he now has an image that is deformed but not lost, and the goal is to refigure (reconfigure, one might say today) or to re-form the lost image of God in man. Re-formation took on meaning within the history of salvation, based on the theology of the image. It is the end point of this history, in which form, deformation, and reformation echo creation, original sin, and redemption. Re-formation is the re-formation of original traits on the model of the divine exemplar within a soteriological design. In this sense, re-formation is the tension of the creature desiring its creator: an intentionality in the phenomenological sense of the term. It is an ontological aspiration.

From this perspective, hardship can also be read as permission from God to pursue reform. For Henry of Langenstein, the Great Western Schism was an opportunity for reform because it signaled God's permission: The ordeal was not in vain, nor was it gratuitous, but necessary and useful for the conversion of the Church.[63] The point of the schism was to awaken people from torpor and numbness.[64] Jean Gerson contemplated the moral reform that was called for as a consequence of reform: "The present schism does not prevent penitence, to the contrary, it propels induces people to it as the precipit, the antidote, and the means to reach the port of salvation."[65]

Reformatio, a Limitatio

The meaning of *reformatio* did not stay the same from the start of the Great Western Schism until its end. It evolved in the sense of a conceptual densification and a definitional fixation. From the start, in fact, there was nothing vaguer than *reformatio*: It was assimilated, as tradition suggests, to a reparation, a moral correction, and a fight against the centralism of and taxation by Rome. It was only in the 1410s, and particularly in 1415, at the Council of Constance, that a more concrete meaning became fixed; at that point, *reformatio* was, for the first time, clearly formulated as a *limitatio*. The council was the authority behind this reform, which was understood as a *limitatio* despite lacking the capacity to suppress the *plenitudo potestatis* entrusted to the pope by Christ. It nevertheless had the function of limiting this *plenitudo potestatis* in usage and according to precise conditions, with a view to the edification of the Church. "This is the firm foundation of the whole Church," Gerson wrote.[66] The abuse of pontifical power was the target of this limitation. The aim was limiting, channeling, and regulating this power, as well as its tendency toward absolutism—not suppressing, diminishing, or fighting it. In this sense, *reformatio* was the exact opposite of absolutist pontifical centralism.[67]

Reformatio as Political Program

Toward the end of the period of the Great Western Schism, in 1417–1418, reform became an authentic political program within the Church. More precisely, two political programs of reform confronted each other, like two identity-based affiliations. The substance of this conflict concerned epikie or *aequitas* (equity), its equivalent in Roman law. The concept belonged to the great legal tradition of the Middle Ages, particularly the thought of Gratian, for whom equity was the source, mother, and origin of justice.[68]

Starting in 1402, Pierre d'Ailly and Jean Gerson championed the concept of epikie within the context of a general movement of silent opposition to the canonists, decretists, and decretalists that corresponded to aspirations of restituting obedience. D'Ailly and Gerson deployed their opposition to all literalism, legalism, and formalism by virtue of the Pauline adage "the letter kills, but the spirit gives life," which itself recalls another pericope, "Ubi spiritus Dei, ibi libertas" (Where the spirit of God is, there is liberty).[69] Although neither was a conciliarist in the manner of Henry of Langenstein or Conrad de Gelnhausen, especially in 1402, d'Ailly and Gerson nevertheless felt that epikie could provide a way out from the impasse, implement reform, and resolve the schism.[70] Gerson's particular fondness for the concept of epikie has become a well-established fact.[71] For him, however, the use of the concept was aimed as much toward mitigating the schism in the interest of rediscovering unity—as the historiography has clearly shown—as it was toward fostering a reformist program. This program's epikie provided the key to approaching it in a discreet, masked way, serving as a signal for reformist desires within the political tradition of the French kingdom that was perhaps coded, but nevertheless active—something the historiography has shown less clearly.

The strength of the Gersonian approach lay in its constituting a sort of casuistry. For the chancellor, it served to reaffirm how solutions varied according to the contingency of situations, *variatio in contingentibus*.[72] Different times had different customs.[73] Gerson emphasized the diversity of places and times in the application of laws and rules.[74] He used history as a witness, showing its evolutions and mutations. The manner in which laws were embodied was not fixed; instead, it was intended to be evolving and historical.

The concept of epikie, though present from 1402, truly emerged in the debates that took place starting in the year 1409 around the Council of Pisa. Gerson's *Tractatus de unitate* established epikie as a reformist slogan. It should be no surprise that, in discussions around the Council of Pisa, the opposing party refuted the pertinence of the term. Indeed, in order to counter the Council of Pisa, three of Benedict XIII's canonists simultaneously produced a discourse aimed at dismantling the notion: For them, epikie was not only inadequate for casuistry but, moreover, antithetical to the truth. Pierre Ravat, a pontificalist canonist, focused his syllogism on the predictability of unique cases. Those who claimed that unique cases could not be foreseen were wrong, because every case was predictable. But epikie was based on the unpredictability of unique cases. Thus, he had to conclude that there was no casuistry beyond epikie for predictable cases. All cases were predictable because Christ assured that the Holy Spirit would teach the truth.[75]

Epikie versus truth. All the pontifical jurists repeated this sentiment, each in his own manner. Charles d'Urries wrote that the Church was never in danger to the point of having recourse to epikie, which remained contrary to divine and human law, as well as to all of Church law.[76] This was because these canonists understood the vagueness of the law as result of Peter's fallibility. This was the connection they drew. They countered the fragility of the law by insisting upon the infallibility of Peter and his faith. For Pierre Ravat, if any doubt in the silences of the law existed, it would suffice to defer to superiors in the letter of the law and not its spirit, as epikie allowed.[77] For him, obedience was better than prudence, which he interpreted as common-sense discernment in the Aristotelian sense. This reflects the distrust the pontifical canonists held toward Aristotelian epikie, which they claimed at the time to prefer, at least, to equity/*aequitas*, its decretist version.

It cannot be denied that epikie contains within itself an obviously controversial charge. For the pope's jurists, who pushed it aside, it represented the partisans of reform beyond the pope. For Gerson, on the other hand, it was a latent offensive, one directed against jurists both pontifical and academic, both of whom followed the letter of the law and did not implement epikie. Thus, it is no surprise that Gerson, whose irritation with the canonists—regardless of their pontificalist or academic orientation—is well-known, made epikie the spearhead of an identity-based vision of reform, that of the moralist theologians.[78] To use epikie discursively would be one way of ensuring the triumph of one reform program over another: On the one hand was a program close to moral theology, focused on a reformism colored by mercy, moral action according to the demands of conscience, an understanding of the social bond according to charity and a measured ecclesiology, tinged with conditional obedience, and balanced by a harmonious arrangement of powers.[79] On the other hand was a more juridical program of reform that was marked by the intransigence of an opposition to pontifical power, oriented by the national conception of the Church, habituated to an opposition to any clemency or practice of mercy on the part of the king, and that refused royal grace as a mark of weakness.[80]

Epikie was both a watershed at the very heart of the discourse around reform in the kingdom of France and an index of identity-based affiliations. Or rather, in view of the stakes to come—namely, conciliar works and the holding of an announced council; at this point, that of Pisa—epikie was a question of the predominance of one party over the other. This meant it was a question of the victory of one ecclesiological vision of reform, that of the theologians, over another, that of the jurists.[81] For Gerson, the wise men of the coming council needed to be theologians, paradigms of prudence, full of epikie, virtuosos of interpretive finesse—in short, men who were spiritual in the Pauline manner, receptive to what God showed them.[82] The issue at hand had to do with the function of counseling the king: Theologians and jurists, two learned bodies with the same ambitions, were locked in tight competition over their ability to advise the king. However, the withdrawal of the theologians caused a reaction, something confirmed by the jurists' penetration into the administrative bodies of the state during the reign of Charles VI. Gerson represented this attempt—which could be qualified as desperate—to establish the institutional character of the theologians of the University of Paris as advisers to the king:[83] "They could do no greater service than to constantly demonstrate [to the kings and the lords] the truth of the faith, the sound doctrine of good morals, against the false informants who are at a remove and in darkness."[84] This seems to have been the fundamental issue at stake in his harangue *Vivat rex*.

ANTIREFORMISM, OR THE POTENTIAL SUBVERSIVENESS OF THE CONCEPT OF *REFORMATIO*

A history of antireformism remains to be written. Some possible leads for one are proposed here. As a preliminary point, it should be emphasized that the primary cause of antireformism may well have issued from certain popes themselves, who argued against the need for reform in the Church. Hence, amid the turmoil of 1832, Gregory XVI declared, "It is obviously absurd and injurious to propose a certain 'restoration and regeneration' for her [the Church] as though necessary for her safety and growth, as if she could be considered subject to defect or obscuration or other misfortune."[85] The bottom line was that the Catholic Church did not need reform. The term "reform" was derogatory from the outset. Hence the sarcastic title of Robert McNally's study *The Unreformed Church*, published in 1965, which points to the paradox between a strong reformist ideology and the frequent practical failures of its implementation.[86]

On the Concrete Implementation of Reform: Resistance and Reticence

The first observation made in any history of antireformism must be the contrast between the theoretical meaning of an ideological reform and the practical resistance to its implementation. In 2004, Birgit Studt published a biography of Martin V that was centered around the theme of reform: *Papst Martin V (1417–1431) und die Kirchenreform in Deutschland*. In it, Studt showed how in Martin V's hands reform became a tool of the pope, no longer solely claimed by the council. In a word, it became the tool of choice for the restoration of the pontifical monarchy. In fact, the pope emphasized the reform of dioceses (Mainz, Cologne, Trier) as a papal instrument of reform. Likewise, in order to reform members, the pope leveraged provincial synods, which had by then also become instruments of reform that were ordered and controlled by the pope, just like pontifical legations and curial reform commissions. Similarly, the Curia was conceived as a bearer and agent of reform for an impeccable life, strictly speaking, and a conscious fulfillment of its duty. Through this reorganization, the Curia aimed *ad exaltationem Romae Urbis et curiae nostrae decorem*.[87] Likewise, the activity of legates was dynamic, incessant, and urgent—all terms that could be used to describe Branda da Castiglione, for example.[88]

In this context, the resistance that sprung up across Germany was no surprise. At Cologne, an appeal was launched against Branda's reformist statutes. At Trier, opposition was signaled against another papal legate, Henry Beaufort. Job Vener, through his writings, became the great critic of Branda's reformist activity. This history of the Germanic reception of reforms—namely, those due to pontifical legates—was grim.[89] This has been demonstrated by Johannes Helmrath in a pioneering article published in 1992.[90] In it, he showed members' resistance to reform in the conciliar period, concluding that reform was desirable but being reformed less so. Likewise, numerous studies have discussed resistance in the Germanic world against the actions of Nicholas of Cusa, the reform legate appointed to Germany.

Curialism and Antireformism

During the Avignon period, appeals to reform were concentrated on the head alone, not the members, but these appeals to reform were made against the Avignon Curia. Hence Petrarch, Bridget of Sweden, and Catherine of Siena formulated their virulence against prelates and cardinals with provocative lifestyles. In this sense, reformist currents merged as a result of the actions of certain Avignon popes, such as Benedict XII (1334–1342), who punished absenteeism by expelling all prelates who had pastoral responsibilities elsewhere. He demanded higher and higher standards in the selection of priests and bishops.[91] Innocent VI and Urban V furthered Benedict XII's reforms concerning absenteeism, the evaluation of candidates, and the education of priests.[92] At the same time, "reform" became a powerful political slogan in the conflict between Philip IV the Fair and Boniface VIII.[93]

The historiography and the documentation concerning the cardinalate at the time of the Avignon period, and then the Great Western Schism, elucidate the history of antireformism. The Great Western Schism is often understood as the refusal of cardinals in the face of the brutal reforms of Urban VI, who had never been a cardinal himself. In 1378, Jacques de Sève narrated how Urban VI's implementation of reform was the root cause of the rebellion of the cardinals, and particularly the French ones. This explanation of the Great Western Schism as the result of antireformism on the part of cardinals and curialists merits further exploration, as the sources touch on it repeatedly. For Henry of Langenstein, for example, the schism began due to the French cardinals who resisted Urban VI's attempts at reform.[94] This position must be qualified and refined, however, considering that Urban VI, though not a cardinal, was nevertheless a former curialist from Avignon, which is sufficient proof that both reformist and antireformist tendencies circulated within the Curia. It may have been true that the cardinals had the upper hand at the beginning of the schism, since they alone were present to narrate the facts through the testimony of their presence and experience, but it was also true that the College of Cardinals was experiencing one of the strongest crises in its history. Noël Valois wrote of a "terrible crisis at the time of the Council of Constance."[95] "One might say that the cardinals were the great losers of the Schism," he added. It is true that John XXIII's flight to Constance on March 20, 1415, aggravated the fragility of the cardinals' position. Conscious of having less influence at Constance than they had at Pisa, the cardinals felt all the more destabilized when, on May 2, 1415, before the seventh session opened, they were informed that they would no longer have the right to vote as cardinals but instead would have to vote as members of their respective nations. In his treatise *De emendatione Ecclesiae*, Pierre d'Ailly complained about this attack on the cardinals' presence, as well as their authority at the core of the conciliar body.[96] Reporting on the crisis of the College of Cardinals, he then donned his historian's hat and related the origin of the Sacred College—hence the ideological offensive of an ecclesiology of cardinals and the debate around the election of the pope before the reform. Likewise, at Basel this ideology failed, as did the entire College of Cardinals.

In curialist circles, the figure of the reformer was disturbing, both subjectively and objectively. A reformer could, in fact, fall within the field of dissidence. When Jean-Pierre Albert, a scholar of the historical anthropology of Christianity, reflected upon dissident figures, he was inspired by both Max Weber and Pierre Bourdieu.[97] He drew up a schematic for identifying the profiles of religious scholars: the priest, the prophet, the sorcerer (or magician), and the reformer. Corresponding to these four virtuosos of religion, Albert identified four types of dissidence (heresy, reform, schism, magic). Between the legitimate priest or theologian and the reformer lay expertise and scriptural exegesis, the foundations of the latter scholars' competence, but this was a competence that could either serve or work against the institution. At the heart of his discussion of dissidence, Jean-Pierre Albert pointed to the tension between truth and restraint. The truth proclaimed by each camp—whether orthodox or heretical—was in this case a restrained truth, he declared. Hence the superiority of the dissident over the inquisitor: The dissident has no need for any institutional framework to assert his claim to speak the truth. Therefore, the superiority of the reformer over the curialist, in some sense, led to the notable antireformism of curialist circles.

The Perfection of the Church and the Imperfection of Reform

If it is true that reformism and conciliarism could sometime cancel and neutralize each other, and that conciliarism could sometimes eclipse reformism, it is also true that both could come together to insinuate a latent anti-pontificalism. In both cases, the papacy and its claim to primacy became the targets of the respective currents. Also in both cases, emphasis on the council or on reform was a potential challenge to the central authority of Rome. Furthermore, in the way the official Roman historiography has stifled the memory of conciliarism, it may be seen that the term "reform" has been dismissed, just as any hint of reformism has been dismissed in the construction of the great narratives of Church history. At the time of Vatican II, the official discourse chose to speak of renewal or *aggiornamento* rather than reform, with renewal understood not as a list of points to be revised but instead as a process, an experiment rather than an achievement.

The Church is therefore called to be reformed so that it conforms to the model that underlies it, that of the *societas perfecta*. With constant reference to and idealization of the *ecclesia primitiva*, the Church thought of itself as a *societas perfecta* (François Jankowiak). Must its reform be perfect, however? Jean-Jacques Allmen's words of praise for imperfect reform, inspired by Karl Barth, are worth reflecting upon: "Without overshadowing the full commitment of those who think of it, want it, and carry it out, a reform in the Church is neither Pentecost nor the Last Judgment, nor is it the foundation of the Kingdom of God. It does not found, it does not end, it does not replace the Church. It helps her to be who she is and to do what she must better—modestly, partially, but also joyfully, freely, and courageously."[98]

A brief mention of the *Lex fundamentalis Ecclesiae* project, on which Alain Rauwel has recently written,[99] serves to close this brief survey of the history of antireformism. The idea for it came from a project to rewrite the two canonical codes, the Latin Code and the Eastern Code, to provide them with common principles in the interest of greater ecclesial unity. Seven successive versions were published between 1960 and 1970 in ninety-five canons and twenty-two pages. In them, pontificalism is affirmed in an outrageous manner that seemingly issues directly from the *Dictatus papae*. The three thousand bishops who received the text were very critical of it, to be sure, but the idea of an authoritarian refocusing in the wake of the audacity of Vatican II also recalled the refocusing that took place after the era of the reformist councils of the fifteenth century. Rauwel has proposed the simple idea of a "return to the center": Following an effervescence of reformist desires and openness to the action of the local churches, the recovery of authority came from the Roman center and from the Curia. The same might be said for the situation in Church history, a structural phenomenon in which antireformism had the last word.

5

ANTI-ROMANISM AND ITS HITHERTO UNRECOGNIZED MEDIEVAL ROOTS

Within Catholicism, there is a current that rebels against the necessity of Roman centrality.

—Sylvio Hermann De Franceschi, "Bruno Neveu et la romanité. Sources historiographiques et méthode," *Chrétiens et sociétés* 14 (2007): 104

Catholic anti-Romanism is a singularly porous and vulnerable confessional sensibility that attempts to hold the middle ground between heresy and orthodoxy—that is, an ecclesiological concept of limitation that is aware of its own excesses.

—Sylvio Hermann De Franceschi, *La crise théologico-politique du premier âge baroque. Antiromanisme doctrinal, pouvoir pastoral et raison du prince: Le Saint-Siège face au prisme français (1607–1627)* (École Française de Rome, 2009), 557

Anti-Romanism, the counterpart to Romanism, is a concept that was essentially constructed out of modern and contemporary historiographies. To date, it has not fully entered the field of medieval historiography. However, a close reading of the sources and texts of the late medieval period, and particularly those of the Great Western Schism and the reformist councils, leads to the following question: Is it possible to speak of a late medieval anti-Romanism?

ANTI-ROMANISM AND HISTORIOGRAPHY: AN ESSENTIALLY MODERN SUBJECT

The adjective "anti-Roman" emerged progressively over the nineteenth century. It was initially applied to Josephinism, the great movement of resistance to Rome that sprang up around the Habsburg monarch Joseph II in the Holy Roman Empire. Prior to that, the term "Romanism," used commonly by English authors and distinct from "Papism," belonged to the polemical traditions found in Protestantism, and particularly Anglicanism. In 1860, Prince Jakob G. Pitzipios (1802–1869) wrote a work titled *Le Romanisme.*[1] A scholar of the Byzantine Empire and the Eastern Church who was Orthodox by confession, he questioned the supremacy of the vicariate of Saint Peter and the transmission of its privileges to the Roman popes. In the long anti-Roman tradition of the Greeks, he thus condemned what he called "Romanism" or "the revival of the despotic government of pagan Rome under the cloak of Christian religion,"[2] the chronology of which he traced century by century down to Pius IX and Napoleon III. He concluded with the "legal assassination" of Christ by the Roman government.[3] For Pitzipios, Romanism was in a sense anti-Christian.

In volume 18 of the *Histoire de l'Église depuis les origines jusqu'à nos jours*, published in 1960 and edited by Augustin Fliche and Victor Martin, Léopold Willaert was the first to describe the currents of opposition to Roman influence in the Church:

> We have no word for this resistance. The well-known term *Gallicanism* technically means *French* opposition to Roman centralization. It

ANTI-ROMANISM ❧ 135

has been thought possible to discuss *Gallicanism outside France*. But doesn't it sound strange to speak of a German, Italian, or English Gallicanism? There can be no question of a term derived from *ultramontanism*, which is too relative considering that in Italy it means the opposite of what we mean on this side of the Alps. On the other hand, neither *episcopalism* nor *regalism* covers the entire trend of opposition to Rome. This trend, in its various degrees, is essential to and therefore common to all the undertakings of the more-or-less autonomous Churches, ranging from Gallicanism (faithful to Rome despite it all) to the separated Churches. *Anti-curialism* has the disadvantage of taking aim above all at the Curia; it is critical to distinguish between the Pope and the Curia, because the two sometimes oppose each other. *Anti-Romanism* simply indicates resistance to the absolutism of Rome (both pope and Curia). *Romanism*, in this sense, is borrowed from the Protestant usage.[4]

After this initial explanation, the term became definitively official in 1974, with Hans Urs von Balthasar's *Der antirömische Affekt*, translated into English in 1986 as *The Office of Peter and the Structure of the Church*. According to Balthasar, it was necessary to "show that there is a deep-seated anti-Roman attitude within the Catholic Church . . . and that this attitude has not only sociological and historical grounds but also a theological basis."[5]

Balthasar drew on work written by the young John Henry Newman before his conversion from Anglicanism to Catholicism for an initial definition of Romanism. He was also especially influenced by the work of Congar, which, by Balthasar's own admission, remained definitive.[6] According to Balthasar, in fact, before he wrote his book on anti-Romanism Congar wrote his own study, a paper titled "Le Complexe antiromain," which he had intended to have translated into German. In his introduction, Balthasar included the following footnote thanking Congar for calling his attention to a quotation from

Luther: "I am indebted for this quotation to Fr. Yves Congar, who, a few days before I finished the present work, most graciously lent me his paper on *Le Complexe antiromain*. He concentrates nearly exclusively on this attitude in the Middle Ages and in the sects which dissociated themselves from the Catholic Church. This is exactly the topic that we have excluded from our study."[7]

What was this study by Congar? No direct trace of it can be found, at least under this title. There is no sign of it in bibliographies or in the analytical tables of scholarly journals. On the other hand, a famous article published by the French theologian in the *Revue des sciences théologiques et philosophiques* in 1987 defined these concepts. Its title was "Romanité et catholicité. Histoire de la conjonction changeante de deux dimensions de l'Église" (Romanity and Catholicity: History of the changing conjunction of the two dimensions of the church).[8] Contrary to what Balthasar wrote, Congar chronologically located Romanism after Luther's rupture with the Church: "The Catholic Church insisted on its Roman center or principle as a condition of divine institution in the face of the Greek Church following the rupture of communion, but especially in the face of the Churches that resulted from the Reformation."[9]

The problem Congar raised consisted of understanding the link between "Catholic" and "Roman": Was this a constitutive link, a descriptive and historical link, or a combination of both? In order to better analyze and approach the phenomenon, Congar described Tridentine Catholicism as being centered around the Roman Curia in its omnipotence. He explained: "Those who do not love this type of Catholicism sometimes speak of Romanism."[10] The concepts thus became clearer.

In the 2000s, Sylvio Hermann De Franceschi, a student of Bruno Neveu and a scholar of modern history, placed anti-Romanism at the heart of his doctoral research, which appeared, following numerous articles, in book form in 2009. That book, published by the École française de Rome, had the title *La crise théologico-politique du pre-mier âge baroque. Antiromanisme doctrinal, pouvoir pastoral et raison du prince: Le Saint-Siège face au prisme français (1607–1627)* (The theological-political crisis of the first baroque age: Doctrinal anti-Romanism, pastoral power, and reason of the prince: The Holy See in the face of the French prism, 1607–1627). Within the context of a post-Tridentine Catholicism and, more precisely, of the absolute monarchy of the post-Tridentine pontificate, Sylvio Hermann De Franceschi described a context of anti-Romanism that had diverse European sensibilities and was based on a constellation of three historical events: the Venetian anti-Romanism that sprang up around Paulo Sarpi and the Venetian Interdict (1606–1607); anti-Romanism in England at the time the Oath of Allegiance of 1606, which James I imposed on English Catholics as a profession of political loyalty following the fail-ure of the Gunpowder Plot; and, finally, French anti-Romanism fol-lowing the assassination of Henry IV on May 15, 1610, which caused latent anti-Roman hostility to explode, "a wave of anti-Romanism and anti-Jesuitism then surg[ing] across Europe."[11] Several dozen articles have deepened and enriched the concept. Finally, a series of colloquia (in 2007, 2009, 2010, and 2012) have steadily developed anti-Romanism as a subject.[12]

Drawing on these scholarly works, how might the concept of anti-Romanism be most closely approached today? Anti-Romanism is fundamentally a sensibility of resistance that exists within a straight-forward adherence to Catholicism—a Catholic but anti-Roman sen-timent, incontestably Catholic but reflexively anti-Roman. Sylvio Hermann De Franceschi has defined it as "confronting the papacy without abandoning confessional adherence to Catholicity."[13] Such a definition only makes sense within a context in which a rupture—that of Luther and the Protestants, in this case—has already taken place. Other definitions are sketched out here and there in De Fran-ceschi's work, which consistently emphasizes the "refusal of the

Roman tropism established in the Church by the Council of Trent."[14] He has written of a "critical refusal or even a knee-jerk rejection of Roman control over the ecclesial community,"[15] of a "questioning of pontifical tropism brought about by the Tridentine achievements."[16] In sum, it was a new way of considering the relationship between politics and religion.[17]

Presented in this way, the phenomenon of anti-Romanism can only have been a modern phenomenon, since it is linked to the Tridentine context and to the triumphalism of ecclesiological Romanity that followed the Council of Trent. De Franceschi has traced its genesis as follows:

> In the first half of the sixteenth century, the attacks of the Protestant reformers violently called the Romanity of the Church of Christ into question. The council of Trent . . . then reaffirmed and considerably reinforced the legitimacy of a Roman tropism within Catholicity by virtue of a *potentior principalitas* recognized in the Chair of St. Peter. . . . After Trent, the Roman authority in the Church experienced an unprecedented development, to the detriment of the so-called episcopalist traditions. In other words, the council tacitly established a monstrous Roman tropism.[18]

With this causal link established, it nevertheless remains the case that in De Franceschi's analyses anti-Romanism is not a homogenous phenomenon. For him, anti-Romanism has encompassed multiple sensibilities, sometimes discordant ones; these sensibilities have often not been in dialogue with each other, and their boundaries have been calibrated differently. It would be better, De Franceschi has written, to speak of a "range of Catholic anti-Roman movements,"[19] or, rather, of anti-Tridentinism, which "alone makes it possible to bring the different currents that make up the European spectrum of anti-Roman Catholicism into a coherent whole."[20] Anti-Tridentinism, then distinct from anti-Romanism, was established in reaction to the concept of Tridentinism as formulated by Giuseppe Alberigo or, more recently, Paolo Prodi.[21] At any rate, "there is obviously a gradation within anti-Roman Catholicism, of which the arc of intensity must be evaluated."[22] In its generic form, the term does not account for the multiplicity of realities of resistance to Roman centralism that were historically expressed as Gallicanism, Jansenism, episcopalism, parochialism, anti-Curialism, regalism, anti-Tridentinism, Richerism, Josephinism, Febronianism, jurisdictionalism, even Catholic anti-Jesuitism, Anglican Erastianism (subordination of the interests of the Church to those of the state), or even conciliarism, parliamentarism, constitutionalism, Ferrism (a product of the doctrine of Jérémie Ferrier, a moderate anti-Romanist who asserted the superiority of the reason of state over the service of the Church), etc. Philippe Boutry also rightly wrote of "the universality of forms of a historical hatred," "from Venetian anti-Curialism to British anti-papism, by way of French Gallicanism,"[23] in order to "grasp the extent of the antipathy aroused by the Roman pontiff" and to approach historical intelligibility.[24]

Finally, the political dimension of the concept should be examined. "Anti-Romanism" is controversial in its essence and even its terminology, since the term is based on its original antithesis, "Romanism," a term that is itself controversial, which is to say it is understood as a "particular religion, that which the papacy has created in order to establish its universal domination."[25] Anti-Romanism has also been controversial in its historiographical reception. Against Balthasar, Jean-Luis Quantin has rejected the use of the term by asking whether it makes sense at all to speak of anti-Romanism. The notion is anachronistic because the term and the concept were forged in the context of the crisis of Germanic Catholicism after Vatican II. Quantin thus has warned against the improper and anachronistic usage of the term: "It seems unnecessary, at best, to transpose this notion of an 'anti-Roman complex' into modern times. For both apologetic and polemical purposes, it developed in the context of the crisis of Germanic Catholicism after Vatican II."[26]

De Franceschi himself has recognized the nonuniformity or nonhomogeneity of the phenomenon behind the term. He has emphasized the very different sensibilities of resistance, which in no way constitute a coherent doctrinal body. In his own way, Thierry Wanegffelen has preferred to speak of a "critical Catholicism" to account for the difficulty inherent in the term "non-Tridentine Catholic": "It became more and more impossible to be and to call oneself a non-Tridentine Catholic, since it was now necessary to live as a Roman Catholic or otherwise be a Protestant."[27]

Another debate, then, could open up in order to discuss what a post-Tridentine, Catholic anti-Romanism might owe to late medieval thought and, in particular, to the subversive currents of the era of the Great Western Schism. In other words, what late medieval legacy authorized Richer to draw his ecclesiological presuppositions from Gerson? How might post-Tridentine anti-Romanism be considered rooted in and fueled by centuries-old traditions implemented in the Middle Ages?

The question therefore arises of whether it is strictly possible to speak of anti-Romanism in the late Middle Ages. To put it another way, what role would the particular moment of dissension expressed in the Great Western Schism and the fifteenth-century reformist councils play in the crystallization and transmission of the earlier material that would be bequeathed to later eras?

THE ABSENCE OF ANTI-ROMANISM IN MEDIEVAL THOUGHT

If the locus of our demonstration remains the period of the Great Western Schism, the constituent elements of resistance that form what might be called anti-Romanism can be found before the late medieval period. Numerous attestations of resistance to pontifical supremacy appear in sources as early as Gratian's *Dictatus Papae* and the debates around pontifical theocracy; the episode surrounding Boniface VIII and Philip the Fair (1296–1303) was merely one of the most obvious. Anti-Romanism remained a strong dimension of the Gregorian conflicts toward the end of the eleventh century, as well as in the moments of dissidence of the twelfth and thirteenth centuries. Among other examples, the Gregorian-era quarrels over liturgical reforms sufficiently prove the persistence of local traditions—such as those of the Church of Spain or the Church of Milan and the Ambrosian rite—in the face of the militant Gregorians' push for liturgical unification. In this case, the anti-Gregorianism visible in several areas of Christianity appears to be nothing other than an expression of anti-Romanism.[28]

The Anti-Romanism of the University of Paris

From dissidence to anti-Romanism: What nuance might be found in the medieval period? Starting in the fourteenth century, there were the theses of Marsilius of Padoa as well as those of John of Jandun and even William of Ockham; a few generations later, those of Wycliff and Jean Hus. The former thinkers influenced the latter, and the documents are well-known. In the *Defensor pacis* (1324), Marsilius of Padua undertook to eradicate the doctrine of the pope's plenitude of power. The offensive charge of these authors and their influence on hostility toward the Church and the pope are well-known. But is it possible to describe this as anti-Romanism? For Marsilius, the pope did not exist: He was the bishop of Rome, and he took on responsibilities that did not properly belong to him.[29] Additionally, the laws of the Church of Rome had no normative value. Only the general council could claim the function of fulfilling Christ's promise, "I am with you always until the end of time." Marsilius aimed to construct a new, radical ecclesiology that would defeat the clergy and destroy the ecclesiological structure of Rome: He intended to work toward a substitution of ecclesiological models and a transfer of the *plenitudo potestatis* from the pope to the emperor.[30]

The genesis of the elements of resistance that could be described as anti-Roman can be better approached at the University of Paris during the dark hours of the Great Western Schism and, particularly, during the time of the subtraction of obedience in France, 1398–1403. For Victor Martin, echoed by De Franceschi, the Great Western Schism saw the birth of Gallicanism when the Parisian theologians developed the idea of subtracting obedience starting in 1396, followed by the declaration of neutrality toward the popes (1408) under the authority of Charles VI, the defense of the *libertates gallicanae*, and the refusal of the clergy in the face of the fiscal demands of the Avignon Curia. Finally, in 1438, the Pragmatic Sanction proclaimed the limitation of pontifical authority by conciliar acts.[31] In a sense, Gallicanism as it was defined by Victor Martin was the same thing as anti-Romanism as defined by De Franceschi: "Victor Martin takes the prize for being first to emphasize two essential dimensions of Gallicanism: its desire to remain always, and contradictorily, in ecclesial communion with the pope, as well as its vital rooting in the institutional, legal, political, and social worlds offered by the old French monarchy."[32]

On closer inspection, however, an authentic anti-pontificalism emerged at this time from the University of Paris. In fact, starting in 1394 and especially after the failure of the embassies in the spring of 1395, the University of Paris as a whole manifested open hostility toward the pope to which it was obedient, the former Aragonese nuncio Pedro de Luna, who became successor to Clement VII on September 16, 1394, under the name Benedict XIII. *Hostili animo animati sunt*, the texts say.[33] The issue at stake was a spiritual hostility between the academics and their pontiff. The salvo of offensives in late August 1395 marked the end of the discussions and embassies that had sought to convince the pope to opt for the path of cession. It was now the time for confrontation and the balance of power, inaugurated by the publication of the *Novem quaestiones* addressed to Benedict XIII.[34] The pope was clearly suspected of heresy and schism to the extent that he did not respect the oath of the conclave, which he had taken as a cardinal and which bound him to use any and all means, *including cession*, to work toward unity in the event of an election.

At precisely the same time, on August 25, 1395, the famous second *Epistola Parisiensis* was published. This text was a programmatic manifesto for the path of cession (*via cessionis*).[35] To be sure, the letter's evocations of scandal and ignominy, its descriptions of bad shepherds and their corruption, and its description of the backdrop of the desolation of the Church were not new. Instead, they were parts of the *topoi* used by reformist traditions of the eleventh and twelfth centuries. However, the tone used in these *topoi* had become imperious, moving from invective to hostility. This indignation led to animosity against a pope who was deemed to have caused the schism.[36] Above all, under the pretext of zeal for the Church's benefit, this animosity tended to mask a feeling that was less acknowledged and less speakable: authentic hatred toward the very person of Benedict XIII, as recounted by Michel Pintoin, the "Religieux of Saint-Denis."[37]

Benedict XIII became a hated figure in the context of the Great Western Schism, but he could also be described as a hateful pope himself. There were many complaints about this. Because hatred responds to hatred, the University of Paris regularly appealed to the king, the council, and even the future pope to prevent Benedict XIII's hateful behavior. The insults, persecutions, and attacks Benedict XIII inflicted on the university were laid out in these appeals. Jean Gerson, the theologian and chancellor of the University of Paris, noted this toxic climate in his writings, in which he called for moderation. In an attempt to calm things down, he invoked the reciprocal respect that the respective parties owed each other, and particularly that which the pope owed the university. He invited the *via oblivionis*, the practice of amnesty, in order to mitigate the resentment and vindictiveness that Benedict XIII might experience when obedience was restored in 1402.[38] He warned against being too blinded by passion to judge matters serenely and lucidly.[39]

In sum, relations between the University of Paris and the pope of their own obedience were tense, hostile, and woven with animosity, resentment, and grievances. Passions were everywhere and hatred was capital, which is to say it was the source of other fatal passions in the same way that sins that generate other sins are capital. Hatred was crucial in that it united all the degrees of this disastrous sentiment, ranging from "simple hatred," or even "great hatred,"[40] all the way to mortal hatred. An example of this transition from word to deed is the assassination of the Duke of Orleans by his cousin, the Duke of Burgundy, in 1407. It was rumored that the pope pursued those who no longer obeyed him, whether cardinals or subjects, with his capital hatred (*odio capitali*) taking the form of threats and actions against them.[41] The university complained about the pope's insults, and its *appellatio* was aimed at protecting itself against them. The university's *Prima appellatio* against Benedict XIII, dated March 21, 1396, was framed as protection against the pontiff's hatred. Hence the picture of a hateful pope and the context of persecution and aggression. The *appellatio* was intended to protect the university from the dangers of persecution. The New Testament references within it relate to Paul's proselytizing and the persecutions brought against him on account of it: "If the blessed Paul had less readily preached the deposit of holy truth to the people of the Jews and especially the Pharisees, he would in no way have been persecuted by them, as he was from city to city.

If the Preacher of this truth had not feared persecution, he would not have appealed to Caesar. And if he had not appealed, he would hardly have escaped the trouble of his persecutors."[42]

The point was to protect the university from being unjustly attacked by Benedict XIII (*indebite molestari*). The university aimed to legally protect itself against the pope's excesses, and this protection also involved a campaign of slander: "Commovebant populum contra dominum nostrum" (They stirred up the people against our Lord), wrote Guillaume Benoît.[43]

Simon de Cramaud and Subtractionism: Anti-Pontificalism and Personal Hatred

Of all the examples of this personal hatred against Benedict XIII, the most paradigmatic remains that of Simon de Cramaud (1345–1423).[44] This hatred was directed at the pope not as a public person, but as a private individual. From 1394 to 1417, Cramaud's policy was exclusively one of hostility and hatred toward Benedict XIII. Martin de Alpartil, a chronicler of the time of Benedict XIII, witnessed this hatred. It was based on de Alpartil's work that Howard Kaminsky traced the genesis of the hatred between Cramaud and Pedro de Luna to before the latter was elevated to the pontificate.[45] Subsequently, Cramaud's entire ecclesiology seems to have been conditioned by and oriented around his personal hatred, which recalled the relationship between Guillaume de Nogaret and Boniface VIII. Cessionist ecclesiology, of which Cramaud was the main theorist, was aimed at Benedict XIII's resignation just as much as (if not more than) the union of the Church. Everything known about the man and his career confirms Martin de Alpartil's explanation of why Simon led a policy of union against Benedict XIII, who, while still merely the Cardinal

Pedro de Luna, had blocked the Duke of Berry's very "urgent" efforts to have Clement VII name Simon a cardinal. This was why Cramaud harbored hatred against Benedict XIII.[46]

After that, according to Martin de Alpartil, Simon hated Benedict. For Howard Kaminsky, whose interpretation is followed here, France's policy of union, which lasted from September 16, 1394, until the Council of Pisa, was a period that can be understood as a personal confrontation between Cramaud and Benedict XIII.[47] This hateful confrontation concerned their political opinions, their ecclesiological views, their representations of Church and state, and their personal ideas. Their positions were not the same, and neither were the traditions each came from: Benedict XIII, the "great tragic figure,"[48] aimed to be part of the secular tradition of the papacy and emphasized the expression of his pontifical sovereignty. Cramaud, for his part, was the political agent of the Valois dukes, and he became the mobilizer of a Church that Kaminsky has described as "Gallican," even if this anachronistic use of the term may be debatable.[49] Simon was also the theorist of the *via cessionis*, a statesman, and a diplomat of European stature. For Cramaud, Benedict XIII was an intruder,[50] but also the father of error and of schism: "If he is as true a pope as Saint Gregory was, he is bound to give in; if by cession he can have union, and if he does not do so, he is not *Pater Patrum*, but *Pater errorum*. I can prove it: if the pope *non colligit ad Christum* [does not gather to Christ], he is called the Father of Schism, *c. quoniam verus*, 24, q. v."

In other words, Benedict was illegitimate. He was worse than schismatic. Any syllogism could persuade the pope to pertinacity and heresy: "When could it be more appropriate to say that a pope is contumacious than when he keeps the Church of God in schism? Where will one find a bigger heretic? But Benedict thus holds the Church in this schism, *per praedicta*."[51]

Over the course of the speech, Cramaud's legal arguments slide toward personal invective: "He says that I said Benedict was a good man: I did say that, when he was Cardinal, he was of good reputation: he speaks the truth. I swear in my conscience that if I had had a voice in the election, I would willingly have elected him, but truly I would not do so now, if I had the power. He played the Lamb-God: it seemed that he was a marvel, but it was nothing but an illusion."[52]

Finally, he compares the pope to Lucifer: "This pope, who by his lust and ambition holds the Church in schism, is worthy of being condemned like Lucifer, without any mercy, *7 q. I. Praesul.*"[53]

Elsewhere, he compares the pope to Pharaoh in his hardness.[54]

After his arrival in Constance, on March 28, 1417, Simon de Cramaud tirelessly took up his arguments and ideas to remove Pedro de Luna from the pontificate. His tenacious hatred of his lifelong adversary continued in his *Mémoire pour l'élection du pape.*[55] Anti-Romanism as a rejection of monarcho-Roman tropism could draw its intensity from personal conflicts in this way, such as with the Venetian anti-Romanism against Paul V at the time of Paolo Sarpi, about which De Franceschi wrote, "Sarpian anti-Romanism was the work of a personality, not a movement."[56]

Hatred of the Pontifical Office

When he wrote his *Tractatus* of 1398, Bernard Alaman was drafting a critique of the pontifical office within a tradition, then already centuries old, of criticizing papal supremacy. The virulence of his critique did not betray a real hatred toward the pontifical function itself. The explosion of passion against the Petrine figure—and no longer against the pope as an individual—took a rather unprecedented turn into classic anti-pontifical rhetoric, even if it took part in a specific anticlericalism that resulted from hierarchical changes in the ecclesial structure, which provoked great reluctance and strong hostility.[57] Over the course of the *Quinta pars*, the author asks, "Quid sit Petrus in Ecclesia?" (What is Peter within the Church?) Alaman emphasized the ministerial function of the pope, which functions through the delegation of authority. In short, the pope is only the servant (*minister*) of the Church and not its head, who remains Christ.[58] Writing within the tradition of criticism of the expression *Vicarius Christi*, Alaman proposed a new path of criticism that denies Peter the legitimacy of his claim to be the head of the Church.[59] The author heightened the virulence of his words in the *Nona pars*. Here, the pope appears more Satan than Peter. And, like any tyrant, he works for himself more than for Christ.[60] In a clever bit of rhetorical symmetry, Alaman concludes that "we should say not Peter but rather Satan the shepherd, not the shepherd but rather the thief and robber, not the Roman pontiff [*pontifex*] but rather the Roman feces [*fex*]."[61]

The English translation loses the Latin alliteration but keeps the violence of the metaphor. In any case, Alaman insistently identifies the pope with the devil: "Serpens igitur ille adulter antiquus" (He is therefore the ancient deceitful serpent).[62] This demonization of the Petrine function proves that the author's hatred was not personally addressed to the two popes, both of whom he rejects with an aggressive neutrality.[63] He clearly turns his back on both contenders for the pontificate, seeing them as adversaries both to each other as well as to Christ. This intrinsic division of their authority originated, for Alaman, in a type of power that was diabolical in the quasi-etymological sense of the term—namely, a power of division.[64] The reign of the devil through his agent: such was the Petrine power and the pontifical office in Alaman's discourse, which took on the appearance of a doctrine of hatred—even an ecclesiology of hatred. His remarks, therefore, are undeniably part of the literature of the highly distinctive anti-theocratic tradition that ran from the eleventh century to well into the modern era.

Subtractionism as a Type of Anti-Pontificalism

At the time when the path of cession (*via cessionis*)—that is, the abdication of the pope—was advocated by the University of Paris as the only viable solution and held up as an official program of the monarchy, cessionism-subtractionism became a form of hatred toward the pope and of an anti-Romanist sensibility. It was a matter of withholding obedience from a pope who had been declared perjured, and therefore schismatic and heretical. Indeed, to point out the pope's perjury was to convict him of heresy. And the significance of an accusation of heresy as a card to be played is well-known.[65]

Since Gratian's *Decretum*, heresy had, formally, been the only reason to depose a pope.[66] Not only would obedience be withdrawn from a perjured pope, but he would also become inferior to any of his Catholic subjects.[67] This forfeiture would be due to his status as a sinner, perjurer, schismatic, and heretic. Ultimately, the pope was caught in a bind between the voluntary abdication of the *via cessionis* and ipso facto forfeiture. From the perspective of the faithful, it was better to subtract than to obey: "And thus it appears that it is no evil, so it is lawful to resist the pope in order to acquire and procure union."[68] Just as Paul resisted Peter, disobedience was advocated. The pope was presented as a tyrant, a mercenary who must be resisted. This situation of scandal, subversion, and danger for many souls in the Church required urgent recourse with a radical solution—such was the fundamental teaching of the *Decretum*.

Ultimately, the canonist Simon de Cramaud emphasized this context of scandal.[69] The scandal demanded resistance in order to convict the pope of heresy and contumaciousness. Cramaud exploited the

Decretum, down to its smallest details, in order to wield the canons in the service of his thesis. He pointed out exceptions and reservations as well as commentators' inflections: The evangelical precept of brotherly correction thus allowed him to circumvent the canonical prohibition against the pope being judged by anyone. The end of the passage from the Gospel signals permission for subtraction: If, after having corrected your brother, he does not repent, let him be to you like the tax collectors and foreigners. What remained? The refusal of obedience as sanction and as right of resistance.[70]

Anti-Romanism and Paulinism

Following the first historiographical milestones, which had been erected by Bruno Neveu and Sylvio Hermann De Franceschi, a study of anti-Roman Paulinism remained to be written.[71] The two modernist historians borrowed a clever metaphor from Henry Chadwick, the Anglican historian, and laid out the theory of the Petrine and Pauline double focus using the two images of a circle and an ellipse: "The elliptical figure conveniently allowed anti-Roman Catholics to call into question the unique prestige of the primacy of Peter. The thesis of the apostolic twinship of Peter and Paul was rejected without concession. The supreme pontificate preferred to stick to an integral Petrinity, which ensured that it would keep the deposit of faith unobscured."[72]

De Franceschi then suggested the formidable subversiveness of the specter of Paul, who had resisted Peter. Anti-Roman theorists of the seventeenth century defended the idea of a perfect *aequalitas* between the two apostles, which Simon Vigor and Martin de Barcos had affirmed. Bellarmine conceded this point: Saint Peter and Saint Paul, he said, jointly deserved the title of *Princeps Apostolorum*.[73] In his preface to Antoine Arnauld's work, the Jansenist

Barcos showed his Pauline bias by declaring the absence of hierarchy between the two apostles. "He desired, or at least he claimed, to combine Paulinity and Petrinity in order to finally fully justify pontifical primacy."[74]

At the time of the Great Western Schism, an anti-Roman Paulinism emerged in cessionist and subtractionist writings, particularly surrounding the exegesis of Galatians 2:11, a verse central to polemics of the time. In his letter to the Galatians, Paul wrote, "Cum autem venisset Cephas Antiocham, in faciem ei restiti, quia reprehensibilis erat."[75] What the Acts of the Apostles calls the "controversy at Antioch" gave rise to the Council of Jerusalem, in which the questions of circumcision as well as the observance of ritual purity by Christian converts from paganism were resolved.[76] What Paul reproached Peter for at Antioch was his failure to have discerned the impropriety of an obligation to follow Jewish law for pagan converts. He summoned Peter for this error and confronted him. A question may be found at the heart of this attitude of resistance: *Cur ita facis?* (What are you doing?) is thus to be understood in the sense of a disapproval of the will of the hierarchical leader. In view of this apparently absolute will, posing this question took courage. *Cur ita facis?* was thus a slogan of refusal of the omnipotence of the prince as much as it was a safeguard against the discretionary and despotic power of the universal rector.[77] Scholars and other subtractionists seized upon it to justify a limitation of the pontiff's *plenitudo potestatis*. The gesture was all the more frontal considering that the *Dictatus pape*, the *Decretum*, and theocratic movements had all, at times and out of turn, affirmed the opposite: that the pope is not indebted to anyone for his actions, that he does not answer to anyone but God, that he is above all discussion, and that he cannot be judged by anyone.[78]

Three lessons derive from the preceding remarks. First, a political purpose can be found behind anti-Romanism—namely, that of the balance of power.[79] In many cases, anti-Romanism was actually a charge against absolutism: "An anti-absolutist in the Church, Richer must also be so in the State: such was Du Perron's conclusion. Richerist conciliarism denounced itself as the ecclesial version of a doctrine that aimed to situate the States General between the king and his subjects."[80]

For the Great Western Schism, anti-Romanism—or anti-Avignonism, in the strict sense—was, more modestly, a way of thinking about a counterpower to the plenitude of pontifical power. That counterpower could be exercised through the cardinals, through councils, through resistance and subtraction, and against the *plenitudo potestatis* of the pontiff, as well as against Gregorian supremacy as rooted in canon law. However, the danger, as some furtively perceived, was that the subtraction of obedience from the person of the pope might one day apply to the person of the king. Political obedience was therefore threatened. Pierre d'Ailly did not fail to note this: The *novitas* of subtraction had all the trappings of something malign, as was often the case for medieval thinkers, because it attacked established institutions.[81] And yet d'Ailly suggested interpreting this as a personal attack on Benedict XIII?[82] The risk of weakening the link of obedience with the king was present.[83] D'Ailly invited his readers to think carefully about the consequences of such a decision.[84] By opting for the radical nature of such a *novitas*, the prelates risked acting against their consciences.[85]

Second, medieval and modern anti-Romanism are both characterized by constancy: A priori, there is no schismatic rupture inherent to anti-Romanism, no more so than there is in Gallicanism. Attachment to the institution remains, even if anti-Romanism plays with its limits—its dangerous margins, delimited by the sulfurous borders of dissidence and critical posturing. In this sense, Sylvio Hermann De Franceschi wrote of "an ecclesiological thought of the limit." However, over the long term, should anti-Romanism not be thought of instead as a discourse of rupture? The critical elements could well push dissidence into a decidedly more frontal opposition.

From here, a third lesson follows: "Anti-Romanism will have created a public space for discussion in which the position the ecclesial power sought to continue to occupy in governing the faithful was called very strongly into question."[86] Hence the question, What link should be established between anti-Romanism and anticlericalism— but also between anti-Romanism and polemology? Following Catherine Maire, Philippe Boutry has stated that "the Civil Constitution of the Clergy constitutes the original schism of revolutionary France and papal Rome, as well as the first act of the process of the destruction of pontifical authority."[87] Why not see in the age of the Great Western Schism the premises of this "process of unbinding that was to lead to secularism"?[88]

Out of this late medieval moment of crisis there emerged the idea of a process of crystallization. Medieval premodernity seems to have gathered and organized a vast amount of material carried over from previous centuries, starting with the implementation of the great papal reform of the eleventh century. What made sense in the fifteenth century was that this material crystallized into what might be called anti-Romanism, which was bequeathed to the modern era. Is it possible, then, to speak of anti-Romanism before anti-Romanism? That the construction of the historiographical category occurred later, well into the nineteenth and then the twentieth century, does not prevent the identification of a perceptible reality at a decisive moment, that of the fifteenth century, at which the material crystallized through concretion and the transmission of a legacy may be identified.

Anti-Romanism is certainly a concept invented by the moderns, but it also finds an abundant and hitherto underutilized textual substrate in the medieval period. Without supporting either a teleological or a continuist narrative, this substrate nevertheless lends credence to the idea, defended here, of a gap between the official discourses found in accounts of religious history and the original medieval sources.

6

MODERNISM'S CHALLENGE
TO THE MIDDLE AGES

Between Medieval Studies and Medievalism

Modernism can be defined as the present-day encounter with and confrontation of a long-established religious past with a present that has found the living sources of its inspiration elsewhere than within itself.

—Émile Poulat, *Histoire, dogme et critique dans la crise moderniste* (Albin Michel, 1996), 15

As a specific episode in the history of contemporary Catholicism dated to the years 1890–1900, the modernist crisis very broadly raises the question of the Church's intellectual regime in the face of modern thought. Modernism offers an invitation to think more globally about the relationships between faith and science, between the tradition of faith and the progress of reason. It is possible to ask whether a form of political modernity existed in the Middle Ages, with the introduction in the West of Aristotle's work, which represented a type of thought exogenous to the Latin theological system. For this reason, the relevance of the idea of a long-term "modernist" crisis is well-founded.

In a sense, the medieval prism calls into question the status of intellectual modernity in the Church, both because the Middle Ages

156 ᴏ MODERNISM'S CHALLENGE TO THE MIDDLE AGES

served as the historical setting for a long-term religious crisis and because, above all, the Middle Ages were a historiographical locus for the ideological divide between modernists and antimodernists.

Rather than systematizing modernism as an archetypal constant across all periods of history—as Herbert L. Stewart did in 1932[1]—the aim of the present chapter is to read the Middle Ages in the light of modernism between medieval studies and medievalism, which is to say between archival studies and narratology, between the documentation and the teleological narrative.

Before identifying the medieval form of this long history of an "antagonism," some definitions should be established. The most successful studies (those by Émile Poulat, Pierre Colin, François Laplanche, or, from the Italian perspective, by Maurilio Guasco and, more recently, Giuseppe Losito,[2] to name only a few) have shown that "modernism" was, above all, the Roman authority and magisterial censorship's reconstruction into a cohesive system of various scattered tendencies, diverse movements, and different disciplines.[3] Today, historians no longer reduce modernism to the definition given in the encyclical *Pascendi* in 1907, which established in the controversy the identity of an enemy—namely, the "modernist" system that in itself never actually existed.[4] Hence the general consensus to use quotation marks around "modernist" and "modernism."

Philippe Boutry's definition allows for forward movement in the long term of history. According to him, "the claim of intellectual autonomy and freedom to study exegetes in relation to the authority of the ecclesiastical magisterium constitutes the heart of the quarrel, whose stakes touch on the very foundations of the Christian faith."[5] The modernist crisis could therefore be defined as a distortion between the progress of the sciences (critical, historical, theological, philosophical) and traditional theology, between new aspirations and established ecclesiastical institutions, between the exogeneity of a thought and the endogeneity of a tradition.

A LONG-TERM RELIGIOUS CRISIS: THE "1270 MOMENT"

Picking up where the 1920s left off, the early 1930s were shaken by "repressive surges" of antimodernism, such as the first, unheeded warning of the Saulchoir.[6] In this context, under the pretext of a 1931 review of Jean Rivière's work, Marie-Dominique Chenu reflected on the "meaning and lessons of a religious crisis," the modernist crisis, of which he identified similar "parallel places" and "critical points" in the medieval period.[7] He considered modernism in the long term of intellectual history, defining it as "a normal effect of intellectual growth in Christian society."[8]

A few centuries earlier, the introduction of Aristotle's work into the Latin West, which had been occurring in staggered waves since the sixth century, was completed in the thirteenth century with the Latin reception of a full "scientific" corpus, the whole Aristotelian body of work accompanied by the Arabic commentaries of Avicenna and, especially, Averroes—in other words, the epistemic universe of Greco-Arab peripateticism. With the arrival of Aristotle's three final, practical works—the *Nicomachean Ethics* (1246–1247), the *Politics* (1260), and the *Pseudo-Economics* (1295)—the medievalists could undertake the great work of acculturing Greek political-moral philosophy to Latin Christian lands. The era was one of intellectual effervescence. In 1255, Aristotelian works entered the official curriculum of the Faculty of Arts at the University of Paris. The question of the assimilation of the work of the Stagirite, exogenous to the Church in metaphysical, physical, and ethical terms, arose acutely for the first great commentators, Albertus Magnus and Thomas Aquinas. Within the ecclesiastical world, in its most learned elite, the slow movement of acculturation took place over three centuries, from the thirteenth to the fifteenth, through the great scholastic genre of the commentary, in the form of *quaestiones* at the Faculty of Arts.[9]

158 ॐ MODERNISM'S CHALLENGE TO THE MIDDLE AGES

Far from pitting Aristotelian philosophy against theological discourse, Albertus Magnus, the first and most encyclopedic of Aristotle's commentators, distinguished between different perspectives, just as he distinguished between faith and reason. A famous phrase from his commentary on *De generatione et corruptione* has become an apothegm of the *Auctoritates Aristotelis*, the anthology of Aristotelian aphorisms for the use of masters: "I do not care much for divine miracles when I discuss natural things."[10] His project was undeniably aimed at a form of philosophical autonomy in relation to theological epistemology. His anthropology, however, remained dependent on a universe of hierarchies, which is to say on a strong Dionysianism in which theology remained the referent and the keystone of the overall structure. Philosophy remained embedded in the gangue of the theological. What Thomas Aquinas attempted, in the same intellectual context of the Dominican order, was a synthesis of the two thoughts, Christian morality and Aristotelian ethics, with a view toward what has been called a "Christian Aristotelianism." According to this synthesis, nature is ordered to the supernatural and the practice of virtue perfected by grace, and philosophical thought is ordered to theological construction as its crowning achievement.[11] Since the early decades of the twentieth century, the philosophical work of Thomas Aquinas has been revisited and reevaluated for its own sake. A pioneer of this line of study, Joseph Maréchal, wrote in 1933, "Saint Thomas . . . claims, against the Augustinian schools, the complete autonomy of the philosophical method: it is incontestably within the light of Christian dogma that Saint Thomas . . . completes Aristotelianism, but he does so without borrowing any logical premise from dogma."[12] More recently, Ruedi Imbach has reiterated the importance of recognizing Aquinas's philosophical inclination toward and genuine interest in the discipline.[13] For his part, James C. Doig has also understood Thomasian commentaries on moral philosophy as the true training provided to Parisian students and teachers and as

MODERNISM'S CHALLENGE TO THE MIDDLE AGES ❧ 159

the substance of Aquinas's moral doctrine, even more so than the *Summa Theologica*.[14]

In the 1260s and 1270s, within the intellectual momentum inspired by the introduction of Aristotle's works to Latin realms and at the University of Paris, the so-called radical Aristotelians wanted to take their penetration into the Aristotelian *intentio* further. What did they teach that could be criticized? Two theses: the eternity of the world and the theory of separate intellect, both of which were in open contradiction to the Christian doctrines of Creation and the immortality of the individual soul. In his *De unitate intellectus*, Thomas expressed offense, although he thought he had settled the score with the Averroist sect in his *Summa contra Gentiles* of a few years earlier. In 1270, he took Siger of Brabant to task (without naming him) by referring to the *Averroistae*, "followers of Averroes." In response to Thomas's attack, Siger, stung to the quick, had to publicly reaffirm that he was a perfect exegete of Aristotle. But he readjusted his interpretation of book 3 of the *De anima*, the subject of the dispute and the stakes of the debate. Being under pressure and, despite everything, under Thomas's guidance, Siger moved away from his initial Averroism to become more strictly Aristotelian. At the same time and in the same generation, other authors, who had voluntarily remained anonymous, transgressed the limits of a strictly Aristotelian philosophy and fell into an exegetical radicalism that was close to so-called Averroism. Anonymous Giele, named for the editor of the Oxford manuscript Merton College 275, wrote his own response to the challenge launched by Thomas between 1270 and 1275. The violence of his tone indicates the degree of the passion and heated spirits.[15]

Then the censures dropped, like guillotines of thought. It was a drama in three acts. Act 1: On December 10, 1270, censure coming from the Bonaventure–Giles of Rome–Thomas Aquinas front was pronounced by the bishop of Paris, Étienne Tempier, who prohibited thirteen philosophical theses. In doing so, it reorganized the errors,

160 ❧ MODERNISM'S CHALLENGE TO THE MIDDLE AGES

structured them, and ordered them to better condemn them. From that moment on, the radical philosophers rethought how their exegeses connected to the given of Revelation. Two years later came act 2: On April 1, 1272, a statute was promulgated by the Faculty of Arts of the University of Paris prohibiting masters and bachelors of arts from disputing a purely theological question: "We rule and order that no master or bachelor of our Faculty of Arts shall claim to determine or even dispute a purely theological question, thereby transgressing the limits assigned to him."[16]

The statute specified three prohibitions on the *magistri artium*: (1) There was a prohibition against deciding or even disputing purely theological questions; (2) when a question was found to be equally relevant to faith and philosophy, there was a prohibition against deciding it in a sense contrary to the faith, under penalty of being considered heretical and excluded from the "society" of masters of arts; and (3) if faced with texts or arguments contrary to the faith, there was an obligation to refute them, to declare them absolutely false and totally erroneous, or to pass them over in silence.

Alain de Libera has commented that "In the event that a philosophical question spills over into theology, the position of the scholar of arts is delicate: If there was opposition between philosophy and theology, he did not have the *right* to decide in favor of philosophy, but only to refute it if he chose to speak about it. He also had the *right to remain silent* if he, more prudently, decided not to address the question."[17]

Contrary to all historiographies, especially that of Pierre Mandonnet, who established Siger of Brabant as an independent thinker and a leader of the opposition against the Faculty of Arts, François-Xavier Putallaz and Ruedi Imbach demonstrated another piece of epistemological logic at work in 1997. According to them, Siger, by proposing the principle of distinguishing between fields, reaffirmed that in the event of a conflict, faith absolutely must prevail in

MODERNISM'S CHALLENGE TO THE MIDDLE AGES ℭ 161

determining the truth.[18] Putallaz and Imbach's interpretation did not win support, and, in 1999, Luca Bianchi wrote, "It seems to me completely unlikely that the intervention of April 1, 1272, is the practical translation, at the institutional level, of the spirit of *De aeternitate mundi* by Boethius of Dacia, or of Siger's *Quaestiones in metaphysicam*."[19] The epistemological conflict to be resolved was that of the double status of truth: Natural knowledge and Christian revelation pose two truths that—far from being contradictory and therefore leading to a monstrous "double truth"—complement each other.[20] Siger opposed Thomas Aquinas, whom he accused of accommodating philosophy to revelation. For Siger, the professional philosopher must present the entirety of Aristotle's thought in all its purity, "without deliberately mutilating the components most openly opposed to Christian beliefs."[21] In a word, there was no need to undermine the sciences' autonomy in order to reconcile them with the truth.[22]

Luca Bianchi has, very rightly, spoken of a distinction between the unicity of truth and the unity of knowledge: Masters of arts did not in any way want to call into question the unicity of truth because, for them as well as for the theologians, the Catholic faith represented the absolute criterion of truth, allowing for the adjudication of a contentious question. On the other hand, they indubitably put the *unity of knowledge* into crisis by seeking to liberate philosophical research from religious tutelage and by proclaiming their intellectual right to make philosophers' thought totally explicit.[23]

In any case, the statute of 1272 was not respected, and on March 7, 1277, in act 3 of the drama, the same Étienne Tempier, based on the expertise of a commission of sixteen theologians including Henri de Gand, prohibited the teaching of 219 theses on the grounds that the *artistae* of Paris "exceed the limits of their specialty" by spreading "execrable errors or, to put it better, their proud and vain insanities." Contrary to the spirits of the statute of 1272 and of Siger of

162 ❧ MODERNISM'S CHALLENGE TO THE MIDDLE AGES

Brabant, Tempier sought to subjugate philosophy to the truth of faith. He imposed what could be described as a tutelage on, or even a takeover or a tightening of control of, the Faculty of Arts.[24]

How, then, to understand the crisis? Did it come from a fierce demand for the autonomy of the Faculty of Arts, of which Siger was the figurehead and the audacities of which the Church would have had the mission to limit? Or did it, rather, come from the ecclesiastical authorities' failure to comprehend the intellectual project of the masters of arts, or even the radical Aristotelians—in other words, the distinction between fields in areas where the boundaries between philosophical investigation and theological investigation were blurred? The ecclesiastical authorities reacted when the answers provided by the academics were incompatible with the articles of the Catholic faith. As in the case of the "modernist" crisis, the crisis of the 1270s came from the institutional Church's inability to conceive of the integration of exogeneity in its intellectual construction: the difficulty of integrating the epistemological radicalism of a new philosophical system, that of Aristotelianism mixed with peripateticism in its Arab elements—intellectual modernity for the thirteenth century. As in the modernist crisis, the Church thus invented its enemy by systematizing it: Latin Averroism and its "double truth," which was a heresy invented by censorship, a myth that had never taken form in textual reality, a hermeneutic drift on the part of the ecclesiastical authorities. As with the modernist crisis, the root of the problem arose not only from a claim for autonomy on the part of the philosophers, but also from a discourse on what method could make better use of all the potentialities of philosophical rationality. In short, the situation of the crisis of the 1270s is comparable to that of the 1900s as in the sense of "parallel places," to use Marie-Dominique Chenu's term. Understood as an object of study, the Middle Ages therefore spur a revival of the meaning of modernism, in its broad sense of openness to intellectual modernity.[25]

However, during the same decade, the 1930s, in which Marie-Dominique Chenu forged a type of medieval studies that claimed to be based on the Middle Ages as an object, another parallel issue emerged in the discourse on the Middle Ages. Philosophical anti-modernism, which may be seen in the reactivation of Thomism in France, was its paradigm. The 1907 encyclical *Pascendi*, promulgated a generation after 1879's *Aeterni Patris*, reaffirmed that Thomism would be the best weapon of defense against modernism. This was a hardened Thomism, a Roman Thomism.[26] It was no longer triumphant, but now defensive.[27] Through this gateway, antimodernism turned into medievalism.[28] Similarly, Thomism, that "Catholicism that has become philosophy,"[29] claimed to be the entirety of Christian thought, or even thought in general: It was a matter of erecting the Middle Ages as the quintessence of Christianity, the heart and the highest expression of Christian culture, even its truth. For antimodernists, the Middle Ages were the time of a radiant Christianity. Daniel Russo has written that medievalism is the opinion according to which "medieval Christianity represented the best possible form of the relationship woven between the Church and history."[30]

MEDIEVALISM CONSTRUCTED AS ANTIMODERNISM

Recent textbooks on the history of philosophy have tended to suggest a certain equivalence: Étienne Gilson's Thomism was the quintessence of the antimodern reaction, which Gilson, a Catholic philosopher, sought to champion. For a time, "Christian philosophy" dominated the narrative of philosophy in the Middle Ages. Thus, Christian philosophy, Thomism or neo-Thomism, antimodernism, and medievalism were all constituent elements of modernism's opposing pole, simultaneously forming this pole's bastion and its front line.

164 ✥ MODERNISM'S CHALLENGE TO THE MIDDLE AGES

To establish this equivalence, Alain de Libera returned to the roots of the debate, around 1931, when Émile Bréhier attacked Étienne Gilson. Indeed, the quarrel over "Christian philosophy," which Bréhier launched against Gilson in 1931, is a condensed version of the whole episode.[31] In the famous lecture he delivered to the French Philosophical Society that year, Bréhier posed the question, "Is there a Christian philosophy?" Taking aim at Gilson, the coiner of the expression, Bréhier denounced the "tendency to endorse the Catholic milieu's judgment of the philosophers of the modernist crisis."[32] In short, he denounced a form of antimodernism found among historians of philosophy. By coining the term "Christian philosophy" in the interwar period, Gilson would serve neo-Thomism, which had been the official philosophy of the Church since Leo XIII promulgated the encyclical *Aeterni Patris* on August 4, 1879.[33] This encyclical reaffirmed Thomas Aquinas's authority in matters of faith, with an emphasis on the balance to be maintained between faith and reason. Against Kantianism and the German idealism of Hegel and Schelling, the program refocused on the *spirit of Saint Thomas*. The pontiff supported the Catholic institutes founded, starting in 1875, to raise the educational level of French clergy. The physical, psychological, and social sciences were to be integrated into the traditional expression of faith, according to this neoscholastic or neo-Thomist perspective. What the encyclical called into question was man's capacity to access God's knowledge by reason alone. When the encyclical *Pascendi* condemned Kantian idealism and the "modernist system" in 1907, this also reaffirmed that Thomism was the best weapon of defense against modernism.[34]

The forging of Gilsonism by its adversaries in the 1930s and its more recent revival by the Liberan school have both solidified its teleology: The golden age was the time of Thomas Aquinas, which represented the peak of the scholastic odyssey. In this view, the vision of the Middle Ages was reorganized around the thirteenth century

MODERNISM'S CHALLENGE TO THE MIDDLE AGES ❧ 165

and the Gilsonian scenario was denounced as a Thomistic teleology. The "perfect world of the thirteenth century" was that of "the victory of theology *within* philosophy," the solid synthesis between faith and reason, in which "all rational knowledge and all the data of faith are presented as so many elements of a single intellectual system.[35] Entities such as Albertino-Thomism or even Christian Aristotelianism, neither of which de Libera judged to be more significant or real than the other, were forged from scratch.[36] According to the same scenario, Gilson considered the fourteenth century a time of decadence after the acme of the thirteenth century. Ockhamism, which is to say the tendency to dissociate philosophy from theology, dominated. That dissociation opened onto fideism (faith without reason), skepticism, criticism, and empty rationalism (reason without faith). As a result, the Gilsonist vision of history was caricatured by its detractors: After the twelfth century, the age of promises, came the thirteenth century, the golden age, followed by the fourteenth century, the age of decadence, and the fifteenth century, the age of emptiness and so-called "scholastic" dryness, in the worst sense of the term.

It is true, and it has been written in various places, that Gilson considered what he called "Christian philosophy" to be the quintessence of medieval philosophy linked to the neoscholastic epistemology of Leo XIII,[37] something Gilson also acknowledged in some of his late writings in the 1960s. In his *Introduction à la philosophie chrétienne* (1960), he wrote,

> By "Christian philosophy" should be understood the manner of philosophizing that Pope Leo XIII described by this term in the encyclical *Aeterni Patris*, as a model for which he gave the doctrine of Saint Thomas Aquinas.[38]

There has been talk of a "hardening" of Gilson himself over the course of his works, and particularly at the end of his career.[39] In his 1960 intellectual autobiography, *Le philosophe et la théologie*, Gilson shed light on his path in relation to the Leonine saying, "This philosophy must live in a sort of symbiosis with the Christian faith."[40] Gilson, however, scrutinized and commented on the encyclical *Aeterni Patris*: Such as it emerges from the encyclical *Aeterni Patris*, he thought, Christian philosophy is therefore the use that the Christian makes of philosophical speculation in his attempt to conquer the intelligence of his faith, both in matters accessible to natural reason and in those that surpass it. Leo XIII did not say that there were no other ways of philosophizing, nor even that no other way is good; he only said that this way was the best, especially for a Christian.[41]

In French institutions of higher education, Thomism as professed by Gilson was precisely a reaction to the modernist atmosphere of the early years of the century. Gilson was, first of all, surprised that Christian philosophy, which is to say the neoscholastic system of Thomism, had been passed over in silence at the time of the modernist crisis: "On the notion of Christian philosophy, we have neither heard nor read any commentary from the time of the modernist crisis."[42] He specified that Christian philosophy had generated the encyclical *Aeterni Patris* of 1879, in contrast to its having been forgotten around 1907.[43] Gilson continued to express his personal judgment of what modernism was: "Modernism was a bundle of errors for which those who supported them were responsible."[44] According to his antimodernist reading, Gilson—though he audited a course Bergson taught at the Collège de France from 1905 to 1907 and was a Bergsonian in his own way—could only inveigh against modernism for having made itself the enemy of Thomas Aquinas, the "scapegoat for all the sins of scholasticism" and the "hated theologian": "The detestation of Aristotelian-Thomist scholarship had ended up commanding its own position on the problem in the mind of Father Laberthonnière."[45] Gilson thus reinvested Thomas Aquinas as a symbolic and strategic object, in parallel with the reinvestment carried out in the same years by Jacques Maritain (1882–1973), who—also a Thomist, if in a different way—coined the term "antimodern" in 1922. Over the decades, Gilson made Thomas the spokesperson for a Christian universalism that broke with the work of Victor Cousin, who, in the previous century, had made Abelard the national figure of his cultural politics. The Gilsonian way of writing the history of philosophy thus turned out, in a way, to be a product of the years following the modernist crisis. Was it, however, merely an antimodernist resurgence?

In his strictly historicist and secularist reading, Alain de Libera hardened Gilson's antimodernist Thomism, making it play as a form of medievalism for the history of philosophy. Thus, the camps were binary: The militantly Catholic Gilson's "Christian philosophy" would be to the history of medieval thought what the Middle Ages were to the history of Christianity, according to the antimodernist sensibility—namely, its quintessence and its truth. The Gilsonian Middle Ages, according to the Liberan reading, played like a projection screen for all antimodernist utopias, a field untouched by any modernist stain. This was an ideologized reference more than an object of history, an invention or reinvention more than a reality. In short, it was what the Liberan generation of historians of philosophy denounced and deconstructed.

De Libera has therefore emphasized his warnings against Gilsonism, which he saw dominating the history of philosophy. It was, to him, a victory of neo-scholasticism, from Albertus Magnus to Wojtyla's personalism: "The history of contemporary French medieval studies is dominated by the work of Étienne Gilson. . . . We do not want to reduce the history of a discipline to the intellectual trajectory of a man."[46] In 2016, Jacques Musset asked, Have we emerged from the crisis of modernism?[47] In response, de Libera would ask in return, Have we emerged from Gilsonian teleology in the history of medieval philosophy?

168 ✒ MODERNISM'S CHALLENGE TO THE MIDDLE AGES

NEW HISTORICIST AND LAICIST
DECONSTRUCTIONS

Scholarship of the 1990s and 2000s sought to rewrite a history of thought that was, if not dispassionate, at least de-ideologized, "without dream or synthesis,"[48] without utopia or projection, in which the medievalism/modernism pairing would no longer function. This desire to escape from Gilsonian teleology and its neo-Thomist Catholic militancy took several paths, both historicist and laicist. The first path was that of a cultural and social history of medieval thought—the path of Alain de Libera. This was a question of returning to the institutional foundations of handling knowledge and its archival foundations.[49] When he wrote *Raison et foi. Archéologie d'une crise, d'Albert le Grand à Jean-Paul II*, de Libera relied on a history of the corpus that allowed him to denounce Gilsonism, the common thread of which he traced back to John Paul II's 1998 encyclical *Fides et ratio*, of which he paints a dark picture: "*Fides et ratio* fundamentally teaches nothing other than what many medieval theologians have said: We must not confuse 'the affirmation of the just autonomy of the philosophical approach' with 'the claim of a self-sufficiency of thought, which clearly proves to be illegitimate.'"[50]

Legitimate autonomy versus illegitimate self-sufficiency: There were, therefore, both good and bad autonomies. Good autonomy distinguishes without separating; it is Thomistic concordism. Rationalist autonomy, that which separates faith and reason, is not acceptable from the perspective of the Church. De Libera has denounced both the double autonomies and the position of the Church, but he has not denounced rationalist autonomy. Understanding the debates of the time requires returning to a reflection anchored in the institutional terrain and in the stakes of power. De Libera has formulated the problem in terms of *territorialization*: "What are the respective limits of philosophy and theology as sciences?"[51] What are their areas

MODERNISM'S CHALLENGE TO THE MIDDLE AGES ᝪ 169

of competency, their principles and their methods, their boundaries? Contesting the Gilsonian schema, which John Paul II continued—namely, the opposition between faith and reason, between philosophy and theology, between science and the authority of Revelation—de Libera has given theology its own rationality. There are religious rationalities, as David L. d'Avray reiterated, in a sense, by opting to use a Weberian grid of analysis in his 2010 book.[52] The separation was not between faith and reason, but between rationalism and irrationalism. Christian theology based on biblical revelation never ceased to be a rational theology. Irrationalism and hostility to philosophy are two different matters.[53] Each science has its own territory. "What distinguishes philosophy and theology is their territory and not their rational argumentation."[54] This "methodological atheism of science," as Pierre Colin wrote, referring to Alfred Loisy, has remained a question of territorialization.[55] Albertus Magnus was first to envisage this "epistemological pluralism,"[56] precisely because he taught within the framework of a Dominican *studium*, which is to say outside the institutional framework of the university, strictly speaking, and therefore not subject to the statute of 1272. Far from the construct of Albertino-Thomism, the Albertine paradigm was that of a Dionysian peripateticism, a "non-Thomasian, non-Gilsonian paradigm of the relationship between faith and reason hidden at the heart of the crisis of the thirteenth century."[57]

The recent movement of historicist medieval studies sought to better justify itself through a hardening of Gilsonism, the antimodernism of the Catholic philosopher Étienne Gilson. To qualify the picture, however, the earlier existence of a powerful alternative current in the French-speaking world should be recalled. It could be summarized by the name "Swiss–Belgian axis," but in reality it is represented by the double axis of Freiburg–Louvain. Within this current, the names Pierre Mandonnet (1858–1936), Maurice de Wulf (1867–1947), and Fernand Van Steenberghen (1904–1993) in

170 ✠ MODERNISM'S CHALLENGE TO THE MIDDLE AGES

Belgium and Gallus M. Manser (1866–1950) in Switzerland qualify the picture: Medievalism was not merely a recourse against a triumphant modernism. Mandonnet was accused of modernism for his early work on Siger of Brabant, notably for his critical method and his rationalism. Even better, Mandonnet attacked Gilson for his theory of Christian philosophy, which argued that philosophy had always had absolute autonomy. And Fernand Van Steenberghen, in 1974, wrote against Gilson: "A philosophy would cease to be philosophy to the extent it became Christian."[58] This meant that the equivalence between medievalism, antimodernism, Gilsonism, and even Thomism was also a recent construction, an optical effect resulting from the work of the Liberan movement.

The second path out of the so-called domination of Gilsonism, a corollary of the first: The return to Paul Vignaux of the 2000s, orchestrated and coordinated by Ruedi Imbach and Kurt Flasch, among others. Indeed, the 2004 reissue of Vignaux's book *La Pensée au Moyen Âge* signaled a paradigm shift in the form of anti-Gilsonism. Ruedi Imbach, in his preface to the reissue published by Vrin, sought to compare the intellectual work of the two great French historians of medieval philosophy. Vignaux (1904–1987), elected to the École Pratique des Hautes Études in 1934, was Gilson's successor to the fifth section. The following anecdote about him has been told: One day, in the Latin Quarter, Léon Brunschvicg called out to Vignaux and pointed out to him that the Middle Ages as presented in his book "did not resemble those of Gilson."[59] And for good reason. Ruedi Imbach has recalled that Vignaux was a trade unionist; he was the founder of the Syndicat Général de l'Éducation Nationale in 1937 and its general secretary from 1948 to 1970. In 1964, he contributed to deconfessionalizing the Confédération Française des Travailleurs Chrétiens, which became the Confédération Française Démocratique du Travail. The contrast between his biography and that of Gilson, a

MODERNISM'S CHALLENGE TO THE MIDDLE AGES ᴄᴙ 171

practicing Catholic, is clear. On the epistemological and historical levels, Vignaux sought to rehabilitate the fourteenth and even the fifteenth century, both of which had been neglected and forgotten by the Gilsonian construction. In his textual methodology, Vignaux focused on arguments more than doctrines. Among his chosen fields, he preferred logic to metaphysics, and nominalism to Thomism. Similarly, he revisited the thirteenth century *beyond Thomism*. In a sense, Imbach's Vignaux sought to re-historicize and to de-ideologize the thought of Thomas Aquinas.[60] The return to Vignaux seemed to play out more like a story than a reality, like an optical effect confirmed by Vignaux's few written works. As evidence, Vignaux's own analyses of Gilson contradict the 2004 story. In an article on Gilson and the scholasticism of the fourteenth and fifteenth centuries, Vignaux wrote, "The philosopher remained a historian by confirming that his choice of a thirteenth-century metaphysics did not, in the face of the following centuries, restrict his horizon as a researcher whose free-ranging curiosity remained exemplary."[61]

Not content with republishing this work, Ruedi Imbach himself took other shortcuts to deconstruct the historiographical constructions dependent on Gilsonism. In 2013 he set out to highlight the "secular challenge"—that is, a cultural and social history that could claim to escape the antimodernist and Catholic schemata of the history of philosophy, perhaps in the tradition of the work undertaken by Georges de Lagarde in his monumental, six-volume *Naissance de l'esprit laïque au déclin du Moyen Âge*, which presented Ockhamian nominalism as the founding moment of modern thought.[62] Imbach is interested in the sociopolitical position and intellectual work of secular actors, whom he sees as no less historical than the clergy. He has focused on the great figures, such as Dante, Petrarch, and Ramon Llull, but he has also considered anonymous and minor authors who witnessed intellectual labor in the daily life of the university at the time.

Through this pursuit of the margins and this appetite for dissidence, mystical figures, or masters of the secondary arts, secularist medieval studies sought to establish itself against the clerical medieval studies of the previous generation—or generations. However, it is important to recall that many great historians of medieval philosophy in the early twentieth century saw inspiration for a the twentieth-century renewal of theology in the nonorthodox currents of the Middle Ages. One example is the work of Edmond Vansteenberghe (1881–1943), a defiant bishop from Bayonne who studied Nicholas of Cusa and the mystics.

Against the picture of a uniform and monolithic antimodernist Thomism, it once again happened that all medievalist readings of a progressive sort were opposed—among them, those of the art historian Élie Faure concerning the cathedral and the non-medievalist modernist Marie-Joseph Lagrange, or the Thomism of Cardinal Mercier, the founder of the Louvain school and yet a non-reactionary Thomist. Thus, medievalism has not exclusively been a recourse against triumphant modernism, except insomuch as it has helped to construct the narrative of a clear-cut opposition: that between a Catholic Middle Ages and a secularizing Middle Ages.

Beyond the role of the Middle Ages in the current debates, it should be noted that the Middle Ages have been called upon to constitute a paradigm against modernity: The other pole has been drawn in the face of the question of modernism and, then, of intellectual modernity.

In any case, what the Middle Ages continue to offer is the relevance of questioning modernity, including its status and its challenges. As a historiographical site of division, the Middle Ages have given rise to ideological readings, the interpretation of which remains of great hermeneutic interest. It is, of course, itself the period of choice for those who study it, but it is also important for what it reveals about the passions of the contemporary world as well as the long-term passions in the history of the Church and in the history of intellectual regimes of truth within the Church.

7

INFALLIBILISM

Anatomy of a Misinterpretation

[On the topic of infallibility], it seems that almost everything that could be said has been said.

—Yves-Marie Congar, "Infaillibilité et indéfectibilité," in *Ministères et communion ecclésiale* (Cerf, 1971), 141

The way in which the Church has existed is that truth has been without contestation, or if it has been contested, there has been the Pope, or, failing him, there has been the Church.

—Blaise Pascal, *Thoughts*, trans. W. F. Trotter (Collier Press, 1910), 302, no. 849

Papal infallibility, which was defined in 1870 at the First Vatican Council, has a particular characteristic: It is the concept that most symbolizes the arbitrariness of the pontiff in the eyes of non-Catholics, but also in public opinion. As the Jansenists of Port-Royal said, infallibility is a tyranny. Hans Küng called it the "insurpassable peak of the concentration of teaching authority in the pope."[1] For Karl Rahner it was a "kind of blank check" for "despotism," the abuses of theocratic authority.[2] At the same time, many Catholics have tended to exaggerate the concept of papal infallibility, even though it was defined very precisely in 1870, by the texts of the council.

176 ⁊ INFALLIBILISM

Nevertheless, a paradox emerges when the sources are read. In the fourteenth century, within the context of debates on evangelical poverty, the concept of papal infallibility emerged as a weapon directed *against* the pope himself. The point has been fully established today in the scholarly literature.[3] At the time, thinking about the infallibility of the pontiff was a way of thinking about the limitation of papal power. Infallibility protected the sovereignty of the pontiff: A future pontiff could not invalidate a decision taken by a previous pontiff. Infallibility functioned as a constitutionalizing limit in the face of the risk of an absolutist drift of *plenitudo potestatis*.

How should such a historical reversal be understood?

THE CONTEXTS OF THE DEBATE: 1870 AND 1970

To conduct an archaeology of infallibilism and to undo the historiographical constructs of the dominant narrative within a critical thought, it is first of all necessary to trace the terms of a double debate, that of the context of the First Vatican Council in 1870 and that of its centennial anniversary, in 1970, which took place during the upheavals of the post-1968 years, post–*Humanae vitae* (1968), and post–Vatican II (1962–1965).

In 1870, the council that Pope Pius IX had convened at the Vatican took place within the troubled double context of the Roman question and the Franco-Prussian War. The council opened on December 8, 1869, and adopted only two dogmatic constitutions before it was suspended on October 20, 1870, due to the previous month's entry of Italian troops into Rome and in the aftermath of the dissolution of the Papal States, which had been united with the rest of Italy by popular referendum around ten days earlier. Only the final chapter of the second dogmatic constitution, the so-called *Pastor Aeternus* concerning papal infallibility, was voted on July 18, 1870, and promulgated by Pope Pius IX. It affirmed two theses: The universal primacy of the pope's jurisdiction, and his personal infallibility with regard to defining truths of faith or morals. A minority of opponents, particularly German ones (von Döllinger) but also French (Dupanloup), fought to subordinate infallibility to the consent of the bishops. They did so in vain. Fifty-five bishops left the council before Pius IX's proclamation of infallibility.

Historians have shown how the dogma of infallibility as proclaimed at Vatican I testified to the new power of the current of ultramontane intransigentism with a strong anti-Gallican sensibility, with infallibilism representing only one of its constituent elements. Indeed, even if papal infallibility was, to a certain extent, a theological doctrine that had been current for several centuries in the Roman Catholic Church, or at least the post-Tridentine Church, its sudden promotion in the nineteenth century, which resulted from its ideologization, made it a new phenomenon.[4] In the context of the upheavals resulting from the French Revolution and the transformations resulting from the Industrial Revolution, political democratization, and the rise of nationalities in Europe in the mid-nineteenth century, the counterrevolutionary ideological apparatus gave another dimension to papal infallibility. According to the views of Joseph de Maistre (*Du pape*, 1819) or of the younger Lamennais, infallibility was synonymous with sovereignty: The infallibility of the head of the Church appeared to be a point-by-point response to the revolutionary theory of the infallible sovereignty of the people, on the one hand, and to the positivist theory of the infallible sovereignty of science, on the other. The dogma proclaimed in 1870 was a defensive reaction within the context of aggression against the Church (academic history, Darwinism, the laicization of education, the direct attack on the Papal States) and ultramontane exaltation of the personal power of the pope. The Church sought to distinguish itself from civil society by defining itself as a counter-society or "perfect society," marked by Caesarism and doctrinal intransigence "as a resurgence of a counter-revolutionary apocalyptic."[5]

During the council, the two parties of the infallibilists and the anti-infallibilists clashed in a translation into other terms of the confrontation between "ultramontanes" and "Gallicans" or between "conciliarists" and "papalists"—another way of describing "Catholic anti-infallibilism as anti-Romanism."[6] Starting in the seventeenth century, with Bellarmine and Suarez, for example, "papal infallibilism went hand in hand with an obvious and uncompromising anti-conciliarism."[7] Proof can be found in the proliferation of treatises with eloquent titles in the same years: Under the pseudonym Janus, Ignaz von Döllinger, the leader of the anti-infallibilist minority, published a treatise titled *Le pape et le concile* (The pope and the council). "If we define papal infallibility, councils will forever be superfluous," he wrote. In September 1869, in the context of the pre-conciliar controversies, Henri Maret (1805–1884), a proponent of moderate Gallicanism and anti-absolutist episcopalism, published *Du concile général et de la paix religieuse*, a book in two volumes: According to him, "the pontiff gives infallibility to his judgments by receiving it from the episcopal body." And, in 1869, one of the representatives of the infallibilist party, Victor Dechamps, archbishop of Malines, wrote *L'Infaillibilité et le Concile général. Étude de science religieuse à l'usage des gens du monde.*[8] This showed the collusion and close affinity between conciliarist movements and the anti-infallibilist sensibility. The question was that of an ecclesiology of the relations between the pope and the Church, which is to say a reflection on the structures of the Church: Who held the power? Who was infallible, the pope or the Church?

A century later, in 1970, the debate on infallibilism took off again. Was this due to the celebration of its centenary? Perhaps. More securely, it was due to the atmosphere of protest that followed the encyclical *Humanae vitae*, published by Paul VI on July 25, 1968, as well as the broader context of the crisis of authority resulting from the revolutions of 1968. The encyclical focused on marriage and birth control. The contraceptive pill had, in fact, been on the market since 1956, and public opinion demanded a softening of the Church's doctrinal position on artificial contraception. In response, Paul VI reaffirmed the magisterium's opposition to all artificial contraception, as well as abortion and sterilization. A storm of protests and demonstrations of hostility broke out within the Catholic Church. Two hundred Catholic theologians declared that the encyclical was not an infallible teaching, and that contraception could be permitted in conscience. At the heart of an already profound crisis of the ecclesiastical magisterium, the proclamation of the encyclical accelerated the questioning of the very principle of infallibility as well as Catholicism's increasing incompatibility with contemporary culture.[9]

The proliferation of writings by theologians and historians during those years spoke volumes about the intensity and urgency of the debate. It is true that the ecumenical meetings of Chevetogne had, as early as 1961, made room for the topic and had resulted in the appearance, the following year, of the publication titled *L'Infaillibilité de l'Église* (The infallibility of the Church).[10] The first milestone had been erected. The following year, Hans Küng published *Unfehlbar? Eine Anfrage*, which was translated into English as *Infallible? An Inquiry* the following year.[11] The book was the subject of debate.[12] There was talk of the *Unfehlbarkeitsdebatte*, the debate on infallibility. Karl Rahner reacted and joined the argument.[13] Reviews of the book proliferated, including, among many, Claude Langlois's from 1973: "Infallibility, a new idea in the nineteenth century."[14] Over the subsequent years, Hans Küng extended his reasoning: He published *Fehlbar? Eine Bilanz* (Fallible? A review) in 1973, and then *Infallible? An Unresolved Enquiry* in 1994. Gustave Thils, for his part and in his own way, became the other specialist on the subject, starting in the early 1960s with his first article on "L'infaillibilité du peuple chrétien *in credendo*. Notes de théologie post-tridentine" (The infallibility of the Christian people *in credendo*. Notes on post-Tridentine theology).[15] Then, in 1969, he published *L'infaillibilité pontificale: Source, conditions, limites* (Pontifical infallibility: Source, conditions, limits); in 1972, *La primauté pontificale. La doctrine de Vatican I, les voies d'une révision* (Pontifical primacy: The doctrine of Vatican I, paths of a revision), and in 1989, *Primauté et infaillibilité du pontife romain à Vatican I, et autres études d'ecclésiologie* (Primacy and infallibility of the Roman pontiff at Vatican II, and other studies in ecclesiology).[16] On the anglophone side, in 1971 Brian Tierney published his magisterial *Origins of Papal Infallibility, 1150–1350*.[17] He was finishing work on it when the controversy surrounding Küng's book broke out. Yves Congar also wrote numerous articles on the subject.[18] It will not go unnoticed that the authors who focused on the theme of infallibility in the late 1960s and early 1970s were the very same authors (Küng, Tierney, Congar, De Vooght, etc.) who took interest in the structures of the Church and the ecclesiological issues of the debates on conciliarism, ecclesial constitutionalism, and the powers between the pope and the Church.

The 1970s and the decade that preceded them were marked by a return to erudition and to archival sources. Brian Tierney, as was his habit, enjoyed scrutinizing the origins of the problem. The Middle Ages were put to the service of a "new idea," that of the nineteenth century, legitimized in the twentieth century. For the moment, it serves to pause on a question of terminology. In a famous article, Paul De Vooght investigated the word itself, as well as its semantic context.[19] Infallibility, indefectibility, inerrancy, irreformability: The thinkers of the 1960s and 1970s again raised the question. Gustave Thils recalled that "the Fathers of Vatican I did not hold stubbornly to the term infallibility. Many spoke of inerrancy or even of *fidei firmitas, indefectibilitas et ideo inerrantia*."[20] Congar proposed redefining the term by suggesting the idea of "solidity of faith," *fidei firmitas*, which was less ambiguous than that of infallibility.[21] Above all, he worked on the connection between infallibility and indefectibility in a 1970 article: For him, indefectibility meant the permanence of origins within the institution, whereas infallibility applied this permanence to the teachings of the faith and to morals.[22] The surest formula remained the medieval one: *errare non posse* (it is not possible to err). Other terms were related to it: *inobliqualis, indeviabilis, inflexibilis/inflexibilitas ad errorem* (unslanting, unerring, unbendable to error). Gerson also wrote of *veritates quae sint de necessitate salutis credendae* (truths that are necessary to believe for salvation).[23] In German, the terms further confound the perception of nuances and meanings: The root of *Unfehlbarkeit* is *fehlen*, which means "to fail" as much as it means "to sin." Etymologically, the term suggests impeccability. Translating it as "infallibility" gives the German term a technical meaning that it did not originally have. Hans Küng occasionally preferred to speak of doctrinal immunity or inerrancy: *Irrtumfreiheit, Irrtumlosigkeit*.[24]

THE NINETEENTH CENTURY AND ITS NEED FOR LEGITIMACY

What Medieval Infallibility?

The infallibilism of the nineteenth and twentieth centuries needed medieval infallibility. It was necessary to root the term in the distant past in order to legitimize it. Hence there was imposed a litany of the so-called infallibilist authors found in all textbooks and histories of the Church: Bonaventure, Peter John Olivi, William of Ockham, and Guido Terreni, to whom should be added Thomas Aquinas or, more aptly, the Augustinian Hermann of Schildesche. Unsurprisingly, the medieval list of such authors often ends with the figure of Juan de

Torquemada, who has recently been reinterpreted from this angle.[25] The point of this enumeration usually consisted of identifying the first author to have used the term *infallibilis* or *infallibilitas*. Was it Bonaventure? Olivi? Ockham? More securely, it was Guido Terreni.

As early as 1870, Fidelis a Fanna (1838–1881) collected a number of texts by Bonaventure that supported the existence of a doctrine of infallibility, in the modern sense of the term, starting in the thirteenth century.[26] The Quaracchi editors then took over the works of the Seraphic Doctor, and shared the same perspective: According to them, Bonaventure was the first to envisage papal infallibility. Rejecting this position, Brian Tierney chose, in turn, to identify Peter John Olivi as a precursor of Vatican I thanks to Maccarrone's edition of Olivi's *Quaestio de infallibilitate Romani pontificis*. Ulrich Horst and, later, Klaus Schatz firmly refused this identification.[27] However, Paul De Vooght's investigation into the semantics of the term in medieval texts, upon which Bernard Sesboüé has based his work, is clear: Until the fifteenth century, there was not a single theologian who directly or explicitly mentioned infallibility. The word was not used, and when it was, it did not refer to the precise modern concept of infallibility: "Infallibility, *vox et res*, was unknown to the canonists of the twelfth, thirteenth, and fourteenth centuries." He added, "The word was not favored by the scholastics."[28] At most, Guido Terreni (1330) and Juan de Torquemada (1453) possessed the concept of a Church that was without error because it was governed by a pope who could not err.

This was because, in the medieval period, the sovereignty of the pontiff was distinguished from his inerrability. What was conceived of in the Middle Ages was not the infallibility of the person of the pontiff, but rather the constitutionality of his sovereign power. What was of interest was thinking about the limitation of pontifical sovereignty, particularly in the case of the heretical pope, something of an obsession for medieval thinkers. What needed to be safe-guarded at all costs was not so much the magisterial authority of the pontiff—which did not make much sense in the Middle Ages—as the relationship of the pope to his Church when it became conflictual or problematic: What would happen to the truth of the faith in the Church if the pope were to fall into error or heresy? The question was all the more crucial because all medieval canonists admitted the possibility of a heretical pope. The error of the pope was anything but an unconsidered fact of the time. How might the error of the pope and the necessary inerrancy of the Church be connected? During the Middle Ages, how could these two firmly held propositions—that the pope could fall into error and that the Church could not err—be considered simultaneously?

The context of the early fourteenth-century debates around evangelical poverty is, therefore, enlightening. A few elements should be recalled. Since the establishment of the Order of Minors and, in particular, since the death of its founder, Francis of Assisi, the Franciscans have been divided on the interpretation to be given to the practice of poverty and the property of the apostles. Should property be held by individuals or the community? Should certain goods be kept in common, or should everything be donated to the pope? Nicholas III, pope from 1277 to 1280, accepted that the property of the Franciscans should be given to the Holy See, opting for a radical interpretation with clear doctrinal consequences: Christ and the apostles possessed nothing of their own, not even collectively. However, John XXII, pope from 1316 to 1334, qualified the theory of the total poverty of Christ and the apostles and sought to restore Franciscan property to the Franciscans. In 1323, he revoked Nicholas III's bull *Exiit qui seminat* (1279) with the bull *Cum inter nonnullos*.

Peter John Olivi, spiritually a Franciscan in favor of radical poverty, discussed the problem. Michael of Cesena, the order's minister general, and William of Ockham had denounced the pope as a de facto fallen heretic. Olivi posed the following question: Could a pope reconsider what one of his predecessors declared to bring to the faith?

Put another way, could a pope change the position of one of his predecessors in matters of faith? The terms he used were precise: Could a pontifical decision be irrevocable, or even irreformable? Following a strong argument, Olivi concluded that there was no possible revocation of a previous decree made by another pope. He defended the thesis of the irreformability of pontifical decisions, even while he himself was in the camp of anti-pontifical dissent. How can this be understood? It was because for Olivi, as for the notorious anti-papalist Ockham, considering the irreformability of the decisions of a pontiff remained a way to limit the powers of future popes. In short, establishing the irreformability of the pontifical decisions of past popes was a guarantee of the limitation of the sovereignty of future popes, who would henceforth be bound by this irrevocability. The irrevocability—which is not to say the infallibility—of pontifical decisions thus acted as a *limitatio* to the individual sovereignty of the popes. Luca Parisoli has summed up the rationale as follows: "Infallibility is the key to an argument that opposes the assertion of *plenitudo potestatis*, a boundary that aims rather to establish that a pope cannot deviate from the decisions of his predecessors (in faith and in morals); above all, it aims to force the pope himself to recognize that there are decisions that can never be modified."[29]

On the subject of Ockham, Brian Tierney spoke of an anti-pontifical infallibilism:

A widely held point of view suggests that, when Ockham insisted on the proneness to error of a pontiff occupying the Roman see, he was explicitly attacking an old doctrine of papal infallibility. The truth is just the opposite. We should rather say that, when Ockham insisted on the irreformability of a true pope's doctrinal decrees, he was implicitly affirming a new doctrine of papal infallibility. What he was attacking was the old doctrine of papal sovereignty.[30]

The concept was perceived as a disastrous novelty by Pope John XXII himself, to the point that it was only a small step to speak of anti-infallibilism on the part of the very pontiff. Understood in this way, infallibility was, for him, a heavy obstacle to his sovereignty. It was a limitation. Infallibility was a constitutional limit placed on the fullness of sovereignty. In this sense, and only in this sense, infallibility was perceived by medieval thinkers as a limit to *plenitudo potestatis*, precisely because it was not the same thing as sovereignty. There was no synonymy between infallibility and sovereignty in the Middle Ages. The conflation of the two was a confusion, specific to the nineteenth century, that did not take into account the semantic and doctrinal trajectory of the concept in the course of history. In 1819, in fact, Joseph de Maistre, in his treatise *Du pape* (On the pope), articulated the conflation—damaging in retrospect, but since canonized—of infallibility and sovereignty in his famous assertion that "Infallibility in the spiritual order and sovereignty in the temporal order are two perfectly symmetrical words. Infallibility is nothing more than a necessary consequence of supremacy."[31]

Sovereignty and infallibility were actually antagonistic in the Middle Ages,[32] but the historiography has connected—without explicitly saying so—the issues of conciliar theories and infallibilism. Paul De Vooght wrote, "In the thought of the conciliarists, in fact, the pope is a sort of constitutional monarch. He is the supreme organ of the executive in the Church, but he is revocable."[33] For the conciliarists, and for those who followed them—the Gallicans and, more broadly, the anti-Roman Catholics—there was no infallibilism other than the conciliar type, that of the assembly gathered in an ecumenical council. Hence "the impious transfer of a charism originally devolved to the *Ecclesia universalis* for the benefit of a singular and human person."[34]

186 ✷ INFALLIBILISM

From Anti-Pontifical Infallibilism to Anti-Pontifical Fallibilism

More frequently than anyone, the conciliarist thinkers sometimes considered popes heretical and discussed their errors. At the time of the Great Western Schism, the entire exegesis of Galatians 2:11 reflected this: Far from being infallible, Peter erred in faith and was reproached for it by Paul.[35] The apostolic episode during which Paul reprimanded Peter on the subject of circumcision, sometimes called the "Antioch controversy," was read by the conciliarists as an argument for the fallibility of Peter's power, but also for its limitation by "fraternal correction" and collegial government. Starting in 1396–1397, and especially during the Council of Constance, the authors explored the theme of fraternal correction. Simon de Cramaud proposed divesting the pope of his status as master and father, accentuating this divestment by using as pretext the precept of fraternal correction— namely, the famous verse from the Gospel of Matthew, 18, "If your brother sins against you" (*Si peccaverit in te frater tuus*, etc.): The pope was neither the superior nor the father that has been claimed, but a brother, and as a brother, one has the right to correct him.[36] The evangelical precept of fraternal correction thus circumvents the canonical prohibition against the pope being judged by anyone. The end of the evangelical passage signaled permission for the subtraction of obedience: If you correct your brother and he does not repent, let him be to you as the tax collectors and foreigners. What recourse was left? The refusal of obedience as sanction and right to resistance.[37]

Around 1417–1418, Jean Gerson emphasized this point in particular: This was just at the time when the development of the right to resistance and the right to appeal became well established. In this context, a final debate arose after the election of Martin V. It was, in fact, within the context of a particular episode that Gerson specified the nature of the right to appeal: On May 10, 1418, the newly elected

Martin V condemned the appeal of the Poles. The Council of Constance had been closed since April 22. The Poles were agitating to have the propaganda from apologists for the Teutonic Knights condemned. This propaganda would make the Slavs and Lithuanians heretics and would forbid them from appealing to the pope at future councils.[38] Gerson reopened the debate, extending the themes he had already outlined. In 1417–1418, he invoked the evangelical reference of fraternal correction on each page of his treatise. He hammered home its content. This contained several ecclesiological implications, the scope of which was in itself capable of opening a new era for the Church. First of all, he emphasized the precept of fraternal correction, rendering the pope a brother. The pope, according to Gerson, was a son of the Church and a brother to every man; he did not need to be called "Father."[39] This was the new aspect. Demonstrating that the pope was a brother meant being able to subject him to the evangelical precept of fraternal correction, the biblical foundation of the right to reprimand and the right to appeal—there was no impeccability of the pope by the sole fact of his dignity.[40]

Gerson, like Pierre d'Ailly, proposed invoking the right to appeal by broadening the scope of the pope's peccability and not restricting it to heresy alone.[41] In a literal sense, the text of the *Decretum* was outdated. Above all, its spirit was contradicted, since the precept of evangelical correction allowed one to appeal to the pope beyond the motive of heresy, for any crime.[42] Gerson positioned himself against the theocratic principle of the superiority of the pope, which is to say against the refutation that Benedict XIII (Pedro de Luna) himself led against the right to appeal.[43] Not only was the pope subject to the evangelical command and, therefore, answerable to the Church, but also he could be denounced by any inferior.[44] In 1418, in his *Quaestio an liceat in causis fidei a papa appellare*, Gerson used Matthew 18 to bolster the Pauline resistance of Galatians 2:11.[45] The reprobation of the pope needed to be public, just as Paul had acted publicly against

Peter. If Peter had not desisted, he would have been condemned by the Church.[46] It was even up to the theologians to denounce the pope's lack of rectitude, just as Peter had pointed out Paul's attitude.[47] If Gerson's theorization seems much stronger from a modern perspective, it is because he was still up against supporters of papal omnipotence, censorship, and the absolute superiority of the pope over any form of judgment or contestation. Above all, there had only been one pope, Martin V, since November 11, 1417, and he was neither an all-powerful monarch nor an infallible pontiff. Gerson spoke of a resistance to the abusive power of the keys: *abusui clavium resistere*.[48] What he was pointing out, more than ever and in the face of all theocratic theory, was the risk of the pope's deviation, his abuse and peccability. In short, what he was pointing out was the pope's fallibility.

For their part, the proponents of strong monarchical power, the pope's canonists, and other thurifers refuted the fraternal correction argument, which weakened the authority and power of the pontiff. First, Nicholas Eymerich contested the fraternal correction argument, which did not seem to him to apply to the pope. He saw the pontifical position as separate from—which is to say above—the law: "It is the same with the pope: Just as a Christian is subject to the law of fraternal correction of Christ—that he should correct his brother, and if the brother is not corrected, he should tell this to the leader and to the Church—but because he does not follow that law, the role of the pope deviates."[49]

What was at stake was the sacrosanct nonjusticiability of the pope.[50] Hence the implacably decretist argument that he who resists the power established by God's order resists God's order, *quihuic potestati a Deo ordinate resistit, Dei ordinacioni resistit*.[51] Another defense that was put forward was the argument of defamation. For the papal camp, any appeal to the pope, any right of reprimand or right of resistance became a defamation, according to the equivalence that was posed. This was due to the theocratic slogans according to which the pope was above all, protected from all criticism by the asymmetry of his superiority: "No one but God can convict [him] of fault in this world."[52] For Martin de Zalba, even fraternal correction seemed like defamation; he explained, in fact, that if anyone could privately correct his brother, even the pope, as in the present case, the pope would remain within his rights to oppose and prevent it.[53] To reprimand the pope was, therefore, to defame him.[54] Rumors and murmurs were distractions.[55] As for appeal against the pope, it was simply impossible,[56] on the grounds that the pope had no superior on earth.[57] Those who claimed the contrary were thus suspect in their very faith.[58] This shows to what extent the conception of reverential obedience did not tolerate criticism. The omnipotence of pontifical authority was defended only through rejecting that which undermined it. For canonists, the specter of the crime of lèse-majesté in the process of becoming a juridical and scholarly construction was a powerful weapon.[59] The pontifical canonists were quick to pit papal majesty, or even divine majesty, against *jus resistendi*, in light of theocratic principles. By affirming that there was no salvation outside the Church, *extra Ecclesiam non est salus*, the *Epistola Tholosana* suggested, in Bonifacian style, that there was no salvation without obedience to the pontiff.[60]

Thus, within the context of the polemics of the years of the Great Western Schism, the question reemerged of knowing who was infallible—the Church or the pope. Pierre d'Ailly's *De potestate ecclesiastica* was a response to the attacks of Jean Mauroux, the patriarch of Antioch, who in February 1415 had himself composed a treatise supporting the pontifical, or even the theocratic, line within the council. In his response, d'Ailly wrote, "Is the pope subject to the council?"[61] Where Jean Mauroux had advocated the submission of the council to the pope without discussion, Pierre d'Ailly desired the interdependence and balance of the three powers (pope, council, Sacred College) in an ecclesiology that would become more collegial and, above all, more weighted toward the cardinals.[62] By the power of the Holy Spirit, the council was infallible, while the pope could fail.[63]

At that point in the text, Pierre d'Ailly brought up the episode of the Epistle to the Galatians.[64] According to him, Pierre had failed, and the Church needed to obey him only insofar as he built it up and did not destroy it.[65] In the event of destruction, an appeal against the pope could be made to the council.[66] Pierre d'Ailly listed the famous cases of appeal according to canon law, which reflected manifest heresy or notorious tyranny.[67] The concept of tyranny thus came to be included within the polemical literature of the Great Western Schism, whereas heresy, as both fault and fallibility, had been invoked since very early on, with Gratian's *Decretum*, to indict the pope and convict him of error.[68] Pierre d'Ailly's exegesis on Galatians 2:11 further developed the idea:

> Here, it must be considered that, although Peter was rebuked by Paul and was rightly deemed reprehensible because he did not walk the straight path of evangelical truth, neither the text nor the Glossa state that Peter could have been a heretic, nor that he could have erred due to a heretical error. For this reason, in absolute terms, the pope can be rebuked and corrected in certain cases where there is no heresy.... Then, the pope stepped off and deviated from the straight path of evangelical truth, since evangelical truth is the uprightness of faith. But this can happen in many cases other than that of heresy, such as cases of scandal that manifestly disturb and destroy the Church. Consequently, in these cases, he could be corrected, accused, and judged.[69]

The concept of tyranny, or disruption of public order, was greatly reinforced by the portrait of a deviant and fallible pope. Benedict XIII was less a tyrant by usurpation—considering he was recognized as a legitimate pope within his obedience—than he was a tyrant by exercise, which is to say by the abuse and excess of power that was legitimate in origin, according to Bartolus of Sassoferrato's (1314–1357) famous distinction in his tract *De Tyrannia*.

In the fifteenth century, thinkers therefore attributed infallibility to the Church as conceived of as a *congregatio fidelium* or *universitas fidelium*, which is to say the Church in council. Only the universality of the faithful as represented by a council could not err, a thesis that would later become *infallibilitas in credendo*. This was distinct from *infallibilitas in docendo*, the infallibility of the episcopal college in general, and above all from *infallibilitas in definiendo*, that of the pontiff. *Infallibilitas in credendo* was that of the faithful, who, though individually subject to error, could not collectively fall into error on an essential point of faith.[70]

INFALLIBILISM AND THE REGIME OF TRUTH IN THE CHURCH

Writing of the debates around infallibility as a whole, Gustave Thils specified that "Infallibility is at the service of the truth."[71] Charles Moeller likewise wrote as conclusion to the meetings at Chevetogne in 1961, "The term *infallibility* . . . must be placed within the broader context of the biblical term of *truth*."[72] Underlying the debates, therefore, lay the certainty of a faith that involved the truth of its transmission, that the Church could not be mistaken. Such is the axiom. Hence the idea, in the nineteenth and twentieth centuries, of an incontrovertibility of pontifical definitions, following the irreformability of decrees. More precisely, what is the regime of truth in an infallibilist context?

"In this treatise I am about to write, as in all my other writings and statements, I am subject to the Catholic truth and to the doctrine of my sacrosanct mother, the Church."[73] Between 1410 and 1412,

Benedict XIII wrote a *Tractatus adversus conciliabulum Pisanum* to justify himself as never having fallen into heresy. In that text, the truth is assimilated to the doctrine of the Church; for that reason, it is not discussed; it is defended. Moreover, when John Hayton evoked the debates of the University of Paris in 1395, he suggested that they not seek to establish the truth.[74] The magisterial regime of truth and the world of debates hardly overlapped, according to him. The truth of the pontificalists was a reverential truth, one that needed to be discovered if it was hidden and revealed if it was occult, exclusive of other truths and alternatives and, above all, exclusive of any discussion. It was an infallible and immutable truth.[75]

Infallibilis veritas: it consists of dogmatic statements held by the authority for the full and immutable expression of the truth, according to Bruno Neveu.[76] This is a truth that was defended more than it was discussed, against the practices of the polemicists themselves, for whom the debate ventured into innovations and challenges, far from certainties and dogmatisms.

The thinkers thus reconstructed the path of error and its emergence. There was, in fact, a spirit of truth, just as there was a spirit of falsehood. For the authors of the *Epistola Parisiensis*, when the spirit of falsehood prevails, the Spirit of truth—that is, the Holy Spirit—flees. The two spirits confront each other, the Holy Spirit against the spirit of falsehood, the spirit of the devil: "This is the opinion of the majority, although it is impossible for the council to err in matters of faith with the Holy Spirit directing it. However, through bad counsel or lying witnesses, it could, in fact, fail or err (*falli aut errare posse*). That is, the Spirit of truth itself deserts and the spirit of falsehood prevails. . . . And it is enslaved to the devil, the father of liars, [the Holy Spirit] giving no assistance."[77]

The question arises, within the context of a conciliarist reflection, of understanding the situation with regard to conciliar infallibility and the assistance of the Holy Spirit. Using the same anti-pontifical tone, the anonymous scholar against the *Epistola Tholosana* took up the expression of a Spirit of truth, rather than the simple term *veritas*: "The spirit of falsehood exists where the Spirit of truth must dwell."[78] For their part, the canonists of Benedict XIII, opposing the Council of Pisa, recalled the link between the Holy Spirit and the truth according to the Gospel of John, chapter 16, in which it is the Spirit of truth: "Whatever happened, the apostles were full of the grace of the Holy Spirit, as we have in Acts 2, when Christ promised to give them the Holy Spirit, who would teach them the whole truth." Also in John 16, he said to them, "When the Spirit of truth comes, it will teach you the whole truth (John 16:13)."[79]

The truth could be appropriated: It was the "truth of the pope," a magisterial truth that was truth according to the holder of a position and not intrinsically, a truth decreed by a sovereignty that held the power to prescribe and to proscribe, a truth defined by an authority.

Between medieval ecclesiology and the ecclesiology of the Conciliar Fathers of Vatican I, there was a profound gap, as Brian Tierney noted.[80] The back-and-forth between the late medieval period—with its fourteenth-century debates on Franciscan poverty and the fifteenth-century era of the reformist councils—and the nineteenth and twentieth centuries (1870 and 1970) have shown that there is neither linearity nor genealogy in the semantic and ecclesiological approach. When the historians and theologians of the contemporary era constructed their narratives—whether in the service of magisterial historiography or in its countermemory—they reinvented the history of papal power as an upward, even inevitable march with origins in the foundational centuries of the Middle Ages, and particularly the fifteenth century.

By tracing the archaeology of infallibilism, this chapter has sought to show how contemporary narratives and their search for legitimizing origins were, above all, a political gesture and an issue of power.

Through as close a reading as possible of the sources of the fifteenth century, the contrast in narrativities has been pointed out: There is a linear narrative of infallibilist reinvention, and then there is a narrative stemming from the texts themselves that breaks with this linearity. This book was born from this contrast, and it ends in the hopes of having awakened minds to it.

CONCLUSION

The relationship of the modern and contemporary Church to its medieval memory remains, unsurprisingly, one characterized by emotions and passions—those of honor and shame, above all, but also those of love and hate, fear and even mourning. The episode of the conciliar moment and its ideologization into conciliarism perhaps constituted the nodal point of this passionate relationship. The episode was painful for the memory of the Church, as it was a source of humiliation for its pope, its hierarchy, and its prestige. By damaging its ideal of unity, the era of the Great Western Schism and the reforming councils tested the Church's linear discourse. This was a question of a drama rewritten, polished, and inserted into an anesthetic and innervating linearity. This book has attempted to trace how the episode was silenced.

The dark hours of the fifteenth century tarnished the ideals of monarchical authority and uncontested power, particularly in terms of the weaknesses, humiliations, imprisonments, escapes, flights, trials, condemnations, failures, and obstinacy of the pontiffs. It was, therefore, necessary to rewrite history. The official historiography controlled by the magisterial authorities of Roman centralism was, more than ever, an issue of power. It was a question of finding the linearity of an official narrative in order to restore the tarnished honor

196 ❧ CONCLUSION

of the institution and, therefore, to disqualify these shameful episodes as so many accidents of history. Hence the repressions, the avoidances, the gray areas, the things left unspoken, and the silences regarding the restoration of ecclesiastical memory.

The theme of reform has shown that this memory, which functioned through honor and shame, brought about passionate and unstable relationships in which the Church came and went: Sometimes fusional, it reappropriated the theme of *reformatio* in its Catholic affiliation; sometimes distrustful, it repressed it by substituting for it false friends such as *aggiornamento*. No less passionate in its relationships of love and disenchantment, the historiography engaged with anti-Romanism as an object of history but also an unconscious foundation. The theme gained momentum in the modern and contemporary periods. It remained overlooked in the official historiography of the late medieval period, even though it is a category attested in the sources. Most of all, modernism expressed the contemporary passions of the Church in its debates, twisting the outlines of the past and manipulating the Middle Ages in order to better construct its memory. Above all, when it made use of the concepts of "collegialism" and "infallibility," the official memory needed the Middle Ages to better legitimize its discourse: It sought distant roots, the long term, historical continuities, and, ultimately, a reassuring immutability.

In short, the Middle Ages were the key component of a memorial narrative, often at the price of historical forcing (collegialism) or misinterpretation (infallibility). Uncovering the construction of a memory behind the manipulations of history was, indeed, the objective set by the confrontation between the great narratives and the archival sources. It appeared that the official memory of the Church, as relayed by university textbooks, could be considered a history of honor and shame, and could be reread in the light of a heuristically fruitful intersection between historiography and the history of emotions in

CONCLUSION ❧ 197

the Church. This history of ecclesiastical passions from the Church's origins to the present day remains to be written.

This book has also shown the constancy of an obvious fact: the specularity of the debate between continuities and ruptures, and between continuism and discontinuism. An endless debate that has run out of fuel, the question of the medieval legacy and its relationship to modernity—in the form of modernization or secularization—has not, even after many decades, produced the expected heuristic fruits. Today, it would be better to find a way to leave the debate behind. How? A few paths have been outlined along the way. The first path out of the specular debate between continuities and ruptures between the Middle Ages and contemporary modernity may well be that of erudition and a return to the sources. This book has shown how the 2000s and 2010s saw researchers returning to the archives, reediting foundational texts (Michiel Decaluwé) that have underpinned controversies but had previously been incorrectly edited, exhuming the manuscripts of trials and legal proceedings (Sebastian Provvidente, Émilie Rosenblieh), and rereading the texts more closely in order to break down the traditional historiographical front lines (Thomas Prügl). Only a return to the archive, stripped of its interpretative and historiographical traditions, can now attest to some scientific validity. It is also possible to follow the traces of manuscripts and to practice codicological work on the texts in order to see history as it was made day by day, in its materiality and in micro-history: the composition of collections, *marginalia*, the marks of owners, compilers, and annotators, re-borrowings from and affiliations with spheres of polemicism, library circulations, etc.

The second path out of the debate emerged from the young field of the history of knowledge. Indeed, it is not enough to take note of the situation of a historiographical construct. It is not enough to describe, in as much detail as possible, the historiographical constructs induced by official narratives, the reworked memory of the Church

198 ๑ℓ CONCLUSION

and its transpirations in academic works. Now, it is a question of setting historiographical constructs into confrontation with each other: the analysis of argumentative performances, as has been considered here, and the history of normative contexts of production, which is to say the history of disciplinary boundaries, the conditions of the historical possibilities of discursive receptions. To escape this impasse, it is necessary to stop separating the official strategies for constructing a memory from history of theological knowledge itself, connected to a regime of religious authority, as Jean-Pascal Gay has done.[1] This confrontation between historiographical discursivity and an epistemological approach opens with the crisis of the boundaries between the religious and the political (Jean-Pascal Gay) and the crisis of periodizing the Middle Ages and modernity (Kathleen Davis), and ultimately breaks with the teleological linearity of official narratives to arrive at a better historiographical intelligibility of the Middle Ages themselves, on the one hand, and of our relationship to modernity, on the other.

A third path remains to be considered. Michel Foucault suggested speaking of a history of the clergy, breaking with the official ecclesiastical history. As Philippe Büttgen has shown, Foucault also tackled the unfathomable question of the legacy the Middle Ages left to modernity, even if the debates around secularization he considered were precisely those of his own generation.[2] However, Foucault rejected secularization because of its disadvantageously excessive linearity: He rejected the concepts of reports, resumptions, translations, passages, transfers, transitions, and transpositions because he rejected traditional historical causality, all concepts for which he preferred to substitute strategies and tactics. His alternative proposal was that of a history of intensifications—the proliferation of the arts of governing, for example—which departed from causal representations: "The intersection of durations takes place differently from an intersection of causal series."[3] If Foucault was resolutely on the side of the

CONCLUSION ∞ 199

discontinuists, he envisaged an exit from the binary debate through no longer thinking of "the game between the Church and the State, but rather that between the pastorate and the government."[4] Foucault deactivated the confrontation between the Church and the state from within, freeing it "from the simplifying gigantomachy of personified institutions—the Church, the State, Caesar, Christ, the pope."[5] He rejected secularization and the theologico-politics that pitted the state against the Church. In his course on the pastorate, Foucault thus considered the minister as an intermediary figure who implemented the diversity of government practices and strategies, exiting the history of institutions and "institutional centrism." The minister, above all, allowed for an intersection of the analysis of pastoral power and the history of the clergy.[6] This was a way to get away from traditional religious history, at least as it has been practiced in France. Thus, as Philippe Büttgen has written, "the analysis of pastoral power imposes the conviction that it is possible to do religious history with a view toward something other than religion."[7] This book has been the bearer of this conviction.

ACKNOWLEDGMENTS

The individual chapters of this book each served as the subject of a discussion at "Contemporary Uses of the Middle Ages: Ecclesiology and Historiography," a seminar of the École des Hautes Études en Sciences Sociales, in 2016–2017 and 2017–2018. The book therefore owes much to Dominique Iogna-Prat, who generously included me in the seminar.

Likewise, it owes much to each of the speakers who were invited to the seminar to discuss and test the theses the book advances. My gratitude and my friendship go to Émilie Rosenblieh, Fabrice Delivré, Anne Massoni, Christine Barralis, Philippe Boutry, Guillaume Cuchet, Jacob Schmutz, Frédéric Gabriel, Laurent Fonbaustier, Jean-Pascal Gay, and Claude Gauvard, as well as to Alain Rauwel and Sylvain Destephen, for their valuable and stimulating comments, and to Paul Garapon and the Presses Universitaires de France, for their confidence in the work.

NOTES

FOREWORD TO THE ENGLISH TRANSLATION

1. For the interest Catholics will have in this book, see Brenna Moore, "Rethinking Catholic Intellectual History," *Catholic Historical Review* 109, no. 2 (2023): vi and 255–268. For current legal arguments over "originalism" and the American Constitution, see Laurence H. Tribe's review of five books on the Supreme Court in "Constrain the Court—Without Crippling It," *New York Review of Books*, August 17, 2023. For continuing controversy over American historians' use of the past, see the debate that raged in the pages of the American Historical Association's newsmagazine *Perspectives on History* over James Sweet's presidential column "On Presentism and History: Or, We're Doing This Again, Are We?," August 19, 2022. On the debate, see also Malcolm Foley, "History as Love," and Priya Satia, "The Presentist Trap," in *Perspectives on History*, September 7, 2022.

INTRODUCTION

1. See, respectively, Kathleen Davis, *Periodization and Sovereignty: How Ideas of Feudalism and Secularization Govern the Politics of Time* (University of Pennsylvania Press, 2008), and Jean-Claude Monod, *La Querelle de la sécularisation de Hegel à Blumenberg* (Vrin, 2012).
2. Bénédicte Sère, *Les Débats d'opinion à l'heure du Grand Schisme. Ecclésiologie et politique* (Brepols, 2016).
3. Monod, *La Querelle de la sécularisation.*

204 ❧ INTRODUCTION

4. See Reinhart Koselleck, *Futures Past: On the Semantics of Historical Time* (Columbia University Press, 2004).

5. Marie-Dominique Chenu, "Le sens et les leçons d'une crise religieuse," *La Vie intellectuelle* 13 (October–December 1931): 356–380.

6. See Davis, *Periodization and Sovereignty*, and, for example, Dominique Pestre, ed., *Histoire des sciences et des savoirs*, 3 vols. (Seuil, 2015); Dominique Pestre, *Introduction aux Science Studies* (La Découverte, 2006).

7. John Neville Figgis, *Political Thought from Gerson to Grotius, 1414–1625: Seven Studies* (Harper, 1960); Brian Tierney, *Foundations of the Conciliar Theory: The Contribution of the Medieval Canonists from Gratian to the Great Schism* (Cambridge University Press, 1955).

8. Claude Langlois, "L'infaillibilité pontificale, une idée neuve au XIXe siècle," in *Le Continent théologique. Explorations historiques* (Presses Universitaires de Rennes, 2016).

1. CONCILIARISM

1. Jean-Louis Gazzaniga, "L'appel au concile dans la politique gallicane de la monarchie de Charles VII à Louis XII," *Bulletin de littérature ecclésiastique* 85, no. 2 (1984): 111–129.

2. Hermann Josef Sieben, *Traktate und Theorien zum Konzil vom Beginn des Grossen Schismas bis zum Vorabend der Reformation (1378–1521)* (Knecht, 1983).

3. See Aldo Landi, "Conciliarisme," in *Dictionnaire historique de la papauté*, ed. Philippe Levillain (Fayard, 1994).

4. On the same subject, see Bénédicte Sère, "Pierre d'Ailly fut-il un conciliariste? Les effets d'optique de l'état archivistique," in *Pierre d'Ailly. Un esprit universel à l'aube du XVe siècle*, ed. Jean-Patrice Boudet et al. (Peeters, 2019).

5. Hélène Millet, "Pierre d'Ailly et le Concile de Pise (1409)," *Comptes rendus des séances de l'Académie des Inscriptions et Belles-Lettres* 158, no. 2 (2014): 826.

6. On this subject, see Bénédicte Sère, "Gerson ecclésiologue. Les réinventions de la modernité (XVe–XXIe siècle)," in *Jean Gerson écrivain: De l'œuvre latine et française à sa réception européenne (XVe–XVIIIe siècle)*, ed. Isabelle Fabre (Droz, 2024).

7. Philippe Denis, *Edmond Richer et le renouveau du conciliarisme au XVIIe siècle* (Cerf, 2014), 415–433.

I. CONCILIARISM ❧ 205

8. Jean Gerson, *Dialogus de potestate ligandi et solvendi*, starting: "Cum Christus dederit potestatem ligandi et solvendi principaliter Petro" (after February 1417). In Jean Gerson, *Œuvres complètes*, ed. Palémon Glorieux, 11 vols. (Desclée de Brouwer, 1960–1973), 6:251–258 § 284.

9. Jean Gerson, *De auferibilitate pape ab ecclesia* or *De auferibilitate sponsi ab Ecclesia*, starting: "Venient autem dies" (June 15–July 8, 1409; edited at Constance on April 20, 1415, according to Glorieux). In Gerson, *Œuvres complètes*, 3:313 § 102.

10. Daniel Hobbins, *Authorship and Publicity Before Print: Jean Gerson and the Transformation of Late Medieval Learning* (University of Pennsylvania Press, 2009), 208.

11. Hobbins, *Authorship and Publicity Before Print*, 208.

12. Hobbins, 208.

13. Robert Bellarmine, *Risposta di Card. Bellarmino ad un libretto intitulato Trattato e resolutione sopra la validità de la scommuniche di Gileio. Gersono* (Guglielmo Facciotto, 1606). See Francis Oakley, "Complexities of Context: Gerson, Bellarmine, Sarpi, Richer, and the Venetian Interdict of 1606–1607," in *Politics and Eternity: Studies in the History of Medieval and Early-Modern Political Thought* (Brill, 1999).

14. See Sylvio Hermann De Franceschi, *La crise théologico-politique du premier âge baroque. Antiromanisme doctrinal, pouvoir pastoral et raison du prince: Le Saint-Siège face au prisme français (1607–1627)* (École Française de Rome, 2009), esp. chap. 4, "Le richérisme et l'âge d'or du catholicisme antiromain," 325–524; this quotation, 363.

15. Jean Gerson, *Opera multo quam antehac auctiora et castigatiora*, ed. Edmond Richer, 2 vols. (Paris, 1606).

16. For the most recent edition, see Edmond Richer, *De la puissance ecclésiastique et politique. Texte de la première edition latine (1611) et française (1612)* (Cerf, 2014).

17. De Franceschi, *La crise théologico-politique du premier âge baroque*, 325–524.

18. Richer, *De la puissance ecclésiastique et politique*, 72–73 and 102–103.

19. Richer, 47.

20. André Duval, *Libelli de ecclesiastica et politica potestate elenchus pro suprema Romani Pontificis in Ecclesiam authoritate* (Paris, 1612).

21. Bossuet, *Œuvres complètes de Bossuet*, ed. F. Lachat, 31 vols. (Paris, 1863–1867). See also Aimé-Georges Martimort, *Le gallicanisme de Bossuet* (Cerf, 1953);

206 & I. CONCILIARISM

Aimé-Georges Martimort, *L'établissement du texte de la* Defensio declarationis *de Bossuet* (Cerf, 1956).

22. Louis Ellies du Pin, *Traité de la puissance ecclésiastique* (Paris, 1707), 372–542, for example, 441, 443, and 450.

23. Dale Van Kley, *Les origines religieuses de la Révolution française* (Seuil, 2002).

24. Catherine Maire, *De la cause de Dieu à la cause de la nation: Le jansénisme au XVIIIe siècle* (Gallimard, 1998).

25. Émile de Bonnechose, *Réformateurs avant la Réforme, XVe siècle: Gerson, Jean Hus et le concile de Constance, avec des considérations nouvelles sur l'Église gallicane depuis le grand schisme jusqu'à nos jours*, 2 vols. (Paris, 1844).

26. Louis Salembier, "Gerson (Jean le Charlier de)," in *Dictionnaire de théologie catholique*, vol. 6, pt. 2, ed. Alfred Vacant et al. (Letouzey & Ané, 1914). Translation adapted from *The Catholic Encyclopedia*, ed. Charles Herbermann et al. (Encyclopedia Press, 1913), 6:532.

27. Salembier, "Gerson (Jean le Charlier de)," col. 1329, quoted in Frédéric Gabriel, "Idées gallicanes et conceptualités ecclésiales: Parcours et tensions d'une histoire doctrinale dans le *Dictionnaire de théologie catholique*," in *Théologie et érudition de la crise moderniste à Vatican II. Autour du* Dictionnaire de théologie catholique, ed. Silvio Hermann De Franceschi (Presses Universitaires de Limoges, 2014), 248n112.

28. Olivier de La Brosse, *Le Pape et le Concile. La comparaison de leurs pouvoirs à la veille de la réforme* (Cerf, 1995), 115.

29. Francis Rapp, "Le conciliarisme bâillonné, la réforme escamotée," in *Histoire du christianisme des origines à nos jours*, vol. 7, *De la réforme à la réformation (1450–1530)*, ed. Jean-Marie Mayeur et al. (Desclée de Brouwer, 1995), 134.

30. Gazzaniga, "L'appel au concile," 125.

31. Gazzaniga, 126–127.

32. Alain Tallon, *La France et le concile de Trente* (École Française de Rome, 1997), 439n6.

33. Tallon, 431.

34. Tallon, 431.

35. Tallon, 439; John A. F. Thomson, *Popes and Princes 1417–1517: Politics and Polity in the Late Medieval Church* (George Allen & Unwin, 1980), xvi.

36. Rapp, "Le conciliarisme bâilonné, la réforme escamotée," 126–127.

I. CONCILIARISM ❧ 207

37. In the sixteenth century, the Roman Curia seriously attempted to render inoperative the *Haec sancta* and *Frequens* decrees of the Council of Constance.

38. François Rabelais, *Quart livre*, ed. R. Marichal (Droz, 1947), 188, line 4.

39. Oakley, "Complexities of Context"; James H. Burns, *"Politia regalis et optima*: The Political Ideas of John Mair," *History of Political Thought* 2, no. 1 (1981): 41.

40. See Paolo Prodi, *Christianisme et monde moderne. Cinquante ans de recherches* (Seuil, 2006), 253.

41. James H. Burns and Thomas M. Izbicki, eds., *Conciliarism and Papalism* (Cambridge University Press, 1997).

42. Hans Schneider, *Der Konziliarismus als Problem der neueren katholischen Theologie* (De Gruyter, 1976).

43. The expression is from Francis Oakley, *The Conciliarist Tradition: Constitutionalism in the Catholic Church, 1300–1870* (Oxford University Press, 2003), 16.

44. Thomas M. Izbicki, "Papalist Reaction to the Council of Constance: Juan de Torquemada to the Present," *Church History* 55, no. 1 (1986): 14.

45. Eugene IV, *Etsi non dubitemus*, in *Epistolae Pontificiae ad Concilium Florentinum spectantes*, ed. Georg Hoffmann (Pontifical Oriental Institute, 1940), 1:7–9n248. The bull reproduces the text of Juan de Torquemada, *Summa de Ecclesia*, (Venice, 1561), chap. 100, 2. On this subject, see Izbicki, "Papalist Reaction to the Council of Constance." On the bull, see Regimius Bäumer, "Die Stellungnahme Eugens IV. Zum Konstanzer Superioritätsdekret in der Bulle 'Etsi non dubitemus,'" in *Das Konzil von Konstanz. Beiträge zu seiner Geschichte und Theologie*, ed. August Franzen and Wolfgang Müller (Herder, 1964).

46. Heinrich Denzinger, *Enchiridion Symbolorum* (Herder, 1991), § 1375, 472; Emily O'Brien, *The Commentaries of Pope Pius II (1458–1464) and the Crisis of the Fifteenth Century Papacy* (University of Toronto Press, 2015). O'Brien has recently shown how the conciliarist threat continued long after the end of the Council of Basel and further weakened the papacy's legitimacy, authority, relevance, and identity. She speaks of a "revisionist history" and argues that Pius II (Aeneas Piccolomini, 1458–1464), the pope and one of the greatest humanists of the time, in his *Commentaries*, sought to erase conciliarism from the historical record with silences, distractions, and distortions,

208 ❧ I. CONCILIARISM

as if it had barely existed: "The Commentaries opt for the more indirect assault of historical silence" (124), "Silence is a crucial weapon" (139), in contrast with his earlier pro-conciliar writings (157).

47. Denzinger, *Enchiridion Symbolorum*, § 1445, 485–486.

48. Francis Oakley, *Council Over Pope? Towards a Provisional Ecclesiology* (Herder & Herder, 1969), 26.

49. Wilhelm, "Councils (General)," in Herbermann et al., *Catholic Encyclopedia*, 423. The work does contain a single entry on "Gallicanism." See Degart, "Gallicanism," *Catholic Encyclopedia*, 355. In the volume 4 of the *New Catholic Encyclopedia* (2nd ed., Catholic University of America Press, 2003), two entries concerning councils appear: one on their history, 298–303, and the other on their theology, 303–306. In the same work there also appears an entry on "Conciliarism (History of)," by Brian Tierney, 53–56.

50. "Conciles," in *Dictionnaire de théologie catholique*, vol. 3, pt. 1, ed. Alfred Vacant and Eugène Mangeno (Letouzey & Ané, 1908), 636–676. See Oakley, *Council Over Pope?*, 122–124.

51. Henry Hallam, *View of the State of Europe During the Middle Ages* (J. Murray, 1901), 3:243–245.

52. Bernhard Hübler, *Die Constanzer Reformation und die Concordate von 1418* (Leipzig, 1867). See especially Johann Joseph Ignaz von Döllinger, *The Pope and the Council* (London, 1869), 302.

53. Figgis, *Political Thought from Gerson to Grotius*, 28: "The most revolutionary official document in the history of the world is the decree of the Council of Constance asserting its superiority to the Pope, and striving to turn into a tepid constitutionalism the Divine authority of a thousand years."

54. Tierney, *Foundations of the Conciliar Theory*, 177.

55. Tierney, 13.

56. For example, Yves-Marie Congar, "La collégialité de l'épiscopat et la primauté de l'évêque de Rome dans l'histoire," in *Ministères et communion ecclésiale* (Cerf, 1971), 116n32. On the reception of Tierney, see Sère, "Gerson ecclésiologue."

57. Paul De Vooght, *Les pouvoirs du concile et l'autorité du pape au concile de Constance* (Cerf, 1965). For his previous articles, see Paul De Vooght, "Le Conciliarisme aux Conciles de Constance et de Bâle," in *Le Concile et les conciles. Contribution à l'histoire de la vie conciliaire de l'Église*, ed. Bernard Botte (Chevetogne-Cerf, 1960); Paul De Vooght, "Le concile oecuménique de

I. CONCILIARISM ❧ 209

Constance et le conciliarisme," *Istina* 9 (1963): 57–86; Paul De Vooght, "Le Conciliarisme aux conciles de Constance et de Bâle (Compléments et precisions)," *Irénikon* 36 (1963): 61–75.

58. De Vooght, *Les pouvoirs du concile et l'autorité du pape au concile de Constance*, 61.

59. De Vooght, "Les controverses sur les pouvoirs du concile."

60. Hans Küng, *Structures of the Church* (University of Notre Dame Press, 1964), 254–255: "Just what was actually defined at Constance? Conciliar parliamentarism (along the lines of a radical conciliarism) was *not* defined. . . . In any case, however, what was *defined* was a distinct kind of superiority of the council (along the lines of at least moderate 'conciliar theory')."

61. Küng, 257.

62. Küng, 258–259. For Francis Oakley, see the bibliography at the end of this book.

63. See Erich Meuthen, "Das Basler Konzil in römisch-katholischer Sicht," *Theologische Zeitschrift* 38 (1982): 277–278n8.

64. Yves-Marie Congar, *L'Église de saint Augustin à l'époque moderne* (Cerf, 1970), 326.

65. Congar, 327.

66. Yves-Marie Congar, "Avertissement des éditeurs," in *Les pouvoirs du concile et l'autorité du pape au concile de Constance* (Cerf, 1965), 9.

67. Congar, 11: "Beyond this point of doctrine, we undoubtedly attach ourselves to the position of Professor H. Jedin. It seems that, in the decree, some of the determinations were linked to the truly exceptional and dramatic circumstances in which the Church found itself at the time."

68. Joseph Gill, *Constance et Bâle–Florence* (L'Orante, 1965), 50–51. See also Joseph Gill, "The Fifth Session of the Council of Constance," *Heythrop Journal* 5 (1964): 132, 134; Joseph Gill, "The Canonists and the Council of Constance," *Orientalia Christiana periodica* 32 (1966): 528–535; Joseph Gill, "The Representation of the *Universitas Fidelium* in the Councils of the Conciliar Period," in *Councils and Assemblies*, ed. G. J. Cuming and L. C. D. Baker (Cambridge University Press, 1971).

69. Gill, *Constance et Bâle–Florence*, 51.

70. Isfried Hermann Pichler, *Die Verbindlichkeit der Konstanzer Dekrete* (Herder, 1966); Heinz Hürten, "Zur Ekklesiologie der Konzilien von Konstanz und Basel," *Theologische Revue* 59 (1963): 361–372.

210 &) I. CONCILIARISM

71. Hubert Jedin, *Bischöfliches Konzil oder Kirchenparlament? Ein Beitrag zur Ekklesiologie der Konzilien von Konstanz und Basel* (Helbing und Lichtenhahn, 1963), 173.

72. August Franzen, "Le Concile de Constance devant l'histoire, Examen des problèmes qu'il soulève. État actuel de la recherche," *Concilium* 187 (1983): 29–68, especially 54: "None of the participants had the intention of defining an infallible dogma. The decree of Constance was not a dogmatic conciliar definition in the sense defined by Vatican I"; and 57.

73. Regimius Bäumer, *Nachwirkungen des konziliaren Gedankens in der Theologie und Kanonistik des frühen 16. Jahrhunderts* (Aschendorff, 1971).

74. Quoted in Thomas Prügl, *"Antiquis juribus et dictis sanctorum conformare:* Zur antikonziliaristichen Interpretation von *Haec sancta* auf dem Basler Konzil," *Annuarium historiae conciliorum* 31 (1999): 73.

75. Walter Brandmüller, *Das Konzil von Konstanz* (Ferdinand Schöningh, 2000), 2:426, 432, and 436.

76. Brandmüller, *Das Konzil von Konstanz,* 1:326.

77. Jürgen Miethke, review of Brandmüller, *Konzil von Konstanz,* in *Deutsches Archiv* 47 (1991): 692–695, quotation at 693.

78. Jürgen Miethke, review of Brandmüller, *Papst und Konzil im grossen Schisma,* in *Deutsches Archiv* 46 (1990): 667, "Stark legitimisch-römische Standpunkt."

79. Paul De Vooght, "Les controverses sur les pouvoirs du concile et l'autorité du pape au concile de Constance," *Revue théologique de Leuven* 1 (1970): 70–71.

80. Oakley, *Council Over Pope?,* 130; Francis Oakley, "The 'New Conciliarism' and Its Implications: A Problem in History and Hermeneutics," *Journal of Ecumenical Studies* 8 (1971): 829–830.

81. Oakley, *Council Over Pope?,* 74–76, 126, 130–131.

82. See especially Henri Maret, *Du concile général et de la paix religieuse* (Paris, 1869). On Maret, see Claude Bressolette, *Le Pouvoir dans la société et dans l'Église. L'ecclésiologie politique de Mgr Maret, dernier doyen de la faculté de théologie de la Sorbonne* (Cerf, 1984).

83. For a rich, if not exhaustive, bibliography on Oakley, see the bibliography at the end of this book.

84. Philippe Levillain, "Conciles oecuméniques," in *Dictionnaire historique de la papauté,* ed. Philippe Levillain (Fayard, 1994), 429–431. Translated into English as Philippe Levillain, "Councils, Ecumenical," in *The Papacy: An Encyclopedia,* ed. Philippe Levillain (Routledge, 2002), 427–430.

I. CONCILIARISM ❦ 211

85. Levillain, "Councils, Ecumenical," 429.
86. Aldo Landi, "Conciliarisme," in Levillain, *Dictionnaire historique de la papauté*, 436. English translation: Aldo Landi, "Conciliar Movement," in Levillain, *The Papacy*, 389.
87. Jean-Robert Armogathe et al., eds., *Histoire générale du christianisme* (Presses Universitaires de France, 2010).
88. Walter Brandmüller, "Les soubresauts de l'institution ecclésiastique," in Armogathe et al., *Histoire générale du christianisme*, 1339.
89. Brandmüller, 1341.
90. Brandmüller, 1354.
91. Brandmüller, 1355.
92. Brandmüller, 1355.
93. Charles McIlwain, *Constitutionalism: Ancient and Modern* (Cornell University Press, 1940).
94. George H. Sabine, *A History of Political Theory* (Henry Holt, 1956).
95. Cary Nederman, "Conciliarism and Constitutionalism: Jean Gerson and Medieval Political Thought," *History of European Ideas* 12, no. 2 (1990): 192.
96. Nederman, 201.
97. Jürgen Miethke, "Konziliarismus: Die neue Doctrin einer neuen Kirchenverfassung," in *Reform von Kirche und Reiche zur Zeit der Konzilien von Konstanz (1414–1418) und Basel (1431–1449)*, ed. Ivan Hlaváček and Alexander Patschovsy (Konstanz, 1996).
98. Tierney, *Foundations of the Conciliar Theory*, 11n2.
99. Karl Ubl, "Debating the Emergence of an Idea Debating the Emergence of an Idea: John of Paris and Conciliarism," in *John of Paris: Beyond Royal and Papal Power*, ed. Chris Jones (Brepols, 2015); Karl Ubl, "McIlwain und Constitutionalism: Ursprung, Wandel, und Bedeutung eines Forschungskonzepts," *Viator* 42 (2011): 321–342. See also Nederman, "Conciliarism and Constitutionalism."
100. Michiel Decaluwé, "A New and Disputable Edition-Text of the Decree *Haec sancta* of the Council of Constance (1415)," *Cristianesimo nella storia* 32, no. 2 (2006): 417–445; Michiel Decaluwé, "Three Ways to Read the Constance Decree *Haec sancta* (1415): Francis Zabarella, Jean Gerson and the Traditional Papal View of General Councils," in *The Church, the Councils, and Reform: The Legacy of the Fifteenth Century*, ed. Gerald Christianson et al. (Catholic University of America Press, 2008), 122–139.

212 ❧ 1. CONCILIARISM

101. Brandmüller, *Das Konzil von Konstanz*, 1:239–261; Thomas Morrissey, "The Decree *Haec sancta* and Cardinal Zabarella: His Role in Its Formulation and Interpretation," *Annuarium historiae conciliorum* 10 (1978): 145–176.

102. Thomas Prügl, "*Antiquis juribus et dictis sanctorum conformare*: Zur antikonziliaristichen Interpretation von *Haec sancta* auf dem Basler Konzil," *Annuarium historiae conciliorum* 31 (1999): 72–143.

103. Prügl, 83n28; Frantisek Palacky and Birk Ernst, *Monumenta Conciliorum Generalium Seculi Decimi Quinti* (Basel, 1873), 2:253.

104. Sebastian Provvidente, "The Synodial Practices of the Council of Constance (1414–1418): Between Symbol and Trace," in "Les nouveaux horizons de l'ecclésiologie: Du discours clérical à la science du social," ed. Frédéric Gabriel et al., special issue, *Bulletin du centre d'études médiévales d'Auxerre*, no. 7 (2013), https://doi.org/10.4000/cem.12743.

105. Provvidente, § 12.

106. Sebastian Provvidente, "The *Haec sancta synodus* Decree: Between Theology, Canon Law and History. Judicial Practices and *plenitudo potestatis*." *Temas medievales* 20, no. 1 (2012): § 2.

107. Provvidente, § 13.

108. Jean Gerson, *De auferibilitate pape ab ecclesia*, in *Œuvres complètes*, 3:308.

109. Provvidente, "The Synodial Practices of the Council of Constance," § 14.

110. Émilie Rosenblieh, "La violation des décrets conciliaires ou l'hérésie du pape: Le procès d'Eugène IV (1431–1447) au concile de Bâle d'après le manuscrit latin 1511 de la Bibliothèque nationale de France," *Revue belge de philologie et d'histoire* 86, nos. 3–4 (2009): 245–268.

111. Decree *Prospexit dominus*, published in *Amplissima collectio*, vol. 29, col. 180: "violatorem assiduum atque contemptoranem sacrorum canonum synodalium."

112. Émilie Rosenblieh, "L'Esprit saint, ou la légitimation de l'autorité conciliaire: Le procès du pape Eugène IV au concile de Bâle (1431–1439)," in *La Dramatique conciliaire. Coups de théâtre, tactique et sincérité des convictions dans les débats conciliaires de l'Antiquité à Vatican II*, ed. Guillaume Cuchet and Charles Mériaux (Presses Universitaires du Septentrion, 2019).

2. CONSTITUTIONALISM

1. Charles McIlwain, *Constitutionalism: Ancient and Modern* (Cornell University Press, 1940), 21: "All constitutional government is by definition limited

2. CONSTITUTIONALISM ᏩᎡ 213

government. . . . Constitutionalism has one essential quality: it is a legal limitation on government."

2. Carl Schmitt, *Political Theology* (MIT Press, 1985), 36. On secularization, the most recent overview is Monod, *La Querelle de la sécularisation de Hegel à Blumenberg.*

3. Olivier Beaud, "Constitution et constitutionnalisme," in *Dictionnaire de philosophie politique*, ed. Philippe Raynaud and Stéphane Rials (Presses Universitaires de France, 1996), 133.

4. Stéphane Rials, "Sur les origines canoniales des techniques constitutionnelles modernes," *Pouvoirs* 44 (1988): 150.

5. The same author mentions, without exact citation, Léo Moulin, *Le Monde vivant des religieux* (Calmann-Lévy, 1964).

6. Rials, "Sur les origines canoniales des techniques constitutionnelles modernes," esp. 144.

7. James M. Blythe, *Ideal Government and the Mixed Constitution in the Middle Ages* (Princeton University Press, 1992).

8. E. I. Brutus, *De la puissance légitime du Prince sur le peuple et du peuple sur le Prince* (EDHIS, 1977), 108. See Stéphane Rials, "Aux origines du constitutionnalisme écrit. Réflexions en marge d'un projet constitutionnel de la ligue (1588)," *Revue d'histoire des Facultés de droit et de la science juridique* 8 (1989): 234.

9. For this historical deployment, see Beaud, "Constitution et constitutionnalisme," and Olivier Beaud, "L'histoire du concept de constitution en France. De la constitution politique à la constitution comme statut juridique de l'État," *Jus politicum: Autour de la notion de constitution* 3 (2010): 31–59.

10. Thomas Paine, "Constitution, Governments and Charters," in *The Writings of Thomas Paine*, vol. 4, ed. Moncure Daniel Conway (G. P. Putnam's Sons, 1894).

11. Paine.

12. Emmanuel Joseph Sieyès, *Qu'est-ce que le tiers-état?* (Éditions du Boucher, 2002).

13. Carl Schmitt, *Verfassungslehre* (Duncker & Humblot, 1928).

14. Beaud, "Constitution et constitutionnalisme," 141–142.

15. Denis Baranger, *Parlementarisme des origines. Essai sur les conditions de formation d'un exécutif responsable en Angleterre (des années 1740 au début de l'âge victorien)* (Presses Universitaires de France, 1999).

16. See Alain Boureau, "Les cérémonies royales françaises entre performance juridique et compétence liturgique," *Annales ESC* 46, no. 6 (1991): 1256.

214 ❧ 2. CONSTITUTIONALISM

17. Jacques Derrida, *Force de loi* (Galilée, 2005).

18. Carolina Cerda-Guzman, *Cours de droit constitutionnel et des institutions de la Ve République* (Gualino, 2017), 65.

19. Albert Rigaudière, "La *lex vel constitutio* d'août 1374, 'première loi constitutionnelle de la monarchie française,'" in *Un Moyen Âge pour aujourd'hui. Mélanges offerts à Claude Gauvard*, ed. Julie Claustre et al. (Presses Universitaires de France, 2010), 188. See also Albert Rigaudière, "Un grand moment pour l'histoire du droit constitutionnel français: 1374–1409," *Journal des Savants* 2, no. 1 (2012): 281–370; Albert Rigaudière, "Les fonctions du mot constitution dans le discours politique et juridique du bas Moyen Âge français," *Revista internacional de los Estudios Vascos* 4 (2008): 15–51.

20. Rigaudière, "La *lex vel constitutio* d'août 1374," 171 and 187.

21. Rigaudière, 170–171, referencing Raymond Cazelles, *Société politique, noblesse et couronne sous Jean le Bon et Charles V* (Droz, 1982), 580. Alongside the British, American, and French traditions, further topics of discussion include the geo-cultural inscription of the German tradition, which will be discussed in the final section of this chapter, the Italian tradition around Enzo Sciacca, Francesco Donati, and Diego Quaglioni, or even the Spanish tradition. In 2014, François Foronda gathered case studies and invited historians from the Iberian Peninsula (José Manuel Nieto Soria, Carlos Laliena Corbera, and Sixto Sánchez-Lauro for Aragon; José Domingues for Portugal; and Pablo Fernandez Albaladejo for the modern era and the constitutional crisis of 1640) to reflect on them.

22. John Neville Figgis, *Political Thought from Gerson to Grotius, 1414–1625: Seven Studies* (Harper, 1960).

23. Brian Tierney, *Religion, Law, and the Growth of Constitutional Thought, 1150–1650* (Cambridge University Press, 1982), xi; Brian Tierney, "'Divided Sovereignty' at Constance: A Problem of Medieval and Early Modern Political Theory," *Annuarium historiae conciliorum* 7 (1975): 238–256.

24. Harold S. Laski, "Political Theory in the Later Middle Ages," in *Cambridge Medieval History*, vol. 8, *The Close of the Middle Ages*, ed. Charles V. Prévité-Orton and Zachary N. Brooke (Cambridge University Press, 1936), 638. See also Francis Oakley, "On the Road from Constance to 1688: The Political Thought of John Major and George Buchanan," *Journal of British Studies* 1, no. 2 (1962): 1–31.

2. CONSTITUTIONALISM ᘉ 215

25. Figgis, *Political Thought from Gerson to Grotius*, 28. See also Tierney, "'Divided Sovereignty' at Constance," 256.

26. "It was Figgis's great insight to see that the ideas of the fifteenth-century conciliarists did not die away altogether, that they had a continuing afterlife in writings on secular constitutional theory." Tierney, *Religion, Law, and the Growth of Constitutional Thought*, 3.

27. Tierney, *Foundations of the Conciliar Theory*.

28. Tierney, *Religion, Law, and the Growth of Constitutional Thought*, 2.

29. Brian Tierney, "'The Prince Is Not Bound by the Laws': Accursius and the Origins of the Modern State," *Comparative Studies in Society and History* 5, no. 4 (1963): 378–400; Charles McIlwain, *Growth of Political Thought in the West* (Macmillan, 1932).

30. Tierney, "'The Prince Is Not Bound by the Laws,'" 378–380. See also Adhémar Esmein, "La maxime *Princeps legitus solutus est* dans l'ancien droit public français," in *Essays in Legal History*, ed. Paul Vinogradoff (Oxford University Press, 1913), 210–214; and Alexander James Carlyle and Robert Warrand Carlyle, *A History of Medieval Political Theory in the West*, vol. 2 (W. Blackwood, 1922), 75.

31. McIlwain, "Constitutionalism in the Middle Ages," chap. 4 in *Constitutionalism*, 61–83.

32. On the debate regarding whether there existed a state in the Middle Ages, see Tierney, "'The Prince Is Not Bound by the Laws,'" 379–380, in which he cites Gaines Post's survey article arguing against those for whom the state was merely a postmedieval phenomenon, such as Meinecke, Kern, Gilbert, and Friedrich. See Gaines Post, "*Ratio publicae utilitatis, ratio status* und 'Staatsräson' (1100–1300)," *Die Welt als Geschichte* 21, no. 2 (1961): 8–28, 71–99.

33. McIlwain, *Constitutionalism*, 107, 133, and 136.

34. Tierney, *Religion, Law, and the Growth of Constitutional Thought*, 17.

35. For some amendments, see the introduction to the second edition of Tierney, *Foundations of the Conciliar Theory*, i–xxix, and the third edition, published by Cambridge University Press in 2010.

36. On this subject, see Bénédicte Sère, "La réception de Brian Tierney, *Foundations of the Conciliar Theory*, 1955," in *Ecclésiologies: Éléments d'histoire et d'historiographie*, ed. Frédéric Gabriel et al. (Beauchesne, forthcoming).

37. Antony Black, *Monarchy and Community: Political Ideas in the Later Conciliar Controversy, 1430–1450* (Cambridge University Press, 1970).

216 & 2. CONSTITUTIONALISM

38. Blythe, *Ideal Government and the Mixed Constitution in the Middle Ages.*

39. Blythe's list of targets was long: John Morall, Quentin Skinner, Charles McIlwain, Jean Dunbabin, Francis Wormuth, Georges de Lagarde, Robert W. Carlyle, Michael Wilks, and Thomas Gilby. See Blythe, 30n19.

40. Blythe, 243.

41. For a bibliography of Oakley, see sources cited in chapter 1, "Conciliarism."

42. Constantin Fasolt, "*Quod omnes tangit ab omnibus approbari debet*: The Words and the Meaning," in *In Jure veritas: Studies in Canon Law in Memory of Schafer Williams*, ed. Steven B. Bowman and Blanche E. Cody (University of Cincinnati College of Law, 1991), 21–55.

43. I thank Richard Figuier for this remark.

44. Gabriel Le Bras, *Les Origines canoniques du droit administratif* (Sirey, 1956).

45. Paul Ourliac, "Souveraineté et lois fondamentales dans le droit canonique du XVe siècle," in *Herrschaftsverträge, Wahlkapitulationen, Fundamentalgesetze*, ed. Rudolf Vierhaus (Vandenhoeck und Ruprecht, 1977), 22–33; Patrick Arabeyre, *Les idées politiques à Toulouse à la veille de la réforme: Recherches autour de l'œuvre de Guillaume Benoît (1455–1516)* (Presses de l'Université de Sciences Sociales de Toulouse, 2003). See also Tyler Lange, "Constitutional Thought and Practice in Early Sixteenth-Century France: Revisiting the Legacy of Ernst Kantorowicz," *Sixteenth Century Journal* 42, no. 4 (2011): 1018.

46. Tyler Lange, "Gallicanisme et Réforme: Le constitutionnalisme de Cosme Guymier (1486)," *Revue de l'histoire des religions* 226, no. 3 (2009): 293–313. On Cosme Guymier, see also Arabeyre, "Un enseignement de science politique."

47. Lange, "Gallicanisme et Réforme," 307.

48. Hubert Jedin, *Bischöfliches Konzil oder Kirchenparlament? Ein Beitrag zur Ekklesiologie der Konzilien von Konstanz und Basel* (Helbing und Lichtenhahn, 1963).

49. Tyler Lange, "L'ecclésiologie du royaume de France: L'hérésie devant le Parlement de Paris dans les années 1520," in "Les nouveaux horizons de l'ecclésiologie: Du discours clérical à la science du social," ed. Frédéric Gabriel et al., special issue, *Bulletin du centre d'études médiévales d'Auxerre*, no. 7 (2013), https://doi.org/10.4000/cem.12743.

50. Julien Théry, "Une hérésie d'État. Philippe le Bel, le procès des 'perfides templiers' et la pontificalisation de la royauté française," *Médiévales* 60 (2011): 157–186.

2. CONSTITUTIONALISM ❧ 217

51. Rials, "Sur les origines canoniales des techniques constitutionnelles modernes," 144.

52. Rials, 144.

53. Laurent Fonbaustier, *La déposition du pape hérétique. Une origine du constitutionnalisme?* (Mare et Martin, 2016).

54. For a reflection on the link between Whiggish historiography and the movement of the First Vatican Council in the nineteenth century, see Francis Oakley, "Anxieties of Influence: Skinner, Figgis, Conciliarism and Early Modern Constitutionalism," *Past and Present* 151, no. 1 (1996): 77.

55. Harold Berman, *Law and Revolution: The Formation of the Western Legal Tradition* (Harvard University Press, 1983), 250; Peter Moore, "Synodical Scenario," in *The Synod of Westminster: Do We Need It?* (SPCK Publishing, 1986), 1–9, quoted in Paul Vallière, *Conciliarism: A History of Decision-Making in the Church* (Cambridge University Press, 2012), 228n5.

56. Cary Nederman, "Constitutionalism—Medieval and Modern: Against Neo-Figgist Orthodoxy (Again)," *History of Political Thought* 17 (1996): 179–194, republished as chapter 3 in Cary Nederman, *Lineages of European Political Thought* (Catholic University of America Press, 2009).

57. Nederman, "Conciliarism and Constitutionalism."

58. Karl Ubl, "McIlwain und Constitutionalism: Ursprung, Wandel, und Bedeutung eines Forschungskonzepts," *Viator* 42 (2011): 321–342; Karl Ubl, "Debating the Emergence of an Idea: John of Paris and Conciliarism," in *John of Paris: Beyond Royal and Papal Power*, ed. Chris Jones (Brepols, 2015).

59. Beaud, "Constitution et constitutionnalisme," 134: "Only the *stricto sensu* meaning of constitutionalism will be retained here, because ancient or medieval constitutionalism has become obsolete since the birth of sovereignty and the modern State. . . . Contrary to what McIlwain asserts, the appearance of the modern State (which is sovereign) has completely downgraded medieval constitutionalism to the extent that sovereignty places non-State law at the disposal of the sovereign—customary law, for example."

60. Tierney, "'The Prince Is Not Bound by the Laws,'" relying on Post, *"Ratio publicae utilitatis, ratio status* und 'Staatsräson.'" Post discusses Meinecke, Kern, Gilbert, and Friedrich, for whom the emergence of the state was a postmedieval phenomenon. See also Brian Tierney, "Medieval Canon Law and Western Constitutionalism," *Catholic Historical Review* 52 (1966): 2n2, citing Ernst Kantorowicz, *The King's Two Bodies* (Princeton University Press,

218 ᛝ 2. CONSTITUTIONALISM

1957), and Gaines Post, *Studies in Medieval Legal Thought* (Princeton University Press, 1964).

61. The rest of this passage owes much to Olivier Beaud's preface, "Carl Schmitt ou le juriste engagé," in Carl Schmitt, *Théorie de la constitution* (Presses Universitaires de France, 1993), 5–113.

62. Beaud, 55.

63. Beaud, 93; and Carl Schmitt, *The Nomos of the Earth in the International Law of* Jus Publicum Europaeum (Telos Press, 2006). See also Carl Schmitt, *Hugo Preuss. Sein Staatsbegriff und seine Stellung in der deutschen Staatslehre* (Mohr Siebeck, 1930), 71: "The critical moment in the history of the concept is when the adversary disappears."

64. Kantorowicz, *The King's Two Bodies.*

65. Alain Boureau, *Kantorowicz: Stories of a Historian* (Johns Hopkins University Press, 2001), 103–105.

66. Ernst Kantorowicz, "Mysteries of State: An Absolutist Concept and Its Late Medieval Origins," *Harvard Theological Review* 48, no. 1 (1955): 65–91.

67. Cf. Boureau, *Kantorowicz*, 100.

68. Boureau, 106.

69. Marcel Gauchet, *The Disenchantment of the World: A Political History of Religion* (Princeton University Press, 1997), 146.

70. Boureau, *Kantorowicz*, 100.

71. Jean-François Courtine, "L'héritage scolastique dans la problématique théologico-politique de l'âge classique," in *L'État baroque (1610–1652). Regards sur la pensée politique de la France du premier XVIIe siècle*, ed. Henry Méchoulan (Vrin, 1985).

72. Figgis, *Political Thought from Gerson to Grotius*, 41 and 43, quoted in Courtine, "L'héritage scolastique," 97.

73. Courtine, 109.

74. Courtine, 109.

75. Alain Boureau, "Les cérémonies royales françaises entre performance juridique et compétence liturgique," *Annales ESC* 46, no. 6 (1991): 1253–1264.

76. Boureau, 1261.

77. Boureau, 1260.

78. Among other titles, see especially François Foronda, ed., *Avant le contrat social. Le contrat politique dans l'Occident médiéval (XIIIe–XVe siècle)* (Éditions de la Sorbonne, 2011), and François Foronda and Ana Isabel Carrasco,

3. COLLEGIALISM ❧ 219

Du contrat d'alliance au contrat politique. Cultures et sociétés politiques dans la péninsule Ibérique à la fin du Moyen Âge (Méridiennes, 2007).

79. Jean-Philippe Genet, "Du contrat à la constitution," in *Avant le contrat social. Le contrat politique dans l'Occident médiéval (XIIIe–XVe siècle)*, ed. François Foronda (Publications de la Sorbonne, 2011), esp. 703.

80. Christine Carpenter, *The Wars of the Roses: Politics and the Constitution in England, c. 1437–1509* (Cambridge University Press, 1997), esp. 21–26. See also Watts, "Community and Contract in Later Medieval England."

81. Genet, "Du contrat à la constitution," 704–705.

3. COLLEGIALISM

1. Translator's note: In the original French, the word used for the "ism" discussed in this chapter is *collégialité*, which does not have a perfect English equivalent; in American usage, "collegiality" is broadly understood as referring to positive working relationships in general, rather than referring to the specific theory of Church polity intended here. Instead, *collégialité* has here been translated as "collegialism," which the *Merriam-Webster Dictionary* defines as "a theory of church polity that defines the church as a society of voluntary members independent of the state, self-governing, and with authority vested in the members." Another valid translation would be "corporatism," meaning the organization of a society—here, the Church—into separate individual organs, each with their own jurisdiction.

2. Bernard Sesboüé, preface to *Heurs et malheurs de la "collégialité." Pontificats et synodes face à la réception de Vatican II*, by Jan Grootaers (Peeters, 2012), xi: "La collégialité épiscopale est le nom nouveau du thème classique, et chargé d'une histoire conflictuelle, du rapport entre le primat romain et l'épiscopat. La supériorité d'autorité du pape sur le Concile a été l'objet de nombre de conflits qui sont allés jusqu'à la crise du conciliarisme." (Episcopal collegialism is the new name for the classic theme of the relationship between Roman primacy and the episcopate, and it is charged with this conflicting history. The papal authority's superiority over the council was the subject of a number of conflicts, which went as far as the crisis of conciliarism.)

3. Hervé Legrand, "Collégialité," in *Dictionnaire critique de théologie*, ed. Jean-Yves Lacoste (Presses Universitaires de France, 1998), 233.

220 ∽ 3. COLLEGIALISM

4. "Constitution on the Church," in *The Third Session: The Debates and Decrees of Vatican Council II, September 14 to November 21, 1964*, ed. Xavier Rynne (Farrar, Straus and Giroux, 1965), 320 § 28.

5. "Constitution on the Church," 313, § 22.

6. Legrand, "Collegialité," 233–234.

7. "Constitution on the Church," 318, § 26: "This power, which they personally exercise in Christ's name, is proper, ordinary, and immediate."

8. "Constitution on the Church," 318, § 26: "Bishops, as vicars and ambassadors of Christ, govern the particular Churches entrusted to them."

9. "Constitution on the Church," 318, § 26: "Nor are they to be regarded as vicars of the Roman pontiffs, for they exercise an authority that is proper to them, and are quite correctly called 'prelates,' heads of the people whom they govern."

10. "Constitution on the Church," § 23.

11. "Constitution on the Church," § 23.

12. On this subject, see André de Halleux, "La collégialité dans l'Église ancienne," *Revue théologique de Leuven* 24 (1993): 433–454; Hervé Legrand et al., eds., *Les Conférences épiscopales. Théologie, statut canonique, avenir* (Cerf, 1988)

13. See Yves-Marie Congar, "Le peuple fidèle et la fonction prophétique de l'Église (seconde partie)," *Irénikon* 24 (1951): 440–466. Grootaers rightly remarked that around the same time other pioneers translated *sobornost* as "communion." Grootaers, *Heurs et malheurs de la "collégialité,"* 55n40.

14. Yves-Marie Congar, *Ministères et communion ecclésiale* (Cerf, 1971), 132.

15. On collegialism at the First Vatican Council, see Jérôme Hamer, "Le corps épiscopal uni au pape, son autorité dans l'Église, d'après les documents du 1er concile du Vatican," *Revue des sciences philosophiques et théologiques* 45 (1961): 21–31; Jean-Pierre Torrell, *La théologie de l'episcopat au 1er concile du Vatican* (Cerf, 1961).

16. Yves-Marie Congar, *Journal d'un théologien* (Cerf, 2005), 333.

17. Yves-Marie Congar, *Mon journal du concile* (Cerf, 2002), 2:164.

18. Congar, 1:472.

19. Congar, 1:535. Original emphasis.

20. Congar, 1:438.

21. Congar, 1:469.

22. Congar, 1:469.

23. Congar, 1:471.

3. COLLEGIALISM ❧ 221

24. Congar, 2:37.

25. Congar, 2:39.

26. Congar, 2:59.

27. Congar, 2:26. Original emphasis.

28. Yves-Marie Congar, "Primauté et collégialilté. À propos du synode des évêques (octobre 1969)," occasional paper of the *Recherches et dialogues Saint-Jacques* 8 (1969): 2.

29. Sesboüé, preface to Grootaers, *Heurs et malheurs de la "collégialité,"* xi.

30. B. C. Butler and Jean Marie R. Tillard, "The Pope with the Bishops," *Tablet*, October 11, 1980, 988.

31. See Hervé Legrand, "Collégialité des évêques et communion des Églises dans la réception de Vatican II," *Revue des sciences philosophiques et théologiques* 75 (1991): 545–568

32. Congar, *Mon journal du concile*, 2:243.

33. Eric Maheu, introduction to Congar, *Mon journal du concile*, 1:lv.

34. Grootaers, *Heurs et malheurs de la "collégialité,"* 44.

35. "Explanatory Note," in Rynne, *The Third Session*, 349, § 2: "'*Communion*' is a concept which was held in high honor in the ancient Church (as it is even today, especially in the East). But it does not mean a kind of vague *affection*, but an *organic* relationship which demands juridical form and at the same time is animated by charity."

36. Quoted in Congar, *Mon journal du concile*, 2:223.

37. John Paul II, *Post-Synodal Apostolic Exhortation* Christifideles Laici *of His Holiness John Paul II on the Vocation and the Mission of the Lay Faithful in the Church and the World* (Vatican Polyglot Press, 1988), 48, § 19.

38. Quoting Paul VI: Joël-Benoît D'Onorio, "Primauté collégiale: Sur une imprécision conciliaire et sa correction pontificale," in "La Synodalité. La participation au gouvernement dans l'Église. Actes du VIIe Congrès international de Droit canonique, Paris, UNESCO, 21–28 September 1990," special issue, *L'année canonique* (1992): 223.

39. Quoted in Grootaers, *Heurs et malheurs de la "collégialité,"* 47.

40. Quoted in Grootaers, 180.

41. Quoted in Grootaers, 21.

42. Sesboüé, preface to Grootaers, x.

43. "Explanatory Note," in Rynne, *The Third Session*, 349–350, § 3–4.

44. "Explanatory Note," 350.

222 ∞ 3. COLLEGIALISM

45. Jean Colson, *L'épiscopat catholique. Collégialité et primauté dans les trois premiers siècles de l'Église* (Cerf, 1963), 133.

46. Congar, "Primauté et collégialité," 5.

47. Bernard-Dominique Dupuy, preface to Congar, *Mon journal du concile*, 1:xv. Bernard Dupuy succeeded Congar as chair of fundamental theology at Saulchoir in 1960. At Vatican II, he was an expert on ecumenical issues in the service of the French bishops. Before the council, he, at Congar's invitation, coedited the 1962 volume *L'épiscopat et l'Église universelle*.

48. Yves-Marie Congar, *L'Église de saint Augustin à l'époque moderne* (Cerf, 1970), 337.

49. Yves-Marie Congar, "Notes sur le destin de l'idée de collégialité épiscopale en Occident au Moyen Âge (VIIe–XVIe siècle)," in *La collégialité épiscopale. Histoire et théologie* (Cerf, 1965), 118. See also 127: "With the growth of the role of cardinals, brilliant minds were for almost two centuries deceived by the chimera of a divine institution of cardinals: The ideas of apostolic succession and collegialism were thus quite broadly seized upon by the ideology of a function of cardinals to which, moreover, was attributed something that had never been claimed for episcopal collegialism—namely, the sharing of the very function and primacy of the pope." And on 128: "The Middle Ages were inclined to see universal office and authority of the collegiate type only through participation in a sort of mystical personality of the pope in the college of cardinals."

50. Congar, *L'Église de saint Augustin à l'époque moderne*, 308.

51. Pierre d'Ailly, *Tractatus de potestate ecclesiastica* (October 1, 1416), in Jean Gerson, *Opera omnia*, ed. Louis Ellies du Pin (Peter de Hondt, 1728), 2:940.

52. D'Ailly in Gerson, 940.

53. D'Ailly in Gerson, 930: "Apostoli coassistebant Petro."

54. D'Ailly in Gerson, 946.

55. D'Ailly in Gerson, 935.

56. Hostiensis was quoted in Tierney, *Foundations of the Conciliar Theory*, 151–153, and in Congar, "Notes sur le destin de l'idée de collégialité épiscopale," 120.

57. Congar, "Notes sur le destin de l'idée de collégialité épiscopale," 120.

58. Congar, 120.

59. Congar, 120.

3. COLLEGIALISM ☙ 223

60. Cf. Brian Tierney, *Foundations of the Conciliar Theory: The Contribution of the Medieval Canonists from Gratian to the Great Schism* (Cambridge University Press, 1955), 150.

61. Tierney, 152–153, quoting Hostiensis: "Dictum est non *judicabis* in singulari sed *judicabitis* in plurali, ut non solum papa sed et cardinales includerentur etiam in expressione plenitudinis potestatis" (What was said was not *judicabis* in the singular but *judicabitis* in the plural, and not only the pope but also even the cardinals would be included in the expression of *plenitudo potestatis*) (Hostiensis, *Lectura in quinque Decretalium Gregorianarum Libros* [Rembolt, 1512], here *Lectura ad* IV, XVII, 3 fol., 38v) and "Sed numquid collegium cardinalium habet jurisdictionem papae et etiam exercitium ipsius . . . tu teneas quod sic" (But does the college of cardinals have the jurisdiction of the pope and also the exercise thereof? . . . You hold that it is so) (*Lectura ad* V, XXXVIII, 14 fol., 102r).

62. Jean Gerson, *De auctoritate concilii*, starting: "In sequenti opere ad videndum de auctoritate congregationis fidelium" (between November 15, 1408, and March 25, 1409), in *Œuvres complètes*, ed. Palémon Glorieux, 11 vols. (Desclée de Brouwer, 1960–1973), 6:114 § 269, *quinta conclusio*.

63. Charles Moeller, "La collégialité au concile de Constance," in *La collégialité épiscopale: Histoire et théologie*, ed. Jacques Dupont and Yves-Marie Congar (Cerf, 1965), 142.

64. Véronique Beaulande-Barraud, "Jean Gerson et les cas réservés: Un enjeu ecclésiologique et pastoral," *Revue d'histoire de l'Église de France* 100 (2014): 301–318.

65. Jean Gerson, *De plenitude potestatis ecclesiasticae*, starting: "Concordia quod plenitudo potestatis ecclesiasticae sit in summo pontifice et in Ecclesia," in *Œuvres complètes*, 6:§ 250, *secunda conclusio*. See also Rowan Dorin, "The Bishop as Lawmaker in Late Medieval Europe," *Past and Present* 253, no. 1 (2021): 45–82.

66. Jean Gerson, *Conclusiones octo de jure episcoporum*, starting: "Ad justificationem condemnationis factae" (February 2, 1416), in *Œuvres complètes*, 6:175–178 § 278.

67. The use of the term *collegium* without a qualifier usually referred in general to the collegialism of cardinals. For example, Jean Gerson, *Acta de schismate tollendo*, starting: Pensata diuturnitate schismatis et extraneitate" (late December 1406–early January 1407), in *Œuvres complètes*, 6:98 § 265.

224   3. COLLEGIALISM

68. Jean Gerson, *De auctoritate concilii*, starting: "In sequenti opere ad videndum de auctoritate congregationis fidelium" (between November 15, 1408, and March 25, 1409), in *Œuvres complètes*, 6:115, § 269.

69. Gerson, *De auctoritate concilii*, 115, *quarta conclusio*. Charles Moeller has noted that Hermann de Schildesche used the term *inobliquabilis* regarding the pope. Moeller, "La collégialité au concile de Constance," 138n22.

70. Gerson, *De auctoritate concilii*, 115, *quinta conclusio*.

71. Jean Gerson, *De consiliis evangelicis et statu perfectionis*, starting: "Quaestio determinanda utrum aurora mane rubens," in *Œuvres complètes*, 3:25 § 88.

72. Moeller, "La collégialité au concile de Constance," 138.

73. Gerson, *De auctoritate concilii*, in *Œuvres complètes*, 6:116.

74. Gerson, *De auctoritate concilii*, 117.

75. On the connection between collegialism and representivity, see also Gerson, *De auctoritate concilii*, 118.

76. Jean Gerson, *Nova positio*, starting: "Voluimus propter elucidationem veritatis" (September 1415), in *Œuvres complètes*, 6:151 § 273.

77. See Francis Oakley, "Conciliarism at the Fifth Lateran Council?," *Church History* 29 (1972): 452–463; Benoît Schmitz, "La pragmatique sanction de Bourges et ses usages dans les controverses ecclésiologiques autour des conciles de Pise II et Latran V," unpublished manuscript, May 2011.

78. Cf. Yves-Marie Congar, "Notes sur le destin de l'idée de collégialité épiscopale en Occident au Moyen Âge (VIIe–XVIe siècle)," in *La collégialité épiscopale. Histoire et théologie* (Cerf, 1965), 10.

79. Congar, 10.

80. Congar, 12: "D'un autre côté, la notion de collège avait, chez les canonistes ou les juristes médiévaux, une précision qui la disposait mal à exprimer l'idée théologique de collégialité épiscopale" (Among medieval canonists or jurists, on the other hand, the concept of the college had a specificity that made it difficult to express the theological concept of episcopal collegialism).

81. Congar, 12.

82. Cf. Michel Parisse, "Collégiale," in *Dictionnaire du Moyen Âge*, ed. Claude Gauvard et al. (Presses Universitaires de France, 2002), 307; Henri-Jacques Légier, "Les églises collégiales en France, des origines au XVe siècle" (PhD diss., Faculté de droit de Paris, Panthéon-Sorbonne University, 1995).

83. Anne Massoni, *La collégiale Saint-Germain l'Auxerrois de Paris (1380–1510)* (Presse Universitaires de Limoges, 2009), 39.

84. Massoni, 39 and 45.

4. RETHINKING REFORM ❧ 225

85. Massoni, 45 and 54.

86. Massoni, 51.

87. Massoni, 53.

88. Massoni, 57 and 59.

89. Hélène Millet, "La participation des abbayes aux assemblées du clergé réunies par le roi de France de 1395 à 1408," in *L'Église du Grand Schisme, 1378–1417* (Picard, 2009), 55.

90. Albert Rigaudière, "Assemblées politiques," in Gauvard et al., *Dictionnaire du Moyen Âge*, 97–101.

91. Rigaudière, 97.

92. Rigaudière, 100.

93. Vincent Tabbagh, *Les évêques dans le royaume de France au XIVe siècle* (Éditions Universitaires de Dijon, 2015).

94. Tabbagh, 10.

95. Hélène Millet, "Du conseil au consile," in *L'Église du Grand Schisme*, 44.

96. Millet, 42–43.

97. See Bruno Lemesle, *Le gouvernement des évêques. La charge pastorale au milieu du Moyen Âge* (Presses Universitaires de Rennes, 2015), for example 216: "Les canonistes raisonnaient en fonction de la plénitude de puissance du pape dont ils justifiaient l'accroissement et dont l'un des effets était la réduction de la faculté pour les évêques d'accorder des dispenses" (The canonists reasoned according to the plenitude of power of the pope, the increase of which they justified and one of the effects of which was the reduction of the faculty for bishops to grant dispensations).

4. RETHINKING REFORM

1. Étienne Delaruelle, *L'Église au temps du Grand Schisme et de la crise conciliaire (1378–1449)*, vol. 14 of *Histoire de l'Église*, ed. Augustin Fliche and Victor Martin (Bloud & Gay, 1964), 883.

2. Delaruelle, 883. On this subject, see also Pierre Chaunu, *Le temps des réformes. La crise de la chrétienté. L'éclatement 1250–1550* (Fayard, 1975).

3. Delaruelle, 884. Delaruelle titled his first chapter "La question de la réforme à la fin du XIVe siècle" (The question of reform in the late fourteenth century).

4. Gerd Tellenbach, *Die westliche Kirche vom 10. bis zum frühen 12. Jahrhundert* (Vandenhoeck & Ruprecht, 1998); Florian Mazel, "Pour une redéfinition de

226 &3 4. RETHINKING REFORM

la réforme grégorienne. Éléments d'introduction," *Cahiers de Fanjeaux* 48 (2013): 9–38.

5. Yves-Marie Congar, "Le mouvement réformateur," in *Cardinal Yves Congar. Écrits réformateurs*, ed. Jean-Pierre Jossua (Cerf, 1995), 184.

6. Congar, 177. See also John O'Malley, "Reform, Historical Consciousness, and Vatican II's Aggiornamento," *Theological Studies* 32 (1971): 573–601; John O'Malley, *Trent and All That* (Harvard University Press, 2000), 2; and Xavier de Montclos, *Réformer l'Église. Histoire du réformisme catholique en France de la Révolution jusqu'à nos jours* (Cerf, 1998), 156: "*Aggiornamento*. One might remark that this expression—'update'—was a subtle understatement, somewhere between two unspeakable terms: 'reform,' which has been in delicate usage since the sixteenth century, and 'self-criticism.' At the same time, it meant that the council would not be directed against anyone, and that it was above all addressed to the Church itself."

7. Hubert Jedin, *Geschichte der Konzils von Trent*, 2nd ed. (Herder, 1951), 1:11.

8. Isnard Wilhelm Frank, "Ein antikonziliarer Traktat des Wiener Dominikaners Leonhard Huntpichler von 1447/1448," *Freiburger Zeitschrift für Theologie und Philosophie* 18 (1971): 66.

9. Miramon, "L'invention de la Réforme grégorienne."

10. Johannes Voigt, *Hildebrand als Pabst Gregorius VII und sein Zeitalter*, rev. ed. (Landes Industrie Comptoirs, 1846).

11. See Julia Barrow, "Ideas and Applications of Reform," in *Early Medieval Chistianities, c. 600–c. 1100*, vol. 3 of *The Cambridge History of Christianity*, ed. Thomas F. X. Noble and Julia M. H. Smith (Cambridge University Press, 2008), 347.

12. The following lines owe much to Phillip H. Stump, "The Influence of Gerhart Ladner's *The Idea of Reform*," in *Reform and Renewal in the Middle Ages and the Renaissance: Studies in Honor of Louis Pascoe, SJ*, ed. Thomas M. Izbicki and Christopher M. Bellitto (Brill, 2000).

13. Gerhart B. Ladner, *The Idea of Reform: Its Impact on Christian Thought and Action in the Age of the Fathers* (Harvard University Press, 1959), 35.

14. Henri-Irénée Marrou, "Review of Gr. B. Ladner, *The Idea of Reform. Its Impact on Christian Thought and Action in the Age of the Fathers*," *Revue d'Histoire Ecclésiastique* 57 (1962): 139.

15. Herbert Musirillo, "Book Review: *The Idea of Reform: Its Impact on Christian Thought and Action in the Age of the Fathers*," *Theological Studies* 21, no. 3

(1960): 472–474. The reviewer was the author of *The Acts of the Christian Martyrs* (Clarendon Press, 1972).

16. Robert M. Grant, "Book Review: *The Idea of Reform: Its Impact on Christian Thought and Action in the Age of the Fathers*," *Speculum* 36, no. 1 (1961): 140–142.

17. Christine Mohrmann, "Review: *The Idea of Reform, Its Impact on Christian Thought and Action in the Age of the Fathers* by Gerhart B. Ladner," *Vigiliae Christianae* 16, nos. 3–4 (1962): 235–237.

18. H. Fichtenau, "Ladner, Gerhart B., *The Idea of Reform. Its Impact on Christian Thought and Action in the Age of the Fathers*," *Institut für Österreichische Geschichtsforschung, Mitteilungen* 69 (1961): 116–118.

19. Friedrich Kempf, "*The Idea of Reform. Its Impact on Christian Thought and Action in the Age of the Fathers*," *Historisches Jahrbuch* 82 (1962): 235–237.

20. Klaus Thraede, "*The Idea of Reform: Its Impact on Christian Thought and Action in the Age of the Fathers*," *Jahrbuch für Antike und Christentum* 4 (1961): 168–170.

21. Lived 1912–2000. Austrian medievalist at the University of Vienna (1962–1983); director of the Institute of Austrian Historical Research.

22. Born 1934. Austrian medieval historian at the University of Vienna; director of the Institute of Austrian Historical Research.

23. Born 1953. Austrian high medievalist specializing in human migration in late antiquity; director of the Institute of Institut für Mittelalterforschung at the Austrian Academy of Sciences and professor at the University of Vienna.

24. Gerhart B. Ladner, *Erinnerungen*, ed. Herwig Wolfram and Walter Pohl (Verlag der österreichischen Akademie der Wissenschaften, 1994).

25. Particularly John O'Malley, *Praise and Blame in Renaissance Rome: Rhetoric, Doctrine and Reform in the Sacred Orators of the Papal Court, c. 1450–1521* (Duke University Press, 1979). See also John O'Malley, *Giles of Viterbo on Church and Reform: A Study in Renaissance Thought* (Brill, 1968).

26. Steven Ozment, *The Age of Reform, 1250–1550: An Intellectual and Religious History of Late Medieval and Reformation Europe* (Yale University Press, 1980).

27. John Van Engen, *Sisters and Brothers of the Common Life: The Devotio moderna and the World of the Later Middle Ages* (University of Pennsylvania Press, 2008). See also Dieter Mertens, "Monastische Reformbewegungen des 15. Jh: Ideen-Ziele-Resultate," in *Reform von Kirche und Reich zur Zeit der Konzilien von Konstanz (1414–1418), und Basel (1431–1449). Konstanz-Prager*

228 ❧ 4. RETHINKING REFORM

historisches Kolloquium (11–17 Oktober 1993), ed. Ivan Hlaváček and Alexander Patschovsky (Universitätsverlag Konstanz, 1996).

28. Ladner's debate with Tellenbach opened with the following article: Gerd Tellenbach, "Aspects of Mediaeval Thought on Church and State," *Review of Politics* 9 (1947): 403–422, which was reprinted in Ladner, *Images and Ideas in the Middle Ages*, 435–456, 1028–1029, and 1045. See also Karl F. Morrison, *The Mimetic Tradition of Reform in the West* (Princeton University Press, 2014).

29. Louis B. Pascoe, "Gerhart Ladner's *The Idea of Reform*. Reflections on Terminology and Ideology," in *Reassessing Reform: A Historical Investigation into Church Renewal*, ed. Christopher M. Bellitto and David Zachariah Flanagin (Catholic University of America Press, 2012), 31.

30. Louis B. Pascoe, *Jean Gerson: Principles of Church Reform* (Brill, 1973).

31. Louis B. Pascoe, *Church and Reform: Bishops, Theologians and Canon Lawyers in the Thought of Pierre d'Ailly* (Brill, 2005).

32. His articles most narrowly focused on reform were Louis B. Pascoe, "Jean Gerson: Mysticism, Conciliarism and Reform," *Annuarium historiae conciliorum* 6 (1974): 135–153, and Louis B. Pascoe, "Jean Gerson: The *Ecclesia primitiva* and Reform," *Traditio* 30 (1974): 379–409.

33. Hélène Millet and Monique Maillard-Luypaert, *Le Schisme et la Pourpre: Le cardinal Pierre d'Ailly, homme de science et de foi* (Cerf, 2015), 207.

34. Millet and Maillard-Luypaert, 209.

35. Yves-Marie Congar, *Vraie et fausse réforme dans l'Église*, 2nd ed. (Cerf, 1968). The book was planned in 1944–1946, although it was not published until 1950.

36. Yves-Marie Congar, "Renouvellement de l'Esprit et réforme de l'Institution," in Jean-Pierre Jossua, *Cardinal Yves Congar*, 199.

37. Congar, 199.

38. Yves-Marie Congar, "La pensée de Möhler et l'ecclésiologie orthodoxe," *Irénikon* 12 (1935): 328. "L'Église est à la fois Corps mystique et Société hiérarchique, organisme de vie et organisation; plus profondément Corps mystique que Société hiérarchique et organisme qu'organisation indissolublement l'un et l'autre" (The Church is both mystical body and hierarchical society, an organism of life and organization; it is more profoundly a mystical body than a hierarchical society and an organism more than an organization, both indissolubly).

39. Congar, 196. In this work, Congar proposed four historical examples of reforms that were both spiritual and structural—for example, on 200: "Aussi

4. RETHINKING REFORM ❧ 229

l'histoire nous offre-t-elle des exemples significatifs de réformes qui furent à la fois spirituelles et de structures. En voici quatre: la réforme du XIe siècle dite grégorienne, celle des ordres mendiants au XIIIe siècle, celle issue du concile de Trente, celle de Vatican II" (History also offers us significant examples of reforms that were both spiritual and structural. Here are four: the so-called Gregorian reform of the eleventh century, the reform of the mendicant orders in the thirteenth century, the reform resulting from the Council of Trent, and the reform of Vatican II).

40. Congar, 198–199.

41. Congar, "Renouvellement de l'Esprit et réforme de l'Institution," 204–205.

42. Congar, 205.

43. Giuseppe Alberigo, "L'amore alla chiesa: Dalla riforma all'aggiornamento," in *"Con tutte le tue forze." I nodi della fede cristiana oggi. Omaggio a Giuseppe Dossetti*, ed. Angelina Alberigo and Giuseppe Alberigo (Marietti, 1993).

44. Philippe Levillain, "Vatican II en contre-chant," in *Rome, l'unique objet de mon ressentiment: Regards critiques sur la papauté*, ed. Philippe Levillain (École Française de Rome, 2011), 280.

45. Étienne Fouilloux, "Recherche théologique et magistère romain en 1952. Une 'affaire' parmi d'autres," *Le Magistère, Revue des sciences religieuses* 71, no. 2 (1983): 269–286.

46. Étienne Fouilloux, "La phase antépréparatoire (1959–1960)," in *Histoire du concile Vatican II*, ed. Giuseppe Alberigo (Cerf, 1997), 1:87. On the neologism, which John XXIII did not invent, see note 2 on the same page: "Convoqué à Rome en novembre-décembre 1950, le premier congrès international des religieux a pour but la *'accomodata renovatio, ossia, in volgare, l'aggiornamento'* des ordres et congrégations, selon le cardinal Piazza" (Convened in Rome in November and December 1950, the first international congress of clergy aimed at the 'accomodata renovatio, ossia, in volgare, l'aggiornamento' of orders and parishes, according to Cardinal Piazza), citing *La Documentation Catholique*, 31 December, col. 1699. See also Alberigo, "L'amore alla chiesa."

47. Giuseppe Alberigo, "Réforme en tant que critère de l'histoire de l'Église," *Revue d'histoire ecclésiastique* 76 (1981): 72–81. Alberigo's conclusions are followed here. On the bibliography for Jedin, which includes 662 titles up to the year 1976 alone, see Robert Samulski, "Bibliographie Hubert Jedin," in *Reformata Reformanda. Festgabe für Hubert Jedin zum 17 Juni 1965*, edited by

230   4. RETHINKING REFORM

Erwin Iserloh and Konrad Repgen (Aschendorff, 1965), 2:665–715, and Robert Samulski, "Bibliographie Hubert Jedin, 1965–1976," *Annuarium historiae conciliorum* 8 (1976): 612–637.

48. Jedin, *Geschichte der Konzils von Trient*.

49. Alberigo, "Réforme en tant que critère de l'histoire de l'Église."

50. Alberigo, 73. See also Hubert Jedin, *Die Erforschung der kirchlichen Reformationsgeschichte seit 1876. Leistungen und Aufgaben der deutschen Katholiken* (Aschendorff, 1931).

51. Alberigo, "Réforme en tant que critère de l'histoire de l'Église," 74.

52. Alberigo, 74.

53. Alberigo, 75.

54. Alberigo, 76, quoting Hubert Jedin, *Storia del Concilio di Trento* (Morcelliana, 1949), 1:14.

55. See Alberigo, 78.

56. Hubert Jedin, *La Storia della Chiesa e teologia e storia* (Vita e pensiero, 1968), 8–9, quoted in Alberigo, 78.

57. Alberigo, 78.

58. Jedin, *La Storia della Chiesa e teologia e storia*, 11.

59. Alberigo, "Réforme en tant que critère de l'histoire de l'Église," 79.

60. Alberigo, 80.

61. On this point, I take the liberty of repeating some analyses developed in Bénédicte Sère, *Les débats d'opinion à l'heure du Grand Schisme. Ecclésiologie et politique* (Brepols, 2016), particularly in chapter 4, "Le débat, un contre-pouvoir: *Reformatio* et *limitatio*."

62. See the example of Guillaume de Diguleville, as discussed in Bénédicte Sère, "*Forme, déformation, reformation*: Les corps difformes et la théologie de l'image de Dieu en l'homme dans le *Pèlerinage de l'âme*," in *Regards croisés sur le* Pèlerinage de l'âme *de Guillaume de Digulleville*, ed. Marie Bassano et al. (Brepols, 2015), 137–143.

63. Henry of Langenstein, *Concilium pacis de unione et reformation ecclesiae in concilio universali quaerenda*, starting: "Epistola concilii pacis ad universos. Capitulum primum scismatis causam," in Jean Gerson, *Opera omnia*, ed. Louis Ellies du Pin (Peter de Hondt, 1728), 2:810.

64. Henry of Langenstein, in Gerson, *Concilium pacis de unione*, 2:825.

65. Jean Gerson, "Sermo de vita clericorum," starting: "Poenitemini et crediti evangelio," in *Œuvres complètes*, ed. Palémon Glorieux, 11 vols. (Desclée de Brouwer, 1960–1973), 5:456 § 239.

4. RETHINKING REFORM ᘓ 231

66. Jean Gerson, Sermon of March 23, 1415, starting: "Ambulate dum lucem habetis," in *Œuvres complètes*, 5:45 § 210.

67. Might one go so far as to say that reform was part of the long-term movement of a modality of anti-Romanism in the sense of an opposition to Roman predominance? Hence the collusion, historical and historiographical, between anti-Romanist reformism and conciliarism. Hence the thought of counterpowers: the council, the bishop, the cardinals, and the king, which would, in their controversial theories, become conciliarism, episcopalism, the ideology of cardinals, and regalism or even Gallicanism.

68. On epikie, see Charles Lefebvre, "Épikie," in Raoul Naz, ed., *Dictionnaire de droit canonique*, vol. 5 (Letouzey & Ané, 1953), col. 364–375; Gabriel Le Bras et al., eds., *L'age classique*, vol. 7 of *Histoire du Droit et des Institutions de l'Église en Occident* (Cujas, 1965), 352–366 and 406–420. See also Pier G. Caron, "*Æquitas" romana, "Misericordia" patristica ed "Epicheia" aristotelica nella dotrina dell'"Aequitas" canonica (dalle origini al Rinascimento)* (Giuffrè, 1971), here 70–72. See also the excellent, if slightly outdated, study by Guido Kisch, "*Summum ius summa iniuria. Baseler Humanisten und Juristen über Aequitas un Epieikeia*," in *Aequitas und bona fides. Festschrift für August Simonius* (Helbing und Lichtenhahn, 1955), 195–211; expanded upon in Guido Kisch, *Erasmus und die Jurisprudenz seiner Zeit. Studien zum humanistische Rechtsdenken* (Helbing und Lichtenhahn, 1960). See the previously mentioned volume *Æquitas und bona fides. Festschrift für August Simonius*; and finally, and earliest, Lawrence Joseph Riley, *The History, Nature and Use of Epikeia in Moral Theology* (Catholic University of America Press, 1948), here 52–54.

69. 2 Cor. 3:6: "Littera enim occidit, spiritus autem vivificat," and 2 Cor. 3:17. See Pierre D'Ailly, *Tractatus de varietate viarum ad unionem*, starting: "Ad unionem Ecclesie sancte Dei propterantibus nobis opus," in *Martin de Alpartil chronica actitatorum temporibus domini Benedicti XIII*, ed. Franz Ehrle (Ferdinand Schöningh, 1906), 918.

70. The hypothesis could well be validated by Gerson's influence on Pierre d'Ailly regarding the use of the concept of *epikeia*, because it is in the work of the chancellor that the finest analyses can be found. For the historiography of the problems of affiliation between Gerson and d'Ailly and the meaning of influences, see the middle path offered in Francis Oakley, "Gerson and d'Ailly," *Speculum* 40 (1965): 74–83. In contrast with Louis-Joseph Salembier, André Combes, John B. Morrall, and M. Liebermann more readily see the influence of Gerson over Pierre d'Ailly.

232 &? 4. RETHINKING REFORM

71. See G. H. M. Posthumus Meyjes, "The Concept of Epikie," in *Jean Gerson— Apostle of Unity: His Church Politics and Ecclesiology*, trans. J. C. Grayson (Brill, 1999). See also the more contestable article by Z. Rueger, "Le *De auctoritate concilii* de Gerson," *Revue d'histoire ecclésiastique* 53, no. 4 (1958): 775–795; Jean Gerson, *Regules morales* or *Flores spiritualium moralium* ou *Regules mandatorum*, starting: "Agamus interim," in *Œuvres complètes*, 9:95–96 § 434.

72. Jean Gerson, *De modo se habendi tempore schismatis*, starting: "Ad tollendam quorumdam in praesenti schismate," in *Œuvres complètes*, 6:34 § 256.

73. Henry of Langenstein, *Concilium pacis de unione et reformation ecclesiae in concilio universali quaerenda*, starting: "Epistola concilii pacis ad universos. Capitulum primum scismatis causam," in Gerson, *Opera omnia*, 2:821.

74. Jean Gerson, *Tractatus de unitate Ecclesiae*, starting: "Unitatis ecclesiasticae tractatoribus unus" (January 29, 1409), in *Œuvres complètes*, 6:142 § 272.

75. Pierre Ravat, "Questio de concilio Pisani," starting: "Pater sancte, salva semper determinatione," Paris, Bibliothèque nationale de France, Departement des manuscrits, lat. 1479, fol. 5r–10v, here fol. 8v–9r.

76. Charles d'Urries, *Allegations pro Benedicto XIII*, Paris, Bibliothèque nationale de France, Departement des manuscrits, lat. 1450, fol. 50r–55v, here fol. 56r.

77. Pierre Ravat, "Questio de concilio Pisani," Paris, Bibliothèque nationale de France, Departement des manuscrits, lat. 1479, fol. 9r.

78. On the conflicts between canonists and theologians according to Gerson, see Daniel Hobbins, *Authorship and Publicity Before Print: Jean Gerson and the Transformation of Late Medieval Learning* (University of Pennsylvania Press, 2009), 60–61, in which Hobbins writes of "professional jealousy"; Meyjes, *Jean Gerson—Apostle of Unity*, 88; G. H. M. Posthumus Meyjes, "Exponents of Sovereignty: Canonists as Seen by Theologians in the Late Middle Ages," in *The Church and Sovereignty, c. 590–1918: Essays in Honor of Michael Wilks*, ed. Dianna Wood (Blackwell, 1991), 299–312, especially 308– 311 on Gerson; and finally Jacques Krynen, "Les légistes 'idiots politiques': Sur l'hostilité des théologiens à l'égard des juristes, en France au temps de Charles V," in *Théologie et droit dans la science politique de l'État moderne (Actes de la Table ronde EFR, CNRS, Rome, 1987)* (École Française de Rome, 1991), 193–198, especially 197: "Assurément, il y a chez ces théologiens formés à Paris à la fin du XIVe siècle beaucoup de crispation corporatiste. . . . Au vrai, ce qu d'Ailly et Gerson manifestent à travers leurs diatribes, c'est une

4. RETHINKING REFORM ❧ 233

indéfectible croyance en la vocation éminente de leur savoir. . . . Vers 1400, les grands représentants de l'université de Paris sacrifient encore à cette vision scientiste de la théologie, qui fait les théologiens s'attribuer eux-mêmes une fonction sociale, et qui les apparente aux philosophes de la cité platonicienne" (To be sure, there was much corporatist tension among these theologians trained in Paris at the end of the fourteenth century. . . . In truth, what d'Ailly and Gerson demonstrated through their diatribes was an unwavering belief in the eminent vocation of their knowledge. . . . Around 1400, the great representatives of the University of Paris still sacrificed to this scientific vision of theology, which made theologians attribute a social function to themselves and which set them in comparison to the philosophers of the Platonic city). See also Jacques Krynen, "Un exemple de critique médiévale des juristes professionnels. Philippe de Mézières et les gens du Parlement de Paris," in *Histoire du droit. Mélanges en hommage à Jean Imbert*, ed. J.-L. Harouel (Presses Universitaires de France, 1989), 333–344. Likewise for Pierre d'Ailly, see Krynen, "Les légistes 'idiots politiques,' " 194: "C'est d'une haine véritable qu'il poursuit les juristes, singulièrement les canonistes" (He pursued jurists, particularly canonists, with real hatred). See also Bernard Guenée, *Entre l'Église et l'État. Quatre vies de prélats français à la fin du Moyen Âge (XIIIe–XVe siècle)* (Gallimard, 1987), 183. Next, see Yves-Marie Congar, "Un témoignage des désaccords entre canonistes et théologiens," in *Études d'histoire du droit canonique dédiées à Gabriel Le Bras*, ed. G. Vedel (Sirey, 1965), 2:861–884, especially 884: "Le conflit, malgré tout pacifique, entre théologiens et canonistes, touche à des valeurs ecclésiologiques" (Despite being totally peaceful, the conflict between theologians and canonists touched on ecclesiological values); Takashi Shogimen, "The Relationship Between Theology and Canon Law: Another Context of Political Thought in the Early Fourteenth Century," *Journal of the History of Ideas* 60, no. 3 (1999): 417–431. For the same dissensions that could be found at the time of the Council of Basel, see Thomas Prügl, "Modelle konziliarer Kontroverstheologie. Johannes von Ragusa und Johannes von Torquemada," in *Die Konzilien von Pisa (1409), Konstanz (1414–1418) und Basel (1431–1449), Institution und Personen*, ed. Herbert Müller and Johannes Helmrath, (Thorbecke, 2007), 257–287, especially starting 268. See also Walther's distinction between a conciliarism of theologians and a conciliarism of canonists in Helmut G. Walther,

234 ❧ 4. RETHINKING REFORM

"Konziliarismus als politische Theorie? Konzilsvorstellungen im 15. Jahrhundert zwischen Notlösungen und Kirchenmodellen," in *Die Konzilien von Pisa (1409), Konstanz (1414–1418) und Basel (1431–1449), Institution und Personen*, ed. Herbert Müller and Johannes Helmrath, (Thorbecke, 2007), 31–60, especially 55. On the connections between theology and law in ecclesiological thought, see also Thomas Woelki, "Theologische und juristische Argumente in den Konzilstraktaten des Lodovico Pontano († 1439)," in *Proceedings of the Thirteenth International Congress of Medieval Canon Law, Esztergom 3–8 August 2008*, ed. Peter Erdö and Sz. Anselm Szuromi (Biblioteca apostolica vaticana, 2010), 747–763.

79. For epikie in the service of charity, see Jean Gerson, *Sermo Apparuit*, in *Œuvres complètes*, 5:73.

80. See Claude Gauvard, "De grace especial," in *Crime, État et société en France à la fin du Moyen Âge* (Publications de la Sorbonne, 1991), 2:907–920. Starting with letters of remission, Claude Gauvard showed that epikie was not the same thing as pardon. The reformers of the reign of Charles VI were reluctant regarding pardon but put forth epikie as a reasoned application of the law. See also Ludovic Viallet, *Les Sens de l'observance. Enquête sur les réformes franciscaines entre l'Elbe et l'Oder, de Capistran à Luther (vers 1450–vers 1520)* (Lit, 2014), especially chap. 2 on the middle path that allowed balance to be maintained in the interest of the common good and on *epikeia* as the superiority of the equitable over the just, and even as a synonym for "temperance" in the sources of the observant friars minor and in particular in the reform program of John of Capistrano (210–213). On the two opposing reformist parties, see also Laurent Tournier, "Jean sans Peur et l'université de Paris," in *Paris, capitale des ducs de Bourgogne*, ed. Werner Paravicini and Bertrand Schnerb (Thorbecke, 2007), 310–311.

81. The jurists' preoccupation with affirming the excellence of their training or even the "nobility of the law" in the face of theologians has been well studied. Cf. Patrick Gilli, *La Noblesse du droit. Débats et controverses sur la culture juridique et le rôle des juristes dans l'Italie médiévale (XIIe–XV siècle)* (Honoré Champion, 2003); Corinne Leveleux-Teixeira, "Controverses juridiques et désarmement herméneutique, ou la brève histoire d'un espace public doctrinal chez les juristes (XIIe–XIIIe siècles)," in *L'espace public au Moyen Âge. Débats autour de Jürgen Habermas*, ed. Patrick Boucheron and Nicolas Offenstadt (Presses Universitaires de France, 2011), 263–275, especially 265.

4. RETHINKING REFORM ❧ 235

82. Jean Gerson, *Tractatus de unitate Ecclesiae*, in *Œuvres complètes*, 6:145.

83. Serge Lusignan, "Vérité garde le roy: *La Construction d'une identité universitaire en France (XIIIe–XVe siècle)* (Publications de la Sorbonne, 1999), 260–261.

84. Jean Gerson, *Vivat rex* ou *Pour la réforme du royaume,* starting: "Vivat rex" (November 7, 1405), in *Œuvres complètes*, 7:1155 § 398.

85. Claudia Carlen, *The Papal Encyclicals 1740–1878* (McGrath Publishing Company, 1981), 237.

86. Robert E. McNally, *The Unreformed Church* (Sheed and Ward, 1965).

87. Birgit Studt, *Papst Martin V (1417–1431) und die Kirchenreform in Deutschland* (Böhlau, 2004), 712–713.

88. Studt, 716.

89. Studt, 721.

90. Johannes Helmrath, "Theorie und Praxis der Kirchenreform im Spätmittelalter," *Rottenburger Jahrbuch für Kirchengeschichte* 11 (1992): 47, for example.

91. On the reforms of Benedict XII, see Jan Ballweg, *Konziliare oder Päpstliche Ordensreform: Benedikt XII und die Reformdiskussion im frühen 14. Jh.* (Mohr Siebeck, 2001).

92. See Ludwig Vones, *Urban V (1362–1370): Kirchenreform zwischen Kardinalkollegium, Kurie, und Klientel* (Hiersemann, 1998).

93. The term *reformatio* was exported from the clerical sphere to the secular political world. Demonstrating this was the aim of Marie Dejoux, who saw it as an indication of the pontificalization of the Capetian monarchy under Philip the Fair: "Le roi répliquait au pape dans ses propres termes" (The king responded to the pope in his own words): Marie Dejoux, *Les enquêtes de Saint Louis. Gouverner et sauver son âme* (Presses Universitaires de France, 2014), 252. The concern for the king to conform to the ideal of the public good and to respond to the complaints of the kingdom's ecclesiastics was a matter of reforming the kingdom in place of the pope, so as to avoid accusations of *rex inutilis* or of *regulus*. For his part, Olivier Canteaut was able to show that the noun *reformator* was attested in Latin in 1302 and transposed into French in 1323, sometimes alone and sometimes attached to the term *enquêteur*. Olivier Canteaut, "Le juge et le financier: Les enquêteurs-réformateurs des derniers Capétiens (1314–1328)," in *L'enquête au Moyen Âge*, ed. Claude Gauvard (École Française de Rome, 2018), 269–318. This is a fine example of

historical intelligibility through the secularization of a concept, in line with linear theories of modernization.

94. See R. N. Swanson, *Universities, Academics and the Great Schism* (Cambridge University Press, 1979), 8, 61–62, 181, and 197.

95. Noël Valois, *La France et le Grand Schisme d'Occident* (Picard, 1896–1902), 4:386 and 483–485. See also Swanson, "The Problem of the Cardinalate in the Great Schism," in *Authority and Power: Studies on Medieval Law and Government*, ed. Brian Tierney and Peter Linehan (Cambridge University Press, 1980); Philippe Généquand, "Des ombres aux chapeaux rouges. Pour une nouvelle histoire des cardinaux à la fin du Moyen Âge," in *Église et État, Église ou État?*, ed. Christine Barralis et al. (Éditions de la Sorbonne and École Française de Rome, 2015); and Philippe Généquand, "Kardinäle Schisma und Konzil. Der Kardinalskolleg im Grossen Abedländischen Schisma," in *Geschichte des Kardinalats im Mittelalter*, ed. Jürgen Dendorfer and Ralf Lützelschab (Hiersemann, 2011).

96. Pierre d'Ailly, *Tractatus de emendatione Ecclesiae* (also called *De reformatione*), starting: "De reformatione Ecclesiae dudum" (November 1, 1416), in *Quellen zur Kirchenreform im Zeitalter der großen Konzilien des 15. Jahrhunderts*, ed. Jürgen Miethke and Lorenz Weinrich (Darmstadt, 2015), 338–377.

97. Jean-Pierre Albert et al., eds., *Dissidences en Occident des débuts du christianisme au XXe siècle. Le religieux et le politique* (Presses Universitaires du Midi, 2015), especially the schematic on 21.

98. Jean-Jacques Von Allmen, *Une réforme dans l'Église. Possibilités-critères-acteurs-étapes* (Duculot, 1971).

99. Alain Rauwel, "Loi," in *Dictionnaire critique de l'Église*, ed. Dominique Iogna-Prat et al. (Presses Universitaires de France, 2023), 640–642.

5. ANTI-ROMANISM AND ITS HITHERTO UNRECOGNIZED MEDIEVAL ROOTS

1. Iakovos G. Pitzipios, *Le Romanisme* (Bern, 1860).

2. For this quotation, see Pitzipios, 23. See also 435: "The sovereign pontiffs gave their government the external forms of the ecclesiastical regime while exercising their Roman despotism using means that were purely worldly and, so to speak, *mechanical* for both temporal and spiritual matters."

5. ANTI-ROMANISM ❧ 237

3. Pitzipios, 436: "The incompatibility of the liberal principles of Jesus Christ's teachings with such a system pushed the Roman government to legally assassinate the divine Savior."

4. Léopold Willaert, *Après le concile de Trente. La restauration catholique (1563–1648)*, vol. 18 of *Histoire de l'Église depuis les origines jusqu'à nos jours*, ed. Augustin Fliche and Victor Martin (Bloud & Gay, 1960).

5. Hans Urs Von Balthasar, *The Office of Peter and the Structure of the Church* (Ignatius Press, 1986), 9.

6. John Henry Newman, *On the Prophetical Office of the Church*, in *The Via Media of the Anglican Church* (London, 1891), 1:102–104: "Romanism, by its pretence of Infallibility, lowers the standard and quality of Gospel obedience as well as impairs its mysterious and sacred character; and this in various ways. When religion is reduced in all its parts to a system, there is hazard of something earthly being made the chief object of our contemplation instead of our Maker."

7. Von Balthasar, *The Office of Peter and the Structure of the Church*, 16n4.

8. Yves-Marie Congar, "Romanité et catholicité. Histoire de la conjonc- tion changeante de deux dimensions de l'Église," *Revue des sciences philosophiques et théologiques* 71 (1987): 161–190.

9. Congar, 176.

10. Congar, 187.

11. Sylvio Hermann De Franceschi, "Paolo Sarpi et Fulgenzio Micanzio. L'extrémisme catholique antiromain du débat du XVIIe siècle," in *Antiromanisme doctrinal et romanité ecclésiale: Dans le catholicisme posttridentin (XVIe–XXe siècles)*, ed. Sylvio Hermann De Franceschi (Laboratoire de recherche historique Rhône-Alpes, 2008), 46.

12. Respectively published as Sylvio Hermann De Franceschi, ed., *Antiromanisme doctrinal et romanité ecclésiale: Dans le catholicisme posttridentin (XVIe–XXe siècles)* (Laboratoire de recherche historique Rhône-Alpes, 2008); Sylvio Hermann De Franceschi, ed., *Le Pontife et l'erreur: Anti-infaillibilisme catholique et romanité ecclésiale aux temps posttridentins (XVIIe–XXe siècles)* (Laboratoire de recherche historique Rhône-Alpes, 2010); Sylvio Hermann De Franceschi, ed., *Histoires antiromaines: Antiromanisme et critique dans l'historiographie catholique (XVIe–XXe siècles)* (Laboratoire de recherche historique Rhône-Alpes, 2010); and François-Xavier Bischof and Sylvio Hermann De Franceschi, eds., *Histoires antiromaines II. L'antiromanisme dans*

238 &? 5. ANTI-ROMANISM

l'historiographie ecclésiastique catholique (XVIe–XXe siècles) (Laboratoire de recherche historique Rhône-Alpes, 2014).

13. De Franceschi, "Antiromanisme doctrinal et romanité ecclésiale dans le catholicisme posttridentin," 49.

14. De Franceschi, 52.

15. Sylvio Hermann De Franceschi, *La crise théologico-politique du premier âge baroque. Antiromanisme doctrinal, pouvoir pastoral et raison du prince: Le Saint-Siège face au prisme français (1607–1627)* (École Française de Rome, 2009), 2.

16. De Franceschi, 158.

17. De Franceschi, 915: "Des îles Britanniques à la cité lagunaire en passant par la capitale parisienne, une manière catholique antiromaine d'appréhender les rapports du politique et du religieux se confirmait" (From the British Isles to the lagoon city via the Parisian capital, an anti-Roman Catholic way of understanding the relationship between politics and religion was confirmed).

18. De Franceschi, 2–3.

19. Sylvio Hermann De Franceschi, "Les théologiens parisiens face à un anti-romanisme catholique extrême au temps du richérisme. La condamnation du *De republica ecclesiastica* de Marc'Antonio De Dominis par la Sorbonne (15 décembre 1617)," *Chrétiens et sociétés, XVIe–XXe siècles* 11 (2004): 12.

20. De Franceschi, 12.

21. Giuseppe Alberigo, "L'ecclesiologia del Concilio di Trento," in *Il Concilio Tridentino. Prospettive storiografiche e problemi storici*, ed. Paolo Brezzi et al. (Vita e pensiero, 1965); Paolo Prodi, *Il paradigma tridentino. Un'epoca della storia della Chiesa* (Morcelliana, 2010).

22. De Franceschi, "Antiromanisme doctrinal et romanité ecclésiale," 50.

23. Philippe Boutry, "Introduction," in *"Rome, l'unique objet de mon ressentiment": Regards critiques sur la papauté*, ed. Philippe Levillain (École Française de Rome, 2011), 4.

24. Boutry, 5.

25. De Franceschi, "Antiromanisme doctrinal et romanité ecclésiale," 70.

26. Jean-Louis Quantin, "La menace des faits: Érudition moderne et condamnations romaines," in Levillain, *"Rome, l'unique objet de mon ressentiment,"* 31.

27. Thierry Wanegffelen, *Ni Rome ni Genève. Des fidèles entre deux chaires en France au XVIe siècle* (Honoré Champion, 1997), 31.

5. ANTI-ROMANISM ❧ 239

28. For the expression and development of the argument in this paragraph, see Alain Rauwel, "Concurrence des rits et jugement de Dieu: Une originalité espagnole?" *Cahiers de civilisation médiévale* 58 (2015): 371–376.

29. On Marsilius of Padua, see Jeannine Quillet, *Le Défenseur de la paix. Traduction, introduction et commentaire* (Vrin, 1968), and, more recently, Gianluca Briguglia, *Marsilo da Padova* (Carocci, 2013).

30. On the influence of Marsilius of Padua, see Gregorio Piaia, *Marsilio da Padova nella Riforma e nella Controriforma. Fortuna ed interpretazione* (Antenore, 1977). See also Sylvio Hermann De Franceschi, "Hybridation doctrinale au temps de l'Interdit: Calvinisme, marsilisme et wycliffisme aux sources de l'antiromanisme sarpien," in *Frontières religieuses dans le monde moderne*, ed. Denis Crouzet and Francisco Bethencourt (Sorbonne Université Presses, 2013).

31. De Franceschi, *La crise théologico-politique*, 24 and 26, quoting Victor Martin, *Les origines du gallicanisme* (Bloud & Gay, 1939), 1:29–31.

32. De Franceschi, 26.

33. G. Benoît, "Traité autour des Novem quaestiones," Archivio Segreto Vaticano, *Armarium* LIV, vol. 36, fol. 5r–35v, here fol. 17r, discussing professors at the university: "Isti declarando et publicando papam haereticum vel scismaticum hostili animo animati sunt" (By declaring and making public a heretical or schismatic pope, they are animated by a hostile spirit), quoted in Howard Kaminsky, *Simon de Cramaud and the Great Schism* (Rutgers University Press, 1983), 159n45.

34. University of Paris, "Novem Quaestiones," starting: "Utrum Papa teneatur acceptare viam cessionis" (late August 1395), Paris, Bibliothèque nationale de France, Departement des manuscrits, lat. 14643, fol. 71r; César-Egasse du Boulay, ed., *Historia universitatis Parisiensis*, 6 vols. (Paris, 1665–1673), 4:753a–735b.

35. University of Paris, *Epistola Parisiensis* (secunda), starting: "Sanctissimo in Christo Patri D. Benedicto divina providentia sancte romane ecclesie" (April 14, 1395, rewritten August 25, 1395), Paris, Bibliothèque nationale de France, Departement des manuscrits, lat. 14643, fol. 49r–52r; Du Boulay, *Historia universitatis Parisiensis*, 4:740–747b.

36. See the addition of the explanation in the infra-paginal margin of fol. 52r, University of Paris, *Epistola Parisiensis* (secunda).

37. Religieux de Saint-Denis, *Chronique du Religieux de Saint-Denys, contenant le règne de Charles VI, de 1380 à 1422*, ed. Bernard Guenée (Editions du Comité

240 ❧ 5. ANTI-ROMANISM

des travaux historiques et scientifiques, 1994), 3:468 and 486: "Tous furent aiguillonnés par l'indignation. Chez quelques-uns, même, la haine latente éclata de façon indécente. De part et d'autre, on ose déclamer des invectives et des satires qui salissaient publiquement la réputation des gens d'âge et d'autorité" (All were goaded by indignation. Among a few, even, latent hatred broke out indecently. On both sides, we dare to declaim the invectives and satires that publicly sully the reputation of people of age and authority), quoted by Bernard Guenée, *L'opinion publique à la fin du Moyen Âge d'après la "Chronique de Charles VI" du Religieux de Saint-Denis* (Perrin, 2002), 72: "La haine resurgit par cinq fois dans le récit que Michel Pintoin fit des affaires religieuses" (Hatred resurfaced five times in Michel Pintoin's account of religious affairs), with the following citations: Religieux de Saint-Denis, *Chronique du Religieux de Saint-Denys*, 3:580, 582, and 638; 4:18 and 60. He concludes, "Ainsi, dans la longue histoire du Schisme, du début du règne à 1417, la simple attention portée au mot *odium* permet de suivre, dans ses grands traits, l'état d'esprit des clercs et de bien distinguer les trois années, 1406–1408, où les passions atteignent leur paroxysme" (Thus, in the long history of the schism, from the beginning of the reign to 1417, simply paying attention to the word *odium* makes it broadly possible to trace the clerics' states of mind and to clearly determine the three years in which passions reached their peak, 1406–1408).

38. See Bénédicte Sère, "Entre rigeur et indulgence: La voie de l'oubli chez Gerson à l'heure de la restitution d'obédience (c. 1402)," in *Justice et miséricorde*, ed. Catherine Vincent (Presses Universitaires de Limoges, 2015), 241–256.

39. Jean Gerson, *De schismate*, starting: "Praesupposito quod papa possit fieri haereticus et schismaticus" (around April 15, 1402), in *Œuvres complètes*, 6:47 § 259: "Favor et amor multum impediunt judicia hominum etiam justorum, licet hoc non credant vel videant" (Favor and love greatly hinder the judgements even of just men, though they do not believe or see this).

40. Claude Gauvard, "De grace especial," in *Crime, État et société en France à la fin du Moyen Âge* (Publications de la Sorbonne, 1991), 686. Regarding *odium capitale*, the author adds, "At that point he who was only an adversary became an 'enemy,' and then a 'capital enemy.'"

41. Gerson, *De Schismate*, 44 § 259. See also Jean Gerson, *Considerations de restitutione* and the first part of *De restitutione obedientiae considerationes*,

5. ANTI-ROMANISM ❧ 241

starting: "Ad videndum quid expediat" (around April 15–16, 1402), in *Œuvres complètes*, 6:58 § 261.

42. University of Paris, "Prima appellatio Universitatis a Benedicto XIII" (March 21, 1396, against Benedict XIII), starting: "Si tramitem veritatis vas electionis beatissimus Paulus judeorum," Paris, Bibliothèque national de France, Departement des manuscrits, lat. 14643, fol. 309r–315v; Du Boulay, *Historia universitatis Parisiensis*, 4:803–820, here 804.

43. G. Benoît, "Traité autour des Novem quaestiones," Archivio Segreto Vaticano, *Armarium* LIV, vol. 36, fol. 5r–35v, here fol. 17r.

44. On Simon de Cramaud, see Kaminsky, *Simon de Cramaud and the Great Schism*.

45. Kaminsky, 33–34.

46. Kaminsky, 105, quoting Martin de Alpartil, *Cronica actitatorum temporibus domini Benedicti XIII. Einleitung, Text der Chronik, Anhang Ungedruckter Aktenstücke*, ed. Franz Ehrle (Ferdinand Schöningh, 1906), 118, 29–34.

47. Kaminsky, 108.

48. Kaminsky, 109.

49. Kaminsky, 109, "mobilizer of the Gallican Church."

50. Simon de Cramaud, *Premier discours à la IVe assemblée du clergé de Paris* (December 2, 1406), starting: "Tres redoutés Seigneurs, il vous a plus ordonner aucuns pour debattre la matiere," in *Preuves de la nouvelle histoire du concile de Constance*, ed. L. Bourgeois du Chastenet (Paris, 1718), 122.

51. *Premier discours à l'assemblée du clergé de Paris* (December 8, 1406), "Sire, en vostre absence autrefois je fu chargiés de parler en cette matiere," in *Preuves de la nouvelle histoire du concile de Constance*, 215.

52. *Premier discours à l'assemblée du clergé de Paris*, 216.

53. *Premier discours à l'assemblée du clergé de Paris*, 217; Simon de Cramaud, *Gloses sur le traité de Johannes Dominici adressé à Sigismond* (Summer 1414), Hanover, Landesbibliothek, I, 176; Munich, Staatsbibliothek, 15183, fol. 127–144; Vienna, Nationalbibliothek, 5100, fol. 50; on the *lemmata* of the text of Johannes Dominici on pages 272–275, see *Acta Concilii Constantiensis*, ed. Heinrich Finke (Regensbergsche Buchhandlung, 1826–1928), 1:277–289, here 281.

54. Finke, *Acta Concilii Constantiensis*, 1:280.

55. Simon de Cramaud, *Mémoire pour l'élection du pape*, the modern title given to the manuscript, Paris, Bibliothèque nationale de France, Departement des

manuscrits, lat. 18378, 566, starting: "Quoniam sicut scribitur in canone" (May 28, 1416; the date is given on page 551 of the modern manuscript, although, according to Kaminsky's edition of 1984, the date should be between June 18 and July 26, 1417).

56. De Franceschi, *La Crise théologico-politique*, 67: "Venetian anti-Romanism took on a personal dimension: the hatred directed against Paul V, the person, reflected on the sovereign pontificate in general," and 71.

57. On this subject, see Jacques Paul, ed., "L'anticléricalisme en France méridionale (milieu XIIe–début XIVe siècle)," special issue, *Cahiers de Fanjeaux* 38 (2003), especially the introduction by Jean-Louis Biget, p. 11.

58. Bernard Alaman, *Tractatus*, starting: "Christianissimo Dei gratia Francorum regi Karolo illustrissimo Dei pacienti" (1398), Paris, Bibliothèque nationale de France, Departement des manuscrits, lat. 14644, fol. 13r–47v, here fol. 30r.

59. Alaman, *Tractatus*, fol. 26r: "Ergo apparet quod nec Petrus, nec Paulus sed Christus est hostium" (Therefore it appears that neither Peter nor Paul but Christ is the enemy). On this point, see Hugues Labarthe, "Bernard Alaman, un évêque lecteur de saint Augustin en vue de résoudre le Grand Schisme d'Occident," *Revue Mabillon* 18 (2007): 193–216.

60. Interlocutors of the modern and contemporary eras have legitimated this hatred of the tyrant as a positive hatred. See, for example, Marc Deleplace, "Peut-on fonder la République sur la haine? Une interrogation sur la république directoriale (1795–1799)," in *La haine. Histoire et actualité*, ed. Frédéric Chauvaud and Ludovic Gaussot (Presses Universitaires de Rennes, 2008), 206, where the author highlights a phrase used by some revolutionaries: "Haïr la royauté, c'est aimer le peuple" (To hate royalty is to love the people).

61. Alaman, *Tractatus*, fol. 36r, repeated at fol. 46r: "Tunc potius non Petrus sed Sathan pastor, non pastor sed fur et latro, non Romanus pontifex sed fex romana potius dici debet."

62. Alaman, fol. 37r.

63. Alaman, fol. 18r.

64. Alaman, fol. 18v.

65. See Karen Bollerman et al., eds., *Religion, Power and Resistance from the Eleventh to the Sixteenth Centuries: Playing the Heresy Card* (Palgrave Macmillan, 2014).

5. ANTI-ROMANISM ❦ 243

66. Cf. Gratian, *Decretum*, D. 40 c. 6, *Si Papa*, in Emil Friedberg, ed., *Decretum Magistri Gratiani*, vol. 1 of *Corpus Iuris Canonici* (Leipzig, 1879). Huguccio understood the general meaning of heresy as an offshoot of the concept of notorious crime, a category that included simony, *fornicatio, furtum*, and anything else that scandalized the Church (*scandalizare Ecclesiam*). On the broadening of the meaning of heresy to condemn any form of opposition to Rome and any type of challenge to hierarchical power, see Willem Lourdaux and Daniël Verhest, eds., *The Concept of Heresy in the Middle Ages (11th–13th c.)* (Nijhoff, 1973); Monique Zerner, "Hérésie," in *Dictionnaire raisonné de l'Occident médiéval*, ed. Jacques Le Goff and Jean-Claude Schmitt (Fayard, 1999); Dominique Iogna-Prat, "La formation d'un paradigme ecclésial de la violence intellectuelle dans l'Occident latin aux XIe et XIIe siècles," in *Le mot qui tue. Une histoire des violences intellectuelles de l'Antiquité à nos jours*, ed. Vincent Azoulay and Patrick Boucheron (Champ Vallon, 2009), 325. Finally, regarding accusations of heresy against Benedetto Caetani/Boniface VIII, which serves as a good comparative example, see Agostino Paravicini Pagliani, *Boniface VIII. Un pape hérétique?* (Payot, 2003), as well as the introduction to Jean Coste, *Boniface VIII en procès. Articles d'accusation et déposition des témoins (1303–1311)* (École Française de Rome, 1995); Agostino Paravicini Bagliani, *Le corps du pape* (Seuil, 1997). See also J. A. Mirus, "On the Deposition of the Pope for Heresy," *Archivium historiae pontificiae* 13 (1975): 231–248, and Ludwig Buisson, "Der häretische Papst," chap. 4 of *Potestas und caritas, Die päpstliche Gewalt im Spätmittelalter* (Böhlau, 1958).

67. *Alique conclusiones circa juramentum conclavis*, starting: "Nos omnis et singuli sancte ratione Ecclesie cardinales congregati pro electione" (1395), Paris, Bibliothèque nationale de France, Departement des manuscrits, lat. 14643, fol. 265r–267r, here fol. 267r.

68. Cramaud, *Discours à la IVe assemblée du clergé*, in *Preuves de la nouvelle histoire du concile de Constance*, 168.

69. Cramaud, 90–91. See Brian Tierney, *Foundations of the Conciliar Theory: The Contribution of the Medieval Canonists from Gratian to the Great Schism* (Cambridge University Press, 1955); Yves-Marie Congar, "Status Ecclesiae," *Studia Gratiana* 15 (1972): 3–31.

70. Simon de Cramaud, *De substraccione obediencie*, ed. H. Kaminsky (Medieval Academy of America, 1984), 116.

244   5. ANTI-ROMANISM

71. Bruno Neveu, "Saint Paul et Rome: À propos d'une controverse sur la primauté pontificale," in *Homo religiosus. Autour de Jean Delumeau* (Fayard, 1997), 446–452.

72. Sylvio Hermann De Franceschi, "Saint Pierre et saint Paul: Deux chefs de l'Église qui n'en font qu'un. Primauté romaine et pétrinité aux temps posttridentins," in Levillain, *"Rome, l'unique objet de mon ressentiment,"* 244. See also Neveu, "Saint Paul et Rome," and Henry Chadwick, *The Circle and the Ellipse: Rival Concepts of Authority* (Clarendon Press, 1959).

73. Quoted in De Franceschi, "Saint Pierre et saint Paul," 237n24; Robert Bellarmine, *De Romano pontifice*, vol. 1 of *Disputationes de controversiis christianae fidei* (Naples, 1586), 361.

74. De Franceschi, "Saint Pierre et saint Paul," 251. It should be kept in mind, following De Franceschi, that Pius X intransigently asserted that the doctrine of the equality of Saint Peter and Saint Paul had been proscribed by Innocent X.

75. In the New International Version, this verse is translated as "When Cephas came to Antioch, I opposed him to his face, because he was stood condemned." The New Jerusalem Bible has this as follows: "However, when Cephas came to Antioch, then I did oppose him to his face since he was manifestly in the wrong."

76. See Hermann Josef Sieben, *Vom Apostelkonzil zum Ersten Vatikanum: Studien zur Geschichte der Konzilsidee* (Ferdinand Schöningh, 1996).

77. Cf. Yves-Marie Congar, "La 'réception' comme réalité ecclésiologique," *Revue des sciences philosophiques et théologiques* 56 (1972): 374.

78. Among other examples, see the canonist Tancredus (1235), *Gloss ad Comp. III*, 1.5.3: "Nec est quid dicat ei, cur ita facis?," quoted in Tierney, *Foundations of the Conciliar Theory*, 147, and the theocrat Alvarez Pelayo (d. 1353), quoted in Nicolas Jung, *Un franciscain, théologien du pouvoir pontifical au XIVe siècle Alvaro Pelayo, évêque et penitentier de Jean XXII* (Vrin, 1931), 107n1.

79. See Pierre-Jean Souriac, "Écrits historiques et excommunication sous Henri III et Henri IV," in Levillain, *"Rome, l'unique objet de mon ressentiment,"* 44.

80. De Franceschi, *La crise théologico-politique*, 854. See also De Franceschi, "Antiromanisme doctrinal et romanité ecclésiale," 52: "Opposed to absolutism in the Church, the trustee of the theological faculty of Paris necessarily had to be so in the state. . . . Richerist conciliarism denounced itself as the ecclesial version of a doctrine that aimed to situate intermediary bodies

6. MODERNISM'S CHALLENGE TO THE MIDDLE AGES ❧ 245

between the king and his subjects and to carry out a dismemberment of sovereign power. . . . Very few zealous Catholic polemicists were able to discern the seeds of a doctrine diametrically opposed to nascent absolutism behind the syndic's anti-Roman charge."

81. Pierre d'Ailly, "Secunda schedula" (before September 1396), in de Alpartil, *Cronica actitatorum temporibus domini Benedicti XIII*, 477.

82. D'Ailly, 477.

83. D'Ailly, 479.

84. D'Ailly, 478.

85. D'Ailly, 484.

86. De Franceschi, *La crise théologico-politique*, 853.

87. Philippe Boutry, "La tentative française de destruction du Saint Siège (1789–1814)," in Levillain, *"Rome, l'unique objet de mon ressentiment,"* 82.

88. De Franceschi, *La crise théologico-politique*, 929.

6. MODERNISM'S CHALLENGE TO THE MIDDLE AGES

1. Herbert Leslie Stewart, *Modernism: Past and Present* (J. Murray, 1932).

2. Among others, see most recently Giacomo Losito, ed., *La crisi modernista nella cultura europea* (Istitutio della Enciclopedia Italiana, 2012).

3. Émile Poulat, *Histoire, dogme et critique dans la crise moderniste* (Albin Michel, 1996); Pierre Colin, *L'Audace et le Soupçon: La crise moderniste dans le catholicisme français, 1893–1914* (Desclée de Brouwer, 1997); François Laplanche, *La crise de l'origine. La science catholique des Évangiles et l'histoire du XXe siècle* (Albin Michel, 2006).

4. It should be noted that the two historiographies, that of modernism and that of the thirteenth-century censure of radical Aristotelianism, have never really intersected any more than those of medieval and modernist censorship have. They do, however, conclude with the same principle: It is the censor who creates heresy. Averroism was constructed from scratch by theologians and is a "theological construct taken directly from the theological reading of the 1260s." Alain de Libera, *Raison et foi: Archéologie d'une crise d'Albert le Grand à Jean-Paul II* (Seuil, 2003), 202.

5. Philippe Boutry, "Modernisme," in *Dictionnaire des faits religieux*, ed. Régine Azria and Danièle Hervieu-Léger (Presses Universitaires de France, 2010), 737.

246 &⁓ 6. MODERNISM'S CHALLENGE TO THE MIDDLE AGES

6. For the expression, see Étienne Fouilloux, *Une Église en quête de liberté. La pensée catholique française entre modernisme et Vatican II, 1914–1962* (Desclée de Brouwer, 1998), 25. See also 68–84 on the weakening of antimodernist repression; Étienne Fouilloux, "Première alerte sur le Saulchoir (1932)," *Revue des sciences philosophiques et théologiques* 96, no. 1 (2012): 93–105.

7. Marie-Dominique Chenu, "Le sens et les leçons d'une crise religieuse," *La vie intellectuelle* 13 (October–December 1931): 359, 367. The idea was restated in the 1950s, 1960s, and 1980s by, respectively, Gilson, Balic, and Hissette: Étienne Gilson, *Jean Duns Scot. Introduction à ses positions fondamentales* (Vrin, 1952), 643: "Around 1300, a theologian found himself in roughly the same situation with regard to the decree of 1277 as those of our time were in after the condemnation of modernism. In fact, Étienne Tempier's decree had been a reminder of tradition"; Charles Balic, "Johannes Duns Scotus und die Lehrentscheidung von 1277," *Wissenschaft und Weisheit* 29 (1966): 211; and Roland Hissette, "Note sur la réaction 'antimoderniste' d'Étienne Tempier," *Bulletin de philosophie médiévale* 22 (1980): 88. Marie-Dominique Chenu's article in *La vie intellectuelle* is, from the outset, a review of Jean Rivière, *Le Modernisme dans l'Église. Étude d'histoire religieuse contemporaine* (Letouzey & Ané, 1929).

8. Chenu, "Le sens et les leçons d'une crise religieuse," 367.

9. On this subject, see Bénédicte Sère, *Penser l'amitié au Moyen Âge. Étude historique des livres VIII et IX de l'*Éthique à Nicomaque, *XIIIe–XVe siècle* (Brepols, 2007).

10. Albertus Magnus, *De generatione et corruptione*, ed. Paul Hossfeld, vol. 5, pt. 2 of *Opera Omnia*, ed. Bernhard Geyer and Wilhelm Kübel (Aschendorff, 1980), bk. 1, chap. 1, 22: "Dico quod nihil ad me de Dei miraculis cum ego de naturalibus disseram," which passed into the *Auctoritates Aristoteles* as "Quid mihi de miraculis divinis cum de rebus naturalibus loquor?" (What are divine miracles to me when I am speaking of natural things?); Jacqueline Hamesse, *Auctoritates Aristotelis. Un florilège médiéval. Étude historique et édition critique* (Nauwelaerts, 1974), 168n21.

11. This teleological aim must, however, not reduce philosophy to remaining the "handmaid of theology," as the "neoscholastic fiction of 'Albertino-Thomism'" would have it in Gilsonian historiography. On the expression, see de Libera, *Raison et foi*, 35. See also Étienne Gilson, *Le Philosophe et la Théologie* (Vrin, 2005), 189: "Saint Thomas is only a commentator in his

6. MODERNISM'S CHALLENGE TO THE MIDDLE AGES ᏋᏜ 247

writings on Aristotle; it is in the two *Summae* and other writings of the same genre that he is properly an author, and it is therefore there that we must seek his personal thought."

12. Joseph Maréchal, *De la Renaissance à Kant*, vol. 1 of *Précis d'histoire de la philosophie moderne* (L'édition universelle, 1951), 16–17.

13. Ruedi Imbach, "Thomas d'Aquin 1224/1225–1274," in *Dictionnaire du Moyen Âge*, ed. Claude Gauvard et al. (Presses Universitaires de France, 2002), 1389.

14. James C. Doig, *Aquinas's Philosophical Commentary on the* Ethics: *A Historical Perspective* (Kluwer, 2001), 273–274.

15. On the handling of this affair, see Sère, "Thomas d'Aquin contre Siger de Brabant, 1270. Chronique d'une dispute," in *Le mot qui tue. Une histoire des violences intellectuelles de l'Antiquité à nos jours*, ed. Vincent Azoulay and Patrick Boucheron (Champ Vallon, 2009).

16. Full text: Heinrich Denifle and Emile Chatelain, eds., *Chartularium Universitatis Parisiensis*, 5 vols. (Paris, 1897), 1:499–500n441.

17. Alain de Libera, *La philosophie médiévale* (Presses Universitaires de France, 1993), 415.

18. François-Xavier Putallaz and Ruedi Imbach, *Profession: Philosophe. Siger de Brabant* (Cerf, 1997), 147.

19. Luca Bianchi, *Censure et liberté intellectuelle à l'Université de Paris (XIIIe–XIVe siècles)* (Les Belles Lettres, 1999), 194.

20. Bianchi, 191.

21. Bianchi, 188.

22. Bianchi, 198.

23. Luca Bianchi and Eugenio Randi, *Vérités dissonantes. Aristote à la fin du Moyen Âge* (Éditions Universitaires Fribourg Suisse, 1993), 52–53, repeated in Luca Bianchi, *Pour une histoire de la "double vérité"* (Vrin, 2008), 17. See also David Piché, *La condamnation parisienne de 1277. Nouvelle édition du texte latin, traduction, introduction et commentaire* (Vrin, 1999), 215.

24. Piché, *La condamnation parisienne de 1277*, 163: "Il est évident que la liberté intellectuelle des artiens se trouvait grandement compromise par ces dispositions qui leur commandaient d'arrimer leur enseignement aux impératifs d'une entreprise d'apologie de la foi chrétienne" (It is obvious that the intellectual freedom of the scholars of the arts was greatly compromised by these provisions, which required them to align their teaching with the imperatives of an enterprise of apology for the Christian faith).

248 ❧ 6. MODERNISM'S CHALLENGE TO THE MIDDLE AGES

25. This should, however, be qualified. It is critical to correctly understand the famous question of the "invention of heresy," or "modernism" in this case, by the censor, and therefore the need not only to put scare quotes around the term but also to take full measure of the theological construction and its associated conspiratorial fantasy; otherwise, one risks falling into a historiographical commonplace that understands censors as incompetent or delusional. As proof, a certain number of the authors targeted by Pascendi, starting with Loisy himself, in fact, recognized themselves in part of the picture drawn up of their ideas. The fantasy lay only in the idea that there was a hidden, global modernist "system," all the manifestations of which (exegetic, theological, philosophical, pastoral) would be articulated, and with which a conspiracy would be associated. But there indeed has been a "modernist" or "modernizing" current in the Church, consisting of networks (which make extensive use of the term "pseudo," in particular), ideas, and even a certain sociological basis for the phenomenon consisting of seminarians, young priests, and members of the cultivated liberal bourgeoisie (for example, the circle around the Lyon magazine *Demain*).

26. Colin, *L'Audace et le Soupçon*, 249.

27. Fouilloux, *Une Église en quête de liberté*, 39.

28. See Alain Rauwel, "Anti-moderne et médiéval," in *Catholicisme et Monde moderne aux XIXe et XXe siècles. Autour du "Modernisme*," ed. François Chaubet (Éditions Universitaires de Dijon, 2008), 59–65.

29. Fouilloux, *Une Église en quête de liberté*, 61.

30. Daniel Russo, "Les lectures de l'art sacré en France et en Europe au tournant des années 1880–1920. Autour du 'médiévalisme,'" in Chaubet, *Catholicisme et Monde moderne aux XIXe et XXe siècles*, 97.

31. On Étienne Gilson see, most recently, Florian Michel, *Étienne Gilson. Une biographie intellectuelle et politique* (Vrin, 2018). See also Monique Couratier, ed., *Étienne Gilson et nous. La philosophie et son histoire. Colloque sur l'actualité de la pensée d'Étienne Gilson* (Vrin, 1980); Alain de Libera, "Les études de philosophie médiévale en France d'Étienne Gilson à nos jours," in *Gli studi di filosofia medievale fra Otto e Novecento. Contributo a un bilancio storiografico. Atti del convegno internazionale Rome, 21–23 settembre 1989*, ed. Ruedi Imbach and Alfonso Maierù (Edizioni di Storia e Letturatura, 1991); Jacques Prévotat, "Étienne Gilson est-il un chrétien modéré?," in *Les chrétiens modérés*

6. MODERNISM'S CHALLENGE TO THE MIDDLE AGES ᏋᎡ 249

en France et en Europe, 1870–1960, ed. Jacques Prévotat and Jean Vavasseur-Desperriers (Presses Universitaires du Septentrion, 2013).

32. Cf. Émile Bréhier, "Y a-t-il une philosophie chrétienne?," *Revue de métaphysique et de morale* 38, no. 2 (1931): 133–162. See also Pierre Colin, "Les historiens de la philosophie et le modernisme," in *Penser la foi. Mélanges offerts à Joseph Moingt*, ed. Joseph Doré and Christoph Theobald (Cerf, 1993).

33. Leo XIII, of course, did not speak of "Christian philosophy," a phrase coined by Gilson himself. He did, however, speak of *philosophia christiana ad mentem Sancti Thomae Aquinatis* (Christian philosophy according to the mind of Saint Thomas Aquinas), which for Gilson referred to the same thing. It is also not appropriate to consider the promulgation of the *Aeterni Patris* the beginning of the history of the debate over the relationship between Christianity and philosophy in that era. There were many earlier discussions on the subject, illustrated in particular by figures like Lamennais, Maine de Biran ("our master over all," Cousin wrote), Louis Bautain, Alphonse Gratry, and more generally in the discussions on philosophical "traditionalism" that constitute a very rich prehistory for the debate of the 1930s, but which had doubtless been partly forgotten by the time the question resurfaced. Étienne Gilson caught a glimpse of it in his "Notes bibliographiques pour servir à l'histoire de la notion de philosophie chrétienne" (republished in the 1943 and 1989 editions of *L'Esprit de la philosophie médiévale* [413–440 in the 1943 edition]), when he noted that the expression dates back to the nineteenth century. In 1835, in fact, Bautain published a *Philosophie du christianisme*. In 1861, Gratry published a *Philosophie du credo*. In this area, Louis Foucher's great 1955 book *La Philosophie catholique en France au XIXe siècle avant la renaissance thomiste et dans son rapport avec elle (1800–1880)* must also be mentioned. A scholar like Maurice Blondel, who would become the main philosopher of the modernist crisis and who participated in the debate of the 1930s, would in the late nineteenth century become heir to this independent current of Thomism by way of figures like Gratry and Léon Ollé-Laprune. I thank Guillaume Cuchet for these reflections.

34. Colin, *L'Audace et le Soupçon*, 249.

35. De Libera, *Raison et foi*, 35.

36. De Libera, 35.

37. Ruedi Imbach and Catherine König-Pralong, *Le Défi laïque* (Vrin, 2013), 34.

38. Étienne Gilson, *Introduction à la philosophie chrétienne* (Vrin, 1960), 9.

250 ☙ 6. MODERNISM'S CHALLENGE TO THE MIDDLE AGES

39. See especially Fernand Van Steenberghen, "Étienne Gilson, historien de la pensée médiévale," *Revue philosophique de Leuven* 77 (1979): 494: "His ideas evolved, unfortunately in the sense of a hardening of his positions, since he ended by declaring that 'the true *scholastic philosophers* will always be theologians.'"

40. Gilson, *Le Philosophe et la Théologie*, 172.

41. Gilson, 177: "As far as can be judged, Pope Leo XIII did not intend to prescribe, recommend, or even advise the use of the formula 'Christian philosophy.' However, since it appears in the title, it is reasonable to think that something corresponds to it in the body of the encyclical. As soon as the question is thus posed, the answer presents itself to the mind. The Pope says: 'Speak of Christian philosophy, if you wish, provided that you understand by these words the Christian manner of philosophizing, of which the doctrine of Saint Thomas must remain for you both model and rule."

42. Gilson, 158.

43. Gilson, 158: "It was nonetheless one of the most certain origins of the document, because, though forgotten in 1907, where it survived only in the title of a review, it had very much been alive in the years just before 1879."

44. Gilson, 48.

45. Gilson, 49–50: "Saint Thomas Aquinas, this scapegoat charged with all the sins of scholasticism, was much talked about and he was made to say many things, but he was not often quoted, and when he was, the opinions attributed to him were not without surprises. . . . There was little concern over doing justice to this hated theologian. He was capable of anything. The consequences of this state of mind were serious."

46. De Libera, "Les études de philosophie médiévale en France d'Étienne Gilson à nos jours," 22.

47. Jacques Musset, *Sommes-nous sortis de la crise du modernisme? Enquête sur le XXe siècle catholique et l'après-concile Vatican II* (Karthala, 2016).

48. De Libera, *Raison et foi*, 35.

49. De Libera, 70.

50. De Libera, 10.

51. De Libera, 69.

52. David D'Avray, *Medieval Religious Rationalities: A Weberian Analysis* (Cambridge University Press, 2010).

53. Cf. De Libera, *Raison et foi*, 29–30.

7. INFALLIBILISM   ❧   251

54. De Libera, 76.
55. Colin, *L'Audace et le Soupçon*, 252.
56. Colin, 268.
57. Colin, 262.
58. Van Steenberghen, *Introduction à l'étude de la pensée médiévale*, 96.
59. Paul Vignaux, *Philosophie au Moyen Âge* (Vrin, 2004), 10.
60. Quoted in Vignaux, *Philosophie au Moyen Âge*, 287–288: "Because it was Christian, the thought of Saint Thomas remained historical, like Christianity itself. But, because it was rational, because it attacked (in the chemical sense of the word) the Christian component by means of a reagent as powerfully ahistorical as Aristotle's thought was, it actually resulted in a particularly lucid understanding of what from this component was *irreducibly historical*."
61. Paul Vignaux, "Situation d'un historien philosophe devant la scolastique des XIVe et XVe siècles," in Couratier, *Étienne Gilson et nous*, 58.
62. Georges de Lagarde, *Naissance de l'esprit laïque au déclin du Moyen Âge* (Presses Universitaires de France, 1942–1947). The work's six volumes had the following titles and publication dates: vol. 1, *Bilan du XIIIe siècle*, 1947; vol. 2, *Marsile de Padoue ou le premier théoricien de l'État laïque*, 1947; vol. 3, *Secteur social de la Scolastique*, 1942; vol. 4, *Ockham et son temps*, 1942; vol. 5, *Ockham: Bases de départ*, 1946; vol. 6, *Ockham: La morale et le droit*, 1946. See also Georges de Lagarde, "Individualisme et corporatisme au Moyen Âge," in *L'Organisation corporative du Moyen Âge à la fin de l'Ancien Régime*, ed. Émile Lousse (Presses Universitaires de Louvain, 1937).

7. INFALLIBILISM

1. Hans Küng, *Structures of the Church* (University of Notre Dame Press, 1964), 327.
2. Respectively, Karl Rahner, "Quelques considérations sur le problème de l'infaillibilité dans la théologie catholique," in *L'Infaillibilité. Son aspect philosophique et théologique*, ed. Enrico Castelli (Aubier, 1970), 64; and Karl Barth, *Dogmatique* (Labor et Fides, 1955), 1:93–95.
3. See, among other titles, Luca Parisoli, "L'émergence de l'infaillibilité pontificale de Pierre de Jean Olieu à Guillaume d'Ockham," *L'Année Canonique* 41 (1999): 143–164.

4. Claude Langlois, "L'infaillibilité pontificale, une idée neuve au XIXe siècle," in *Le continent théologique. Explorations historiques* (Presses Universitaires de Rennes, 2016), 52.

5. Langlois, 57.

6. Sylvio Hermann De Franceschi, "Le catholicisme antiromain et l'infaillibilité pontificale du XVIIe siècle," in *Le Pontife et l'erreur: Anti-infaillibilisme catholique et romanité ecclésiale aux temps posttridentins (XVIIe–XXe siècles)*, ed. Sylvio Hermann De Franceschi (Laboratoire de recherche historique Rhône-Alpes, 2010), 56.

7. Sylvio Hermann De Franceschi, 58.

8. Victor Auguste Dechamps, *L'infaillibilité et le Concile général. Étude de science religieuse à l'usage des gens du monde* (Liége, 1869).

9. On the concept of exculturation, see Danièle Hervieu-Léger, *Catholicisme, la fin d'un monde* (Bayard, 2003).

10. Olivier Rousseau et al., eds., *L'Infaillibilité de l'Église, Journées œcuméniques de Chevetogne* (Éditions de Chevetogne, 1962).

11. Küng, *Infallible? An Inquiry* (Doubleday, 1971).

12. See a remark in Gérard Dejaifve, "Un débat sur l'infaillibilité. La discussion entre K. Rahner et H. Küng," *Nouvelle Revue théologique* 93 (1971): 583: "Even though none of H. Küng's books have gone unnoticed for a long time, we can say that his most recent one, *Infallible?*, has caused more than a stir within the Catholic Church and even well beyond its confessional borders."

13. Karl Rahner, ed., *Zum Problem Unfehlbarkeit: Antworten auf die Anfrage von H. Küng* (Herder, 1971). See also Karl Rahner, "Quelques considérations sur le problème de l'infaillibilité dans la théologie catholique," in *L'infaillibilité. Son aspect philosophique et théologique*, ed. Enrico Castelli (Aubier, 1970); Karl Rahner, "Zum Begriff der Unfehlbarkeit in der Katholischen Theologie," *Stimmen der Zeit* 186 (1970): 18–31; Karl Rahner, "Kritik an Has Küng: Zur frage der Unfehlbarkeit theologischer Sätze. Antwort an Karl Rahner," *Stimmen der Zeit* 187 (1971): 43–64 and 105–122. Following Küng's response, "Im Interresse der Sache," see also Rahner, "Replik. Bemerkungen zu: Hans Küng, Im Interesse der Sache," *Stimmen der Zeit* 187 (1971): 145–160. For a summary of the debate, see Dejaifve, "Un débat sur l'infaillibilité."

14. Langlois, "L'infallibilite pontificale."

7. INFALLIBILISM ❧ 253

15. Gustave Thils, *L'infaillibilité du peuple chrétien* "in credendo." *Notes de théologie post-tridentine* (Bibliotheca Ephemeridum Theologicarum Lovaniensium, 1963).

16. Gustave Thils, *L'infaillibilité pontificale: Source, conditions, limites* (Duculot, 1969); Gustave Thils, *La primauté pontificale: La doctrine de Vatican I, les voies d'une révision* (Duculot, 1972); Gustave Thils, *Primauté et infaillibilité du Pontife romain à Vatican I, et autres études d'ecclésiologie* (Leuven University Press, 1989).

17. Brian Tierney, *Origins of Papal Infallibility: A Study on the Concepts of Infallibility (1150–1350), Sovereignty, and Tradition in the Middle Ages* (Brill, 1972).

18. Among other examples, see Yves-Marie Congar, "Infaillibilité et indéfectibilité," in *Ministères et communion ecclésiale*, ed. Yves-Marie Congar (Cerf, 1971); Yves-Marie Congar, "Saint Thomas Aquinas and the Infallibility of the Papal Magisterium: *Summa theologiae*, IIa IIae, q. 1, art. 10." *Thomist* 38 (1974): 81–105.

19. Paul De Vooght, "Esquisse d'une enquête sur le mot 'infaillibilité' durant la période scolastique," in Rousseau et al., *L'infaillibilité de l'Église*.

20. Thils, *L'infaillibilité pontificale*.

21. Congar, "Infaillibilité et indéfectibilité," 154.

22. Congar, 142.

23. Jean Gerson, *Quae veritates sint de necessitate salutis credendae*, starting: "Declaration compendiosa quae veritates sint" (after September 8, 1416), in *Œuvres complètes*, 6:181–189 § 280.

24. Küng, *Structures of the Church*, 376.

25. Thomas M. Izbicki, "Infallibility and the Erring Pope: Guido Terreni and Johannes de Turrecremata," in *Law, Church, and Society: Essays in Honor of Stephan Kuttner*, ed. Kenneth Pennington and Robert Sommerville (University of Pennsylvania Press, 1977).

26. Fidelis a Fanna, *Bonaventurae doctrina de Romani Pontificis primatu et infallibilitate* (Turin, 1870).

27. Tierney, *Origins of Papal Infallibility*, 96, and Peter John Olivi, *Quaestio de infallibilitate Romani pontificis*, ed. M. Maccarrone, *Rivista di storia della chiesa in Italia* 3 (1949): 309–343. See also Marco Bartoli, "Olivi et le pouvoir du pape," in *Pierre de Jean Olivi (1248–1298): Pensée scolastique, dissidence spirituelle et société. Actes du colloque de Narbonne*, ed. Alain Boureau and Sylvain Piron (Vrin, 1999), 179–180; Ulrich Horst, "Infallibilität und Geschichte. Ein

Rückblick," in *Unfehlbarkeit und Geschichte, Studien zur Unfehlbarkeitdiskussion von Melchior Cano zum I. Vatikanischen Konzil*, ed. Ulrich Horst (Matthias Grünewald-Verlag, 1982), 251; and Klaus Schatz, *La primauté du pape. Son histoire, des origines à nos jours* (Cerf, 1992), 180: "Olivi and the authors who follow him have not yet taken the new and decisive step: It will only be taken in the wake of the discussion around conciliarism from the fifteenth century onward."

28. De Vooght, "Esquisse d'une enquête sur le mot 'infaillibilité' durant la période scolastique," 100, 144.

29. Luca Parisoli, "L'émergence de l'infaillibilité pontificale de Pierre de Jean Olieu à Guillaume d'Ockham," *L'Année Canonique* 41 (1999): 143–164.

30. Tierney, *Origins of Papal Infallibility*, 205.

31. Joseph de Maistre, *Du Pape. Édition critique*, ed. Jacques Lovie and Joannès Chetail (Droz, 1966), 27.

32. De Franceschi, *Le Pontife et l'erreur*, 8.

33. De Vooght, *Les pouvoirs du concile et l'autorité du pape au concile de Constance* (Cerf, 1965), 27.

34. De Franceschi, *Le Pontife et l'erreur*, 9.

35. On the bibliography for the exegesis of Galatians 2:11, see Thomas M. Izbicki, "The Authority of Peter and Paul: The Use of Biblical Authority During the Great Schism," in *A Companion to the Great Western Schism (1378–1417)*, ed. Joëlle Rollo-Koster and Thomas M. Izbicki (Brill, 2009); and G. H. M. Posthumus Meyjes, *De controverse tussen Petrus en Paulus. Galaten 2: 11 in de historie* (M. Nijhoff, 1967), many elements of which were republished in French in G. H. M. Posthumus Meyjes, *Jean Gerson et l'Assemblée de Vincennes (1329). Ses conceptions de la juridiction temporelle de l'Église* (Brill, 1978). On the same subject, see G. H. M. Posthumus Meyjes, "Iconografie en Primaat. Petrus en Paulus op het pauselijk zegel," *Nederlands Archief voor Kerkgeschiedenis* 49 (1968): 4–36. See also Karlfried Froehlich, "New Testament Models of Conflict Resolution: Observations on the Biblical Argument of Paris Conciliarists During the Great Schism," in *Conciliation and Confession: The Struggle for Unity in the Age of Reform, 1415–1648*, ed. Howard P. Louthan and Randall C. Zachman (University of Notre Dame Press, 2004), 26–27, and especially Karlfried Froehlich, "Fallibility Instead of Infallibility? A Brief History of the Interpretation of Ga. 2, 11–14," in *Teaching Authority and Infallibility in the Church*, ed. Paul Empie et al. (Augsburg

7. INFALLIBILISM ⪼ 255

Fortress, 1980), 259–269, 351–357. For informational purposes, note should also be made of the very old Franz Overbeck, *Über die Auffassung des Streits des Paulus mit Petrus in Antiochien (Gal 2, 11), bei den Kirchenvätern* (Wissenschaftliche Buchgesellschaft, 1968), which was originally published in 1877. Finally, it should be mentioned that the verse was one of the favorite subjects of Hus and a leitmotif in the controversy of Hussite writings. See Paul De Vooght, *Hussiana* (Nauwelaerts, 1960), 193. For the Lutheran exegesis, see Inge Lönning, "Paulus und Petrus. Gal 2,11 ff. als kontroverstheologisches fundamental Problem," *Studia Theologica: Scandinavian Journal of Theology* 24 (1970): 1–69; and Helmut Feld, "Christus Diener der Sünde. Zum Ausgang des Streits zwischen Petrus und Paulus," *Theologische Quartalschrift* 153 (1973): 119–131.

36. De Franceschi, *Le Pontife et l'erreur*, 115, 116. On the subject of Matthew 18:17, see Froehlich, "New Testament Models of Conflict Resolution," 19–21.

37. Simon de Cramaud, *De substraccione obediencie*, starting: "Nunc reges intelligite," in Howard Kaminsky, *Simon de Cramaud and the Great Schism* (Rutgers University Press, 1983), 116.

38. See Thomas Wünsch, *Konziliarismus und Polen* (Ferdinand Schöningh, 1998), 66.

39. Jean Gerson, *Libellus articulorum contra Petrum de Luna*, starting: "Libellus articulorum theologicorum et scolastice compositorum contra Petrum de Luna" (April 26, 1417), in *Œuvres complètes*, 6:267–274 § 286.

40. Gerson, 267–274 § 286.

41. Gerson, 267–274 § 286.

42. Gerson, 267–274 § 286.

43. Gerson, 271, art. 2, and 272–273.

44. Gerson, 274.

45. Jean Gerson, *An liceat in causis fidei a papa appellare*, in *Œuvres complètes*, 6:283–290.

46. Gerson, 283–290.

47. Gerson, 283–290.

48. Gerson, 296.

49. Nicolas Eymerich, *Contra emissum in conclavi per papam promissorum juramentum*, Grenoble, Bibliothèque Municipale, 988, fol. 103r–117v, here fol. 111v–112r: "Sic est et de papa: ut enim christianus Christi fraterne

256 ⁊ 7. INFALLIBILISM

correctionis legi est subditus, ut fratrem corrigat et si non corrigitur presidenti et Ecclesie dicat, sed quod legem illam non teneat, status papatus obviat."

50. Eymerich, fol. 112r.

51. Eymerich, fol. 112r. It should be noted that when he defined political obedience in his 1405 speech *Vivat rex*, Gerson referred to the same quotation from Romans 13: "I demonstrate and pronounce that such a one does not show himself to be a loyal son of the holy Church or a good subject of the king, and that, worse, he resists God and his ordinance. *Omnis potestas a Deo, et qui potestati resistit, Dei ordinatione resistit*, Rom. 13. All power, as Saint Paul said, is from God, and whoever resists power resists a divine ordinance."

52. Jean Mauroux, "Propositio in Constantiensi concilio facta, quod papa a negotiis concilii excludi non possit," starting: "Utrum papa subjiciatur concilio" (February 1415), in *Magnum oecumenicum Constantiense concilium*, ed. Hermann von der Hardt (Leipzig, 1697–1700), vol. 2, chap. 297.

53. For Pierre Plaoul, anyone (*quilibet*) could stand up against a faulty pope. See Pierre Plaoul, "Discours de clôture des débats avant le vote," in *Historia universitatis Parisiensis*, ed. César-Egasse du Boulay, 6 vols. (Paris, 1665–1673), 4:835, 843.

54. Martin de Zalba, "Allegationes domini cardinalis sancti Angeli," starting: "Qui potestatem pape," Grenoble, Bibliothèque Municipale, 988, fol. 117r–127r, here fol. 125r.

55. University of Toulouse, *Epistola Tholosana*, in Du Boulay, *Historia universitatis Parisiensis*, 5:4–24, here 11, according to Pierre de Blois.

56. De Zalba, "Allegationes domini cardinalis sancti Angeli," fol. 126v.

57. Eymerich, *Contra universitatem Parisiensis*, fol. 43r–72v, fol. 70v: "Papa autem hominem in terris non habet superiorem, de hoc saepe dictum est prius et dicitur *De elec. Licet* et ix. Q. iii *Aliorum* et c. *Facta* et c. *Cuncta* et c. *Patet* et in Extravagante Bonifacii *Unam Sanctam*. Et quia papa non habet superiorem, non potest aliqualiter ab eo appellari" (But the pope has no superior on earth, as has often been said and is still said in *De elec. Licet* and ix. Q. iii *Aliorum* and c. *Facta* and c. *Cuncta* and c. *Patet* and in Boniface's extravagant *Unam sanctam*. And because the pope has no superior, he cannot in any way be addressed by one). The citations refer, respectively, to X.1.6.6, and to Gratian, *Decretum magistri Gratiani*, C. 24, q. 3, chap. 9 and C. 15, q. 3, chap. 9.

7. INFALLIBILISM ❧ 257

58. Eymerich, *Contra universitatem Parisiensis*, fol. 71r.

59. See, among others, Jacques Chiffoleau, "Sur le crime de majesté médiéval," in *Genèse de l'État moderne en Méditerranée. Approches historique et anthropologique des pratiques et des représentations. Actes des tables rondes internationales tenues à Paris (24–26 septembre 1987 et 18–19 mars 1988)* (École Française de Rome, 1993).

60. University of Toulouse, *Epistola Tholosana*, in Du Boulay, *Historia universitatis Parisiensis*, 5:12. On the axiom *extra Ecclesiam nulla salus*, see Bernard Sesboüé, *"Hors de l'Église pas de salut." Histoire d'une formule et problèmes d'interprétation* (Desclée de Brouwer, 2004). See also David Zachariah, *"Extra Ecclesiam salus non est—sed quae Ecclesia?*: Ecclesiology and Authority in the Later Middle Ages," in Rollo-Koster and Izbicki, *A Companion to the Great Western Schism*.

61. Pierre d'Ailly, *Tractatus de potestate ecclesiastica* (October 1, 1416), in Jean Gerson, *Opera omnia*, ed. Louis Ellies du Pin (Peter de Hondt, 1728), 2:925–960; Mauroux, *Propositio in Constantiensi concilio facta*, in Von der Hardt, *Magnum oecumenicum Constantiense concilium*, 2:297.

62. See Jürgen Dendorfer and Ralf Lützelschwab, eds., *Geschichte des Kardinalats im Mittelalter* (Hiersemann, 2011).

63. D'Ailly, *Tractatus de potestate ecclesiastica*, 958.

64. D'Ailly, 958.

65. D'Ailly, 959.

66. D'Ailly, 959.

67. D'Ailly, 959.

68. See Gratian, *Decretum magistri Gratiani*, D. 40 c. 6: "Papa a nemine est judicandus, nisi deprehendatur a fide devius" (The pope is to be judged by no one, unless he is found to have deviated from the faith). On this subject, see Tierney, *Foundations of the Conciliar Theory*, 57, and, in his appendix, 248–250: "Huguccio's gloss on the words *Nisi deprehendatur a fide devius*."

69. D'Ailly, *Tractatus de potestate ecclesiastica*, 959–960.

70. Paul De Vooght, "Les dimensions réelles de l'infaillibilité papale," in *L'infaillibilité. Son aspect philosophique et théologique*, ed. Enrico Castelli (Aubier, 1970).

71. Thils, *L'infaillibilité pontificale*, 8.

72. Charles Moeller, "Infaillibilité et vérité," in Olivier Rousseau et al., *L'infaillibilité de l'Église*.

258   7. INFALLIBILISM

73. Pedro de Luna (Benedict XIII), "Tractatus adversus conciliabulum Pisanum," starting: "Quia nonnulli quondam" (1410–1412), among others Paris, Bibliothèque nationale de France, Departement des manuscrits, lat. 1474, fol. 1r–33v, partially edited by Ehrle in Heinrich Denifle and Franz Ehrle, eds., *Archiv für Litteratur- und Kirchengeschichte des Mittelalters*, 7 vols. (Freiburg im Breisgau, 1885–1900), 7:533–540, this passage 536.

74. John Hayton, "Contra viam cessionis credo Magister Johannis Aton," starting: "Pater beatissime, iste proponens sequentes cum ipsarum" (after July 1395), Grenoble, Bibliothèque Municipale, 988, fol. 74r–77v, fol. 76r.

75. Leonardo da Giffoni, "Allegationes domini cardinalis de Giffoni contra papam," ed. Clement Schmitt, *Archivum franciscanum historicum* 21 (1958): 51.

76. Bruno Neveu, *L'erreur et son juge. Remarques sur les censures doctrinales à l'époque moderne* (Bibliopolis, 1993), 34.

77. University of Paris, *Epistola Parisiensis*, Paris, Bibliothèque nationale de France, Departement des manuscrits, lat. 14643, fol. 49v.

78. "Contre l'épitre des Toulousains à Charles VI," Paris, Bibliothèque nationale de France, Departement des manuscrits, lat. 14644, fol. 202v–211v, in Du Boulay, *Historia universitatis Parisiensis*, 5:31.

79. Pierre Ravat, "Questio de concilio Pisani," starting: "Pater sancte, salva semper determinatione," Paris, Bibliothèque nationale de France, Departement des manuscrits, lat. 1479, fol. 8v.

80. Tierney, *Origins of Papal Infallibility*, 57.

CONCLUSION

1. See Jean-Pascal Gay, "Théophile Raynaud et le choix de la théologie comme rhétorique en soi. Partages disciplinaires, ordre confessionel et apologétique catholique au XVIIe siècle," *Histoire, monde et cultures religieuses* 35, no. 3 (2015): 35–52; Jean-Pascal Gay, *Le Dernier théologien? Théophile Raynaud, histoire d'une obsolescence* (Beauchesne, 2018).

2. Philippe Büttgen, "Théologie politique et pouvoir pastoral," *Annales HSS* 5 (September–October 2007): 1129–1154.

3. Büttgen, 1144.

4. Quoted in Büttgen, 1148; Michel Foucault, *Sécurité, territoire, population: Cours au Collège de France, 1977–1978*, ed. Michel Senellart et al. (Gallimard-Seuil, 2004), 195.

CONCLUSION ☙ 259

5. Büttgen, "Théologie politique et pouvoir pastoral," 1149.
6. For the history of the clergy, see, for example, Anne Bonzon, *L'esprit de clocher. Prêtres et paroisses dans le diocèse de Beauvais (1535–1560)* (Cerf, 1999); Gérald Chaix, ed., *Le diocèse. Espaces, représentations, pouvoirs (France, XVe–XXe siècle)* (Cerf, 2002).
7. Büttgen, "Théologie politique et pouvoir pastoral," 1154.

BIBLIOGRAPHY

Alberigo, Giuseppe. *Cardinalato e collegialita. Studi sull'ecclesiologia tra l'XI e il XIV secolo.* Vallecchi, 1969.

Alberigo, Giuseppe. *Chiesa conciliare: Identità e significato del conciliarismo.* Paideia, 1981.

Alberigo, Giuseppe. "Ecclésiologie et démocratie. Convergences et divergences." *Concilium* 243 (1992): 29–44.

Alberigo, Giuseppe. "Élection, consensus, réception dans l'expérience chrétienne." *Concilium* 77 (1972): 7–17.

Alberigo, Giuseppe. *Histoire du concile Vatican II (1959–1965). L'Église en tant que communion. La troisième session et la troisième intersession (septembre 1964–septembre 1965).* Cerf, 2003.

Alberigo, Giuseppe. "Hubert Jedin storiografo (1900–1980)." *Cristianesimo nella storia* 22 (2001): 315–338.

Alberigo, Giuseppe. "Il movimento conciliare (XIV–XV sec.) nella ricerca storica recente." *Studi medievali* 19, no. 2 (1978): 913–950.

Alberigo, Giuseppe. "Institutions exprimant la communion entre l'épiscopat universel et l'évêque de Rome." in *Les églises après Vatican II: Dynamique et perspective.* Beauchesne, 1981.

Alberigo, Giuseppe. "L'amore alla chiesa: Dalla riforma all'aggiornamento." In *"Con tutte le tue forze." I nodi della fede cristiana oggi. Omaggio a Giuseppe Dossetti,* edited by Angelina Alberigo and Giuseppe Alberigo. Marietti, 1993.

Alberigo, Giuseppe, ed. *Le catholicisme vers une nouvelle époque. L'annonce et la préparation (janvier 1959–octobre 1962).* Vol. 1 of *Histoire du concile Vatican II (1959–1965).* Cerf, 1997.

Alberigo, Giuseppe. "L'ecclesiologia del Concilio di Trento." In *Il Concilio Tridentino. Prospettive storiografiche e problemi storici*, by Paolo Brezzi, Enrico Cattaneo, and Giuseppe Alberigo. Vita e pensiero, 1965.

Alberigo, Giuseppe. "Réforme en tant que critère de l'histoire de l'Église." *Revue d'histoire ecclésiastique* 76 (1981): 72–81.

Alberigo, Giuseppe. "Réforme et unité de l'Église." In *Cardinal Yves Congar (1904–1995)*, edited by André Vauchez. Cerf, 1999.

Alberigo, Giuseppe, and Anton Weiler, eds. *Election and Consensus in the Church.* Herder & Herder, 1972.

Albert, Jean-Pierre, Anne Brenon, and Pilar Jiménez, eds. *Dissidences en Occident des débuts du christianisme au XXe siècle. Le religieux et le politique.* Presses Universitaires du Midi, 2015.

Albertus Magnus. *De generatione et corruptione*, edited by Paul Hossfeld. Vol. 5, part 2 of *Opera Omnia*, edited by Bernhard Geyer and Wilhelm Kübel. Aschendorff, 1980.

Album Helen Maud Cam: Studies Presented to the International Commission for the History of Representative and Parliamentary Institutions. Nauwelaerts, 1961.

Amargier, Paul. *Une Église du renouveau: Réformes et réformateurs de Charlemagne à Jean Hus, 750–1415.* Cerf, 1998.

Arabeyre, Patrick. *Les idées politiques à Toulouse à la veille de la réforme: Recherches autour de l'œuvre de Guillaume Benoît (1455–1516).* Presses de l'Université de Sciences Sociales de Toulouse, 2003.

Arabeyre, Patrick. "Un enseignement de science politique dans les facultés de droit canonique françaises de la fin du XVe siècle et du début du XVI siècle (Paris, Cahors, Toulouse)." In *Science politique et droit publique dans les facultés de droit européenes (XIIIe–XVIIIe siècle)*, edited by Jacques Krynen and Michael Stolleis. V. Klostermann, 2008.

Armogathe, Jean-Robert, Pascal Montaubin, and Michel-Yves Perrin, eds. *Histoire générale du christianisme.* Presses Universitaires de France, 2010.

Atwood, Craig D. *Always Reforming: A History of Christianity since 1300.* Mercer University Press, 2001.

Baker, Derek, ed. *Renaissance and Renewal in Christian History.* Blackwell, 1977.

Balic, Charles. "Johannes Duns Scotus und die Lehrentscheidung von 1277." *Wissenschaft und Weisheit* 29 (1966): 210–229.

Ballweg, Jan. *Konziliare oder Päpstliche Ordensreform: Benedikt XII und die Reformdiskussion im frühen 14. Jh.* Mohr Siebeck, 2001.

BIBLIOGRAPHY ◌ 263

Baranger, Denis. *Parlementarisme des origines. Essai sur les conditions de formation d'un exécutif responsable en Angleterre (des années 1740 au début de l'âge victorien)*. Presses Universitaires de France, 1999.

Barrow, Julia. "Ideas and Applications of Reform." In *Early Medieval Chistianities, c. 600–c. 1100*. Vol. 3 of *The Cambridge History of Christianity*, edited by Thomas F. X. Noble and Julia M. H. Smith. Cambridge University Press, 2008.

Barth, Karl. *Dogmatique*. Vol. 1, part 2 of *La doctrine de la parole de dieu: Prolégomènes à la dogmatique*. Labor et Fides, 1955.

Barthe, Claude. *Les Oppositions romaines au Pape*. Hora Decima, 2009.

Bartoli, Marco. "Olivi et le pouvoir du pape." In *Pierre de Jean Olivi (1248–1298): Pensée scolastique, dissidence spirituelle et société. Actes du colloque de Narbonne*, edited by Alain Boureau and Sylvain Piron. Vrin, 1999.

Bastid, Paul. *L'idée de constitution*. Economica, 1985.

Bäumer, Remigius. "Antwort an Tierney." *Theologische Revue* 70 (1974): 193–194.

Bäumer, Remigius. *Die Entwicklung des Konziliarismus*. Wissenschaftliche Buchgesellschaft, 1976.

Bäumer, Regimius. "Die Stellungnahme Eugens IV. Zum Konstanzer Superioritätsdekret in der Bulle 'Etsi non dubitemus.'" In *Das Konzil von Konstanz. Beiträge zu seiner Geschichte und Theologie*, edited by August Franzen and Wolfgang Müller. Herder, 1964.

Bäumer, Remigius. *Nachwirkungen des konziliaren Gedankens in der Theologie und Kanonistik des frühen 16. Jahrhunderts*. Aschendorff, 1971.

Baümer, Remigius. "Um die Anfänge der päpstlichen Unfehlbarkeitslehre." *Theologische Revue* 69 (1973): 441–450.

Beaud, Olivier. "Carl Schmitt ou le juriste engagé." Preface to *Théorie de la Constitution*, by Carl Schmitt. Presses Universitaires de France, 1993.

Beaud, Olivier. "Constitution et constitutionnalisme." In *Dictionnaire de philosophie politique*, edited by Philippe Raynaud and Stéphane Rials, 133–142. Presses Universitaires de France, 1996.

Beaud, Olivier. "L'histoire du concept de constitution en France. De la constitution politique à la constitution comme statut juridique de l'État." *Jus politicum: Autour de la notion de constitution* 3 (2010): 31–59.

Beaulande-Barraud, Véronique. "Jean Gerson et les cas réservés: Un enjeu ecclésiologique et pastoral." *Revue d'histoire de l'Église de France* 100 (2014): 301–318.

264 ❧ BIBLIOGRAPHY

Bellarmine, Robert. *De Romano pontifice.* Vol. 1 of *Disputationes de controversiis christianae fidei.* Naples, 1586.

Bellarmine, Robert. *Risposta di Card. Bellarmino ad un libretto intitulato Trattato e resolutione sopra la validità de la scommuniche di Gileio. Gersono.* Guglielmo Facciotto, 1606.

Bellitto, Christopher M. "Ancient Precedents and Historical Case Studies: Recent Reform Scholarship." *Catholic Library World* 75 (2005): 277–289.

Bellitto, Christopher M. "Councils and Reform: Challenging Misconceptions." In *The Church, the Councils and Reform: The Legacy of the Fifteenth Century,* edited by Gerald Christianson, Thomas M. Izbicki, and Christopher M. Bellitto. Catholic University of America Press, 2008.

Bellitto, Christopher M. *General Councils: A History of the Twenty-one Church Councils from Nicaea to Vatican II.* Paulist Press, 2002.

Bellitto, Christopher M. "The Reform Context of the Great Western Schism." In *A Companion to the Great Western Schism (1378–1417),* edited by Joëlle Rollo-Koster and Thomas M. Izbicki. Brill, 2009.

Bellitto, Christopher M. *Renewing Christianity: A History of Church Reform from Day One to Vatican II.* Paulist Press, 2001.

Bellitto, Christopher M., and David Zachariah Flanagin, eds. *Reassessing Reform: A Historical Investigation into Church Renewal.* Catholic University of America Press, 2012.

Berman, Harold. *Law and Revolution: The Formation of the Western Legal Tradition.* Harvard University Press, 1983.

Bianchi, Luca. *Censure et liberté intellectuelle à l'université de Paris (XIIIe–XIVe siècles).* Les Belles Lettres, 1999.

Bianchi, Luca. *Pour une histoire de la "double vérité."* Vrin, 2008.

Bianchi, Luca, and Eugenio Randi. *Vérités dissonantes. Aristote à la fin du Moyen Âge.* Éditions Universitaires Fribourg Suisse, 1993.

Bischof, François-Xavier, and Sylvio Hermann De Franceschi, eds. *Histoires antiromaines II. L'antiromanisme dans l'historiographie ecclésiastique catholique (XVIe–XXe siècles).* Laboratoire de recherche historique Rhône-Alpes, 2014.

Black, Antony. *Council and Commune: The Conciliar Movement and the Fifteenth-Century Heritage.* Burns & Oates, 1979.

Black, Antony. *Monarchy and Community: Political Ideas in the Later Conciliar Controversy, 1430–1450.* Cambridge University Press, 1970.

BIBLIOGRAPHY ❧ 265

Black, Antony. "What Was Conciliarism? Conciliar Theory in Historical Perspective." In *Authority and Power: Studies on Medieval Law and Government Presented to Walter Ullman*, edited by Brian Tierney and Peter Linehan. Cambridge University Press, 1980.

Blanc de Saint-Bonnet, Antoine. *L'Infaillibilité*. Nouvelles éditions latines, 1956.

Blythe, James M. *Ideal Government and the Mixed Constitution in the Middle Ages*. Princeton University Press, 1992.

Bollerman, Karen, Thomas M. Izbicki, and Cary J. Nederman, eds. *Religion, Power and Resistance from the Eleventh to the Sixteenth Centuries: Playing the Heresy Card*. Palgrave Macmillan, 2014.

Bonzon, Anne. *L'esprit de clocher. Prêtres et paroisses dans le diocèse de Beauvais (1535–1560)*. Cerf, 1999.

Bossuet, Jacques Bénigne. *Œuvres complètes de Bossuet*. Edited by F. Lachat. 31 vols. L. Vivès, 1863–1867.

Boureau, Alain. *Histoires d'un historien, Kantorowicz*. Rev. ed. Gallimard, 2000.

Boureau, Alain. *Kantorowicz: Stories of a Historian*. Translated by Stephen G. Nichols and Gabrielle M. Spiegel. Johns Hopkins University Press, 2001.

Boureau, Alain. "Les cérémonies royales françaises entre performance juridique et compétence liturgique." *Annales ESC* 46, no. 6 (1991): 1253–1264.

Boutry, Philippe. "Introduction." In *"Rome, l'unique objet de mon ressentiment"*: *Regards critiques sur la papauté*, edited by Philippe Levillain. École Française de Rome, 2011.

Boutry, Philippe. "La tentative française de destruction du Saint Siège (1789–1814)." In *"Rome, l'unique objet de mon ressentiment"*: *Regards critiques sur la papauté*, edited by Philippe Levillain. École Française de Rome, 2011.

Boutry, Philippe. "Modernisme." In *Dictionnaire des faits religieux*, edited by Régine Azria and Danièle Hervieu-Léger. Presses Universitaires de France, 2010.

Brandmüller, Walter. "Causa reformationis. Ergebnisse und Probleme der Reformen des Konstanzer Konzils." *Annuarium historiae conciliorum* 13 (1981): 49–66.

Brandmüller, Walter. *Das Konzil von Konstanz*. 2 vols. Rev. ed. Ferdinand Schöningh, 2000. Reviews: Klaus-Rederic Johannes, *Zeitschrift der Savigny-Stiftung für Rechtsgeschichte, Kanonistische Abteilung* 121 (2004): 605–608; Jiri Kejr, *Zeitschrift der Savigny-Stiftung für Rechtsgeschichte, Kanonistische Abteilung* 79 (1993): 494–498, and 117 (2000): 583–586; Andreas Kraus, *Zeitschrift für Bayerische Landesgeschichte* 61 (1998): 455–463; Jürgen Miethke, *Deutsches Archiv* 47 (1991): 692–695, and 56 (2000): 313–314.

266 ❧ BIBLIOGRAPHY

Bréhier, Émile. "Y a-t-il une philosophie chrétienne?" *Revue de métaphysique et de morale* 38, no. 2 (1931): 133–162.

Bressolette, Claude. *Le Pouvoir dans la société et dans l'Église. L'ecclésiologie politique de Mgr Maret, dernier doyen de la faculté de théologie de la Sorbonne.* Cerf, 1984.

Bressolette, Claude. "Modernisme." In *Dictionnaire critique de théologie*, edited by Jean-Yves Lacoste. Presses Universitaires de France, 1998.

Briguglia, Gianluca. *Marsilo da Padova.* Carocci, 2013.

Brown, Elizabeth A. R. *"Unctus ad executionem justitie*: Philippe le Bel, Boniface VIII et la grande ordonnance pour la réforme du royaume (du 18 mars 1303)." In *Le roi fontaine de justice. Pouvoir justicier et pouvoir royal au Moyen Âge et à la Renaissance*, edited by Silvère Menegaldo and Bernard Ribémont. Klincksieck, 2012.

Brutus, E. I. *De la puissance légitime du Prince sur le peuple et du peuple sur le Prince.* EDHIS, 1977.

Buisson, Ludwig. *Potestas und caritas: Die päpstliche Gewalt im Spätmittelalter.* Böhlau, 1958.

Burns, James H. *"Politia regalis and optima:* The Political Ideas of John Mair." *History of Political Thought* 2, no. 1 (1981): 31–61.

Burns, James H., and Thomas M. Izbicki, eds. *Conciliarism and Papalism.* Cambridge University Press, 1997.

Burns, J. H., and Thomas M. Izbicki, eds. *Conciliarism and Papalism.* Cambridge University Press, 1997.

Butler, B. C., and Jean Marie R. Tillard. "The Pope with the Bishops." *Tablet*, October 11, 1980, 987–989.

Butterfield, Herbert. *The Whig Interpretation of History.* Bell, 1931.

Büttgen, Philippe. "Théologie politique et pouvoir pastoral." *Annales HSS* 5 (September–October 2007): 1129–1154.

Camadini, Giuseppe. *Paolo VI e la collegialità episcopale.* Studium, 1995.

Canning, Joseph P. "The Corporation in the Political Thought of the Jurists of the Thirteenth and Fourteenth Centuries." *History of Political Theory* 1 (1980): 9–32.

Canning, Joseph P. "Law, Sovereignty and Corporation Theory, 1300–1450." In *The Cambridge History of Medieval Political Thought, c. 350–1450*, edited by James H. Burns. Cambridge University Press, 1988.

Carlen, Claudia, ed. *The Papal Encyclicals 1740–1878.* McGrath Publishing Company, 1981.

BIBLIOGRAPHY ○ 267

Carlyle, Alexander James, and Robert Warrand Carlyle. *A History of Medieval Political Theory in the West*, vol. 2. W. Blackwood, 1922.

Caron, Pier G. *"Æquitas" romana, "Misericordia" patristica ed "Epicheia" aristotelica nella dotrina dell' "Aequitas" canonica (dalle origini al Rinascimento)*. Giuffrè, 1971.

Carpenter, Christine. *The Wars of the Roses: Politics and the Constitution in England, c. 1437–1509*. Cambridge University Press, 1997.

Castelli, Enrico, ed. *L'Infaillibilité. Son aspect philosophique et théologique*. Aubier, 1970.

Cazelles, Raymond. *Société politique, noblesse et couronne sous Jean le Bon et Charles V*. Droz, 1982.

Cazelles, Raymond. "Une exigence de l'opinion depuis saint Louis: La réformation du royaume." *Annuaire-Bulletin de la Société de l'Histoire de France* (1962–1963): 91–99.

Cerda-Guzman, Carolina. *Cours de droit constitutionnel et des institutions de la Ve République*. Gualino, 2017.

Certeau, Michel de. "L'histoire religieuse du XVIIe siècle. Problèmes de méthode.'" *Recherches de sciences religieuses* 57 (1969): 231–250.

Chadwick, Henry. *The Circle and the Ellipse: Rival Concepts of Authority*. Clarendon Press, 1959.

Chaix, Gérald, ed. *Le diocèse. Espaces, représentations, pouvoirs (France, XVe–XXe siècle)*. Cerf, 2002.

Chaunu, Pierre. *Le temps des réformes. La crise de la chrétienté. L'éclatement 1250–1550*. Fayard, 1975.

Chenu, Marie-Dominique. "Le sens et les leçons d'une crise religieuse." *La vie intellectuelle* 13 (October–December 1931): 356–380.

Chenu, Marie-Dominique. *Moyen Âge et modernité*. Centre d'études du Saulchoir, 1997.

Chenu, Marie-Dominique. "Phénomènes de contestation dans l'histoire de l'Église." *Concilium* 68 (1971): 91–96.

Chiffoleau, Jacques. "Sur le crime de majesté médiéval." In *Genèse de l'État moderne en Méditerranée. Approches historique et anthropologique des pratiques et des représentations. Actes des tables rondes internationales tenues à Paris (24–26 septembre 1987 et 18–19 mars 1988)*. École Française de Rome, 1993.

Chiron, Jean-François. *L'infaillibilité et son objet. L'autorité du magistère infaillible de l'Église s'étend-elle aux vérités non révélées?* Cerf, 1999.

268 ❧ BIBLIOGRAPHY

Chrismes, Stanley Bertram. *English Constitutional Ideas in the Fifteenth Century.* Cambridge University Press, 1936.

Christianson, Gerald. "From Conciliar to Curial Reform in the Late Middle Ages." In *The Reformation as Christianization. Essays on Scott Hendrix's Christianization Thesis*, edited by Anna Marie Johnson and John A. Maxfield. Siebeck, 2012.

Christianson, Gerald, Thomas M. Izbicki, and Christopher M. Bellitto, eds. *The Church, the Councils, and Reform: The Legacy of the Fifteenth Century.* Catholic University of America Press, 2008.

Church, William Farr. *Constitutional Thought in Sixteenth Century France.* Harvard University Press, 1941.

Clarke, Maude Violet. *Medieval Representation and Consent: A Study of Early Parliaments in England and Ireland, with Special Reference to the* modus tenendi parliamentum. Russell & Russell, 1964.

Coleman, Janet. "The Interrelationship Between Church and State During the Conciliar Period: Theory and Practice." In *État et Église dans la genèse de l'État moderne. Actes du colloque organisé à la Casa de Velázquez*, edited by Jean-Philippe Genet and Bernard Vincent. Casa de Velázquez Library, 1986.

Colin, Pierre. *L'Audace et le Soupçon. La crise moderniste dans le catholicisme français, 1893–1914.* Desclée de Brouwer, 1997.

Colin, Pierre. "Les historiens de la philosophie et le modernisme." In *Penser la foi. Mélanges offerts à Joseph Moingt*, edited by Joseph Doré and Christoph Theobald. Cerf, 1993.

Colson, Jean. *L'épiscopat catholique. Collégialité et primauté dans les trois premiers siècles de l'Église.* Cerf, 1963.

Congar, Yves-Marie. "Avertissement des éditeurs." In *Les Pouvoirs du concile et l'autorité du pape au concile de Constance.* Cerf, 1965.

Congar, Yves-Marie. "De la communion des Églises à une ecclésiologie de l'Église universelle." In *L'épiscopat et l'Église universelle.* Cerf, 1962.

Congar, Yves-Marie. "Deux facteurs de la sacralisation de la vie sociale au Moyen Âge (en Occident)." *Concilium* 47 (1969): 53–63.

Congar, Yves-Marie. *Église et papauté: Regards historiques.* Rev. ed. Cerf, 2002.

Congar, Yves-Marie. "Infaillibilité et indéfectibilité." In *Ministères et communion ecclésiale*, edited by Yves-Marie Congar. Cerf, 1971.

Congar, Yves-Marie. *Journal d'un théologien.* Cerf, 2005.

Congar, Yves-Marie. "La pensée de Möhler et l'ecclésiologie orthodoxe." *Irénikon* 12 (1935): 321–329.

Congar, Yves-Marie. "La 'réception' comme réalité ecclésiologique." *Revue des sciences philosophiques et théologiques* 56 (1972): 369–403.

Congar, Yves-Marie. *L'Église de saint Augustin à l'époque moderne*. Cerf, 1970.

Congar, Yves-Marie. "Le mouvement réformateur." In *Cardinal Yves Congar. Écrits réformateurs*, edited by Jean-Pierre Jossua. Cerf, 1995.

Congar, Yves-Marie. "Le peuple fidèle et la fonction prophétique de l'Église (seconde partie)." *Irénikon* 24 (1951): 440–466.

Congar, Yves-Marie. *Ministères et communion ecclésiale*. Cerf, 1971.

Congar, Yves-Marie. *Mon journal du concile*. 2 vols. Cerf, 2002.

Congar, Yves-Marie. "Notes sur le destin de l'idée de collégialité épiscopale en Occident au Moyen Âge (VIIe–XVIe siècle)." In *La collégialité épiscopale. Histoire et théologie*. Cerf, 1965.

Congar, Yves-Marie. "Primauté et collégialilté. À propos du synode des évêques (octobre 1969)." Occasional paper of the *Recherches et dialogues Saint-Jacques* 8 (1969): 1–23.

Congar, Yves-Marie. "Quod omnes tangit, ab omnibus tractari et approbari debet." *Revue historique de droit français et étranger* 81 (1958): 210–259.

Congar, Yves-Marie. "Remarques sur le concile comme assemblée et sur la conciliarité de l'Église." In *Le concile au jour le jour, deuxième session*. Cerf, 1964.

Congar, Yves-Marie. "Renouvellement de l'Esprit et réforme de l'Institution." In *Cardinal Yves Congar. Écrits réformateurs*, edited by Jean-Pierre Jossua. Cerf, 1995.

Congar, Yves-Marie. "Romanité et catholicité. Histoire de la conjonction changeante de deux dimensions de l'Église." *Revue des sciences philosophiques et théologiques* 71 (1987): 161–190.

Congar, Yves-Marie. "Saint Thomas Aquinas and the Infallibility of the Papal Magisterium: *Summa theologiae*, IIa IIae, q. 1, art. 10." *Thomist* 38 (1974): 81–105.

Congar, Yves-Marie. "Status Ecclesiae." *Studia Gratiana* 15 (1972): 3–31.

Congar, Yves-Marie. "Structures ecclésiales et conciles dans les relations entre Orient et Occident." *Revue des sciences philosophiques et théologiques* 5 (1974): 355–390.

Congar, Yves-Marie. "Un témoignage des désaccords entre canonistes et théologiens." In *Études d'histoire du droit canonique dédiées à Gabriel Le Bras*, edited by G. Vedel. Sirey, 1965.

Congar, Yves-Marie. *Vraie et fausse réforme dans l'Église*. 2nd ed. Cerf, 1968.

270 ✼ BIBLIOGRAPHY

Congar, Yves-Marie, and Bernard-Dominique Dupuy, eds. *L'Épiscopat et l'Église universelle*. Cerf, 1962.

Contamine, Philippe. "Le vocabulaire politique en France à la fin du Moyen Âge: L'idée de réformation." In *Église et État dans la genèse de l'État moderne*, edited by Jean-Philippe Genet and Bernard Vincent. Library of the Casa de Velázquez, 1986.

Coste, Jean. *Boniface VIII en procès. Articles d'accusation et déposition des témoins (1303–1311)*. École Française de Rome, 1995.

Cottret, Monique. "Edmond Richer (1559–1631): Le politique et le sacré." In *L'État baroque 1610–1652. Regards sur la pensée politique de la France du premier XVIIe siècle*, edited by Henry Méchoulan. Vrin, 1985.

Couratier, Monique, ed. *Étienne Gilson et nous. La philosophie et son histoire. Colloque sur l'actualité de la pensée d'Étienne Gilson*. Vrin, 1980.

Courtine, Jean-François. "L'héritage scolastique dans la problématique théologico-politique de l'âge classique." In *L'État baroque (1610–1652). Regards sur la pensée politique de la France du premier XVIIe siècle*, edited by Henry Méchoulan. Vrin, 1985.

Crowder, Christopher M. D. "Le concile de Constance et l'édition de von der Hardt." *Revue d'histoire ecclésiastique* 57 (1962): 409–445.

Crowder, Christopher M. D. *Unity, Heresy and Reform, 1378–1460: The Conciliar Response to the Great Schism*. St. Martin's Press, 1977.

D'Ailly, Pierre. *Tractatus de emendatione Ecclesiae*. In *Quellen zur Kirchenreform im Zeitalter der großen Konzilien des 15. Jahrhunderts*, edited by Jürgen Miethke and Lorenz Weinrich. Darmstadt, 2015.

Davis, Kathleen. *Periodization and Sovereignty: How Ideas of Feudalism and Secularization Govern the Politics of Time*. University of Pennsylvania Press, 2008.

D'Avray, David. *Medieval Religious Rationalities: A Weberian Analysis*. Cambridge University Press, 2010.

De Bonnechose, Émile. *Réformateurs avant la Réforme, XVe siècle: Gerson, Jean Hus et le concile de Constance, avec des considérations nouvelles sur l'Église gallicane depuis le grand schisme jusqu'à nos jours*. 2 vols. Paris, 1844.

De Franceschi, Sylvio Hermann, ed. *Antiromanisme doctrinal et romanité ecclésiale: Dans le catholicisme posttridentin (XVIe–XXe siècles)*. Laboratoire de recherche historique Rhône-Alpes, 2008.

De Franceschi, Sylvio Hermann. "Bruno Neveu et la romanité. Sources historiographiques et méthode." *Chrétiens et sociétés* 14 (2007): 101–122.

BIBLIOGRAPHY ∝ 271

De Franceschi, Sylvio Hermann, ed. *Histoires antiromaines: Antiromanisme et critique dans l'historiographie catholique (XVIe–XXe siècles)*. Laboratoire de recherche historique Rhône-Alpes, 2010.

De Franceschi, Sylvio Hermann. "Hybridation doctrinale au temps de l'Interdit: Calvinisme, marsilisme et wycliffisme aux sources de l'antiromanisme sarpien." In *Frontières religieuses dans le monde moderne*, edited by Denis Crouzet and Francisco Bethencourt. Sorbonne Université Presses, 2013.

De Franceschi, Sylvio Hermann. *La crise théologico-politique du premier âge baroque. Antiromanisme doctrinal, pouvoir pastoral et raison du prince: Le Saint-Siège face au prisme français (1607–1627)*. École Française de Rome, 2009.

De Franceschi, Sylvio Hermann. "Le catholicisme antiromain et l'infaillibilité pontificale du XVIIe siècle." In *Le Pontife et l'erreur: Anti-infaillibilisme catholique et romanité ecclésiale aux temps posttridentins (XVIIe–XXe siècles)*. Laboratoire de recherche historique Rhône-Alpes, 2010.

De Franceschi, Sylvio Hermann, ed. *Le Pontife et l'erreur: Anti-infaillibilisme catholique et romanité ecclésiale aux temps posttridentins (XVIIe–XXe siècles)*. Laboratoire de recherche historique Rhône-Alpes, 2010.

De Franceschi, Sylvio Hermann. "Les théologiens face à un antiromanisme catholique extrême au temps du richérisme. La condamnation du De Republica ecclesiastica de Marc'Antonio De Dominis par la Sorbonne (15 décembre 1617)." *Chrétiens et sociétés*, no. 11 (2004) : 11–32.

De Franceschi, Sylvio Hermann. "Paolo Sarpi et Fulgenzio Micanzio. L'extrémisme catholique antiromain du début du XVIIe siècle." In *Antiromanisme doctrinal et romanité ecclésiale: Dans le catholicisme posttridentin (XVIe–XXe siècles)*, edited by Sylvio Hermann De Franceschi. Laboratoire de recherche historique Rhône-Alpes, 2008.

De Franceschi, Sylvio Hermann. "Saint Pierre et saint Paul: deux chefs de l'Église qui n'en font qu'un. Primauté romaine et pétrinité aux temps post-tridentins." In *"Rome, l'unique objet de mon ressentiment": Regards critiques sur la papauté*, edited by Philippe Levillain. École Française de Rome, 2011.

De La Brosse, Olivier. *Le pape et le concile. La comparaison de leurs pouvoirs à la veille de la réforme*. Cerf, 1995.

De Lagarde, Georges. "Individualisme et corporatisme au Moyen Âge." In *L'Organisation corporative du Moyen Âge à la fin de l'Ancien Régime*, edited by Émile Lousse. Presses Universitaires de Louvain, 1937.

De Lagarde, Georges. *Naissance de l'esprit laïque au déclin du Moyen Âge*. 6 vols. Presses Universitaires de France, 1942–1947.

De Libera, Alain. *La philosophie médiévale*. Presses Universitaires de France, 1993.

De Libera, Alain. "Les études de philosophie médiévale en France d'Étienne Gilson à nos jours." In *Gli studi di filosofia medievale fra Otto e Novecento. Contributo a un bilancio storiografico. Atti del convegno internazionale Rome, 21–23 settembre 1989*, edited by Ruedi Imbach and Alfonso Maierù. Edizioni di Storia e Letteratura, 1991.

De Libera, Alain. *Raison et foi. Archéologie d'une crise d'Albert le Grand à Jean-Paul II*. Seuil, 2003.

De Maistre, Joseph. *Du Pape. Édition critique*. Edited by Jacques Lovie and Joannès Chetail. Droz, 1966.

De Vooght, Paul. "Esquisse d'une enquête sur le mot 'infaillibilité' durant la période scolastique." In *L'infaillibilité de l'Église. Journées oecuméniques*, edited by Olivier Rousseau, Jean-Jacques Von Allmen, Bernard-Dominique Dupuy et al. Éditions de Chevetogne, 1962.

De Vooght, Paul. "Gerson et le conciliarisme." *Revue d'histoire ecclésiastique* 63 (1968): 857–867.

De Vooght, Paul. *Hussiana*. Nauwelaerts, 1960.

De Vooght, Paul. "Le concile oecuménique de Constance et le conciliarisme." *Istina* 9 (1963): 57–86.

De Vooght, Paul. "Le Conciliarisme aux Conciles de Constance et de Bâle." In *Le Concile et les conciles. Contribution à l'histoire de la vie conciliaire de l'Église*, edited Bernard Botte. Chevetogne-Cerf, 1960.

De Vooght, Paul. "Les controverses sur les pouvoirs du concile et l'autorité du pape au concile de Constance." *Revue théologique de Leuven* 1 (1970): 45–75.

De Vooght, Paul. "Les dimensions réelles de l'infaillibilité papale." In *L'infaillibilité. Son aspect philosophique et théologique*, edited by Enrico Castelli. Aubier, 1970.

De Vooght, Paul. "Les résultats de la recherche récente sur le conciliarisme." *Concilium* 64 (1971): 133–140.

De Vooght, Paul. *Les pouvoirs du concile et l'autorité du pape au concile de Constance*. Cerf, 1965.

Decaluwé, Michiel. "A New and Disputable Edition-Text of the Decree *Haec Sancta* of the Council of Constance (1415)." *Cristianesimo nella storia* 32, no. 2 (2006): 417–445.

BIBLIOGRAPHY ᏅᎦ 273

Decaluwé, Michiel. "Three Ways to Read the Constance Decree *Haec Sancta* (1415): Francis Zabarella, Jean Gerson and the Traditional Papal View of General Councils." In *The Church, the Councils, and Reform: The Legacy of the Fifteenth Century*, edited by Gerald Christianson, Thomas M. Izbicki, and Christopher M. Bellitto. Catholic University of America Press, 2008.

Dechamps, Victor Auguste. *L'infaillibilité et le Concile général. Étude de science religieuse à l'usage des gens du monde.* Liége, 1869.

Degart, A. "Gallicanism." *Catholic Encyclopedia*, vol. 6. Robert Appleton, 1909.

Dejaifve, Gérard. *Non ex consensu Ecclesiae. De doctrina concilii Vaticani Primi.* Libera Editrice Vaticane, 1969.

Dejaifve, Gérard. "Où en est le problème de l'infaillibilité?" *Nouvelle Revue théologique* 100 (1978): 372–388.

Dejaifve, Gérard. "Un débat sur l'infaillibilité. La discussion entre K. Rahner et H. Küng." *Nouvelle Revue théologique* 93 (1971): 583–601.

Dejoux, Marie. *Les enquêtes de saint Louis. Gouverner et sauver son âme.* Presses Universitaires de France, 2014.

Delaruelle, Étienne. *L'Église au temps du Grand Schisme et de la crise conciliaire (1378–1449).* Vol. 14 of *Histoire de l'Église*, edited by Augustin Fliche and Victor Martin. Bloud & Gay, 1964.

Deleplace, Marc. "Peut-on fonder la République sur la haine? Une interrogation sur la république directoriale (1795–1799)." In *La haine. Histoire et actualité*, edited by Frédéric Chauvaud and Ludovic Gaussot. Presses Universitaires de Rennes, 2008.

De Montclos, Xavier. *Réformer l'Église. Histoire du réformisme catholique en France de la Révolution jusqu'à nos jours.* Cerf, 1998.

Dendorfer, Jürgen, and Ralf Lützelschwab, eds. *Geschichte des Kardinalats im Mittelalter.* Hiersemann, 2011.

Denifle, Heinrich, and Emile Chatelain, eds. *Chartularium Universitatis Parisiensis.* 5 vols. Paris, 1897.

Denifle, Heinrich, and Franz Ehrle, eds. *Archiv für Litteratur- und Kirchengeschichte des Mittelalters.* 7 vols. Berlin, 1885–1900.

Denis, Philippe. *Edmond Richer et le renouveau du conciliarisme au XVIIe siècle.* Cerf, 2014.

Denzinger, Heinrich. *Enchiridion Symbolorum.* Edited by Peter Hünermann. Herder, 1991.

Derrida, Jacques. *Force de loi.* Galilée, 2005.

274 ᎒Ꮽ BIBLIOGRAPHY

Doig, James C. *Aquinas's Philosophical Commentary on the* Ethics: *A Historical Perspective.* Kluwer, 2001.

Döllinger, Ignaz von. *Der Papst und das Konzil.* Steinacker, 1869.

D'Onorio, Joël-Benoît. "Primauté collégiale: Sur une imprécision conciliaire et sa correction pontificale." In *La Synodalité. La participation au gouvernement dans l'Église. Actes du VIIe Congrès international de Droit canonique, Paris, UNESCO, 21–28 September 1990.* Special issue, *L'année canonique* (1992).

Dorin, Rowan. "The Bishop as Lawmaker in Late Medieval Europe." *Past and Present* 253, no. 1 (2021): 45–82.

Du Boulay, César-Egasse, ed. *Historia universitatis Parisiensis.* 6 vols. Paris, 1665–1673.

Du Pin, Louis Ellies. *Traité de la puissance ecclésiastique.* Paris, 1707.

Dublanchy, Edmond. "Église." In *Dictionnaire de théologie catholique,* vol. 4, part 2, edited by A. Vacant and E. Mangenot. Letouzey & Ané, 1911.

Dublanchy, Edmond. "Infaillibilité du pape." In *Dictionnaire de théologie Catholique,* vol. 7, edited by A. Vacant and E. Mangenot. Letouzey et Ané, 1923.

Dulac, Raymond. *La collégialité épiscopale au deuxième concile de Vatican.* Cèdre, 1979.

Dupont, Jacques, and Yves-Marie Congar, *La collégialité épiscopale: histoire et théologie.* Cerf, 1965.

Duval, André. *Libelli de ecclesiastica et politica potestate elenchus pro suprema Romani Pontificis in Ecclesiam authoritate.* Paris, 1612.

Elliot van Liere, Katherine. "Vitoria, Cajetan and the Conciliarists." *Journal of the History of Ideas* 58, no. 4 (1997): 597–616.

Empie, Paul C., T. Austin Murphy, and Joseph A. Burgess, eds. *Teaching Authority and Infallibility in the Church.* Augsburg Fortress, 1980.

Esmain, Adhémar. *Éléments de droit constitutionnel.* 6th ed. Sirey, 1914.

Esmein, Adhémar. "La maxime *Princeps legitus solutus est* dans l'ancien droit public français." In *Essays in Legal History,* edited by Paul Vinogradoff. Oxford University Press, 1913.

Eyt, Pierre. "La collégialité." *Publications de l'École Française de Rome* 113, no. 1 (1989): 539–548.

Faggioli, Massimo and Alberto Melloni, ed. *Repraesentatio: Mapping a Keyword for Churches and Governance, Proceedings of the San Miniato International Workshop, October 2004.* Lit, 2006.

Fasolt, Constantin. "*Quod omnes tangit ab omnibus approbari debet*: The Words and the Meaning." In *In Jure veritas: Studies in Canon Law in Memory of Schafer*

Williams, edited by Steven B. Bowman and Blanche E. Cody. University of Cincinnati College of Law, 1991.

Fasolt, Constantin. "Voluntarism and Conciliarism in the Work of Francis Oakley." *History of Political Thought* 22 (2001): 41–52.

Feld, Helmut. "Christus Diener der Sünde. Zum Ausgang des Streits zwischen Petrus und Paulus." *Theologische Quartalschrift* 153 (1973): 119–131.

Feuchter, Jörg, and Johannes Helmrath, eds. *Parlamentarische Kulturen vom Mittelalter bis in die Moderne. Reden-Raüme-Bilder.* Droste, 2013.

Fichtenau, H. "Ladner, Gerhart B., The Idea of Reform. Its Impact on Christian Thought and Action in the Age of the Fathers." *Institut für Österreichische Geschichtsforschung, Mitteilungen* 69 (1961): 116–118.

Fidelis a Fanna. *Bonaventurae doctrina de Romani Pontificis primatu et infallibilitate.* Turin, 1870.

Figgis, John Neville. "The Conciliar Movement and the Papal Reaction." In *Political Thought from Gerson to Grotius, 1414–1625: Seven Studies.* Harper, 1960.

Figgis, John Neville. *Political Thought from Gerson to Grotius, 1414–1625: Seven Studies.* Harper, 1960.

Finke, Heinrich, ed. *Acta Concilii Constantiensis.* 4 vols. Münster, 1826–1928.

Flanagin, David Zachariah. *"Extra Ecclesiam salus non est—sed quae Ecclesia?* Ecclesiology and Authority in the Later Middle Ages." In *A Companion to the Great Western Schism (1378–1417),* edited by Joëlle Rollo-Koster and Thomas M. Izbicki. Brill, 2009.

Fois, Mario. "L'ecclesiologia di emergenza stimulata dallo Scisma." In *Genèse et débuts du Grand Schisme d'Occident (1362–1394).* CNRS, 1980.

Fonbaustier, Laurent. *La déposition du pape hérétique. Une origine du constitutionnalisme?* Mare et Martin, 2016.

Fonbaustier, Laurent. "L'influence des modèles ecclésiologiques et des institutions de l'Église sur les modèles et institutions étatiques." *Droits* 59, no. 1 (2014): 123–144.

Foronda, François, ed. *Avant le contrat social. Le contrat politique dans l'Occident médiéval (XIIIe–XVe siècle).* Éditions de la Sorbonne, 2011.

Foronda, François. *El espanto y el mideo. Golpismo, emociones políticas y constitucionalismo en la Edad Media.* Dykinson, 2013.

Foronda, François, and Ana Isabel Carrasco, eds. *Du contrat d'alliance au contrat politique. Cultures et sociétés politiques dans la péninsule Ibérique à la fin du Moyen Âge.* Méridiennes, 2007.

276 ᔥ BIBLIOGRAPHY

Foronda, François, and Genet, Jean-Philippe, eds. *Des chartes aux constitutions. Autour de l'idée constitutionnelle en Europe, XIIe–XVIIe siècle.* Éditions de la Sorbonne, 2020.

Fossier, François. "Rapports Église-État. Le Grand Schisme vu par les historiens du XIVe au XVIIe siècle." In *État et Église dans la genèse de l'État moderne,* edited by Jean-Philippe Genet and Bernard Vincent. Casa de Velázquez Library, 1986.

Foucault, Michel. *Sécurité, territoire, population: Cours au Collège de France, 1977–1978.* Edited by Michel Senellart, François Ewald, and Alessandro Fontana. Gallimard-Seuil, 2004.

Fouilloux, Étienne. "La phase antépréparatoire (1959–1960)." In *Histoire du concile Vatican II,* edited by Giuseppe Alberigo. Cerf, 1997.

Fouilloux, Étienne. "Première alerte sur le Saulchoir (1932)." *Revue des sciences philosophiques et théologiques* 96, no. 1 (2012): 93–105.

Fouilloux, Étienne. "Recherche théologique et magistère romain en 1952. Une 'affaire' parmi d'autres." *Le Magistère, Revue des sciences religieuses* 71, no. 2 (1983): 269–286.

Fouilloux, Étienne. *Une Église en quête de liberté. La pensée catholique française entre modernisme et Vatican II, 1914–1962.* Desclée de Brouwer, 1998.

Fourcade, Michel. "Thomisme et anti-thomisme à l'heure de Vatican II." *Revue thomiste* 108 (2008): 301–325.

Frank, Isnard Wilhelm. "Ein antikonziliarer Traktat des Wiener Dominikaners Leonhard Huntpichler von 1447/1448." *Freiburger Zeitschrift für Theologie und Philosophie* 18 (1971): 36–71.

Franzen, August. "Le concile de Constance devant l'histoire. Examen des problèmes qu'il soulève. État actuel de la recherche." *Concilium* 187 (1983): 29–68.

Frenken, Ansgar. *Das Konstanzer Konzil.* Kohlhammer, 2015.

Frenken, Ansgar. *Die Erforschung des Konstanzer Konzils (1414–1418) in den letzten 100 Jahren.* Ferdinand Schöningh, 1995. Originally published in *Annuarium historiae conciliorum* 25 (1993): 1–512.

Gratian. *Decretum Magistri Gratiani.* Edited by Emil Friedberg. Vol. 1 of *Corpus Iuris Canonici.* Leipzig, 1879.

Froehlich, Karlfried. "Fallibility Instead of Infallibility? A Brief History of the Interpretation of Ga. 2, 11–14." In *Teaching Authority and Infallibility in the Church,* edited by Paul Empie, T. Austin Murphy, and Joseph A. Burgess. Augsburg Fortress, 1980.

BIBLIOGRAPHY ❧ 277

Froehlich, Karlfried. "New Testament Models of Conflict Resolution: Observations on the Biblical Argument of Paris Conciliarists during the Great Schism." In *Conciliation and Confession: The Struggle for Unity in the Age of Reform, 1415–1648*, edited by Howard P. Louthan and Randall C. Zachman. University of Notre Dame Press, 2004.

Gabriel, Frédéric. "Idées gallicanes et conceptualités ecclésiales: Parcours et tensions d'une histoire doctrinale dans le *Dictionnaire de théologie catholique*." In *Théologie et érudition de la crise moderniste à Vatican II. Autour du* Dictionnaire de théologie catholique, edited by Silvio Hermann De Franceschi. Presses Universitaires de Limoges, 2014.

Gagnebet, Rosaire. *Il primato del pontefice e la collegialità dell'episcopato*. Editrice Domenicana Italiana, 1964.

Gagnebet, Rosaire. *L'origine de la juridiction collégiale du corps épiscopal au Concile selon Bolgeni*. Libreria editrice della pontifica università Lateranense, 1961.

Gauchet, Marcel. *The Disenchantment of the World: A Political History of Religion*. Princeton University Press, 1997.

Gaudemet, Jean. *Les sources du droit canonique, VIIIe–XXe siècle*. Cerf, 1993.

Gauvard, Claude, ed. *L'Enquête au Moyen Âge*. École Française de Rome, 2018.

Gauvard, Claude. "De grace especial." In *Crime, État et société en France à la fin du Moyen Âge*. Publications de la Sorbonne, 1991.

Gauvard, Claude. "Réforme." In *Dictionnaire du Moyen Âge*, edited by Claude Gauvard, Alain de Libera, and Michel Zink. Presses Universitaires de France, 2002.

Gay, Jean-Pascal. *Le Dernier théologien? Théophile Raynaud, histoire d'une obsolescence*. Beauchesne, 2018.

Gay, Jean-Pascal. "Théophile Raynaud et le choix de la théologie comme rhétorique en soi. Partages disciplinaires, ordre confessionel et apologétique catholique au XVIIe siècle." *Histoire, monde et cultures religieuses* 35, no. 3 (2015): 35–52.

Gazzaniga, Jean-Louis. "L'appel au concile dans la politique gallicane de la monarchie de Charles VII à Louis XII." *Bulletin de littérature ecclésiastique* 85, no. 2 (1984): 111–129.

Gazzaniga, Jean-Louis. "Mandat et représentation dans l'ancien droit." *Droits. Revue française de théorie juridique* 6 (1987): 21–30.

Généquand, Philippe. "Des ombres aux chapeaux rouges. Pour une nouvelle histoire des cardinaux à la fin du Moyen Âge." In *Église et État, Église ou État?*,

278   BIBLIOGRAPHY

edited by Christine Barralis, Jean-Patrice Boudet, Fabrice Delivré, and Jean-Philippe Genet. Éditions de la Sorbonne and École Française de Rome, 2015.

Généquand, Philippe. "Kardinäle Schisma und Konzil. Der Kardinalskolleg im Grossen Abedländischen Schisma." In *Geschichte des Kardinalats im Mittelalter*, edited by Jürgen Dendorfer and Ralf Lützelschab. Hiersemann, 2011.

Genet, Jean-Philippe. "Du contrat à la constitution." In *Avant le contrat social. Le contrat politique dans l'Occident médiéval (XIIIe–XVe siècle)*, edited by François Foronda. Publications de la Sorbonne, 2011.

Gerson, Jean. *Joannis Gersonii Opera omnia*. Edited by Louis Ellies du Pin. 5 vols. Dublin, 1728.

Gerson, Jean. *Œuvres Complètes*. Edited by Palémon Glorieux. 11 vols. Desclée de Brouwer, 1960–1973.

Gerson, Jean. *Opera multo quam antehac auctiora et castigatiora*. Edited by Edmond Richer. 2 vols. Paris, 1606.

Giesey, Ralph. "*Quod omnes tangit*: A post scriptum." *Studia Gratiana* 15 (1972): 319–332.

Giffoni, Leonardo da. "Allegationes domini cardinalis de Giffoni contra papam." Edited by Clement Schmitt. *Archivum franciscanum historicum* 21 (1958): 45–72.

Gill, Joseph. "The Canonists and the Council of Constance." *Orientalia Christiana Periodica* 32 (1966): 528–535.

Gill, Joseph. "The Fifth Session of the Council of Constance." *Heythrop Journal* 5 (1964): 131–143.

Gill, Joseph. "The Representation of the *Universitas Fidelium* in the Councils of the Conciliar Period." In *Councils and Assemblies*, edited by G. J. Cuming and L. C. D. Baker. Cambridge University Press, 1971.

Gill, Joseph. *Constance et Bâle–Florence*. Translated by P. de Sainte-Marguerite and J. Thevenet. In *Histoire des conciles oecuméniques*, vol. 9, edited by Gervais Dumeige. L'Orante, 1965.

Gilli, Patrick. *La noblesse du droit. Débats et controverses sur la culture juridique et le rôle des juristes dans l'Italie médiévale (XIIe–XV siècle)*. Honoré Champion, 2003

Gilson, Étienne. *Introduction à la philosophie chrétienne*. Vrin, 1960.

Gilson, Étienne. *Jean Duns Scot. Introduction à ses positions fondamentales*. Vrin, 1952.

Gilson, Étienne. *Le Philosophe et la Théologie*. Vrin, 2005.

Gilson, Étienne. "Notes bibliographiques pour servir à l'histoire de la notion de philosophie chrétienne." In *L'esprit de la philosophie médiévale*. Vrin, 1989.

Goichot, Émile. *Alfred Loisy et ses amis*. Cerf, 2002.

BIBLIOGRAPHY ❧ 279

Grant, Robert M. "Book Review: The Idea of Reform: Its Impact on Christian Thought and Action in the Age of the Fathers." *Speculum* 36, no. 1 (1961): 140–142.

Grootaers, Jan. *Heurs et malheurs de la "collégialité." Pontificats et synodes face à la réception de Vatican II*. Peeters, 2012.

Grootaers, Jan. *Primauté et Collégialité. Le dossier de Gérard Philips sur la* Nota Explicativa Praevia (*Lumen gentium*, chap. III). Leuven University Press; Peeters, 1986.

Guenée, Bernard. *Entre l'Église et l'État. Quatre vies de prélats français à la fin du Moyen Âge (XIIIe–XVe siècle)*. Gallimard, 1987.

Guenée, Bernard. *L'opinion publique à la fin du Moyen Âge d'après la "Chronique de Charles VI" du Religieux de Saint-Denis*. Perrin, 2002.

Hallam, Henry. *View of the State of Europe During the Middle Ages*. 3 vols. J. Murray, 1901.

Halleux, André de. "La collégialité dans l'Église ancienne." *Revue théologique de Leuven* 24 (1993): 433–454.

Hamer, Jérôme. "Le corps épiscopal uni au pape, son autorité dans l'Église, d'après les documents du 1er concile du Vatican." *Revue des sciences philosophiques et théologiques* 45 (1961): 21–31.

Hamesse, Jacqueline. *Auctoritates Aristotelis. Un florilège médiéval. Étude historique et édition critique*. Nauwelaerts, 1974.

Hayden, J. Michael, and Malcolm R. Greenshields. *Six Hundred Years of Reform: Bishops and the French Church, 1190–1789*. McGill-Queen's University Press, 2005.

Hébert, Michel. *Parlementer. Assemblées représentatives et échange politique en Europe occidentale à la fin du Moyen Âge*. De Boccard, 2013.

Helmrath, Johannes. "Reform als Thema der Konzilien des Spätmittelalters." In *Christian Unity: The Council of Ferrara-Florence 1438/9–1989*, edited by Giuseppe Alberigo. Leuven University Press, 1991.

Helmrath, Johannes. "Theorie und Praxis der Kirchenreform im Spätmittelalter." *Rottenburger Jahrbuch für Kirchengeschichte* 11 (1992): 41–70.

Hendrix, Scott. "In Quest of the *Vera ecclesia:* The Crises of Late Medieval Ecclesiology." *Viator: Medieval and Renaissance Studies* 7 (1976): 347–378.

Herbermann, Charles, A. Pace, Condé B. Pallen, Thomas J. Shahan, and John J. Wynne, eds. *The Catholic Encyclopedia*, vol. 6. Encyclopedia Press, 1913.

280 & otimes; BIBLIOGRAPHY

Hervieu-Léger, Danièle. *Catholicisme, la fin d'un monde.* Bayard, 2003.

Hildesheimer, Françoise. "Entre droit et théologie. L'absolutisme gallican." In *Les Cours d'Es- pagne et de France au XVIIe siècle,* edited by Chantal Grell and Benoît Pellistrandi. Library of the Casa de Velázquez, 2007.

Hissette, Roland. "Note sur la réaction 'antimoderniste' d'Étienne Tempier." *Bulletin de philosophie médiévale* 22 (1980): 88–97.

Hlaváček, Ivan, and Alexander Patschovsky, eds. *Reform von Kirche und Reich zur Zeit Konzilien von Konstanz (1414–1418) und Basel (1431–1449).* Universitätsverlag Konstanz, 1996.

Hobbins, Daniel. *Authorship and Publicity Before Print: Jean Gerson and the Transformation of Late Medieval Learning.* University of Pennsylvania Press, 2009.

Hoffman, Georg, ed. *Epistolae Pontificiae ad Concilium Florentinum spectantes.* Pontifical Oriental Institute, 1940.

Horst, Ulrich. "Infallibilität und Geschichte. Ein Rückblick." In *Unfehlbarkeit und Geschichte, Studien zur Unfehlbarkeitdiskussion von Melchior Cano zum I. Vatikanischen Konzil,* edited by Ulrich Horst. Matthias Grünewald-Verlag, 1982.

Horst, Ulrich. *Päpstliche Unfehlbarkeit wider konziliare Superiorität? Studien zur Geschichte eines (ekklesiologischen) Antagonismus vom 15. bis zum 19. Jahrhundert.* Ferdinand Schöningh, 2016.

Hübler, Bernhard. *Die Constanzer Reformation und die Concordate von 1418.* Leipzig, 1867.

Hürten, Heinz. "Zur Ekklesiologie der Konzilien von Konstanz und Basel." *Theologische Revue* 59 (1963): 361–372.

Imbach, Ruedi. "Démocratie ou monarchie? La discussion sur le meilleur régime politique chez quelques interprètes français de Thomas d'Aquin (1893–1925)." In *Saint Thomas au XXe siècle. Colloque du centenaire de la* Revue thomiste, *(1893–1992), Toulouse 25–28 mars 1993,* edited by Serge-Thomas Bonino. Saint-Paul Éditions, 1994.

Imbach, Ruedi. "Thomas d'Aquin 1224/1225–1274." In *Dictionnaire du Moyen Âge,* edited by Claude Gauvard, Alain de Libera, and Michel Zink. Presses Universitaires de France, 2002.

Imbach, Ruedi, and Catherine König-Pralong. *Le Défi laïque.* Vrin, 2013.

Iogna-Prat, Dominique. "La formation d'un paradigme ecclésial de la violence intellectuelle dans l'Occident latin aux XIe et XIIe siècles." In *Le mot qui tue.*

BIBLIOGRAPHY ᴄᴫ 281

Une histoire des violences intellectuelles de l'Antiquité à nos jours, edited by Vincent Azoulay and Patrick Boucheron. Champ Vallon, 2009.

Iogna-Prat, Dominique, Alain Rauwel, and Frédéric Gabriel, eds. *Dictionnaire critique de l'Église*. Presses Universitaires de France, 2023.

Izbicki, Thomas M. "The Authority of Peter and Paul: The Use of Biblical Authority During the Great Schism." In *A Companion to the Great Western Schism (1378–1417)*, edited by Joëlle Rollo-Koster and Thomas M. Izbicki. Brill, 2009.

Izbicki, Thomas M. "Infallibility and the Erring Pope: Guido Terreni and Johannes de Turrecremata." In *Law, Church, and Society: Essays in Honor of Stephan Kuttner*, edited by Kenneth Pennington and Robert Sommerville. University of Pennsylvania Press, 1977.

Izbicki, Thomas M. "Papalist Reaction to the Council of Constance: Juan de Torquemada to the Present." *Church History* 55 (1986): 7–20.

Izbicki, Thomas M. *Reform, Ecclesiology and the Christian Life in the Late Middle Ages*. Routledge, 2008.

Jedin, Hubert. *Bischöfliches Konzil oder Kirchenparlament? Ein Beitrag zur Ekklesiologie der Konzilien von Konstanz und Basel*. Helbing und Lichtenhahn, 1963.

Jedin, Hubert. *Die Erforschung der kirchlichen Reformationsgeschichte seit 1876. Leistungen und Aufgaben der deutschen Katholiken*. Aschendorff, 1931.

Jedin, Hubert. *Geschichte der Konzils von Trent*, vol. 1. 2nd ed. Herder, 1951.

Jedin, Hubert. *La Storia della Chiesa e teologia e storia*. Vita e pensiero, 1968.

Jedin, Hubert. *Storia del Concilio di Trento*, vol. 1. Morcelliana, 1949.

John Paul II. *Post-Synodal Apostolic Exhortation* Christifideles Laici *of His Holiness John Paul II on the Vocation and the Mission of the Lay Faithful in the Church and the World*. Vatican Polyglot Press, 1988.

Johnson, Anna Marie, and John A. Maxfield, eds. *The Reformation as Christianization. Essays on Scott Hendrix's Christianization Thesis*. Mohr Siebeck, 2012.

Jossua, Jean-Pierre, ed. *Cardinal Yves Congar. Écrits réformateurs*. Cerf, 1995.

Juan de Torquemada, *Summa de Ecclesia*. Venice, 1561.

Jung, Nicolas. *Un franciscain, théologien du pouvoir pontifical au XIVe siècle Alvaro Pelayo, évêque et penitentier de Jean XXII*. Vrin, 1931.

Kaminsky, Howard. *Simon de Cramaud and the Great Schism*. Rutgers University Press, 1983.

Kantorowicz, Ernst. *The King's Two Bodies*. Princeton University Press, 1957.

282 ❧ BIBLIOGRAPHY

Kantorowicz, Ernst. "Mysteries of State: An Absolutist Concept and Its Late Medieval Origins." *Harvard Theological Review* 48, no. 1 (1955): 65–91.

Kempf, Friedrich. "The Idea of Reform. Its Impact on Christian Thought and Action in the Age of the Fathers." *Historisches Jahrbuch* 82 (1962): 235–237.

Kisch, Guido. *Erasmus und die Jurisprudenz seiner Zeit. Studien zum humanistische Rechtsdenken.* Helbing und Lichtenhahn, 1960.

Kisch, Guido. "*Summum ius summa iniuria.* Baseler Humanisten und Juristen über *Aequitas* un *Epieikeia.*" In *Aequitas und bona fides. Festschrift für August Simonius.* Helbing und Lichtenhahn, 1955.

König, Franz. *Die Konzilsidee von Konstanz bis Vatikanum II.* Bachem, 1963.

König-Pralong, Catherine. "Découverte et colonisation françaises de la philosophie médiévale (1730–1850)." *Revue des sciences philosophiques et théologiques* 96 (2012): 663–701.

König-Pralong, Catherine. "L'histoire de la philosophie médiévale depuis 1950: Méthodes, textes, débats." *Annales HSS* 64, no. 1 (2009): 143–169.

König-Pralong, Catherine. *Médiévisme philosophique et raison moderne.* Vrin, 2016.

Koselleck, Reinhart. *Futures Past: On the Semantics of Historical Time.* Columbia University Press, 2004.

Krynen, Jacques. "La représentation politique dans l'ancienne France: L'expérience des États généraux." *Droits. Revue française de théorie juridique* 7 (1987): 31–44.

Krynen, Jacques. "Les légistes 'idiots politiques': Sur l'hostilité des théologiens à l'égard des juristes, en France au temps de Charles V." In *Théologie et droit dans la science politique de l'État moderne, Actes de la Table ronde EFR, CNRS, Rome, 1987.* École Française de Rome, 1991.

Krynen, Jacques. "Réflexion sur les idées politiques aux États généraux de Tours de 1484." *Revue historique de droit français et étranger* 62 (1984): 183–204.

Krynen, Jacques. "Un exemple de critique médiévale des juristes professionnels. Philippe de Mézières et les gens du Parlement de Paris." In *Histoire du droit. Mélanges en hommage à Jean Imbert,* edited by Jean-Louis Harouel. Presses Universitaires de France, 1989.

Küng, Hans. "Im Interesse der Sache: Antwort an Karl Rahner." *Stimmen der Zeit* 187 (1971): 105–122.

Küng, Hans. *Infallible? An Inquiry.* Doubleday, 1971.

Küng, Hans. *Infallible? An Unresolved Enquiry.* Continuum, 1994.

Küng, Hans. *Konzil und Wiedervereinigung; Erneuerung als Ruf in die Einheit.* Herder, 1960.

BIBLIOGRAPHY ᑐ 283

Küng, Hans. *Structures of the Church*. Translated by Salvator Attanasio. University of Notre Dame Press, 1964.

Küng, Hans. *Strukturen der Kirche*. Herder, 1962.

Labarthe, Hugues. "Bernard Alaman, un évêque lecteur de saint Augustin en vue de résoudre le Grand Schisme d'Occident." *Revue Mabillon* 18 (2007): 193–216.

Ladner, Gerhart B. *Erinnerungen*. Edited by Herwig Wolfram and Walter Pohl. Verlag der österreichischen Akademie der Wissenschaften, 1994.

Ladner, Gerhart B. *The Idea of Reform: Its Impact on Christian Thought and Action in the Age of the Fathers*. Harvard University Press, 1959.

Ladner, Gerhart B. *Images and Ideas in the Middle Ages: Selected Studies in History and Art*. Edizioni di Storia e Letteratura, 1983.

Ladner, Gerhard B. "Reform: Innovation and Tradition in Medieval Christendom." In *Theology and Law in Islam*, edited by G. E. Von Grunebaum. Harrassowitz, 1971. Reprinted in vol. 2 of Gerhart B. Ladner, *Images and Ideas in the Middle Ages: Selected Studies in History and Art*. Edizioni di Storia e Letteratura, 1983.

Ladner, Gerhart B. "St. Augustine's Conception of the Reformation of Man to the Image of God." In *Augustinus Magister*. Études augustiniennes, 1954.

Lagarde, Georges de. "Individualisme et corporatisme au Moyen Âge." In *L'organisation corporative du Moyen Âge à la fin de l'Ancien Régime*. Bibliothèque de l'Université, 1937.

Lagarde, Georges de. "Les théories représentatives des XIVe–XVe siècles et l'Église." In *Études présentées à la Commission internationale pour l'histoire des assemblées d'États*. Nauwelaerts, 1958.

Landi, Aldo. "Conciliarisme." In *Dictionnaire historique de la papauté*, edited by Philippe Levillain. Fayard, 1994.

Lange, Tyler. "Constitutional Thought and Practice in Early Sixteenth-Century France: Revisiting the Legacy of Ernst Kantorowicz." *Sixteenth Century Journal* 42, no. 4 (2011): 1003–1026.

Lange, Tyler. "Gallicanisme et Réforme: Le constitutionnalisme de Cosme Guymier (1486)." *Revue de l'histoire des religions* 226, no. 3 (2009): 293–313.

Lange, Tyler. *Heresy and Absolute Power: Constitutional Politics in Early Reformation France*. University of California Press, 2009.

Lange, Tyler. "L'ecclésiologie du royaume de France: L'hérésie devant le Parlement de Paris dans les années 1520." In "Les nouveaux horizons de l'ecclésiologie: Du discours clérical à la science du social," edited by Frédéric Gabriel,

Dominique Iogna-Prat, and Alain Rauwel. Special issue, *Bulletin du Centre d'Études médiévales d'Auxerre*, no. 7 (2013). https://doi.org/10.4000/cem.12785.

Langen, Joseph, ed. *Das Vatikanische Dogma von dem Universal-Episcopat und der Unfehlbarkeit des Papstes.* 4 vols. Bonn, 1871–1874.

Langlois, Claude. "L'infaillibilité pontificale, une idée neuve au XIXe siècle." In *Le continent théologique. Explorations historiques.* Presses Universitaires de Rennes, 2016.

Laplanche, François. *La crise de l'origine. La science catholique des Évangiles et l'histoire du XXe siècle.* Albin Michel, 2006.

Laski, Harold S. "Political Theory in the Later Middle Ages." In *The Close of the Middle Ages*, vol. 8 of *Cambridge Medieval History*, edited by Charles V. Prévité-Orton and Zachary N. Brooke. Cambridge University Press, 1936.

Le Bras, Gabriel. *Les Origines canoniques du droit administratif.* Sirey, 1956.

Le Bras, Gabriel, Charles Lefebvre, and J. Rambaud, eds. *L'age classique.* Vol. 7 of *Histoire du Droit et des Institutions de l'Église en Occident.* Cujas, 1965.

Lecler, Jean. *Le Pape ou le Concile? Une interrogation de l'Église médiévale.* Le Chalet, 1973.

Lécuyer, Joseph. *Études sur la collégialité épiscopale.* Mappus, 1964.

Legendre, Pierre. "Du droit privé au droit public: Nouvelles observations sur le mandat chez les canonistes classiques." *Mémoires de la Société pour l'Histoire du Droit et des Institutions des anciens pays bourguignons, comtois et romands* 30 (1970–1971): 7–35.

Légier, Henri-Jacques. *Les églises collégiales en France, des origines au XVe siècle.* PhD diss., Faculté de droit de Paris, Panthéon-Sorbonne University, 1995.

Le Goff, Jacques. "Le concile et la prise de conscience de l'espace de la chrétienté." In *1274, année charnière: Mutations et continuité.* CNRS, 1977.

Legrand, Hervé. "Collégialité des évêques et communion des Églises dans la réception de Vatican II." *Revue des sciences philosophiques et théologiques* 75 (1991): 545–568.

Legrand, Hervé. "Collegialité." In *Dictionnaire critique de théologie*, edited by Jean-Yves Lacoste. Presses Universitaires de France, 1998.

Legrand, Hervé, Julio Manzanares, and Antonio Garcia, ed. *Les Conférences épiscopales. Théologie, statut canonique, avenir.* Cerf, 1988.

Lemaître, Jean-Loup. "Les créations de collégiales en Languedoc par les papes et les cardinaux avignonnais sous les pontificats de Jean XXII et Benoît XII." In *La papauté d'Avignon et le Languedoc (1316–1324).* Privat, 1991.

BIBLIOGRAPHY ᴄ︁ᴙ︁ 285

Lemarignier, Jean-François. "Aspects politiques des fondations de collégiales dans le royaume de France." In *La vita comune del clero nei secoli XI–XIII*, edited by Enrico Cattaneo. Vita e Pensiero, 1962.

Lemesle, Bruno. *Le gouvernement des évêques. La charge pastorale au milieu du Moyen Âge.* Presses Universitaires de Rennes, 2015.

Leveleux-Teixeira, Corinne. "Controverses juridiques et désarmement herméneutique, ou la brève histoire d'un espace public doctrinal chez les juristes (XIIe–XIIIe siècles)." In *L'espace public au Moyen Âge. Débats autour de Jürgen Habermas*, edited by Patrick Boucheron and Nicolas Offenstadt. Presses Universitaires de France, 2011.

Levillain, Philippe, ed. *Dictionnaire historique de la papauté.* Fayard, 1994.

Levillain, Philippe, ed. *The Papacy: An Encyclopedia.* Translated by John W. O'Malley. Routledge, 2002.

Levillain, Philippe, ed. *"Rome, l'unique objet de mon ressentiment": Regards critiques sur la papauté.* École Française de Rome, 2011.

Levillain, Philippe. "Vatican II en contre-chant." In *"Rome, l'unique objet de mon ressentiment": Regards critiques sur la papauté*, edited by Philippe Levillain. École Française de Rome, 2011.

Lloyd, Howell A. "Constitutionnalisme." In *The Cambridge History of Political Thought, 1450–1700*, edited by J. H. Burns. Cambridge University Press, 1991.

Lönning, Inge. "Paulus und Petrus. Gal 2,11 ff. als kontroverstheologisches fundamental Problem." *Studia Theologica. Scandinavian Journal of Theology* 24 (1970): 1–69.

Losito, Giacomo. *Dio s-oggetto della storia, Loisy, Blondel, Laberthonnière.* Loffredo, 2014.

Losito, Giacomo, ed. *La crisi modernista nella cultura europea.* Istitutio della Enciclopedia Italiana, 2012.

Losito, Giacomo, and Charles J. T. Talar, eds. *Modernisme, mystique, mysticisme.* Honoré Champion, 2017.

Lourdaux, Willem, and Daniël Verhest, eds. *The Concept of Heresy in the Middle Ages (11th–13th c.).* Nijhoff, 1973.

Lousse, Émile. "Parlementarisme ou corporatisme? Les origines des assemblées d'états." *Revue historique de droit français et étranger* 14 (1935): 683–706.

Lusignan, Serge. *"Vérité garde le roy": La Construction d'une identité universitaire en France (XIIIe–XVe siècle).* Publications de la Sorbonne, 1999.

286 ∞ BIBLIOGRAPHY

Lyon, Bryce. "Medieval Constitutionalism: A Balance of Power." In *Album Helen Maud Cam: Studies Presented to the International Commission for the History of Representative and Parliamentary Institutions*, vol. 1. Nauwelaerts, 1961.

Lyon, Bryce. "What Made a Medieval King Constitutional." In *Essays in Medieval History Presented to Bertie Wilkinson*, edited by T. A. Sandquist and Michael Powicke. University of Toronto Press, 1969.

Maccarrone, Michele. "Una questione inedita dell'Olivi sull'infallibilità del papa." *Rivista di Storia della Chiesa in Italia* 3 (1949): 309–343.

Maire, Catherine. *De la cause de Dieu à la cause de la nation: Le jansénisme au XVIIIe siècle.* Gallimard, 1998.

Marchetto, Agostino. *"In partem sollicitudinis . . . non in plenitu- dinem potestatis*: Evoluzione di una formula di rapporto Primato- Episcopato." In *Studia in honorem eminentissimi cardinalis Alphonsi M. Stickler*, edited by Rosalio Iosepho Castillo Lara. Libreria Ateneo Salesiano, 1992.

Maréchal, Joseph. *De la Renaissance à Kant.* Vol. 1 of *Précis d'histoire de la philosophie moderne.* L'édition universelle, 1951.

Maret, Henri. *Du concile général et de la paix religieuse.* Paris, 1869.

Marongiu, Antonio. "Préparlements, parlements, États, assemblées d'États." *Revue historique de droit français et étranger* 15 (1979): 631–644.

Marongiu, Antonio. "Q.O.T. Principe fondamental de la démocratie et du consentement au XIVe siècle." In *Album Helen Maud Cam: Studies Presented to the International Commission of the History of Representative and Parliamentary Institutions*, vol. 2. Nauwelaerts, 1961.

Marrou, Henri-Irénée. "Review of Gr. B. Ladner, *The Idea of Reform. Its Impact on Christian Thought and Action in the Age of the Fathers." Revue d'Histoire Ecclésiastique* 57 (1962): 139.

Martimort, Aimé-Georges. *Le gallicanisme de Bossuet.* Cerf, 1953.

Martimort, Aimé-Georges. *L'établissement du texte de la* Defensio declarationis *de Bossuet.* Cerf, 1956.

Martin de Alpartil. *Cronica actitatorum temporibus domini Benedicti XIII. Einleitung, Text der Chronik, Anhang Ungedruckter Aktenstücke.* Edited by Franz Ehrle. Ferdinand Schöningh, 1906.

Martin, Victor. "Comment s'est formée la doctrine de la supériorité du concile sur le pape." *Revue des sciences religieuses* 17 (1937): 121–143, 261–289, 404–427.

Martin, Victor. *Le Gallicanisme et la Réforme catholique. Essai historique sur l'introduction en France des décrets du concile de Trente (1563–1615).* Picard, 1919.

BIBLIOGRAPHY Ꮭ 287

Martin, Victor. *Le Gallicanisme politique et le clergé de France.* Picard, 1929.

Martin, Victor. *Les origines du gallicanisme.* Bloud & Gay, 1939.

Massoni, Anne. *La collégiale Saint-Germain l'Auxerrois de Paris (1380–1510).* Presse Universitaires de Limoges, 2009.

Mazel, Florian. "Pour une redéfinition de la réforme grégorienne. Éléments d'introduction." *Cahiers de Fanjeaux* 48 (2013): 9–38.

Mazzoni, Giampietro. *La collegialità episcopale: Tra teologia e diritto canonico.* Dehoniane, 1986.

McIlwain, Charles. *Constitutionalism: Ancient and Modern.* Cornell University Press, 1940.

McIlwain, Charles. "The English Common Law, Barrier against Absolutism." *American Historical Review* 49, no. 1 (1943): 23–31.

McIlwain, Charles. *Growth of Political Thought in the West.* Macmillan, 1932.

McIlwain, Charles. "Mediaeval Institutions in the Modern World." *Speculum* 16, no. 3 (1941): 275–283.

McNally, Robert E. *The Unreformed Church.* Sheed and Ward, 1965.

McNeil, J. T. "The Relevance of Conciliarism." *Jurist* 31 (1971): 81–112.

Mertens, Dieter. "Monastische Reform bewegungen des 15. Jh: Ideen-Ziele-Resultate." In *Reform von Kirche und Reich zur Zeit der Konzilien von Konstanz (1414–1418), und Basel (1431–1449). Konstanz-Prager historisches Kolloquium (11–17 Oktober 1993),* edited by Ivan Hlaváček and Alexander Patschovsky. Universitätsverlag Konstanz, 1996.

Meuthen, Erich. "Das Basler Konzil in römisch-katholischer Sicht." *Theologische Zeitschrift* 38 (1982): 274–308.

Meyjes, G. H. M. Posthumus. *De controverse tussen Petrus en Paulus. Galaten 2: 11 in de historie.* M. Nijhoff, 1967.

Meyjes, G. H. M. Posthumus. "Exponents of Sovereignty: Canonists as Seen by Theologians in the Late Middle Ages." In *The Church and Sovereignty, c. 590–1918: Essays in Honor of Michael Wilks,* ed. Dianna Wood. Blackwell, 1991.

Meyjes, G. H. M. Posthumus. "Iconografie en Primaat. Petrus en Paulus op het pauselijk zegel." *Nederlands Archief voor Kerkgeschiedenis* 49 (1968): 4–36.

Meyjes, G. H. M. Posthumus. *Jean Gerson—Apostle of Unity: His Church Politics and Ecclesiology.* Translated by J. C. Grayson. Brill, 1999.

Meyjes, G. H. M. Posthumus. *Jean Gerson et l'Assemblée de Vincennes (1329). Ses conceptions de la juridiction temporelle de l'Église.* Brill, 1978.

Michel, Florian. *Étienne Gilson. Une biographie intellectuelle et politique.* Vrin, 2018.

288 &ORD; BIBLIOGRAPHY

Miethke, Jürgen. "Kirchenreform auf den Konzilien des 15. Jahrhunderts. Motive-Methoden-Wirkungen." In *Studien zum 15. Jahrhundert: Festschrift für Erich Meuthen*, 2 vol., edited by Heribert Müller, Johannes Helmrath, and Helmut Wolff. Oldenburg, 1994.

Miethke, Jürgen. "Konziliarismus: Die neue Doctrin einer neuen Kirchenverfassung." In *Reform von Kirche und Reiche zur Zeit der Konzilien von Konstanz (1414–1418) und Basel (1431–1449)*, edited by Ivan Hlaváček and Alexander Patschovsy. Konstanz, 1996.

Miethke, Jürgen and Lorenz Weinrich. *Quellen zur Kirchenreform im Zeitlalter der grossen Konzilien des 15. Jahrhunderts*. Wissenschaftliche Buchgesellschaft, 1995.

Millet, Hélène. "Du conseil au concile (1395–1408). Recherche sur la nature des assemblées du clergé en France pendant le Grand Schisme d'Occident." *Journal des Savants*, nos. 1–3 (1985): 137–159.

Millet, Hélène. "La représentativité, source de la légitimité du concile de Pise (1409)." In *Théologie et Droit dans la science politique de l'État moderne*, edited by Jean-Philippe Genet and Jean-Yves Tillette. École française de Rome, 1991.

Millet, Hélène. *L'Église du Grand Schisme, 1378–1417*. Picard, 2009.

Millet, Hélène. "Pierre d'Ailly et le Concile de Pise (1409)." *Comptes rendus des séances de l'Académie des Inscriptions et Belles-Lettres* 158, no. 2 (2014): 809–827.

Millet, Hélène, and Monique Maillard-Luypaert. *Le Schisme et la Pourpre: Le cardinal Pierre d'Ailly, homme de science et de foi*. Cerf, 2015.

Minnich, Nelson H. "Concepts of Reform Proposed at the Fifth Lateran Council." *Archivum Historiae Pontificiae* 7 (1969): 163–251.

Minnich, Nelson H. *Councils of the Catholic Reformation: Pisa I (1409) to Trent (1545–1563)*. Routledge, 2008.

Minnich, Nelson H. *The Fifth Lateran Council (1512–1517): Studies on Its Membership, Diplomacy and Proposals for Reform*. Ashgate, 1993.

Miramon, Charles de. "L'invention de la Réforme grégorienne: Grégoire VII au XIXe siècle, entre pouvoir spirituel et bureaucratisation de l'Église." *Revue de l'histoire des religions* 236, no. 2 (2019): 283–315.

Mirus, J. A. "On the Deposition of the Pope for Heresy." *Archivium historiae pontificiae* 13 (1975): 231–248.

Moeller, Charles. "Infaillibilité et vérité." In *L'infaillibilité de l'Église. Journées oecuméniques*, edited by Olivier Rousseau, Jean-Jacques Von Allmen, Bernard-Dominique Dupuy et al. Éditions de Chevetogne, 1962.

BIBLIOGRAPHY CR 289

Moeller, Charles. "La collégialité au concile de Constance." In *La collégialité épiscopale: Histoire et théologie*, edited by Jacques Dupont and Yves-Marie Congar. Cerf, 1965.

Mohrmann, Christine. "Review: The Idea of Reform, Its Impact on Christian Thought and Action in the Age of the Fathers by Gerhart B. Ladner." *Vigiliae Christianae* 16, nos. 3–4 (1962): 235–237.

Monahan, Arthur. *Consent, Coercion and Limit: The Medieval Origins of Parliamentary Democracy.* McGill-Queen's University Press, 1987.

Monod, Jean-Claude. *La Querelle de la sécularisation de Hegel à Blumenberg.* Vrin, 2012.

Moore, Peter. "Synodical Scenario." In *The Synod of Westminster: Do We Need It?* SPCK Publishing, 1986.

Morrison, Karl F. *The Mimetic Tradition of Reform in the West.* Princeton University Press, 2014.

Morrissey, Thomas. "After Six Hundred Years: The Great Western Schism, Conciliarism and Constance." *Theological Studies* 40, no. 3 (1979): 495–509.

Morrissey, Thomas. "The Decree *Haec Sancta* and Cardinal Zabarella: His Role in Its Formulation and Interpretation." *Annuarium historiae conciliorum* 10 (1978): 145–176.

Moulin, Léo. "La primauté de l'exécutif et la notion de collégialité dans les Instituts religieux." *Revue internationale des sciences administratives* 19 (1953): 112–149.

Moulin, Léo. *Le Monde vivant des religieux.* Calmann-Lévy, 1964.

Moulin, Léo. "Les origines religieuses des techniques électorales et délibératives modernes." *Politix. Revue des sciences sociales du politique* 11, no. 43 (1998): 117–162.

Moulin, Léo. "SANIOR ET MAIOR PARS: Note sur l'évolution des techniques électorales dans les ordres religieux du VIe Au XIIIe siècle." *Revue Historique de Droit Français et Étranger* 35 (1958): 368–397.

Moulin, Léo. "Une source méconnue de la philosophie marsilienne: l'organisation constitutionnelle des ordres religieux." *Revue française de science politique* 33, no. 1 (1983): 5–13.

Müller, Heribert. *Die kirchliche Krise des Spätmittelalters. Schisma, Konziliarismus und Konzilien.* Oldenburg, 2012.

Müller, Heribert. "L'érudition gallicane et le concile de Bâle." *Francia* 9 (1982): 531–555.

290 &? BIBLIOGRAPHY

Musset, Jacques. *Sommes-nous sortis de la crise du modernisme? Enquête sur le XXe siècle catholique et l'après-concile Vatican II*. Karthala, 2016.

Musurillo, Herbert. "Book Review: The Idea of Reform: Its Impact on Christian Thought and Action in the Age of the Fathers." *Theological Studies* 21, no. 3 (1960): 472–474.

Naegle, Gisela. "D'une cité à l'autre. Bien commun et réforme de l'État à la fin du Moyen Âge (France/Empire)." *Revue française d'histoire des idées* 32 (2010): 325–338.

Naz, Raoul, ed. *Dictionnaire de droit canonique*. 5 vols. Letouzey & Ané, 1953.

Nederman, Cary. "Conciliarism and Constitutionalism: Jean Gerson and Medieval Political Thought." *History of European Ideas* 12, no. 2 (1990): 189–209.

Nederman, Cary. "Constitutionalism—Medieval and Modern: Against Neo-Figgist Orthodoxy (Again)." *History of Political Thought* 17 (1996): 179–194.

Nederman, Cary. *Lineages of European Political Thought*. Catholic University of America Press, 2009.

Neveu, Bruno. "Juge suprême et docteur infaillible: Le pontificat romain de la Bulle *In eminenti* (1643) à la Bulle *Auctorem fidei* (1794)." *Mélanges de l'École française de Rome—Antiquité, Moyen Âge-Temps modernes* 93, no. 1 (1981): 215–275.

Neveu, Bruno. *L'erreur et son juge. Remarques sur les censures doctrinales à l'époque moderne*. Bibliopolis, 1993.

Neveu, Bruno. "Saint Paul et Rome: À propos d'une controverse sur la primauté pontificale." In *Homo religiosus. Autour de Jean Delumeau*. Fayard, 1997.

New Catholic Encyclopedia, vol. 4. 2nd ed. Catholic University of America Press, 2003.

Newman, John Henry. "On the Prophetical Office of the Church." In *The Via Media of the Anglican Church*, vol. 1. London, 1891.

O'Brien, Emily. *The Commentaries of Pope Pius II (1458–1464) and the Crisis of the Fifteenth Century Papacy*. University of Toronto Press, 2015.

O'Malley, John. *Giles of Viterbo on Church and Reform: A Study in Renaissance Thought*. Brill, 1968.

O'Malley, John. *Praise and Blame in Renaissance Rome: Rhetoric, Doctrine and Reform in the Sacred Orators of the Papal Court, c. 1450–1521*. Duke University Press, 1979.

O'Malley, John. "Reform, Historical Consciousness, and Vatican II's Aggiornamento." *Theological Studies* 32, no. 4 (1971): 573–601

O'Malley, John. *Trent and All That*. Harvard University Press, 2000.

BIBLIOGRAPHY ❧ 291

Oakley, Francis. "Anxieties of Influence: Skinner, Figgis, Conciliarism and Early Modern Constitutionalism." *Past and Present* 151 (1996): 60–110.

Oakley, Francis. "Complexities of Context: Gerson, Bellarmine, Sarpi, Richer, and the Venetian Interdict of 1606–1607." In *Politics and Eternity: Studies in the History of Medieval and Early-Modern Political Thought.* Brill, 1999.

Oakley, Francis. "Conciliarism at the Fifth Lateran council?" *Church History* 29 (1972): 452–463.

Oakley, Francis. *The Conciliarist Tradition: Constitutionalism in the Catholic Church, 1300–1870.* Oxford University Press, 2003.

Oakley, Francis. *Council Over Pope? Towards a Provisional Ecclesiology.* Herder & Herder, 1969.

Oakley, Francis. "Figgis, Constance, and the Divines of Paris." *American Historical Review* 75, no. 2 (1969): 368–386.

Oakley, Francis. "Gerson and d'Ailly." *Speculum* 40 (1965): 74–83.

Oakley, Francis. "Legitimation by Consent: The Question of Medieval Roots." *Viator* 14 (1983): 303–335.

Oakley, Francis. "Nederman, Gerson, Conciliar Theory and Constitutionalism: Sed Contra." *History of Political Thought* 16 (1995): 1–19.

Oakley, Francis. "The 'New Conciliarism' and Its Implications: A Problem in History and Hermeneutics." *Journal of Ecumenical Studies* 8 (1971): 815–840.

Oakley, Francis. "On the Road from Constance to 1688: The Political Thought of John Major and George Buchanan." *Journal of British Studies* 1, no. 2 (1962): 1–31.

Oakley, Francis. "Pierre d'Ailly and Papal Infallibility." *Mediaeval Studies* 26 (1964): 353–358. Reprinted in Francis Oakley, *Natural Law, Conciliarism and Consent.* Ashgate, 1984.

Oakley, Francis. "*Verius est licet difficilius*: Tierney's Foundations of the Conciliar Theory After Forty Years." In *Nicholas of Cusa on Christ and The Church: Essays in Memory of Chandler McCuskey Brooks*, edited by Gerald Christianson and Thomas M. Izbicki. Brill, 1996.

Oakley, Francis. *The Western Church in the Later Middle Ages.* Cornell University Press, 1979.

Oberman, Heiko A., ed. *The Dawn of the Reformation: Essays in Late Medieval and Early Reformation Thought.* Eerdmans, 1986.

Olivi, Peter John. *Quaestio de infallibilitate Romani pontificis.* Edited by M. Maccarrone. *Rivista di storia della chiesa in Italia* 3 (1949): 309–343.

292 ₠ BIBLIOGRAPHY

Ourliac, Paul. "Souveraineté et lois fondamentales dans le droit canonique du XVe siècle." In *Herrschaftsverträge, Wahlkapitulationen, Fundamentalgesetze*, edited by Rudolf Vierhaus. Vandenhoeck und Ruprecht, 1977.

Overbeck, Franz. *Über die Auffassung des Streits des Paulus mit Petrus in Antiochien (Gal 2, 11), bei den Kirchenvätern.* Wissenschaftliche Buchgesellschaft, 1968.

Ozment, Steven. *The Age of Reform, 1250–1550: An Intellectual and Religious History of Late Medieval and Reformation Europe.* Yale University Press, 1980.

Paine, Thomas. "Constitution, Governments and Charters." In *The Writings of Thomas Paine*, vol. 4, edited by Moncure Daniel Conway. New York, 1894.

Palacky, Frantisek, and Birk Ernst. *Monumenta Conciliorum Generalium Seculi Decimi Quinti*, vol. 2. C. R. Officinae typographicae, 1873.

Paravicini Pagliani, Agostino. *Boniface VIII. Un pape hérétique?* Payot, 2003.

Paravicini Bagliani, Agostino. *Le corps du pape.* Seuil, 1997.

Parisoli, Luca. "L'émergence de l'infaillibilité pontificale de Pierre de Jean Olieu à Guillaume d'Ockham." *L'Année Canonique* 41 (1999): 143–164.

Parisse, Michel. "Collégiale." In *Dictionnaire du Moyen Âge*, edited by Claude Gauvard, Alain de Libera, and Michel Zink. Presses Universitaires de France, 2002.

Pascal, Blaise. *Thoughts.* Translated by W. F. Trotter. Collier Press, 1910.

Pascoe, Louis B. *Church and Reform: Bishops, Theologians and Canon Lawyers in the Thought of Pierre d'Ailly.* Brill, 2005.

Pascoe, Louis B. "Gerhart Ladner's *The Idea of Reform.* Reflections on Terminology and Ideology." In *Reassessing Reform. A Historical Investigation into Church Renewal*, edited by Christopher M. Bellitto and David Zachariah Flanagin. Catholic University of America Press, 2012.

Pascoe, Louis B. "Gerson and the Donation of Constantine: Growth and Development within the Church." *Viator* 5 (1974): 469–485.

Pascoe, Louis B. "Jean Gerson: Mysticism, Conciliarism and Reform." *Annuarium historiae conciliorum* 6 (1974): 135–153.

Pascoe, Louis B. *Jean Gerson: Principles of Church Reform.* Brill, 1973.

Pascoe, Louis B. "Jean Gerson: The *Ecclesia primitiva* and Reform." *Traditio* 30 (1974): 379–409.

Paul, Jacques, ed. "L'anticléricalisme en France méridionale (milieu XIIe–début XIVe siècle)." Special issue, *Cahiers de Fanjeaux* 38 (2003).

BIBLIOGRAPHY ❧ 293

Pelletier, Denis. "Les savoirs du religieux dans la France du XXe siècle. Trois moments d'une histoire intellectuelle de la sécularisation." *Recherches des Sciences Religieuses* 101 (2013): 167–180.

Pennington, Kenneth. "Sovereignty and Rights in Medieval and Early Modern Jurisprudence: Law and Norms Without a State." In *Rethinking the State in the Age of Globalisation: Catholic Thought and Contemporary Political Theory*, edited by Heinz-Gerhard Justenhoven and James Turner. Lit, 2003.

Pestre, Dominique, ed. *Histoire des sciences et des savoirs*. 3 vols. Seuil, 2015.

Pestre, Dominique. *Introduction aux Sciences Studies*. La Découverte, 2006

Piaia, Gregorio. *Marsilio da Padova nella Riforma e nella Controriforma. Fortuna ed interpretazione*. Antenore, 1977.

Piché, David. *La condamnation parisienne de 1277. Nouvelle édition du texte latin, traduction, introduction et commentaire*. Vrin, 1999.

Pichler, Isfried Hermann. *Die Verbindlichkeit der Konstanzer Dekrete*. Herder, 1966.

Pitzipios, Iakovos G. *Le Romanisme*. Paris, 1860.

Plaoul, Pierre. "Discours de clôture des débats avant le vote." In *Historia universitatis Parisiensis*, edited by César-Egasse du Boulay. 6 vols. Paris, 1665–1673.

Post, Gaines. "*Ratio publicae utilitatis, ratio status* und 'Staatsräson' (1100–1300)." *Die Welt als Geschichte* 21, no. 2 (1961): 8–28, 71–99.

Post, Gaines. *Studies in Medieval Legal Thought*. Princeton University Press, 1964.

Pottmeyer, Hermann J. *Unfehlbarkeit und Souveränität*. Mathias Grünewald, 1975.

Poulat, Émile. *Histoire, dogme et critique dans la crise moderniste*. Albin Michel, 1996.

Prévost, Philippe. *L'Église et le ralliement: Histoire d'une crise, 1892–2000*. Kontre Kulture Éditions, 2016.

Prévotat, Jacques. "Étienne Gilson est-il un chrétien modéré?" In *Les chrétiens modérés en France et en Europe, 1870–1960*, edited by Jacques Prévotat and Jean Vavasseur-Desperriers. Presses Universitaires du Septentrion, 2013.

Prodi, Paolo. *Christianisme et monde moderne. Cinquante ans de recherches*. Seuil, 2006.

Prodi, Paolo. *Il paradigma tridentino. Un'epoca della storia della Chiesa*. Morcelliana, 2010.

Provvidente, Sebastian. "The *Haec Sancta synodus* Decree: Between Theology, Canon Law and History. Judicial Practices and *plenitudo potestatis*." *Temas medievales* 20, no. 1 (2012).

294 ⬥ BIBLIOGRAPHY

Provvidente, Sebastian. "Inquisitorial Process and *plenitudo potestatis* at the Council of Constance (1414–1418)." *Bohemian Reformation and Religious Practice* 8 (2011): 98–114.

Provvidente, Sebastian. "The Synodial Practices of the Council of Constance (1414–1418): Between Symbol and Trace." In "Les nouveaux horizons de l'ecclésiologie: Du discours clérical à la science du social," edited by Frédéric Gabriel, Dominique Iogna-Prat, and Alain Rauwel. Special issue, *Bulletin du Centre d'Études médiévales d'Auxerre*, no. 7 (2013). https://doi.org/10.4000/cem.12784.

Prügl, Thomas. "*Antiquis juribus et dictis sanctorum conformare:* Zur antikonziliaristichen Interpretation von *Haec Sancta* auf dem Basler Konzil." *Annuarium historiae conciliorum* 31 (1999): 72–143.

Prügl, Thomas. "The Concept of Infallibility in Nicholas of Cusa." In *Cusanus: The Legacy of Learned Ignorance*, edited by Peter J. Casarella. Catholic University of America Press, 2006.

Putallaz, François-Xavier and Ruedi Imbach. *Profession: Philosophe. Siger de Brabant.* Cerf, 1997.

Quantin, Jean-Louis. "La menace des faits: Érudition moderne et condamnations romaines." In *"Rome, l'unique objet de mon ressentiment": Regards critiques sur la papauté*, edited by Philippe Levillain. École Française de Rome, 2011.

Quillet, Jeannine. *Le Défenseur de la paix. Traduction, introduction et commentaire.* Vrin, 1968.

Rabelais, François. *Quart Livre.* Edited by R. Marichal. Droz, 1947.

Rahner, Karl. "Kritik an Hans Küng. Zur frage der Unfehlbarkeit theologischer Sätze. Antwort an Karl Rahner." *Stimmen der Zeit* 187 (1971): 43–64 and 105–122.

Rahner, Karl. "Quelques considérations sur le problème de l'infaillibilité dans la théologie catholique." In *L'Infaillibilité. Son aspect philosophique et théologique*, edited by Enrico Castelli. Aubier, 1970.

Rahner, Karl. "Replik. Bemerkungen zu: Hans Küng, Im Interesse der Sache." *Stimmen der Zeit* 187 (1971): 145–160.

Rahner, Karl. "Zum Begriff der Unfehlbarkeit in der Katholischen Theologie." *Stimmen der Zeit* 186 (1970): 18–31.

Rahner, Karl, ed. *Zum Problem Unfehlbarkeit: Antworten auf die Anfrage von H. Küng.* Herder, 1971.

Rapp, Francis. "Le conciliarisme bâillonné, la réforme escamotée." In *De la réforme à la réformation (1450–1530).* Vol. 7 of *Histoire du christianisme des origines à nos*

BIBLIOGRAPHY ⌘ 295

jours, edited by Jean-Marie Mayeur, Charles Pietri, Luce Pietri, André Vauchez, and Marc Venard. Desclée de Brouwer, 1995.

Rathmann, Thomas. *Geschehen und Geschichten des Konstanzer Konzils: Chroniken, Briefe, Lieder, und Sprüche als Konstituenten eines Ereignisses.* Fink, 2000.

Rauwel, Alain. "Anti-moderne et médiéval." In *Catholicisme et Monde moderne aux XIXe et XXe siècles. Autour du "Modernisme,"* edited by François Chaubet. Éditions Universitaires de Dijon, 2008.

Rauwel, Alain. "Concurrence des rits et jugement de Dieu: Une originalité espagnole?" *Cahiers de civilisation médiévale* 58 (2015): 371–376.

Religieux de Saint-Denis. *Chronique du Religieux de Saint-Denys, contenant le règne de Charles VI, de 1380 à 1422.* Edited by Bernard Guenée. Editions du Comité des travaux historiques et scientifiques, 1994.

Rials, Stéphane. "Aux origines du constitutionnalisme écrit. Réflexions en marge d'un projet constitutionnel de la Ligue (1588)." *Revue d'Histoire des Facultés de Droit et de la Science Juridique* 8 (1989): 189–268.

Rials, Stéphane. "Des droits de l'homme aux lois de l'homme. Aux origines de la pensée juridique moderne." *Commentaire* 34 (1986): 281–289.

Rials, Stéphane. "Préface. À l'anglaise: Comment filer l'histoire constitutionnelle?" In *Parlementarisme des origines. Essai sur les conditions de formation d'un exécutif responsable en Angleterre (des années 1740 au début de l'âge victorien),* edited by Denis Baranger. Presses Universitaires de France, 1999.

Rials, Stéphane. "Sur les origines canoniales des techniques constitutionnelles modernes." *Pouvoirs* 44 (1988): 141–153.

Richer, Edmond. *De la puissance ecclésiastique et politique. Texte de la première edition latine (1611) et française (1612).* Cerf, 2014.

Rigaudière, Albert. "Assemblées politiques." In *Dictionnaire du Moyen Âge,* edited by Claude Gauvard, Alain de Libera, and Michel Zink. Presses Universitaires de France, 2002.

Rigaudière, Albert. "La *lex vel constitutio* d'août 1374, 'première loi constitutionnelle de la monarchie française.'" In *Un Moyen Âge pour aujourd'hui. Mélanges offerts à Claude Gauvard,* edited by Julie Claustre, Olivier Mattéoni, and Nicolas Offenstadt. Presses Universitaires de France, 2010.

Rigaudière, Albert. "Les fonctions du mot constitution dans le discours politique et juridique du bas Moyen Âge français." *Revista internacional de los Estudios Vascos* 4 (2008): 15–51.

Rigaudière, Albert. "Un grand moment pour l'histoire du droit constitutionnel français: 1374–1409." *Journal des Savants* 2, no. 1 (2012): 281–370.

296 ❧ BIBLIOGRAPHY

Riley, Lawrence Joseph. *The History, Nature and Use of Epikeia in Moral Theology*. Catholic University of America Press, 1948.

Rivière, Jacques. "In partem sollicitudinis. Evolution d'une formule pontificale." *Revue des Sciences Religieuses* 5 (1925): 210–231.

Rivière, Jean. *Le Modernisme dans l'Église. Étude d'histoire religieuse contemporaine.* Letouzey & Ané, 1929.

Rodríguez, Pedro. "Infallibilis? La Respuesta de Santo Tomás de Aquino. Estudio de la terminología '*infallibilis-infallibiliter-infallibilitas*,' en sus tratados '*De fide*.'" *Scripta Theologica* 7 (1975): 51–123.

Rollo-Koster, Joëlle. *The Great Western Schism, 1378–1417. Performing Legitimacy, Performing Unity*. Cambridge University Press, 2022.

Rosenblieh, Émilie. "Conciliabule, une qualification canonique à l'époque des conciles rivaux (1408–1409 et 1438–1445)." In *Le Concile de Perpignan (15 novembre 1408–26 mars 1409), Études roussillonnaises. Revue d'histoire et d'archéologie méditerranéennes* 24 (2009–2010): 185–186.

Rosenblieh, Émilie. "La violation des décrets conciliaires ou l'hérésie du pape: Le procès d'Eugène IV (1431–1447) au concile de Bâle d'après le manuscrit latin 1511 de la Bibliothèque nationale de France." *Revue belge de philologie et d'histoire* 86, nos. 3–4 (2009): 245–268.

Rosenblieh, Émilie. "Le décret *Frequens* ou la constitutionnalisation de l'autorité conciliaire (première moitié du XVe siècle)." *Annuarium historiae conciliorum* 47 (2015): 153–178.

Rosenblieh, Émilie. "Les conciles réformateurs de la première moitié du XVe siècle, des assemblées européennes?" In *Philippe de Mézières et l'Europe. Nouvelle histoire, nouveaux espaces, nouveaux langages*, edited by Joël Blanchard and Renate Blumenfeld-Kosinski. Droz, 2017.

Rosenblieh, Émilie. "L'Esprit saint, ou la légitimation de l'autorité conciliaire: Le procès du pape Eugène IV au concile de Bâle (1431–1439)." In *La Dramatique conciliaire. Coups de théâtre, tactique et sincérité des convictions dans les débats conciliaires de l'Antiquité à Vatican II*, edited by Guillaume Cuchet and Charles Mériaux. Presses Universitaires du Septentrion, 2019.

Rousseau, O., B. Botte, H. Marot et al. *Le Concile et les conciles. Contribution à l'histoire de la vie conciliaire de l'Église*. Cerf, 1960.

Rousseau, Olivier, Jean-Jacques Von Allmen, Bernard-Dominique Dupuy et al., eds. *L'Infaillibilité de l'Église. Journées œcuméniques de Chevetogne*. Éditions de Chevetogne, 1962.

BIBLIOGRAPHY ❧ 297

Rueger, Z. "Le *De auctoritate concilii* de Gerson." *Revue d'histoire ecclésiastique* 53, no. 4 (1958): 775–795.

Russo, Daniel. "Les lectures de l'art sacré en France et en Europe au tournant des années 1880–1920. Autour du 'médiévalisme.'" In *Catholicisme et Monde moderne aux XIXe et XXe siècles. Autour du "Modernisme,"* edited by François Chaubet. Éditions Universitaires de Dijon, 2008.

Rynne, Xavier, ed. *The Third Session: The Debates and Decrees of Vatican Council II, September 14 to November 21, 1964.* Farrar, Straus and Giroux, 1965.

Sabine, George H. *A History of Political Theory.* Henry Holt, 1956.

Salembier, Louis-Joseph. "Gerson (Jean le Charlier de)." In *Dictionnaire de théologie catholique,* vol. 6, part 1, edited by Alfred Vacant, Eugène Mangenot, and Émile Amann. Letouzey & Ané, 1914.

Sartori, Giovanni. "Constitutionalism: A Preliminary Discussion." *American Political Science Review* 56 (1962): 853–864.

Schatz, Klaus. *La primauté du pape. Son histoire, des origines à nos jours.* Cerf, 1992.

Schatz, Klaus. *Unfehlbarkeitsdiskussion und Rezeption.* Vol. 3 of *Vaticanum I, 1869–1870.* Ferdinand Schöningh, 1994.

Schmitt, Carl. *Hugo Preuss. Sein Staatsbegriff und seine Stellung in der deutschen Staatslehre.* Mohr Siebeck, 1930.

Schmitt, Carl. *The Nomos of the Earth in the International Law of Jus Publicum Europaeum.* Telos Press, 2006.

Schmitt, Carl. *Political Theology.* Translated by George Schwab. MIT Press, 1985.

Schmitt, Carl. *Verfassungslehre.* Duncker & Humblot, 1928.

Schmitz, Benoît. "La pragmatique sanction de Bourges et ses usages dans les controverses ecclésiologiques autour des conciles de Pise II et Latran V." Unpublished manuscript, May 2011.

Schneider, Hans. *Des Konziliarismus als Problem der neueren katholische Theologie.* De Gruyter, 1976.

Schneider, Hans. "Konziliarität/Konziliarismus." In *Religion in Geschichte und Gegenwart,* vol. 4, edited by Hans Dieter Betz, Don S. Browning, Bernd Janowski, and Eberhard Jüngel. Mohr Siebeck, 2001.

Sciacca, Enzo. "L'opposition 'néo-conciliariste' à l'absolutisme monarchique en France: Jacques Almain et Jean Mair." *Parliaments, Estates and Representation* 8 (1948): 149–155.

Sère, Bénédicte. "Entre rigueur et indulgence: La voie de l'oubli chez Gerson à l'heure de la restitution d'obédience (c. 1402)." In *Justice et miséricorde*, edited by Catherine Vincent. Presses Universitaires de Limoges, 2015.

Sère, Bénédicte. "*Forme, déformation, reformation*: Les corps difformes et la théologie de l'image de Dieu en l'homme dans le *Pèlerinage de l'âme*." In *Regards croisés sur le* Pèlerinage de l'âme *de Guillaume de Digulleville*, edited by Marie Bassano, Esther Dehoux, and Catherine Vincent. Brepols, 2015.

Sère, Bénédicte. "Gerson ecclésiologue. Les réinventions de la modernité (XVe–XXIe siècle)." In *Jean Gerson écrivain: De l'œuvre latine et française à sa réception européenne (XVe–XVIIIe siècle)*, edited by Isabelle Fabre. Droz, 2024.

Sère, Bénédicte. "La réception de Brian Tierney, *Foundations of the Conciliar Theory*, 1955." In *Ecclésiologies: Éléments d'histoire et d'historiographie*, edited by Frédéric Gabriel, Dominique Iogna-Prat, and Alain Rauwel. Beauchesne, forthcoming.

Sère, Bénédicte. *Les débats d'opinion à l'heure du Grand Schisme. Ecclésiologie et politique*. Brepols, 2016.

Sère, Bénédicte. *Penser l'amitié au Moyen Âge. Étude historique des livres VIII et IX de l'*Éthique à Nicomaque, *XIIIe–XVe siècle*. Brepols, 2007.

Sère, Bénédicte. "Pierre d'Ailly fut-il un conciliariste? Les effets d'optique de l'état archivistique." In *Pierre d'Ailly. Un esprit universel à l'aube du XVe siècle*, edited by Jean-Patrice Boudet, Monica Brînzei, Fabrice Delivré, Hélène Millet, Jacques Verger, and Michel Zink. Peeters, 2019.

Sère, Bénédicte. "Thomas d'Aquin contre Siger de Brabant, 1270. Chronique d'une dispute." In *Le mot qui tue. Une histoire des violences intellectuelles de l'Antiquité à nos jours*, edited by Vincent Azoulay and Patrick Boucheron. Champ Vallon, 2009.

Sesboüé, Bernard. *Histoire et théologie de l'infaillibilité de l'Église*. Lessius, 2013.

Sesboüé, Bernard. *"Hors de l'Église pas de salut." Histoire d'une formule et problèmes d'interprétation*. Desclée de Brouwer, 2004.

Shogimen, Takashi. "The Relationship Between Theology and Canon Law: Another Context of Political Thought in the Early Fourteenth Century." *Journal of the History of Ideas* 60, no. 3 (1999): 417–431.

Sieben, Hermann Josef. *Konzils und Papstidee. Untersuchungen zu ihrer Geschichte*. Ferdinand Schöningh, 2017.

Sieben, Hermann Josef. *Studien zur Gestalt und Überlieferung der Konzilien*. Ferdinand Schöningh, 2005.

BIBLIOGRAPHY ❧ 299

Sieben, Hermann Josef. *Traktate und Theorien zum Konzil vom Beginn des Grossen Schismas bis zum Vorabend der Reformation (1378–1521).* Knecht, 1983.

Sieben, Hermann Josef. *Vom Apostelkonzil zum Ersten Vatikanum: Studien zur Geschichte der Konzilsidee.* Ferdinand Schöningh, 1996.

Sieyès, Emmanuel Joseph. *Qu'est-ce que le tiers état?* Éditions du Boucher, 2002.

Sigmund, Paul E. "Medieval and Modern Constitutionalism: Nicholas of Cusa and John Locke." In *Cusanus: The Legacy of Learned Ignorance*, edited by Peter J. Casarella. Catholic University of America Press, 2006.

Simon de Cramaud. *De substraccione obediencie.* Edited by Howard Kaminsky. Medieval Academy of America, 1984.

Simon de Cramaud. *Premier discours à la IVe assemblée du clergé de Paris.* In *Preuves de la nouvelle histoire du concile de Constance*, edited by L. Bourgeois du Chastenet. Le Mercier, 1718.

Simons, Francis. *Infallibility and the Evidence.* Templegate, 1968.

Smolinsky, Heribert. "Konziliarismus." In *Lexikon für Theologie und Kirche*, vol. 6, edited by Michael Buchberger and Walter Kasper. Herder, 1961.

Sorrel, Christian. "Conjoncture moderniste et infaillibilité pontificale au début du XXe siècle. Jalons pour une étude." In *Le Pontife et l'erreur: Anti-infaillibilisme catholique et romanité ecclésiale aux temps posttridentins (XVIIe–XXe siècles).* Laboratoire de recherche historique Rhône-Alpes, 2010.

Souriac, Pierre-Jean. "Écrits historiques et excommunication sous Henri III et Henri IV." In *"Rome, l'unique objet de mon ressentiment:" Regards critiques sur la papauté*, edited by Philippe Levillain. École Française de Rome, 2011.

Stewart, Herbert Leslie. *Modernism: Past and Present.* J. Murray, 1932.

Stickler, Alfons Maria. "Papal Infallibility—a Thirteenth Century Invention." *Catholic Historical Review* 65 (1974): 427–441.

Stourzh, Gerald. "Constitution: Changing Meanings of the Term from the Early 17th to the Late 18th Century." In *Conceptual Change and the Constitution*, edited by Terence Ball and J. G. A. Pocock. University Press of Kansas, 1988.

Strauss, Gerald. "Ideas of *Reformatio* and *Renovatio* from the Middle Ages to the Reformation." In *Visions, Programs, and Outcomes*, vol. 2 of *Handbook of European History 1400–1600: Late Middle Ages, Renaissance and Reformation*, edited by Thomas A. Brady Jr., Heiko A. Oberman, and James D. Tracy. Brill, 1995.

Stubbs, William. *The Constitutional History of England*, vol. 1. 6th ed. Clarendon Press, 1903.

300 &) BIBLIOGRAPHY

Studt, Birgit. *Papst Martin V (1417–1431) und die Kirchenreform in Deutschland.* Böhlau, 2004.

Stump, Phillip H. "The Continuing Relevance of *The Idea of Reform.*" In *Reassessing Reform. A Historical Investigation into Church Renewal,* edited by Christopher M. Bellitto and David Zachariah Flanagin. Catholic University of America Press, 2012.

Stump, Phillip H. "The Council of Constance (1414–18) and the End of the Schism." In *Companion to the Great Western Schism,* edited by Joëlle Rollo-Koster and Thomas M. Izbicki. Brill, 2009.

Stump, Phillip H. "The Influence of Gerhart Ladner's *The Idea of Reform.*" In *Reform and Renewal in the Middle Ages and the Renaissance: Studies in Honor of Louis Pascoe, SJ,* edited by Thomas M. Izbicki and Christopher M. Bellitto. Brill, 2000.

Stump, Phillip H. "The Reform of Papal Taxation at the Council of Constance, 1414–1418." *Speculum* 64 (1989): 69–105.

Stump, Phillip H. *The Reforms of the Council of Constance (1414–1418).* Brill, 1994.

Sutto, Claude. "Une controverse ecclésiologique au début du XVIIe siècle: Le *Libellus de ecclesiastica et politica potestate* d'Edmond Richer (1611)." In *Homo religiosus. Autour de Jean Delumeau.* Fayard, 1997.

Swanson, R. N. "The Problem of the Cardinalate in the Great Schism." In *Authority and Power: Studies on Medieval Law and Government,* edited by Brian Tierney and Peter Linehan. Cambridge University Press, 1980.

Swanson, R. N. *Universities, Academics and the Great Schism.* Cambridge University Press, 1979.

Synod and Synodality: Theology, History, Canon Law and Ecumenism in New Contact. International Colloquium Bruges 2003. Lit, 2005.

Tabbagh, Vincent. *Les évêques dans le royaume de France au XIVe siècle.* Éditions Universitaires de Dijon, 2015.

Tallon, Alain. *Conscience nationale et sentiment religieux en France au XVIe siècle. Essai sur la vision gallicane du monde.* Presses Universitaires de France, 2002.

Tallon, Alain. "La fin d'un instrument de paix: Le concile œcuménique." In *Paix des armes, paix des âmes,* edited by Paul Mironneau and Isabelle Pébay-Clottes. Imprimerie Nationale, 2000.

Tallon, Alain. *La France et le concile de Trente.* École Française de Rome, 1997.

Tellenbach, Gerd. "Aspects of Mediaeval Thought on Church and State." *Review of Politics* 9 (1947): 403–422.

BIBLIOGRAPHY ᆼ 301

Tellenbach, Gerd. *Die westliche Kirche vom 10. bis zum frühen 12. Jahrhundert*. Vandenhoeck & Ruprecht, 1998.

Théry, Julien. "Une hérésie d'État. Philippe le Bel, le procès des 'perfides templiers' et la pontificalisation de la royauté française." *Médiévales* 60 (2011): 157–186.

Thils, Gustave. *La primauté pontificale: La doctrine de Vatican I, les voies d'une révision*. Duculot, 1972.

Thils, Gustave. *L'infaillibilité du peuple chrétien* "in credendo." *Notes de théologie post-tridentine*. Bibliotheca Ephemeridum Theologicarum Lovaniensium, 1963.

Thils, Gustave. *L'infaillibilité pontificale: Source, conditions, limites*. Duculot, 1969.

Thils, Gustave. *Primauté et infaillibilité du Pontife romain à Vatican I, et autres études d'ecclésiologie*. Leuven University Press, 1989.

Thomson, John A. F. *Popes and Princes 1417–1517: Politics and Polity in the Late Medieval Church*. George Allen & Unwin, 1980.

Thraede, Klaus. "The Idea of Reform: Its Impact on Christian Thought and Action in the Age of the Fathers." *Jahrbuch für Antike und Christentum* 4 (1961): 168–170.

Tierney, Brian. *Church, Law, and Constitutional Thought in the Middle Ages*. Ashgate, 1979.

Tierney, Brian. "Collegiality in the Middle Ages." *Concilium* 7 (1965): 5–14.

Tierney, Brian. "Divided Sovereignty at Constance: A Problem of Medieval and Early Modern Political Theory." *Annuarium historiae conciliorum* 7 (1975): 238–256.

Tierney, Brian. *Foundations of the Conciliar Theory: The Contribution of the Medieval Canonists from Gratian to the Great Schism*. Cambridge University Press, 1955.

Tierney, Brian. "Hermeneutics and History: The Problem of *Haec Sancta*." In *Essays in Medieval History Presented to Bertie Wilkinson*, edited by T. A. Sandquist and Michael Powicke. University of Toronto Press, 1969.

Tierney, Brian. "Hostiensis and Collegiality." In *Proceedings of the Fourth International Congress of Medieval Canon Law*, edited by Stephan Kuttner. Biblioteca Apostolica Vaticana, 1976.

Tierney, Brian. "Infallibility and the Medieval Canonists: A Discussion with Alfons Stickler." *Theologische Revue* 66 (1975): 265–273.

Tierney, Brian. "La collégialité au Moyen Âge." *Concilium* 7 (1965): 11–18.

Tierney, Brian. "L'idée de représentation dans les conciles d'Occident au Moyen Âge." *Concilium* 187 (1983): 43–51.

302   BIBLIOGRAPHY

Tierney, Brian. "Medieval Canon Law and Western Constitutionalism." *Catholic Historical Review* 52 (1966): 1–17.

Tierney, Brian. "On the History of Papal Infallibility: A Discussion with Remigius Bäumer." *Theologische Revue* 70 (1974): 185–193.

Tierney, Brian. *Origins of Papal Infallibility: A Study on the Concepts of Infallibility (1150–1350), Sovereignty, and Tradition in the Middle Ages.* Brill, 1972.

Tierney, Brian. "'The Prince Is Not Bound by the Laws': Accursius and the Origins of the Modern State." *Comparative Studies in Society and History* 5, no. 4 (1963): 378–400.

Tierney, Brian. *Religion et droit dans le développement de la pensée constitutionnelle.* Translated by J. Ménard. Presses Universitaires de France, 1993.

Tierney, Brian. *Religion, Law, and the Growth of Constitutional Thought, 1150–1650.* Cambridge University Press, 1982.

Tierney, Brian. "Roots of Western Constitutionalism in the Church's Own Tradition: The Significance of the Council of Constance." In *We, The People of God*, edited by James A. Coriden. Canon Law Society of America, 1968.

Tillard, Jean-Marie Roger. "Théologies et 'dévotions' au pape depuis le Moyen Âge. De Jean XXII à Jean XXIII." *Cristianesimo nella storia* 22 (2001): 191–211.

Tillet, Édouard. *La Constitution anglaise, un modèle politique et institutionnel dans la France des Lumières.* Presses Universitaires d'Aix-Marseille, 2001.

Tillet, Édouard. "Les ambiguïtés du concept de constitution au XVIIIe siècle: L'exemple de Montesquieu." In *Pensée politique et droit*, edited by Association française des historiens des idées politiques. Presses Universitaires d'Aix-Marseille, 1998.

Torrell, Jean-Pierre. *La théologie de l'épiscopat au 1er concile du Vatican.* Cerf, 1961.

Torrell, Jean-Pierre. "L'Infaillibilité pontificale est-elle un privilège 'personnel?' Une controverse au premier concile du Vatican." *Revue des sciences philosophiques et théologiques* 45 (1961): 229–245.

Toubert, Pierre. *Les structures du Latium médiéval. Le Latium méridional et la Sabine du IXe siècle à la fin du XIIe siècle.* École Française de Rome, 1973.

Tournier, Laurent. "Jean sans Peur et l'université de Paris." In *Paris, capitale des ducs de Bourgogne*, edited by Werner Paravicini and Bertrand Schnerb. Thorbecke, 2007.

Trippen, Norbert. "Hubert Jedin e il concilio Vaticano II." *Cristianesimo nella storia* 22 (2001): 355–374.

BIBLIOGRAPHY ❧ 303

Ubl, Karl. "Debating the Emergence of an Idea: John of Paris and Conciliarism." In *John of Paris: Beyond Royal and Papal Power*, edited by Chris Jones. Brepols, 2015.

Ubl, Karl. "McIlwain und Constitutionalism: Ursprung, Wandel, und Bedeutung eines Forschungskonzepts." *Viator* 42 (2011): 321–342.

Ullmann, Walter. "Medieval Views Concerning Papal Abdication." *Irish Ecclesiastical Review*, 71 (1949): 125–133.

Vacant, Alfred, Eugène Mangenot, and Émile Amann, eds. *Dictionnaire de théologie catholique*, vol. 6, pt. 2. Letouzey & Ané, 1914.

Vallière, Paul. *Conciliarism: A History of Decision-Making in the Church*. Cambridge University Press, 2012.

Valois, Noël. *La Crise religieuse du XVe siècle. Le pape et le concile (1418–1450)*. 2 vols. Picard, 1909.

Valois, Noël. *La France et le Grand Schisme d'Occident*. 4 vols. Picard, 1896–1902.

Van Engen, John. "Images and Ideas: The Achievements of Gerhart Burian Ladner, with a Bibliography of His Published Works." *Viator* 20 (1989): 85–115.

Van Engen, John. *Sisters and Brothers of the Common Life: The* Devotio moderna *and the World of the Later Middle Ages*. University of Pennsylvania Press, 2008.

Van Kley, Dale. "The Estates General as Ecumenical Council: The Constitutionalism of Corporate Consensus and the Parliaments' Ruling of September 25, 1788." *Journal of Modern History* 61 (1989): 1–52.

Van Kley, Dale. *Les origines religieuses de la Révolution française*. Seuil, 2002.

Van Kley, Dale. *The Religious Origins of the French Revolution: From Calvin to the Civil Constitution, 1560–1791*. Yale University Press, 1996.

Van Steenberghen, Fernand. "Étienne Gilson, historien de la pensée médiévale." *Revue philosophique de Leuven* 77 (1979): 487–508.

Van Steenberghen, Fernand. *Introduction à l'étude de la pensée médiévale*. Nauwelaerts, 1974.

Venard, Marc. "Réforme, Préréforme, Contre-Réforme. Étude de vocabulaire chez les historiens récents de langue française." In *Historiographie de la Réforme*, edited by Philippe Joutard. Delachaux et Niestlé, 1977.

Viallet, Ludovic. *Les Sens de l'observance. Enquête sur les réformes franciscaines entre l'Elbe et l'Oder, de Capistran à Luther (vers 1450–vers 1520)*. Lit, 2014.

Vignaux, Paul. *Philosophie au Moyen Âge*. Selected, edited, and annotated by Ruedi Imbach. Vrin, 2004.

304 ☙ BIBLIOGRAPHY

Vignaux, Paul. "Situation d'un historien philosophe devant la scolastique des XIVe et XVe siècles." In *Étienne Gilson et nous. La philosophie et son histoire. Colloque sur l'actualité de la pensée d'Étienne Gilson*, edited by Monique Couratier. Vrin, 1980.

Voigt, Johannes. *Hildebrand als Pabst Gregorius VII und sein Zeitalter.* Rev. ed. Weimar, 1846.

Von Allmen, Jean-Jacques. *Une réforme dans l'Église. Possibilités-critères-acteursétapes.* Duculot, 1971.

Von Balthasar, Hans Urs, *Der antirömische Affekt*, Herder, 1974.

Von Balthasar, Hans Urs. *The Office of Peter and the Structure of the Church.* Translated by Andrée Emery. Ignatius Press, 1986.

Von Döllinger, Johann Joseph Ignaz. *The Pope and the Council.* London, 1869.

Vones, Ludwig. *Urban V (1362–1370): Kirchenreform zwischen Kardinalkollegium, Kurie, und Klientel.* Hiersemann, 1998.

Von Schulte, Johann Friedrich Ritter. *Die Stellung der Konzilien, Päpste und Bischöfe vom historischen und canonistischen Standpunkte und die päpstliche Constitution vom 18. Juli 1870.* Prague, 1871.

Walther, Helmut. "Konziliarismus als politische Theorie? Konzilsvorstellungen im 15. Jh. zwischen Notlösungen und Kirchenmodellen." In *Die Konzilien von Pisa (1409), Konstanz (1414–1418) und Basel (1431–1449): Institutionen und Personen*, edited by Herbert Müller and Johannes Helmrath. Thorbecke, 2007.

Wanegffelen, Thierry. *Ni Rome ni Genève. Des fidèles entre deux chaires en France au XVIe siècle.* Honoré Champion, 1997.

Watt, John A. "The Constitutional Law of the College of Cardinals: Hostiensis to Johannes Andreae." *Medieval Studies* 23 (1971): 125–151.

Watt, John A. "The Early Medieval Canonists and the Formation of Conciliar Theory." *Irish Theological Quarterly* 25 (1957): 13–31.

Watts, John. "Community and Contract in Later Medieval England." In *Avant le contrat social. Le contrat politique dans l'Occident médiéval (XIIIe-XVe siècle)*, edited by François Foronda. Publications de la Sorbonne, 2011.

Wilhelm, Joseph. "Councils (General)." *Catholic Encyclopedia*, vol. 4. Robert Appleton, 1908.

Willaert, Léopold. *Après le concile de Trente. La restauration catholique (1563–1648).* Vol. 18 of *Histoire de l'Église depuis les origines jusqu'à nos jours*, edited by Augustin Fliche and Victor Martin. Bloud & Gay, 1960.

BIBLIOGRAPHY ⪧ 305

Woelki, Thomas. "Theologische und juristische Argumente in den Konzilstraktaten des Lodovico Pontano († 1439)." In *Proceedings of the Thirteenth International Congress of Medieval Canon Law. Esztergom 3–8 August 2008*, edited by Peter Erdö and Sz. Anselm Szuromi. Biblioteca apostolica vaticana, 2010.

Wohlmuth, Josef. "Conciliarisme et constitution de l'Église." *Concilium* 187 (1983): 53–61.

Wünsch, Thomas. *Konziliarismus und Polen*. Ferdinand Schöningh, 1998.

Zerner, Monique. "Hérésie." In *Dictionnaire raisonné de l'Occident médiéval*, edited by Jacques Le Goff and Jean-Claude Schmitt. Fayard, 1999.

INDEX OF NAMES

Albergati, Nicolas, 52–53

Alberigo, Giuseppe, 32, 46, 50, 115, 116–117, 139

Albertus Magnus, 157–158, 167, 169

Almain, Jacques, 22, 24, 97

Anglicus, Alanus, 54

Aquinas, Thomas, 34, 158–159, 161, 164–166, 171, 181

Arabeyre, Patrick, 68

Armogathe, Jean-Robert, 46

Averroes, 157, 159, 162

Baranger, Denis, 62

Barth, Karl, 130

Bäumer, Remigius, 31, 41

Beaud, Olivier, 60, 61, 78

Bellitto, Christopher, 113

Benedict XIII, 11, 16, 123, 142–146, 152, 187, 190, 192–193

Benoît, Guillaume, 68, 145

Bianchi, Luca, 161

Black, Antony, 67, 72

Blythe, James, 59, 67

Boniface Ferrer, 19

Bossuet, 24, 26, 59

Boureau, Alain, 80

Boutry, Philippe, 139, 153, 156

Brabant, Siger of, 159–162, 170

Brandmüller, Walter, 31, 42, 46–47, 50–52, 54

Bréhier, Émile, 164

Burns, Peter, 31

Büttgen, Philippe, 198–199

Cajetan, 34, 97

Carpenter, Christine, 81

Certeau, Michel de, 83

Chenu, Marie-Dominique, vii, xii, 5, 157, 162–163

Clairvaux, Bernard de, 90–91

Colin, Pierre, 156, 169

Congar, Yves-Marie, xii, 10, 31, 39–40, 85–93, 99, 105–108, 113–115, 119, 135–136, 175, 180

Cosme Guymier, 68

Courtecuisse, Jean, 16

Courtine, Jean-François, 79–80

308 ❧ INDEX OF NAMES

Cramaud, Simon de, 13, 16, 145–147, 149, 186
Cusa, Nicholas of, 18, 127, 172
Cyprian, 90

d'Ailly, Pierre, 8, 16, 18–20, 22, 24–25, 43, 51, 53, 90–95, 112–113, 121–122, 128, 152, 170, 175, 178–180, 187, 189, 190
d'Arezzo, Lorenzo, 18
Davis, Kathleen, 6, 198
De Franceschi, Sylvio Hermann, 133, 137–140, 142, 147, 150, 152
De Vooght, Paul, 37–40, 42–43, 45–46, 55, 180, 182, 185
Decaluwé, Michiel, 50–51, 197
Denis, Philippe, 20, 62, 143
Du Pin, Louis Ellies, 24–26
Durand, Guillaume, 90–91
Duval, André, 23

Eugene IV, 17, 33, 34, 37–39, 47, 55, 57, 79, 91

Fasolt, Constantin, 67
Figgis, John Neville, 8, 35–36, 48–49, 57–58, 64–65, 69, 71–72, 79
Fonbaustier, Laurent, 69–71
Foronda, François, 80–81
Fouilloux, Étienne, xii
Franzen, August, 41

Gauchet, Marcel, 79
Gazzaniga, Jean-Louis, 16, 26, 28
Genet, Jean-Philippe, 81
Gerson, Jean, 8, 16, 18, 20, 21–26, 29, 43, 48–49, 53–54, 57, 64–65, 72–73,

90, 93–97, 112, 120–125, 140, 181, 186–188
Gill, Joseph, 40–41, 47
Gilson, Étienne, vii, 109, 163–171
Gratian, 8, 70, 121, 141, 149, 190
Gregory XII, 34, 40, 92, 107–108, 125, 146

Hallam, Henry, 35
Hegel, Georg Wilhelm Friedrich, 61, 74, 76, 107, 164
Hobbins, Daniel, 22
Hostiensis, 93
Huguccio, 36, 54

Imbach, Ruedi, 158, 160–161, 170–171

Jandun, Jean de, 33, 141
Jedin, Hubert, 41, 51, 68, 107–108, 116–119
John XXIII (Angelo Roncalli), 31, 35, 37, 106, 115, 118
John XXIII (Balthasar Cossa), 17, 35, 41, 54, 128

Kaminsky, Howard, 145–146
Kantorowicz, Ernst, 75, 78–80, 108
Küng, Hans, 38–40, 43, 175, 179–181
Kuttner, Stefan, 44

Ladner, Gerhart, 108–114, 119
Lagarde, Georges de, 171
Lange, Tyler, 68
Langenstein, Henry of, 16, 120, 122, 128
Langlois, Claude, 1, 12, 179

INDEX OF NAMES ❦ 309

Le Bras, Gabriel, 67
Legrand, Hervé, 84
Levillain, Philippe, 45, 115
Libera, Alain de, 12, 160, 164–165,
   167–170

Maire, Catherine, 24, 153
Major, John, 22
Mandonnet, Pierre, 160, 169, 170
Maret, Henri, 44, 178
Maritain, Jacques, 167
Martin V, 17, 33, 37–38, 45–46, 126,
   186–188
Massoni, Anne, 100–101
Mauroux, Jean, 51–52, 189
McIlwain, Charles, vii, xii, 48–49, 57,
   65–66, 74
Miethke, Jürgen, 42, 48
Millet, Hélène, 19, 101, 103, 112
Miramon, Charles de, 107
Möhler, Johann Adam, 113
Morrissey, Thomas, 43, 50

Nederman, Cary, xii, 47–49, 72–74

Oakley, Francis, xii, 30–32, 34, 37, 39,
   41, 43–45, 48–49, 53, 67, 69, 72–73
Ockham, William of, 13, 24, 33, 36, 29,
   42, 47–48, 54, 141, 165, 171, 181–184
Olivi, Peter John, 181–184

Padua, Marsilius of, 33, 36, 39, 41,
   47–48, 141
Paine, Thomas, 60
Palomar, Juan, 51–52
Paris, John of, 22, 36, 48, 73

Pascoe, Louis, 111–113
Pennington, Kenneth, 49
Post, Gaines, 74–75
Poulat, Émile, 155, 156
Prodi, Paolo, 30, 139
Provvidente, Sebastian, 50, 53–54, 197
Prügl, Thomas, xii, 31, 50–53, 197
Putallaz, François-Xavier, 160–161

Rauwel, Alain, 130
Ravat, Pierre, 123
Rials, Stéphane, 59, 68–69
Richer, Edmond, 22–26, 139–140, 152
Rigaudière, Alain, 63, 101–102
Rosenblieh, Émilie, 50, 55, 197

Salembier, Louis-Joseph, 25
Sarpi, Paolo, 22, 137, 147
Schmitt, Carl, 9, 58, 61, 75–80
Schneider, Hans, 31–32
Segovia, John of, 18
Sesboüé, Bernard, 83, 87, 89, 182
Sieben, Hermann Josef, 16, 31, 46
Sieyès, Emmanuel Joseph, 61
Stump, Phillip, 112

Tallon, Alain, 28
Teutonicus, Johannes, 36
Tierney, Brian, vii, xii, 8, 32, 35–39,
   41–43, 46–49, 58, 64–67, 69, 71–75,
   180, 182, 184, 193
Tillard, Jean-Marie, 88
Torquemada, Juan de, 33, 34, 45, 47, 182

Ubl, Karl, 48–49, 73–74
Ullmann, Walter, 37–38

Van Engen, John, xii, 111
Van Steenberghen, Fernand, 169–170
Versailles, Pierre de, 51, 53
Vignaux, Paul, 170–171
Vincelles, Jean de, 51, 53
von Balthasar, Hans Urs, 135–136, 139
von Döllinger, Ignaz, 35, 177–178

Zabarella, Franciscus, 43, 90–91, 93

GPSR Authorized Representative: Easy Access System Europe, Mustamäe tee 50, 10621 Tallinn, Estonia, gpsr.requests@easproject.com

www.ingramcontent.com/pod-product-compliance
Lightning Source LLC
Jackson TN
JSHW081247130925
90962JS00001B/1